POETRY FOCUS

CERTIFICATE POEMS AND NOTES FOR ENGLISH HIGHER LEVEL

Martin Kieran & Frances Rocks

GILL & MACMILLAN

Gill & Macmillan Ltd
Hume Avenue
Park West
Dublin 12
with associated companies throughout the world
www.gillmacmillan.ie

© Martin Kieran and Frances Rocks, 2012
978 07171 5341 1

Design by Liz White Designs
Print origination in Ireland by O'K Graphic Design, Dublin

The paper used in this book is made from the wood pulp of managed forests. For every tree felled, at least one tree is planted, thereby renewing natural resources.

All rights reserved.
No part of this publication may be copied, reproduced or transmitted in any form or by any means without written permission of the publishers or else under the terms of any licence permitting limited copying issued by the Irish Copyright Licensing Agency.

Any links to external websites should not be construed as an endorsement by Gill & Macmillan of the content or view of the linked material.

PICTURE CREDITS

For permission to reproduce photographs, the authors and publisher gratefully acknowledge the following:

© Alamy: 23, 42, 47, 80, 110, 114, 173, 202, 296, 383, 387, 403, 411, 421, 425, 434, 439, 443, 466, 481, 497, 509; © Bridgeman: 84; © Corbis: 12, 355, 399; © Faber & Faber Ltd: 125; © Getty: 6, 30, 53, 60, 76, 128, 133, 138, 154, 178, 182, 231, 246, 254, 259, 263, 278, 284, 289, 318, 323, 340, 346, 350, 361, 367, 374, 378, 407, 430, 461, 476, 492; © Imagefile: 89, 93, 97, 102, 106, 144, 169, 212, 217, 237, 417, 456, 487, 512; © Lebrecht: 224; © Mary Evans Picture Library: 73; © Pd Smith: 504; © Photolibrary: 18; © Press Association: 36, 199; © Scott Hayes/St Patrick's Cathedral: 501; © RTÉ: 314; © Topfoto: 149, 160, 164, 187, 275, 337, 470.

The authors and publisher have made every effort to trace all copyright holders, but if any has been inadvertently overlooked we would be pleased to make the necessary arrangement at the first opportunity.

CONTENTS

INTRODUCTION — vi

Elizabeth Bishop — 1
    The Fish — 4
    The Bight — 11
    At the Fishhouses — 16
    The Prodigal — 23
    Questions of Travel — 28
    The Armadillo — 35
    Sestina — 41
    First Death in Nova Scotia — 46
    Filling Station — 52
    In the Waiting Room — 58
Leaving Cert Sample Essay — 65

Emily Dickinson — 73
    'Hope' is the thing with feathers — 76
    There's a certain Slant of light — 80
    I felt a Funeral, in my Brain — 84
    A Bird came down the Walk — 89
    I Heard a Fly buzz—when I died — 93
    The Soul has Bandaged moments — 97
    I could bring You Jewels—had I a mind to — 102
    A narrow Fellow in the Grass — 106
    I taste a liquor never brewed — 110
    After great pain, a formal feeling comes — 114
Leaving Cert Sample Essay — 118

Seamus Heaney — 125
    The Forge — 128
    Bogland — 132
    The Tollund Man — 137
    Mossbawn: Sunlight — 143
    A Constable Calls — 148
    The Skunk — 154
    The Harvest Bow — 159
    The Underground — 164

• Contents •

Postscript	169
A Call	173
Tate's Avenue	178
The Pitchfork	182
Lightenings viii	187
Leaving Cert Sample Essay	192

Thomas Kinsella — 199

Thinking of Mr D.	202
Dick King	206
Mirror in February	212
Chrysalides	217
from Glenmacnass: VI Littlebody	222
Tear	228
Hen Woman	235
His Father's Hands	243
from Settings: Model School, Inchicore	252
from The Familiar: VII	258
from Belief and Unbelief: Echo	263
Leaving Cert Sample Essay	267

Philip Larkin — 275

Wedding-Wind	278
At Grass	283
Church Going	288
An Arundel Tomb	295
The Whitsun Weddings	301
MCMXIV	308
Ambulances	313
The Trees	318
The Explosion	322
Cut Grass	327
Leaving Cert Sample Essay	331

Derek Mahon — 337

Grandfather	340
Day Trip to Donegal	345
Ecclesiastes	350
After the *Titanic*	355
As It Should Be	361

A Disused Shed in Co. Wexford	366
Rathlin	373
The Chinese Restaurant in Portrush	378
Kinsale	383
Antarctica	387
Leaving Cert Sample Essay	393

Sylvia Plath — 399

Black Rook in Rainy Weather	402
The Times Are Tidy	407
Morning Song	411
Finisterre	416
Mirror	421
Pheasant	425
Elm	429
Poppies in July	434
The Arrival of the Bee Box	438
Child	443
Leaving Cert Sample Essay	447

W. B. Yeats — 453

The Lake Isle of Innisfree	456
September 1913	460
The Wild Swans at Coole	465
An Irish Airman Foresees his Death	470
Easter, 1916	474
The Second Coming	481
Sailing to Byzantium	486
from Meditations in Time of Civil War VI: The Stare's Nest by my Window	492
In Memory of Eva Gore-Booth and Con Markiewicz	496
Swift's Epitaph	501
An Acre of Grass	504
from Under Ben Bulben	508
Politics	512
Leaving Cert Sample Essay	515

GLOSSARY OF COMMON LITERARY TERMS	521
ACKNOWLEDGMENTS	523

Introduction

Poetry Focus is a new, modern poetry textbook for Leaving Certificate Higher Level English. It includes all the prescribed poems for 2014 as well as succinct commentaries on each one. In addition, there are sample student paragraphs on each poem, sample question plans and full graded sample essays. Well-organised and easily accessible study notes provide all the necessary information to allow students to explore the poems and to develop their own individual responses.

- **Explorations** (a series of short questions) follow the text of each poem. These allow students to make initial responses before any in-depth study or analysis. Exploration questions provide a good opportunity for written and/or oral exercises.
- **Study notes** highlight the main features of the poet's subject matter and style. These discussion notes will enhance the student's own critical appreciation through focused group work and/or written exercises. Analytical skills are developed in a coherent, practical way to give students confidence in articulating their own personal responses to the poems and poets.
- **Graded sample paragraphs** aid students in fluently structuring and developing valid points and in using relevant quotations and reference in support.
- **Key quotes** encourage students to select their own individual combination of references from a poem and to write brief commentaries on specific quotations.
- **Sample essay plans** on each poet's work illustrate how to interpret a question and recognise the particular nuances of key words in examination questions. Evaluation of these essay plans increases student confidence in working out clear responses for themselves.
- **There is no single 'correct' approach** to answering the poetry question. Candidates are free to respond in any appropriate way that shows good knowledge of and engagement with the prescribed poems.
- **Full sample Leaving Certificate essays**, graded and accompanied by experienced examiners' comments, show the student exactly what is required to achieve a successful A grade in the Leaving Cert exam and to develop a real enthusiasm for English poetry. This is essential in identifying the task as required by the PCLM marking scheme.

• Leaving Certificate English •

HOW IS THE PRESCRIBED POETRY QUESTION MARKED?

Marking is done (ex. 50 marks) by reference to the PCLM criteria for assessment:
- Clarity of purpose (P): 30% of the total (i.e. 15 marks).
- Coherence of delivery (C): 30% of the total (i.e. 15 marks).
- Efficiency of language use (L): 30% of the total (i.e. 15 marks).
- Accuracy of mechanics (M): 10% of the total (i.e. 5 marks).

Each answer will be in the form of a response to a specific task requiring candidates to:
- Display a clear and purposeful engagement with the set task. (P)
- Sustain the response in an appropriate manner over the entire answer. (C)
- Manage and control language appropriate to the task. (L)
- Display levels of accuracy in spelling and grammar appropriate to the required/chosen register. (M)

GENERAL

'Students at Higher Level will be required to study a representative selection from the work of eight poets: a representative selection would seek to reflect the range of a poet's themes and interests and exhibit his/her characteristic style and viewpoint. Normally the study of at least six poems by each poet would be expected.' (DES English Syllabus, 6.3)

The marking scheme guidelines from the State Examinations Commission state that in the case of each poet, the candidates have **freedom of choice** in relation to the poems studied. In addition, there is **not a finite list of any 'poet's themes and interests'**.

Note that in responding to the question set on any given poet, the candidates must refer to the poem(s) they have studied but **are not required to refer to any *specific* poem(s), nor are they expected to discuss or refer to all the poems they have chosen to study.**

In each of the questions in **Prescribed Poetry**, the underlying nature of the task is the invitation to the candidates to **engage with the poems themselves.**

EXAM ADVICE

- You are not expected to write about any **set number of poems** in the examination. You might decide to focus in detail on a small number of poems, or you could choose to write in a more general way on several poems.

• vii •

- Most candidates write one or two well-developed **paragraphs** on each of the poems they have chosen for discussion. In other cases, a paragraph will focus on one specific aspect of the poet's work. When discussing recurring themes or features of style, appropriate cross-references to other poems may also be useful.

- Reflect on central **themes** and viewpoints in the poems you discuss. Comment also on the use of language and the poet's distinctive **style**. Examine imagery, tone, structure, rhythm and rhyme. Be careful not to simply list aspects of style, such as alliteration or repetition. There's little point in mentioning that a poet uses sound effects or metaphors without discussing the effectiveness of such characteristics.

- Focus on **the task** you have been given in the poetry question. An awareness of audience is important. Are you meant to be writing a letter to the poet? Perhaps you are giving a talk about the poet or writing an article, a review or an introduction to a new collection of the poet's work. If your poetry answer has the appropriate tone and register, it will have an authentic feel and be more convincing.

- Always root your answers in the text of the poems. Support the points you make with **relevant reference and quotation**. Make sure your own expression is fresh and lively. Avoid awkward expressions, such as 'It says in the poem that...'. Look for alternatives: 'There is a sense of...', 'The tone seems to suggest...', 'It's evident that...', etc.

- Neat, **legible handwriting** will help to make a positive impression on examiners. Corrections should be made by simply drawing a line through the mistake. Scored-out words distract attention from the content of your work.

- Keep the emphasis on why particular poets **appeal to you**. Consider the continuing relevance or significance of a poet's work. Perhaps you have shared some of the feelings or experiences expressed in the poems. Avoid starting answers with prepared biographical sketches. Details of a poet's life are better used when discussing how the poems themselves were shaped by such experiences.

- Remember that the examination encourages **individual engagement** with the prescribed poems. Poetry can make us think and feel and imagine. It opens our minds to the wonderful possibilities of language and ideas. Your interaction with the poems is what matters most. Study notes and critical interpretations are all there to be challenged. Read the poems carefully and have confidence in expressing your own personal response.

'The armored cars of dreams, contrived to let us do so many a dangerous thing.'

Elizabeth Bishop (1911–79)

Elizabeth Bishop was born in Worcester, Massachusetts in 1911. During her early life she experienced a series of family tragedies. She spent part of her childhood with her Canadian grandparents following her father's death and mother's hospitalisation. She then lived with various relatives who, according to Bishop, took care of her because they felt sorry for her. These unsettling events, along with the memories of her youth, inspired her to read poetry – and eventually to write it. Like many poets and artists, Bishop was a great observer with a vivid sense of place. After studying English at university, she travelled extensively and lived in New York, Florida and, for 17 years, Brazil. She also taught at several American colleges. Throughout her life she suffered from ill health and depression. As a poet, she wrote sparingly, publishing only five slim volumes in 35 years. However, her work received high acclaim. 'I think geography comes first in my work,' she told an interviewer, 'and then animals. But I like people, too. I've written a few poems about people.' Recurring themes in her refreshing and thought-provoking poetry include childhood experiences, travel, the natural world, loneliness, detachment, and the art of writing itself. Bishop died suddenly in her Boston apartment on 6 October 1979. She was 68 years old. Her poetry continues to gain widespread recognition and study.

PRESCRIBED POEMS (HIGHER LEVEL)

1 'The Fish' (p. 4)

Based on an actual experience from her time in Florida during the 1930s, Elizabeth Bishop gives a detailed description of catching a 'tremendous fish'. Central to the poem is the notion that both nature and human nature share admirable qualities of strength and endurance.

2 'The Bight' (p. 11)

In describing the small, untidy bight (bay), the poet displays a naturally keen observation and an expert use of metaphor. The subtitle '(On my birthday)', suggests a special occasion and, perhaps, a time for reflection and reappraisal of life.

3 'At the Fishhouses' (p. 16)

Bishop travels back to her childhood home in Nova Scotia and notes some of the changes that have taken place. Detailed description leads to intense reflection and she is prompted to review her ideas about origin, identity, knowledge and wisdom.

4 'The Prodigal' (p. 23)

The poem is based on the biblical parable of the Prodigal Son who, on leaving his father's home, is forced to live as a swineherd. Bishop imagines the squalor and degradation brought about by alcoholism. However, determination, hope and human resilience eventually triumph.

5 'Questions of Travel' (p. 28)

The striking Brazilian landscape encourages the poet to consider people's interests in foreign places. She outlines some of the benefits of travel, but asks if there is a good argument for staying at home ('wherever that may be') and visiting imagined worlds.

6 'The Armadillo' (p. 35)

Bishop describes the beautiful – but dangerous – fire balloons that light up the darkness during an annual religious festival in Rio de Janeiro. Unfortunately, defenceless creatures, such as the armadillo, are unable to escape the fire falling from the sky.

7 'Sestina' (p. 41)

In this deeply personal poem, Bishop recalls a painful childhood. Faced with her grandmother's sadness, she retreats to the kitchen of her family home and its familiar comforts. The poem's original title was 'Early Sorrow'. A sestina is a traditional poetic form of six six-line stanzas followed by a final stanza of just three lines.

8 'First Death in Nova Scotia' (p. 46)

Recalling vividly the death of her young cousin Arthur, the poet explores the innocence and bewilderment of childhood. Many of her memories are dominated by the Canadian winter landscape. In her fantasies, she imagines Arthur in a fairytale afterlife as 'the smallest page at court'.

9 'Filling Station' (p. 52)

The description of a run-down filling station leads to other discoveries. Despite the grease and oily dirt, Bishop finds signs of family love and beauty in this unlikely place: 'Somebody loves us all'. Some critics see the poem as an allegory of all human life.

10 'In the Waiting Room' (p. 58)

Set in Worcester, Massachusetts in 1918, the poem returns to the theme of childhood and the loss of innocence. Bishop's experience in a dentist's waiting room at the age of six marks a significant turning point in her development and awakens her to adulthood.

• Poetry Focus •

The Fish

Elizabeth Bishop

I caught a tremendous fish
and held him beside the boat
half out of water, with my hook
fast in a corner of his mouth.
He didn't fight.   5
He hadn't fought at all.
He hung a grunting weight,
battered and venerable
and homely. Here and there
his brown skin hung in strips   10
like ancient wallpaper,
and its pattern of darker brown
was like wallpaper:
shapes like full-blown roses
stained and lost through age.   15
He was speckled with barnacles,
fine rosettes of lime,
and infested
with tiny white sea-lice,
and underneath two or three   20
rags of green weed hung down.
While his gills were breathing in
the terrible oxygen
– the frightening gills,
fresh and crisp with blood,   25
that can cut so badly –
I thought of the coarse white flesh
packed in like feathers,
the big bones and the little bones,
the dramatic reds and blacks   30
of his shiny entrails,
and the pink swim-bladder
like a big peony.
I looked into his eyes
which were far larger than mine   35
but shallower, and yellowed,
the irises backed and packed
with tarnished tinfoil

seen though the lenses
of old scratched isinglass. 40
They shifted a little, but not
to return my stare.
– It was more like the tipping
of an object toward the light.
I admired his sullen face, 45
the mechanism of his jaw,
and then I saw
that from his lower lip
– if you could call it a lip –
grim, wet, and weaponlike, 50
hung five old pieces of fish-line,
or four and a wire leader
with the swivel still attached,
with all their five big hooks
grown firmly in his mouth. 55
A green line, frayed at the end
where he broke it, two heavier lines,
and a fine black thread
still crimped from the strain and snap
when it broke and he got away. 60
Like medals with their ribbons
frayed and wavering,
a five-haired beard of wisdom
trailing from his aching jaw.
I stared and stared 65
and victory filled up
the little rented boat,
from the pool of bilge
where oil had spread a rainbow
around the rusted engine 70
to the bailer rusted orange,
the sun-cracked thwarts,
the oarlocks on their strings,
the gunnels – until everything
was rainbow, rainbow, rainbow! 75
And I let the fish go.

• Poetry Focus •

Elizabeth Bishop

'He hung a grunting weight'

GLOSSARY

1 *tremendous*: huge, startling, fearsome.
8 *venerable*: ancient, worthy of respect.
9 *homely*: comfortable, easy-going, unpretentious, plain.
17 *rosettes*: rose-shaped decorations made of ribbon, often awarded as prizes.
19 *sea-lice*: small parasites that live on the skin of fish.
24 *gills*: breathing organs of fish.
31 *entrails*: internal organs.
33 *peony*: large, flamboyant flower, usually pink.
37 *irises*: coloured parts of an eye.
40 *isinglass*: gelatine-like substance obtained from the bodies of fish, opaque.
45 *sullen*: bad-tempered, sulky.
46 *mechanism*: workings.
52 *leader*: wire connecting fishhook and line.
59 *crimped*: pressed into ridges.
62 *frayed*: unravelled, worn.
68 *bilge*: dirty water that collects in the bottom of a boat.
71 *bailer*: bucket that scoops water out of a boat.
72 *thwarts*: rowers' benches.
73 *oarlocks*: metal devices for holding oars.
74 *gunnels*: upper edges of the side of a boat.

EXPLORATIONS

1 List two details that appealed to you in the description of the fish in lines 1–15. Why did they impact on you? Were they unusual or did they appeal to your senses? Support your response with quotation from the poem.

2 What is the poet's attitude towards the fish? Where does it change as the poem progresses? Give a reason for this change. Refer closely to the poem in your response.

3 Who had the 'victory' in this situation – the fish or Bishop? Why did you come to this conclusion? Support your discussion with clear references from the poem.

STUDY NOTES

'The Fish' is from Elizabeth Bishop's first published collection, *North and South* (1946). She lived in Florida during the 1930s and the poem is based on her experience of catching a large jewfish at Key West. Bishop once said, 'I like painting probably better than I like poetry' and 'The Fish' is certainly a very visual poem. Bishop uses the fish as a way of exploring a 'green' awareness, the respect for nature and all living things.

The poem's **opening line** is direct and forceful ('I caught a tremendous fish'). Bishop's use of the personal pronoun 'I' gives a sense of immediacy and intimacy. The adjective 'tremendous' reflects the **poet's breathless excitement and awe at this magnificent specimen of fish**. The act of catching the fish is described in a personal, down-to-earth way. Bishop once said, 'I always tell the truth in my poems … that's exactly how it happened.' The fish is 'half out of water', no longer in its natural habitat.

In **line 5**, the focus shifts from the person who caught the fish to the fish itself. **It is now given a personality**: 'He didn't fight.' The onomatopoeic 'grunting' allows us to be part of this scene, as we hear the distressed noises from the gasping, ugly ('homely'), exhausted ('battered') fish. Then another facet of the fish is presented to us: it is 'venerable', ancient and worthy of reverence. Bishop the participant is giving way to Bishop the observer. While in college, Bishop met Marianne Moore, a famous American poet whose focus was on the accurate description of a particular thing. This poetic movement was known as **imagism**. We can see the similarity of style between the two poets in Bishop's description of the fish: 'Here and there/his brown skin hung in strips/like ancient wallpaper'.

The surface **detail is painstakingly and imaginatively described** ('like full-blown roses'). There seems to be an attempt to domesticate the creature, but the sordid reality of the blotches on the skin is also noted ('stained and lost through age'). The texture of the fish is described graphically, as if we were examining the skin under a microscope: 'speckled', 'infested', 'rags'. Colours ('lime', 'white' and 'green') help convey this vivid picture. The wildness of the creature is caught in the detailed phrasing ' frightening gills,/fresh and crisp with blood' (**line 24**). Its interior is also imagined ('pink swim-bladder/like a big peony'). These original and striking images appeal to both our visual and tactile senses.

Bishop's delight in catching this fine specimen soon gives way to an **emotional involvement with the fish** and his struggle for survival (line 34). She compares his eyes to her own ('far larger'). She notes the wear and tear from a long, hard life ('yellowed'). The irises are 'backed and packed/with tarnished tinfoil'. Here, assonance and alliteration give emphasis to the image. However, the fish's eyes are unresponsive, so there seems to be no interplay between creature and poet. This suggests both the independence and the vulnerability of the fish.

Progression in the poem is shown in the verbs: 'I caught', 'I thought', 'I looked' and, in line 45, 'I admired'. The **poet admires the resolute nature of the fish** ('his sullen face'). This fish has survived previous battles ('five big hooks/grown firmly in his mouth'). Precise detail emphasises the severity of these battles ('A green line, frayed at the end/where he broke it'). Military language highlights the effort the fish has made to survive: 'weaponlike', 'medals'. Bishop's sympathy is clear as she notes the fish's 'aching jaw'. For the fish, it is clear that the pain of battle remains.

Line 65 shows the poet transfixed ('I stared and stared'). Now the scene expands from a single fisher in a 'little rented boat' to something of **universal significance** ('victory' fills up the boat). Ordinary details (the 'bilge', the 'thwarts' and the 'gunnels') are transformed. The oil has 'spread a rainbow'. Everything is coloured and Bishop's relationship with the fish changes. She exercises mercy. A moment of epiphany occurs and she lets 'the fish go'. The tension in the poem is finally released. The underlying drama contained between the opening line ('I caught a tremendous fish') and the closing line ('And I let the fish go.') has been resolved. **Victory belongs to both the poet and the fish.** The fish is free; the poet has seen and understood.

This poem is a long narrative with a clear beginning, middle and end. Bishop has chosen a suitably unrhymed form. The metre is appropriate for the speaking voice: dimeter (two stresses) and trimeter (three stresses). Short run-on lines suggest the poet excitedly examining her catch and the recurring use of dashes indicates her thought process as she moves from delight to wonder, to empathy and, finally, comprehension. The concluding rhyming couplet brings a definite and satisfying resolution to the dramatic tension.

ANALYSIS

Elizabeth Bishop has been praised for her 'painterly eye'. Discuss this aspect of her style in 'The Fish'. Support your views with close reference to the poem.

SAMPLE PARAGRAPH

An artist looks, then sees, orders, recreates and leads both themselves and their viewers to a new insight. I think Elizabeth Bishop accomplishes all this in her poem 'The Fish'. The poet looks at the event ('I caught a tremendous fish') and then moves to describe the fish, using striking images ('brown skin hung in strips/like ancient wallpaper'). Like a camera, she pans this way and that, making us see also 'its pattern of darker brown' with 'shapes like full-blown roses'. She leads us to imagine the exotic interior of the fish, its 'coarse white flesh/packed in like feathers'. We see the order and symmetry, the 'dramatic reds and blacks'. If Bishop were painting this fish, I could imagine it in glistening oil colours. In her poem, she paints with words: 'the pink swim-bladder/like a peony'. She engages with her subject and has an emotional response to it: 'I looked into his eyes'. She acknowledges this veteran survivor, as she notes his 'medals', the 'five big hooks/grown firmly in his mouth'. They have been there so long that the skin has grown over them and she draws our attention to the fish's 'aching jaw'. Just like a painter leads us to see what they see, Bishop orders her picture so that we can see the 'five-haired beard of wisdom/trailing' from the fish. The poem concludes with a burst of colour ('rainbow, rainbow, rainbow!'). The rainbow from the oil-soaked, dirty bilge water has transformed the poet's relationship with the fish. Like Bishop, we now see the proper relationship between people and nature – one of respect. So the 'painterly eye' of Bishop has led us to see the drama of the occasion, the fish and what it really was, and finally our correct response to the earth and its creatures.

EXAMINER'S COMMENT

A mature and interesting interpretation of the question. The response is very well focused and there is a sustained personal perspective throughout. Judicious use of quotations rounds off the answer. With the exception of the last sentence, expression is generally fluent and assured. Grade A.

CLASS/HOMEWORK EXERCISES

1. Bishop often structures her poems like a mini-drama. Examine the poem 'The Fish' and comment on how a dramatic effect is achieved. Consider setting; characterisation; conflict; the interior debate; tension building to climax; and resolution. Refer closely to the text of the poem in your response.

2. Copy the table below into your own notes and fill in critical comments about the last two quotations.

KEY QUOTES

He hadn't fought at all	The poet's surprise at the fish's lack of engagement in its struggle for life is caught in this colloquial statement.
the frightening gills,/fresh and crisp with blood	An awesome sight is conveyed by the use of the adjective 'frightening'. The onomatopoeic 'crisp' vividly suggests the drying blood on the dangerous, sharp gills.
grim, wet, and weaponlike	Three adjectives describe the fearsome lower lip of the fish as it is pierced. The fish is likened to a veteran soldier.
and victory filled up/the little rented boat	
And I let the fish go	

The Bight

(On my birthday)

At low tide like this how sheer the water is.
White, crumbling ribs of marl protrude and glare
and the boats are dry, the pilings dry as matches.
Absorbing, rather than being absorbed,
the water in the bight doesn't wet anything, 5
the color of the gas flame turned as low as possible.
One can smell it turning to gas; if one were Baudelaire
one could probably hear it turning to marimba music.
The little ocher dredge at work off the end of the dock
already plays the dry perfectly off-beat claves. 10
The birds are outsize. Pelicans crash
into this peculiar gas unnecessarily hard,
it seem to me, like pickaxes,
rarely coming up with anything to show for it,
and going off with humorous elbowings. 15
Black-and-white man-of-war birds soar
on impalpable drafts
and open their tails like scissors on the curves
or tense them like wishbones, till they tremble.
The frowsy sponge boats keep coming in 20
with the obliging air of retrievers,
bristling with jackstraw gaffs and hooks
and decorated with bobbles of sponges.
There is a fence of chicken wire along the dock
where, glinting like little plowshares, 25
the blue-gray shark tails are hung up to dry
for the Chinese-restaurant trade.
Some of the little white boats are still piled up
against each other, or lie on their sides, stove in,
and not yet salvaged, if they ever will be, from the last bad storm, 30
like torn-open, unanswered letters.
The bight is littered with old correspondences.
Click. Click. Goes the dredge,
and brings up a dripping jawful of marl. 35
All the untidy activity continues,
awful but cheerful.

• Poetry Focus •

Elizabeth Bishop

'and the boats are dry'

GLOSSARY

The Bight: refers to a wide bay or inlet.
2 *marl*: rich clay soil.
3 *pilings*: heavy beams supporting a jetty.
7 *Baudelaire*: Charles Baudelaire (1821–67), French symbolist poet.
8 *marimba*: wooden instrument similar to a xylophone, played by African and Central American jazz musicians.
9 *ocher*: ochre; orange-brown colour.
10 *claves*: clefs; musical keys.
17 *impalpable drafts*: slight air currents.
20 *frowsy*: shabby, foul-smelling.
21 *retrievers*: hunting dogs.
22 *bristling*: shining.
22 *jackstraw gaffs*: splinters used as hooks on fishing rods.
23 *bobbles*: trimmings.
25 *plowshares*: ploughing blades.
29 *stove in*: storm-damaged.
30 *salvaged*: repaired.
33 *dredge*: a dredger is a machine for digging underwater.

EXPLORATIONS

1 Using close reference to the text, describe the atmosphere in the first six lines of the poem.
2 Choose one simile that you think is particularly effective in the poem. Briefly explain your choice.
3 Although the poem is not directly personal, what does it suggest to you about Elizabeth Bishop herself? Refer to the text in your answer.

STUDY NOTES

'The Bight' showcases Elizabeth Bishop's aesthetic appreciation of the world around her. The setting for this poem is Garrison Bight in Florida. In describing the small, untidy harbour, Bishop displays a characteristically keen eye for observation and an expert use of metaphor. The subtitle, '(On my birthday)', suggests a special occasion and, perhaps, a time for reflection and reappraisal of life.

The poem begins with an introduction to the bight at 'low tide' and gradually constructs **a vivid picture of an uninviting place**: 'White, crumbling ribs of marl protrude and glare'. Grim personification and a sharp 'r' sound effect emphasise the unsettling atmosphere. There is a sense of unreality about sea water that 'doesn't wet anything'. The description in these opening lines is typically detailed, sensual and precise – all carefully shaped by the poet's own personal vision of the world. References to 'the pilings dry as matches' and the 'gas flame' water are rather disturbing, suggesting that something dangerous might be about to happen.

Bishop's mention of the French poet Charles Baudelaire (line 7) would suggest that she shares his belief in expressing human experience through objects and places around us. The poet imagines Baudelaire being able to 'hear' the water 'turning to marimba music'. She also finds an unexpected jazz rhythm ('perfectly off-beat claves') coming from the machine that is dredging 'off the end of the dock'. In lines 11–19, Bishop depicts the 'outsize' birds through a series of vigorous images. They seem awkward and out of place in this busy, built-up location. **Figurative language illustrates their mechanical movements**: pelicans 'crash' into the sea 'like pickaxes', while man-of-war birds 'open their tails like scissors'. An underlying sense of disquiet can be detected in the detailed observations of these 'tense' birds as they 'tremble' in flight.

The poet's portrayal of the bight is quite realistic: 'frowsy sponge boats keep coming in' to harbour. With wry humour, she acknowledges their unlikely beauty, 'bristling with jackstraw gaffs' and 'decorated with bobbles of sponges'. The cluttered dockside is a busy working environment where 'blue-gray shark tails are hung up to dry' (line 26). The 'little white boats' are a reminder of the local fishing community and its dependence on the sea. Bishop compares the small fishing boats to 'torn-open, unanswered letters'. The bight suddenly reminds her of a cluttered writing-desk – her own, presumably – 'littered with old correspondences'.

This metaphor is developed in lines 33–36. Bishop returns to sharp sounds: the 'Click. Click.' noise of the dredger (compared to an animal unearthing the wet clay) as it 'brings up a dripping jawful of marl'. The ending is highly symbolic of the poet's own impulse to dig deep into her memories. Drawing a close comparison between her own life and the 'untidy activity' of the bight, she concludes that both are 'awful but cheerful'. **The matter-of-fact tone of these closing lines is derisive but good-humoured**. It reflects her realistic approach to the highs and lows of human experience – and the kinds of thoughts that are likely to have crossed her mind as she celebrated yet another birthday.

Elizabeth Bishop

ANALYSIS

'Closely observed description and vivid imagery are striking features of Elizabeth Bishop's poems.' Discuss this statement in relation to 'The Bight'. Refer to the poem in support of your views.

SAMPLE PARAGRAPH

I think 'The Bight' is a good example of how Elizabeth Bishop slowly builds up a picture of a fairly inhospitable place, layer upon layer. At first, she describes the 'sheer' water and the 'crumbling ribs of marl', personifying the loose soil as an emaciated body. This is a vivid and disturbing image that suggests that the bay is bleak and unattractive. We get a sense of the sounds she hears – the 'dredge at work' pounding away in the background. Bishop uses dramatic imagery to bring the birds to life – particularly the vicious man-of-war birds whose tails are 'like scissors' and 'tense' as wishbones. We also see the poet's eye for precise detail in her imaginative description of the damaged fishing boats that lie on the shore 'like torn-open, unanswered letters'. Bishop uses colour imagery very effectively – 'blue-gray shark tails' are hanging out to dry for the local restaurant trade. But she is not restricted to visual effects. Her descriptions appeal to other senses, particularly sound. The poem ends with the rasping sound of the dredger – 'Click. Click' digging up 'a dripping jawful of marl'. This remarkable image suggests to me how the bight keeps bringing back memories to the poet, both pleasant and unpleasant. It is an impressive way of rounding off the poem, as she associates the untidy harbour with her own varied life – 'awful but cheerful'.

EXAMINER'S COMMENT

A very well-focused response, making excellent use of numerous accurate quotations. The various elements of the question are addressed and there is evidence of good personal engagement with the text. Expression throughout is also fluent and controlled. Grade A.

CLASS/HOMEWORK EXERCISES

1. 'Elizabeth Bishop's poetry is both sensuous and reflective.' To what extent is this true of 'The Bight'? Support the points you make with suitable reference to the text of the poem.
2. Copy the table below into your own notes and fill in critical comments about the last two quotations.

Key Quotes

the boats are dry, the pilings dry as matches	The hesitant rhythm and repetition of 'dry' suggest an underlying sense of danger.
open their tails like scissors	This simile is a typically dynamic image, one of many comparisons used to convey the birds' mechanical movements.
The bight is littered with old correspondences	The clutter and disorder of the small harbour reminds Bishop of her own experiences and former relationships.
bristling with jackstraw gaffs and hooks	
Click. Click. Goes the dredge, / and brings up a dripping jawful of marl	

• Poetry Focus •

At the Fishhouses

Elizabeth Bishop

Although it is a cold evening,
down by one of the fishhouses
an old man sits netting,
his net, in the gloaming almost invisible,
a dark purple-brown, 5
and his shuttle worn and polished.
The air smells so strong of codfish
it makes one's nose run and one's eyes water.
The five fishhouses have steeply peaked roofs
and narrow, cleated gangplanks slant up 10
to storerooms in the gables
for the wheelbarrows to be pushed up and down on.
All is silver: the heavy surface of the sea,
swelling slowly as if considering spilling over,
is opaque, but the silver of the benches, 15
the lobster pots, and masts, scattered
among the wild jagged rocks,
is of an apparent translucence
like the small old buildings with an emerald moss
growing on their shoreward walls. 20
The big fish tubs are completely lined
with layers of beautiful herring scales
and the wheelbarrows are similarly plastered
with creamy iridescent coats of mail,
with small iridescent flies crawling on them. 25
Up on the little slope behind the houses,
set in the sparse bright sprinkle of grass,
is an ancient wooden capstan,
cracked, with two long bleached handles
and some melancholy stains, like dried blood, 30
where the ironwork has rusted.
The old man accepts a Lucky Strike.
He was a friend of my grandfather.
We talk of the decline in the population
and of codfish and herring 35
while he waits for a herring boat to come in.
There are sequins on his vest and on his thumb.
He has scraped the scales, the principal beauty,

from unnumbered fish with that black old knife,
the blade of which is almost worn away.

Down at the water's edge, at the place
where they haul up the boats, up the long ramp
descending into the water, thin silver
tree trunks are laid horizontally
across the gray stones, down and down
at intervals of four or five feet.

Cold dark deep and absolutely clear,
element bearable to no mortal,
to fish and seals . . . One seal particularly
I have seen here evening after evening.
He was curious about me. He was interested in music;
like me a believer in total immersion,
so I used to sing him Baptist hymns.
I also sang 'A Mighty Fortress Is Our God.'
He stood up in the water and regarded me
steadily, moving his head a little.
Then he would disappear, then suddenly emerge
almost in the same spot, with a sort of shrug
as if it were against his better judgment.
Cold dark deep and absolutely clear,
the clear gray icy water . . . Back, behind us,
the dignified tall firs begin.
Bluish, associating with their shadows,
a million Christmas trees stand
waiting for Christmas. The water seems suspended
above the rounded gray and blue-gray stones.
I have seen it over and over, the same sea, the same,
slightly, indifferently swinging above the stones,
icily free above the stones,
above the stones and then the world.
If you should dip your hand in,
your wrist would ache immediately,
your bones would begin to ache and your hand would burn
as if the water were a transmutation of fire
that feeds on stones and burns with a dark gray flame.
If you tasted it, it would first taste bitter,
then briny, then surely burn your tongue.

• Poetry Focus •

It is like what we imagine knowledge to be:
dark, salt, clear, moving, utterly free,
drawn from the cold hard mouth   80
of the world, derived from the rocky breasts
forever, flowing and drawn, and since
our knowledge is historical, flowing, and flown.

'in the gloaming'

GLOSSARY

4 *gloaming*: twilight, evening.
6 *shuttle*: tool used for weaving and mending fishing nets.
10 *cleated*: wooden projections nailed to a ladder to prevent slipping.
10 *gangplanks*: removable ramps used for boarding or leaving boats.
15 *opaque*: murky, dark, difficult to see through.
18 *translucence*: semi-transparent, light shining partially through.
24 *iridescent*: glittering, changing colours.
24 *coats of mail*: armour made of metal rings.
28 *capstan*: round machine used for winding or hauling rope.
32 *Lucky Strike*: American cigarette.
37 *sequins*: small, shiny discs used for decorating clothes.
52 *total immersion*: completely covered in liquid; a form of baptism.
63 *associating*: linking.
74 *transmutation*: changing shape.
77 *briny*: very salty.

EXPLORATIONS

1 In your opinion, what role has the old fisherman in the poem? Is he a link with the past, a person in harmony with his environment or something else? Refer closely to the text in your response.

2 Bishop uses a chilling maternal image at the conclusion of the poem. What effect has this startling metaphor on the poem's tone? Support your discussion with clear references from the text.

3 Did you find 'At the Fishhouses' thought-provoking? What questions did the poem raise about the poet and her attitudes? Refer to the text in your answer.

STUDY NOTES

'At the Fishhouses' comes from Elizabeth Bishop's award-winning second collection, *A Cold Spring* (1965). What Bishop sees is never quite what the rest of us see. She challenges us to look again. She gives us poetry as 'normal as sight … as artificial as a glass eye'. An ordinary sight of an old fisherman 'in the gloaming' mending nets in Nova Scotia becomes a strange, exact hallucination examining the essence of knowledge. Bishop saw; now we see. She changes the view.

The poem's opening section (**lines 1–40**) gives us a **detailed, sensuous description** of a scene from Nova Scotia. Bishop has an unerring sense of place. The fishhouses are described so vividly that we can almost smell the fish ('it makes one's nose run and one's eyes water'), see the fish tubs ('completely lined/with layers of beautiful herring scales') and hear the sea ('swelling slowly as if considering spilling over'). The poet draws us right into the scene with microscopic detail, making us pore over the surface of 'benches', 'lobsterpots' and 'masts'. We experience the 'apparent translucence' of the weathered, silvered wood, which matches the cold, opaque, silver sea. Musical language lends beauty to this timeless scene. The long 'o' sound in 'Although' is echoed in 'cold', 'old' and 'gloaming'. All is harmony. The colours of the fisherman's net, 'dark purple-brown', become 'almost invisible'. Nothing jars. The rhythmic work is conveyed in the pulsating phrase 'for the wheelbarrows to be pushed up and down on'. Physical effort is suggested by the assonance of 'u' and 'o'. In **lines 23–25**, the wheelbarrows are described in minute detail ('plastered/with creamy iridescent coats of mail'). The small, circular fish scales are like the metal rings on a medieval knight's coat of armour. Bishop moves in closer to show us similarly coloured little flies, also 'iridescent', moving on the scales.

The poet's eye focuses on 'the little slope behind the houses' and an 'ancient wooden capstan'. Here is a **forlorn reminder of the tough physical work** of the past. The discarded cylinder is 'cracked' and has 'melancholy stains, like dried blood'; the ironwork has also 'rusted'. In **line 32**, a human connection is made when the 'old man accepts a Lucky Strike' cigarette. The personal detail ('a friend of my grandfather') gives a surface intimacy to this chill poem. But there are hidden depths. The man is described as having 'sequins on his vest and on his thumb'. This decorative detail is more usually associated with glamorous ball gowns than an old fisherman's jersey. Does the image of the man's black knife, 'almost worn away', suggest an ebbing life?

In the poem's short second section (lines 41–46), we are at the water's edge and the repetition of 'down' draws us nearer the element of water as we note the 'long ramp/descending'. **The movement seems symbolic of Bishop's own descent into her subconscious mind.** As before, the graceful fish scales have transformed the wooden ramp into 'thin silver/tree trunks'.

The third section (lines 47–83) **changes the view**. We are now not merely looking, but seeing. We are **entering the interior**. We journey with Bishop to examine an element that is 'bearable to no mortal', yet is home 'to fish and to seals'. No human can survive in the icy waters of the North Atlantic Sea: 'Cold dark deep and absolutely clear'. Another figure, a seal, appears in this bleak, surreal sequence. In this compelling episode, seal and poet are linked by a shared belief in 'total immersion'. For the seal, this is into water. Is it some form of baptism for Bishop? The poet, however, finds no comfort in religion, despite singing hymns for the seal ('A Mighty Fortress Is Our God'). Religion, like the distant fir trees, is behind her, waiting to be cut down.

The sea now takes on a nightmarish aspect as Bishop describes it 'indifferently swinging above the stones' (line 68). It is becoming a sea of knowledge. The poet warns us against it, telling us that we will be hurt if we delve in: wrists 'would ache immediately' and hands 'would burn'. Just as in the Garden of Eden, knowledge came with a terrible price. Knowledge gleaned from the world is hard-earned. Mother Nature is depicted with a 'cold hard mouth' and 'rocky breasts'. Here is no warm, comforting, maternal presence. Instead, Bishop's own dark life is suggested. These final lines – filled with harsh sea imagery – are insightful. Place has receded and insight is present. We, together with the poet, realise that knowledge is like water ('flowing'). It is also 'drawn', like waves are moved by the power of the moon. As we recognise that the mysterious waves pass into the past, so we realise that knowledge is 'historical' and ends up 'flown'. **All are part of the flux of nature.** In the end, Bishop seems to accept that the vast ocean – like life itself – defies understanding.

ANALYSIS

'Bishop gives us facts and minute details, sinking or sliding giddily off into the unknown.' Discuss this statement with reference to the poem 'At the Fishhouses'. Support your views with close reference to the text.

SAMPLE PARAGRAPH

I certainly agree that Elizabeth Bishop give us 'facts and minute details'. The 'five fishhouses' are clearly described for the reader to see, with their characteristic 'steeply peaked roofs' and their walkways, 'narrow, cleated' to enable the wheelbarrows to move smoothly. The exchange between the poet and the old man ('a friend of my grandfather') is realistically shown, with even the brand of cigarette identified ('Lucky Strike'). We not only see the fish scales, 'sequins', 'coats of mail', but we also note the 'crawling' flies on the scale-splattered wheelbarrows. Then the poem turns from this detailed scrutiny of the actual to an abstract meditation. Here, the poet is 'sliding giddily off into the unknown'. From contemplating the icy North Atlantic Sea ('Cold dark deep and absolutely clear'), Bishop starts to explore the essence of knowledge – and even of life itself. Knowing hurts, it makes you 'ache', just as the icy water 'burns'. Knowledge is not comfortable; the world is not a nice place, with its 'cold hard mouth'. Experience and knowledge come with an expensive price tag. The last two lines, for me, are dreamlike and surreal. I imagine a sea of knowledge that has been gained in the past ('historical'). This knowledge is always changing and 'flowing' as new discoveries are made. Elizabeth Bishop has brought us from a minute exploration of place to a meditation on an abstract concept.

EXAMINER'S COMMENT

A precise discussion that deals directly with both aspects of the statement: 'facts and minute details' and 'sliding ... into the unknown'. Some good personal engagement and a clear understanding of the poem are evident. There is also effective use of apt quotation. Grade A.

CLASS/HOMEWORK EXERCISES

1. How does Bishop's style contribute to the communication of her themes? Refer to two literary techniques used by the poet in 'At the Fishhouses' and comment on their effectiveness in each case. Refer closely to the text in your response.
2. Copy the table below into your own notes and fill in critical comments about the last two quotations.

• Poetry Focus •

Elizabeth Bishop

Key Quotes

the heavy surface of the sea,/swelling slowly as if considering spilling over,/is opaque	The sluggish movement of the sea is expertly caught by the combined use of alliteration ('s') and broad vowels ('a', 'o', 'u').
The old man accepts a Lucky Strike	By naming a popular brand of American cigarette, Bishop adds a touch of authenticity to this moment of human interaction.
He has scraped the scales	The harsh, grating noise that the old, black knife makes is conveyed by the alliterative 's' sound and the onomatopoeic verb 'scraped'.
Cold dark deep and absolutely clear	
It is like what we imagine knowledge to be	

• Leaving Certificate English •

The Prodigal

The brown enormous odor he lived by
was too close, with its breathing and thick hair,
for him to judge. The floor was rotten; the sty
was plastered halfway up with glass-smooth dung.
Light-lashed, self-righteous, above moving snouts,   5
the pigs' eyes followed him, a cheerful stare –
even to the sow that always ate her young –
till, sickening, he leaned to scratch her head.
But sometimes mornings after drinking bouts
(he hid the pints behind a two-by-four),   10
the sunrise glazed the barnyard mud with red;
the burning puddles seemed to reassure.
And then he thought he almost might endure
his exile yet another year or more.

But evenings the first star came to warn.   15
The farmer whom he worked for came at dark
to shut the cows and horses in the barn
beneath their overhanging clouds of hay,
with pitchforks, faint forked lightnings, catching light,
safe and companionable as in the Ark.   20
The pigs stuck out their little feet and snored.
The lantern – like the sun, going away –
laid on the mud a pacing aureole.
Carrying a bucket along a slimy board,
he felt the bats' uncertain staggering flight,   25
his shuddering insights, beyond his control,
touching him. But it took him a long time
finally to make his mind up to go home.

Elizabeth Bishop

'the pigs' eyes followed him'

Poetry Focus

GLOSSARY

The title comes from the biblical parable of the Prodigal Son, a young man who wasted his inheritance on drunkenness and ended up working as a swineherd. The word 'prodigal' refers to a spendthrift or wastrel.
1 *odor*: odour, smell.
3 *sty*: pig-shed.
5 *snouts*: pigs' noses.
9 *bouts*: sessions.
20 *companionable*: comfortable.
20 *the Ark*: Noah's Ark. In the Bible story, Noah built a boat to save animals from a great flood.
23 *aureole*: circle of light.

EXPLORATIONS

1. In your opinion, is Elizabeth Bishop sympathetic to the central character in this poem? Give reasons for your answer, using close reference to the text.
2. Choose two images that you found particularly memorable in the poem. Comment briefly on the effectiveness of each.
3. Write your personal response to the poem, referring to the text in your answer.

STUDY NOTES

In 'The Prodigal', published in 1951, Elizabeth Bishop returns to the well-known Bible parable of the Prodigal Son. She imagines the squalor and degradation this wayward youth endured when he was forced to live among the pigs he looked after. The poet herself had experienced depression and alcoholism in her own life and could identify with the poem's marginalised central figure. Bishop uses a double-sonnet form to trace the prodigal's struggle from wretchedness to eventual recovery.

The poem's **opening lines** present the repugnant living conditions of the exiled prodigal's everyday life: 'The brown enormous odor' engulfs him. The abhorrent stench and filth of the pig-sty is the only life he knows. Immersed in this animal-like state, he has lost all sense of judgement. Even the odour, 'with its breathing and thick hair', is beyond his notice. **Bishop's graphic imagery is typically precise**, describing the foul-smelling sty's shiny walls as 'plastered halfway up with glass-smooth dung'.

In **lines 5–8**, the 'Light-lashed' pigs are given human traits ('self-righteous', 'a cheerful stare'). The poet conveys **a disturbing sense of the young man's confused and drunken grasp** on reality. In his sub-human state, overwhelmed by nausea and isolation, he now seems almost at home among the pigs. Although he is 'sickening', he can still show odd gestures of affection towards them – 'even to the sow that always ate her young'.

Bishop delves deeper into the alcoholic's secretive world in **lines 9–14**. Ironically, the morning hangovers are not entirely without their compensations: 'burning puddles seemed to reassure'. Despite the ugliness and deprivation of his diminished existence, **he can occasionally recognise unexpected beauty in nature**, such as when 'the sunrise glazed the barnyard mud with red'. It is enough to give him hope: 'then he thought he almost might endure/his exile'. Emphatic broad vowel sounds add a further dimension of pathos to this line.

The poem's second section begins on a more startling note: 'But evenings the first star came to warn' (**line 15**). There is a suggestion that **the prodigal is finally confronting his personal demons**. For the first time, he seems to realise that he is out of place among the orderly routine of farm life that is going on around him. Unlike the sleeping animals ('safe and companionable as in the Ark'), the unfortunate young man is now intensely aware of his dismal alienation. He is poised on the brink of coming to his senses.

For the frustrated prodigal, a defining moment occurs when he finally disassociates himself from the snoring pigs. Yet, ironically, it seems as though he almost envies their simple comfort and security 'beneath their overhanging clouds of hay'. Vivid images of routine farm life, such as 'The lantern – like the sun, going away' (**line 22**) take on a new symbolic significance for the unhappy exile. Is he finally considering the transience of life? Is there still a possibility of regaining his humanity? For an instant, **the young man seems to find a vague kind of hope** in the beautiful 'pacing aureole' of lamplight reflected on the mud.

A renewed vigour and purpose mark the poem's **final lines**. Bishop identifies exactly when the prodigal experiences 'shuddering insights'. This defining instant is symbolised by his acute awareness of 'the bats' uncertain staggering flight'. Taking his cue from nature, **he slowly accepts responsibility for his own destiny**: 'But it took him a long time/finally to make his mind up to go home'. This crucial decision to return from exile is a powerful illustration of human resilience. The poem's affirmative ending is emphasised by the importance placed on 'home' (the only unrhymed end word in the poem). Bishop's reworking of the well-known biblical tale carries a universal message of hope, offering the prospect of recovery not just from alcoholism but from any form of human debasement.

• Poetry Focus •

Elizabeth Bishop

ANALYSIS

'Elizabeth Bishop's mood can vary greatly – from deep depression to quiet optimism.' Discuss this statement, with particular reference to 'The Prodigal'.

SAMPLE PARAGRAPH

Bishop's poem, 'The Prodigal', is extremely grim. The early mood, describing the 'brown enormous odor' (American spelling) is clearly meant to capture the terrible living conditions of the young alcoholic son who had left his home, partied non-stop and fallen on hard times. The description of the outhouse is extremely repulsive. Bishop's tone is one of despair. The prodigal has fallen as low as any person, living among the pigs he looks after. The images are negative – 'rotten', 'sickening', 'barnyard mud'. The stench makes him queasy. But the mood changes when the alcoholic becomes more aware of himself and dares to hope that he will get it together and return to a decent life. Images of light and beauty suggest this – 'catching light', 'a pacing aureole'. The turning point is when the prodigal stumbles on 'shuddering insights' – which refers to his belief that he can regain his dignity and humanity if he really wants to. Although this is extremely difficult and 'took him a long time', he succeeds in the end. The last line emphasises his optimistic mood – as he decides to 'make his mind up to go home'.

EXAMINER'S COMMENT

A well-focused response, in the main, that addresses the question. Effective use of accurate quotation throughout. The answer would have benefited from some discussion on the restrained ('quiet') nature of the final optimism. Expression is weakened by slang and over-use of the word 'extremely'. Grade B.

CLASS/HOMEWORK EXERCISES

1. 'Bishop's poetry often goes beyond description to reveal valuable insights about people's courage and resilience.' Discuss this statement with particular reference to 'The Prodigal'. Refer to the poem in your response.
2. Copy the table below into your own notes and fill in critical comments about the last two quotations.

Key Quotes

The brown enormous odor he lived by	The overpowering filthy condition of the pig-sty is a startling metaphor for human degradation.
he hid the pints behind a two-by-four	Shame and deception are characteristics of Bishop's realistic portrayal of the alcoholic's behaviour.
pitchforks, faint forked lightnings	This striking comparison suggests the clarity, disorientation and paranoia that can accompany alcoholism.
the sunrise glazed the barnyard mud with red	
shuddering insights, beyond his control, /touching him	

Elizabeth Bishop

Questions of Travel

There are too many waterfalls here; the crowded streams
hurry too rapidly down to the sea,
and the pressure of so many clouds on the mountaintops
makes them spill over the sides in soft slow-motion,
turning to waterfalls under our very eyes.   5
– For if those streaks, those mile-long, shiny, tearstains,
aren't waterfalls yet,
in a quick age or so, as ages go here,
they probably will be.
But if the streams and clouds keep travelling, travelling,   10
the mountains look like the hulls of capsized ships,
slime-hung and barnacled.

Think of the long trip home.
Should we have stayed at home and thought of here?
Where should we be today?   15
Is it right to be watching strangers in a play
in this strangest of theatres?
What childishness is it that while there's a breath of life
in our bodies, we are determined to rush
to see the sun the other way around?   20
The tiniest green hummingbird in the world?
To stare at some inexplicable old stonework,
inexplicable and impenetrable,
at any view,
instantly seen and always, always delightful?   25
Oh, must we dream our dreams
and have them, too?
And have we room
for one more folded sunset, still quite warm?

But surely it would have been a pity   30
not to have seen the trees along this road,
really exaggerated in their beauty,
not to have seen them gesturing
like noble pantomimists, robed in pink.

– Not to have had to stop for gas and heard
the sad, two-noted, wooden tune
of disparate wooden clogs
carelessly clacking over
a grease-stained filling-station floor.
(In another country the clogs would all be tested.
Each pair there would have identical pitch.)
– A pity not to have heard
the other, less primitive music of the fat brown bird
who sings above the broken gasoline pump
in a bamboo church of Jesuit baroque:
three towers, five silver crosses.
– Yes, a pity not to have pondered,
blurr'dly and inconclusively,
on what connection can exist for centuries
between the crudest wooden footwear
and, careful and finicky,
the whittled fantasies of wooden cages.
– Never to have studied history in
the weak calligraphy of songbirds' cages.
– And never to have had to listen to rain
so much like politicians' speeches:
two hours of unrelenting oratory
and then a golden silence
in which the traveller takes a notebook, writes:

*'Is it lack of imagination that makes us come
to imagined places, not just stay at home?
Or could Pascal have been not entirely right
about just sitting quietly in one's room?*

*Continent, city, country, society:
the choice is never wide and never free.
And here, or there ... No. Should we have stayed at home,
wherever that may be?'*

• Poetry Focus •

Elizabeth Bishop

'the pressure of so many clouds on the mountaintops'

GLOSSARY

1 *here*: Brazil.
11 *hulls*: main sections of ships.
11 *capsized*: overturned in the water.
12 *barnacled*: covered with small shellfish.
20 *the sun the other way around*: the view of the sun in the southern hemisphere.
22 *inexplicable*: incomprehensible, mysterious.
34 *pantomimists*: people taking part in a pantomime, a slapstick comedy.
37 *disparate*: very different, separate.
45 *church of Jesuit baroque*: ornately decorated 17th-century churches, often found in Brazil.
51 *finicky*: excessively detailed, elaborate.
52 *whittled*: carved.
52 *fantasies*: amazing creations.
54 *calligraphy*: decorative handwriting (in this case, the swirling design of the carved birdcages).
57 *unrelenting*: never stopping, endless.
62 *Pascal*: Blaise Pascal, a 17th-century mathematician and philosopher who wrote that 'man's misfortunes spring from the single cause that he is unable to stay quietly in his room'.

EXPLORATIONS

1 From your reading of lines 1–12, describe Bishop's reaction to the landscape spread before her. How does she feel about this abundance of nature? Is she delighted, unhappy, awestruck? Support your response with quotation from the text.
2 Choose two examples of repetition in the poem. Briefly explain what each example contributes to Bishop's treatment of the poem's theme.
3 Would you consider the ending of the poem conclusive or inconclusive? What does Bishop really feel about travel? Refer closely to the text in your response.

• Leaving Certificate English •

STUDY NOTES

This is the title poem of Elizabeth Bishop's 1965 collection, *Questions of Travel*. Bishop herself was a great traveller, aided by an inheritance from her father. In this poem, she questions the need for travel and the desire that people have to see the world for themselves. The poet provokes the reader by posing a series of questions about the ethics of travel. She places her original observations of Brazil before us and wonders whether it would be better if we simply imagined these places while sitting at home. Finally, she challenges us to consider where our 'home' is.

Elizabeth Bishop

The poem's **opening line** is an **irritable complaint** about Brazil: 'There are too many waterfalls here'. In the first section (**lines 1–12**), Bishop observes the luxuriant, fertile landscape spread out before her. She finds fault with the 'crowded streams' that 'hurry too rapidly' and the 'pressure of so many clouds'. The richness of the misty equatorial landscape is caught in a series of soft sibilant 's' sounds ('spill', 'sides', 'soft slow-motion'). Clouds melt into the 'mile-long, shiny, tearstains'. Everything is on the move, changing position and shape. Both Bishop and the water are 'travelling, travelling'. **Repetition emphasises this restless movement.** The circular motion suggests that neither traveller nor clouds have any real purpose or direction. An original and striking image of a mountain range ('like the hulls of capsized ships') catches our attention. The vegetation is 'slime-hung'; the outcrops of rocks are like the crustaceans of shellfish ('barnacled'). As always, the poet's interest lies in the shape and texture of the words.

A more **reflective mood is found in the poem's second section** (**lines 13–29**). Bishop presents readers with a **series of challenging questions** for consideration. In all, eight 'questions of travel' are posed. Should we remain 'at home' and imagine 'here'? Bishop is uneasy at the prying scrutiny of tourists 'watching strangers in a play'. She is aware that this is how people live; it is not a performance for public consumption. The emphasis here is on the 'childishness' of the tourists as they rush around, greedily consuming sights, viewing the sun from its other side in southern countries, such as Brazil. But as far as Bishop is concerned, historic ruins and 'old stonework' do not speak to the visitor. The repetition of 'inexplicable' stresses the inaccessibility of foreign cultures. The bland, unknowing response of tourists is captured in the conversational phrase 'always delightful'. Their selfish desire for more and more experiences is vividly shown in the image of the traveller nonchalantly packing views, as if they were clothes or souvenirs being placed in a bag at the end of a trip: 'And have we

• 31 •

room/for one more folded sunset, still quite warm?' Perhaps Bishop is asking whether any famous sight ever actually touched the traveller, or was it skimmed over in a frenzy to pack in as much as possible?

Justification for travel is the dominant theme of the third section (lines 30– 59): 'But surely it would have been a pity/not to have seen'; '– A pity not to have heard'; 'a pity not to have pondered'; '– Never to have studied'; 'never to have had to listen'. The repetition of 'pity' beats out a tense rhythm as the poet seeks to condone travel. Bishop's well-known 'painterly eye' provides the evidence, as she presents a series of fresh, first-hand vignettes, e.g. the trees 'gesturing/like noble pantomimists, robed in pink'. The flowing movement of the trees, their flamboyant colour and their suggestion of Brazil's mime plays would be hard to imagine if not really experienced. The sound of this easy-going, carefree society is captured in the hard 'c' sound of 'carelessly clacking', which evokes the slovenly walk of local peasants. The Brazilian love of music is evident in 'clacking', a sound usually associated with the rhythmic castanets. The difference in cultures is wryly noted: 'In another country the clogs would all be tested./Each pair there would have identical pitch.' Elsewhere, all would be sanitised uniformity.

Are these the experiences the traveller would miss by not being in another country? The locals' cavalier attitude to functionality is shown in the contrasting images of the 'broken gasoline pump' and the intricate construction of a 'bamboo church' with 'three towers, five silver crosses'. **The spirit of the people soars in 'Jesuit baroque'**. A similar contrast is seen in wooden carving – the 'crudest wooden footwear' does not have the same importance for this free-spirited people as the 'careful and finicky ... fantasies of wooden cages' (line 51). Another unstoppable force, that of equatorial rainstorms, is likened to the endless rant of a politician bellowing out his 'unrelenting oratory'. Could any of this be imagined from afar?

Lines 58–67 begin in 'golden silence', as Bishop attempts to clarify her own thinking on the value of travel. In the final lines, she **wonders if we travel because we lack the imagination to visualise these places.** However, in the previous section, the poet has graphically shown that nothing can surpass a person **actually hearing and seeing** a place and its people. A reference is made to the 17th-century philosopher Blaise Pascal, who preferred to remain at home. The poet feels that he was not 'entirely right' about this and, by sharing her whimsical images of Brazil with us, she has led us to agree with her.

Another interesting question is posed: How free are we to go where we wish? Bishop states that the choices are 'never wide and never free'; there are always constraints on the traveller. But an emphatic 'No' tells us that this does not take away from the authenticity of the experience.

In the poem's **concluding lines**, Bishop returns to the question of whether or not people should stay at home. She then teases the reader with the follow-up, 'wherever that may be?' (**line 67**). This is a much deeper, philosophical reflection, which reverberates in our minds. **Home is a place of belonging**, from which travellers set out and to which they return. The visited countries are not secure bases; the tourist does not belong there, but is merely a visitor en route to somewhere else. In short, the traveller's role is one of an outsider – observing, but not participating. Bishop's own life experience is revealed here. Perhaps she travelled so extensively because she never felt truly at home in any single place.

ANALYSIS

'Elizabeth Bishop's poems are not only delightful observations, but are also considered meditations on human issues.' Discuss this statement with reference to the poem 'Questions of Travel'. Support your views with close reference to the text.

SAMPLE PARAGRAPH

Elizabeth Bishop was a tireless traveller and in the poem 'Questions of Travel', she presents the reader with evocative images from the lush, misty equatorial landscape of Brazil, where clouds 'spill over the sides' of mountains 'in soft slow-motion'. The giant mountain ranges are imaginatively conjured up before our eyes as upturned ships, and their vegetation and rocky sections are likened to the 'slime-hung and barnacled' appearance of the bottoms of these ships. The sounds of the people intrude upon our consciousness – disparate clogs 'carelessly clacking'. The harsh alliteration mimics the sound of wood hitting floor. No detail is too minute to escape her famous 'eye': 'the broken gasoline pump', 'the whittled fantasies of wooden cages', the 'three towers' and 'five silver crosses' of the small bamboo church. These are Bishop's delightful observations. But the poet also addresses ethical questions surrounding travel, particularly relevant in our times. The reader is asked to ponder 'Questions of Travel'. What right have we to watch people's private lives, as if they were performing in public? Why should we consume experiences and squeeze them up like clothes in a suitcase ('have we room for one more folded sunset ...?'). Why are we rushing around, 'travelling, travelling'? Why do we not 'just stay at home'? These issues have a modern resonance, as we are aware nowadays of the effect of our carbon footprint on the environment when we travel. The poem concludes with a curious question on the meaning of 'home'. Bishop asks us to consider where it is ('home,/wherever that may be'). Suddenly an accepted certainty becomes as hard to define as the disintegrating clouds at the start of the poem.

EXAMINER'S COMMENT

A careful examination of both parts of the statement – the poet's 'delightful observations' and her treatment of issues – is presented by the candidate. The thoughtful approach is referenced accurately with pertinent quotations from the poem. Grade A.

CLASS/HOMEWORK EXERCISES

1. Comment on the different tones in 'Questions of Travel'. Refer closely to the text in your response.
2. Copy the table below into your own notes and fill in critical comments about the last two quotations.

Key Quotes

the crowded streams/hurry too rapidly down to the sea	There is a tone of complaint from the jaded traveller in this run-on line.
Oh, must we dream our dreams/and have them, too?	The poet uses questions throughout this poem to invite the reader to consider accepted ideas in society. Do we have to experience directly as well as imagine?
blurr'dly and inconclusively	The awkward word 'blurr'dly' is made even clumsier by the poet's removal of the vowel 'e'. Bishop's lack of connection with foreign sights is cleverly shown.
weak calligraphy of songbirds' cages	
at home,/wherever that may be?	

The Armadillo

For Robert Lowell

This is the time of year
when almost every night
the frail, illegal fire balloons appear.
Climbing the mountain height,

rising toward a saint   5
still honored in these parts,
the paper chambers flush and fill with light
that comes and goes, like hearts.

Once up against the sky it's hard
to tell them from the stars –   10
planets, that is – the tinted ones:
Venus going down, or Mars,

or the pale green one. With a wind,
they flare and falter, wobble and toss;
but if it's still they steer between   15
the kite sticks of the Southern Cross,

receding, dwindling, solemnly
and steadily forsaking us,
or, in the downdraft from a peak,
suddenly turning dangerous.   20

Last night another big one fell.
It splattered like an egg of fire
against the cliff behind the house.
The flame ran down. We saw the pair

of owls who nest there flying up   25
and up, their whirling black-and-white
stained bright pink underneath, until
they shrieked up out of sight.

The ancient owls' nest must have burned.
Hastily, all alone,   30

Elizabeth Bishop

a glistening armadillo left the scene,
rose-flecked, head down, tail down,

and then a baby rabbit jumped out,
short-eared, to our surprise.
So soft! – a handful of intangible ash   35
with fixed, ignited eyes.

Too pretty, dreamlike mimicry!
O falling fire and piercing cry
and panic, and a weak mailed fist
clenched ignorant against the sky!   40

'the paper chambers flush and fill with light'

GLOSSARY

Elizabeth Bishop dedicated 'The Armadillo' to her friend and fellow poet, Robert Lowell. An armadillo is a nocturnal burrowing creature found mainly in South America. It rolls up into a ball to protect itself from danger.

1 *time of year*: St John's Day (24 June).
3 *fire balloons*: helium-filled balloons carrying colourful paper boxes.
5 *a saint*: St John.
6 *these parts*: Rio de Janeiro, Brazil.
7 *chambers*: hollow boxes.
11 *tinted*: shaded.
13 *the pale green one*: probably the planet Uranus.
16 *kite sticks of the Southern Cross*: cross-shaped constellation of stars.
35 *intangible*: flimsy, insubstantial.
36 *ignited*: lit up.
37 *mimicry*: imitation
39 *weak mailed fist*: the animal's bony armour (defenceless against fire).

EXPLORATIONS

1. Based on your reading of the first four stanzas, how does the poet present the fire balloons? Are they mysterious, beautiful, threatening? Refer to the text in your answer.
2. Comment on Bishop's use of interesting verbs in the poem.
3. In your view, is this an optimistic or pessimistic poem? Give reasons for your response.

STUDY NOTES

'The Armadillo' describes St John's Day (24 June) in Brazil, where Elizabeth Bishop lived for more than 15 years. On this annual feast day, local people would celebrate by lighting fire balloons and releasing them into the night sky. Although this custom was illegal – because of the fire hazard – it still occurred widely.

The **opening lines** introduce us to an exotic, night-time scene. The sense of drama and excitement is palpable as Bishop observes these 'illegal' balloons 'rising toward a saint'. They are also presented as fragile ('frail') but beautiful: 'the paper chambers flush and fill with light'. There is something magical and majestic about their ascent towards the heavens. **The language is simple and conversational**, reflecting the religious faith of the local people. Bishop compares the flickering light of the 'paper chambers' to 'hearts', perhaps suggesting the unpredictability of human feelings and even life itself.

Lines 9–20 associate the drifting balloons with distant planets, adding to their romantic air of mystery. The unsteady rhythm and alliterative description ('With a wind,/they flare and falter') suggest an irregular, buoyant movement. The poet is **increasingly intrigued by the fire balloons** as they 'wobble' out of sight. She notes that they sometimes 'steer between' the stars. Although she appears to be disappointed that the balloons are 'steadily forsaking us', she also worries about them 'suddenly turning dangerous' as a result of downdrafts buffeting and igniting them.

The tone changes dramatically in **line 21**, as Bishop recalls the destructive force of one exploding balloon that fell to earth near her house: 'It splattered like an egg of fire'. This characteristically stirring simile and the onomatopoeic verb highlight the sense of unexpected destruction. The shock is immediately felt by humans and animals alike. Terrified owls – desperate to escape the descending flames – 'shrieked up out of sight' (**line 28**). Contrasting **colour images**

emphasise the garish confusion: the 'whirling black-and-white' bodies of the owls are 'stained bright pink underneath'.

The poet suddenly notices 'a glistening armadillo', isolated and alarmed. Determined to escape the fire, it scurries away: 'rose-flecked, head down, tail down' (line 32). Amid the chaos, a baby rabbit 'jumped out', its urgent movement reflecting the lethal atmosphere. Bishop expresses her intense shock at seeing its burnt ears: 'So soft! – a handful of intangible ash'. **This graphic metaphor emphasises the animal's weakness and suffering.** Its 'fixed, ignited eyes' reflect the fire falling from the sky.

Bishop's emotive voice emerges forcefully in the poem's closing lines. She rejects her earlier description of the elegant fire balloons as being 'Too pretty'. Having witnessed the horrifying reality of the tormented animals, she castigates all her earlier romantic notions about the colourful festivities. Such thoughts are suddenly seen as 'dreamlike mimicry'. **The final image of the trapped armadillo is highly dramatic.** Its 'piercing cry' is harrowing. Bishop imagines the terrified creature in human terms ('a weak mailed fist'). Although the armadillo's helpless body is 'clenched ignorant against the sky', it is unlikely that its coat of armour will save it from fire. The irony of this small creature's last futile act is pitiful. Despite its brave defiance, the armadillo is doomed.

Some critics have commented on the **symbolism** in the poem, seeing the victimised creatures as symbols for powerless and marginalised people everywhere. It has been said that the careless fire balloons signify warfare, mindless violence and ignorant destruction. Is Bishop indicating that people's fate is beyond their control? It has also been suggested that the fire balloons symbolise love ('that comes and goes, like hearts') or even the creative impulse itself – beautiful, elusive and sometimes tragic. As with all poems, readers must decide for themselves.

ANALYSIS

Describe the tone in 'The Armadillo'. Does it change during the course of the poem? Refer to the text in your answer.

SAMPLE PARAGRAPH

The opening section of 'The Armadillo' is dramatic and filled with anticipation. Bishop sets the night-time scene during the noisy Brazilian festival to honour St John. 'This is the time of year' suggests a special occasion. The tone is celebratory and excited as the local community release countless 'illegal fire balloons' which light up the skies. The poet seems in awe of the wonderful spectacle, watching the 'paper chambers flush and fill with light'. The tone changes slightly to sadness as she watches the colourful balloons rise and disappear among the stars, 'steadily forsaking us'. A more dramatic transformation occurs when the exploding balloons start 'turning dangerous'. Due to the careless human activity, fire falls from the air, causing mayhem and destruction for the vulnerable animals below. Terrified owls 'shrieked', a young rabbit is burnt to 'intangible ash' and the armadillo is reduced to 'panic'. Bishop's personal voice is filled with anger and disgust as she rages against the 'falling fire'. The italics and exclamation marks in the final stanza highlight her frustrated tone as she identifies with the unfortunate armadillo whose 'weak mailed fist/clenched ignorant against the sky' represents a useless gesture of resistance.

EXAMINER'S COMMENT

A focused response that traces the development of tone in the poem. There is a real sense of well-informed engagement with the text. Short, accurate quotations are used effectively to illustrate the various changes in tone. The expression is clear, varied and controlled throughout. Grade A.

CLASS/HOMEWORK EXERCISES

1 'In reading the poetry of Elizabeth Bishop, readers can discover moments of quiet reflection and shocking truth.' Discuss this statement in relation to 'The Armadillo', supporting the points you make with reference to the poem.
2 Copy the table below into your own notes and fill in critical comments about the last two quotations.

• Poetry Focus •

Key Quotes

frail, illegal fire balloons appear	Bishop's description suggests both the elegance and menace of the balloons.
rising toward a saint	Might the rising balloons be a symbol of the hopes and prayers of the local people?
they shrieked up out of sight	Sharp, onomatopoeic effects echo the high-pitched sounds made by the fleeing owls.
paper chambers flush and fill with light	
a weak mailed fist/clenched ignorant against the sky!	

Sestina

September rain falls on the house.
In the failing light, the old grandmother
sits in the kitchen with the child
beside the Little Marvel Stove,
reading the jokes from the almanac,
laughing and talking to hide her tears.

She thinks that her equinoctial tears
and the rain that beats on the roof of the house
were both foretold by the almanac,
but only known to a grandmother.
The iron kettle sings on the stove.
She cuts some bread and says to the child,

It's time for tea now; but the child
is watching the teakettle's small hard tears
dance like mad on the hot black stove,
the way the rain must dance on the house.
Tidying up, the old grandmother
hangs up the clever almanac

on its string. Birdlike, the almanac
hovers half open above the child,
hovers above the old grandmother
and her teacup full of dark brown tears.
She shivers and says she thinks the house
feels chilly, and puts more wood in the stove.

It was to be, says the Marvel Stove.
I know what I know, says the almanac.
With crayons the child draws a rigid house
and a winding pathway. Then the child
puts in a man with buttons like tears
and shows it proudly to the grandmother.

But secretly, while the grandmother
busies herself about the stove,
the little moons fall down like tears

Elizabeth Bishop

from between the pages of the almanac
into the flower bed the child   35
has carefully placed in the front of the house.

Time to plant tears, says the almanac.
The grandmother sings to the marvellous stove
and the child draws another
inscrutable house.

'the child draws a rigid house'

GLOSSARY

A sestina is a traditional poetic form of six six-line stanzas followed by a final stanza of just three lines. In Bishop's 'Sestina', the same six words recur at the ends of lines in each stanza: tears, almanac, stove, grandmother, house and child. The final three-line stanza contains all six words.

4   *the Little Marvel Stove*: a heater or cooker that burns wood or coal.
5   *almanac*: calendar giving important dates, information and predictions.
7   *equinoctial*: the time when day and night are of equal length (22 September, 20 March approximately).
39 *inscrutable*: secret; impossible to understand or interpret.

EXPLORATIONS

1 Describe the atmosphere in the house. Is it happy, unhappy, relaxed, secretive? Support your response with quotation from the text.
2 Choose one image that you find particularly interesting and effective in the poem. Briefly explain your choice.
3 Write your personal response to the poem, supporting your views with reference to the text.

STUDY NOTES

'Sestina' was written between 1960 and 1965. For Elizabeth Bishop, the creative act of writing brought shape and order to experience. This poem is autobiographical, as it tells of a home without a mother or father. It is one of Bishop's first poems about her childhood and she was in her fifties, living in Brazil, when she wrote it. The complicated, restrictive structure of the poem can be seen as the poet's attempt to put order on her early childhood trauma.

The poem's **opening stanza** paints a domestic scene, which at first seems cosy and secure. The child and her grandmother sit in the evening light beside a stove. They are reading 'jokes from the almanac' and 'laughing and talking'. However, on closer observation, sadness is layered onto the scene with certain details: 'September rain', 'failing light' and the old grandmother hiding 'her tears'. Bishop adopts the point of view of adult reminiscence. She recollects; she is an observer of her own childhood and the poem's **tone is disturbing and challenging.** We are introduced to someone who looks, but never belongs. The six end-words echo chillingly throughout the poem. Here is a house full of tears with a grandmother and child together, alone.

In **stanza two** the grandmother believes that her autumn tears and the rain were 'foretold by the almanac'. There is a sense of inevitability and tired resignation in the opening lines. But normality enters: 'The iron kettle sings on the stove'. Homely domesticity is seen when the grandmother cuts some bread and says to the child: 'It's time for tea now'. **Bishop suddenly switches from being an observer to being an interpreter,** as she lets the reader see the workings of the child's mind in the **third stanza**: 'but the child/is watching the teakettle's small hard tears'. The child interprets sorrow everywhere; even droplets of steam from a kettle are transformed into the unwept tears of the grandmother. The phrase 'dance like mad' strikes a poignant note as we remember that Bishop's own mother was committed to a mental asylum when Bishop was just five years old; they never met again. A cartoon-like image of the almanac ends this stanza. We view it through the child's eyes, as 'the clever almanac'.

Stanza four focuses on the almanac. It is a **sinister presence,** personified as a bird of ill-omen: 'Birdlike' it hovers, suspended 'half open'. This mood of misgiving is heightened when we are told that the grandmother's cup is not full of tea, but of 'dark brown tears'. However, normality asserts itself again – the grandmother 'shivers' and puts wood on the fire.

Stanza five opens with the eerie personification of the Marvel Stove and the almanac. A **sense of inevitability** ('It was to be') and hidden secrets ('I know what I know') is absorbed by the child. Just as the older Bishop puts order on her traumatic childhood experiences by arranging them into the tightly knit form of the sestina, the child in the poem attempts to order her experiences by drawing houses. But the house is tense, 'rigid', inflexible. The sorrow of this childhood cannot be changed; the situation was as it was. This house can only

• Poetry Focus •

Elizabeth Bishop

be reached by a 'winding pathway'. Does this echo Bishop's later travels, as she searches for home? The sadness of Bishop's situation focuses on the drawing now, as the child sketches a man with 'buttons like tears'.

In **stanza six**, the tears continue to fall, now 'into the flower bed' in the child's drawing. **Fantasy and reality are mixed** in the innocent perception of the child, who feels but does not understand. The **final three lines** contain all six key words as the almanac instructs that it is 'Time to plant tears'. Is the time for regret over? Is the child planting tears that will be wept in the future? Should the grandmother and child be shedding tears now? The 'child draws another inscrutable house'. The secrecy continues. Nothing is as it seems. The future looks chilling.

ANALYSIS

Elizabeth Bishop's poetry is an emotional journey. To what extent do you agree with this? Support your views with close reference to 'Sestina'.

SAMPLE PARAGRAPH

I agree that the reader goes on an emotional journey with Bishop in the poem 'Sestina' as Bishop struggles to come to terms with her traumatic childhood. I think we focus with her, not on her as we observe the little child valiantly drawing 'inscrutable' houses, full of tears and secrets. Our hearts go out to the small, motherless and fatherless little girl, caught in an almost nightmare scenario, as the almanac hangs 'Birdlike' above her, almost like a bird of prey. The child feels, but does not comprehend the awful tragedy in the house and Bishop allows us to see the workings of the little mind as the child blends reality and fantasy, as stoves and books talk. Everything seems to know except the child. The chaotic experiences of Bishop's childhood are strictly contained in the formal structure of the sestina, the song of sixes, with six stanzas containing six lines ending with the same six end-words: house, grandmother, child, stove, almanac and tears. This mirrors the 'rigid' house of the little girl's drawings. Both the older and the younger Bishop are trying desperately to put order and control on this overwhelming situation. The reader experiences the poignancy through the details of the 'failing light', 'the rain that beats on the roof of the house' and the teacup 'full of dark brown tears'. Finally, the reader, like Bishop, is not left comforted, but is faced with enigma as yet another 'inscrutable' house is drawn. It is interesting to note that Bishop was unable to write about her early childhood until her fifties. Was it only then that the planted tears were harvested?

EXAMINER'S COMMENT

A competent and insightful answer focusing on the emotional journey undertaken by both the poet and reader. There is a clear sense of engagement with the poem. Quotations are used effectively throughout. Grade B.

CLASS/HOMEWORK EXERCISES

1. Some critics have said that 'Sestina' is a sentimental poem. Do you agree with this? Support your views with close reference to the poem.
2. Copy the table below into your own notes and fill in critical comments about the last two quotations.

Key Quotes

laughing and talking to hide her tears	This is a poem of pretence, where nothing is as it appears. The grandmother is trying to hide her sorrow as she attempts to entertain her granddaughter.
the clever almanac	The child assumes that the almanac must know many things, since it can foretell the phases of the moon, etc. Is there a sense of desperate curiosity contained in this poem?
It was to be, *says the Marvel Stove*	The blurring of fantasy and reality is shown by Bishop's clever use of personification.
the little moons fall down like tears/ from between the pages of the almanac	
and the child draws another inscrutable house	

• Poetry Focus •

First Death in Nova Scotia

In the cold, cold parlor
my mother laid out Arthur
beneath the chromographs:
Edward, Prince of Wales,
with Princess Alexandra, 5
and King George with Queen Mary.
Below them on the table
stood a stuffed loon
shot and stuffed by Uncle
Arthur, Arthur's father. 10

Since Uncle Arthur fired
a bullet into him,
he hadn't said a word.
He kept his own counsel
on his white, frozen lake, 15
the marble-topped table.
His breast was deep and white,
cold and caressable;
his eyes were red glass,
much to be desired. 20

'Come,' said my mother,
'Come and say good-bye
to your little cousin Arthur.'
I was lifted up and given
one lily of the valley 25
to put in Arthur's hand.
Arthur's coffin was
a little frosted cake,
and the red-eyed loon eyed it
from his white, frozen lake. 30

Arthur was very small.
He was all white, like a doll
that hadn't been painted yet.
Jack Frost had started to paint him

the way he always painted
the Maple Leaf (Forever).
He had just begun on his hair,
a few red strokes, and then
Jack Frost had dropped the brush
and left him white, forever.

The gracious royal couples
were warm in red and ermine;
their feet were well wrapped up
in the ladies' ermine trains.
They invited Arthur to be
the smallest page at court.
But how could Arthur go,
clutching his tiny lily,
with his eyes shut up so tight
and the roads deep in snow?

'the roads deep in snow'

GLOSSARY

1 *parlor*: room set aside for entertaining guests.
3 *chromographs*: coloured copies of pictures.
4 *Edward*: British Royal (1841–1910).
5 *Alexandra*: Edward's wife.
6 *King George*: King George V (1865–1936).
6 *Queen Mary*: wife of King George V (1867–1953).
8 *loon*: great crested grebe, an aquatic diving bird.
14 *counsel*: opinion.
28 *frosted*: iced.
36 *the Maple Leaf*: Canadian national emblem.
42 *ermine*: white fur.
46 *page*: boy attendant.

• Poetry Focus •

Elizabeth Bishop

EXPLORATIONS

1. With reference to lines 1–20 of the poem, describe the mood and atmosphere in the 'parlor'.
2. The poet uses several comparisons in this poem. Select one that you found particularly interesting and comment on its effectiveness.
3. Write your personal response to this poem, referring to the text in your answer.

STUDY NOTES

'First Death in Nova Scotia' was published when Elizabeth Bishop was in her early fifties. Written entirely in the past tense, it is an extraordinarily vivid memory of a disturbing experience. In the poem, Bishop's young narrator recounts the circumstances of an even younger cousin's death.

From the outset, we visualise Cousin Arthur's wake through a child's eyes. Characteristically, Bishop sets the scene in **stanza one** using **carefully chosen descriptive details**. It is winter in Nova Scotia. The dead child has been laid out in a 'cold, cold parlor'. Above the coffin are old photographs of two deceased royal couples. Fragmented memories of unfamiliar objects add to the dreamlike atmosphere. A stuffed loon sits on the marble-topped table. The young girl – in her desperate attempt to comprehend death – describes her cousin as 'all white, like a doll/that hadn't been painted yet'.

The dead boy and the 'dead' room soon become real for the reader, as does the dilemma faced by the **living child who seems increasingly confused**. **Stanza two** focuses on the young narrator's fixation with the stuffed bird. By thinking hard about the death of this 'cold and caressable' loon, she is trying to find a possible explanation for death. She is fascinated by the loon – perhaps an escape mechanism from the unfamiliar atmosphere in the parlour. In any case, the bird – with its desired 'red glass' eyes – might be less threatening than the dead body in the casket. Suddenly, somewhere in the child's imagination, Cousin Arthur and the personified bird become closely associated. Both share an impenetrably cold stillness, suggested by the 'marble-topped table', which is compared to a 'white, frozen lake'.

In **stanza three** the child's mother lifts her up to the coffin so that she can place a lily of the valley in the dead boy's hand. Her mother's insistent invitation ('Come and say good-bye') is chillingly remote. We sense the young girl's vulnerability ('I was lifted up') as she is forced to place the flower in

Arthur's hand. In a poignantly childlike image, she compares her cousin's white coffin to 'a little frosted cake'. **The mood turns progressively surreal** when the apprehensive narrator imagines the stuffed bird as a predator ('the red-eyed loon eyed it'). As always, Bishop's imagery is direct, brisk and to the point.

Bishop continues to explore childhood innocence in stanza four. Using the simplest of language, the child narrator describes her dead cousin: 'He was all white, like a doll'. In a renewed burst of imagination, she creates her own 'story' to explain what has happened to Arthur. His death must be caused by the winter frost that 'paints' the autumn leaves, including the familiar maple leaf. This thought immediately brings to mind the Canadian song 'The Maple Leaf Forever'. To the child, it seems that Jack Frost started to paint Arthur, but 'dropped the brush/and left him white, forever'. This creative **stream of consciousness highlights the child's efforts to make sense of death's mysterious reality.**

The imagery of childhood fairytales continues in stanza five when the narrator pictures Arthur in the company of the royal families whose pictures hang on the parlour walls. He is now 'the smallest page at court'. For the first time, the cold has disappeared and the royals are 'warm in red and ermine'. This fantasy, however, is short-lived. Still shaken by the strangeness of the occasion, the young narrator questions how this could have happened – especially as Arthur could not travel anywhere 'with his eyes shut up so tight/and the roads deep in snow'. The poem's **final, tender image reflects both the child's naivety and a genuine concern** for her cousin. Ironically, all around are symbols of immortality – the heavenly royal images of Arthur's entrance into a new, more glorious life. But the narrator's enduring uncertainty is central to the poem. The deceased boy, like the stuffed loon, seems really dead. Perhaps the dead don't go anywhere.

ANALYSIS

'The unknowable nature of life and death is a central concern of Elizabeth Bishop's poetry.' Discuss this statement with reference to 'First Death in Nova Scotia'. Support the points you make by referring to the poem.

SAMPLE PARAGRAPH

In several poems I have studied, it's clear that Elizabeth Bishop addresses life's mysteries. Sometimes she does this through the eyes of a child, as in 'First Death in Nova Scotia'. The poem describes her first experience of a death and how she struggled to understand it. It is an elegy for her young cousin, Arthur, and Bishop's memories of his funeral are extraordinarily clear. Everything about it confuses her. The formal, domestic setting is uninviting – a 'cold, cold parlor' has strange chromographs of the British Royal Family on the walls and a stuffed loon bird on the marble table. The bird had been shot by the dead child's father. As a young girl, Bishop recalls being forced to place a lily in her dead cousin's cold hand. These objects add to her insecurity. Nothing is explained to her and she escapes into her own imaginary world, comparing Arthur's casket to 'a little frosted cake'. She tries to tell herself that 'Jack Frost' is responsible for leaving Arthur 'white forever'. In the last verse, she imagines her dead cousin in an afterlife – not in heaven, but in a magical royal castle, 'the smallest page at court'. However, the young Elizabeth is caught between make-believe and reason. Her final thoughts challenge her own fantasy about life after death. Common sense tells her that Arthur, 'with his eyes shut up so tight', could not go out into 'roads deep in snow'. I thought Bishop really captured the uncertainty of a young child's mind in this very moving poem. I also got the impression that she was making the point that life and death can never be fully understood, no matter what age a person is.

EXAMINER'S COMMENT

A focused and sustained response, showing good engagement with the text. Starting with a succinct overview, the paragraph traces the progress of thought through the poem, using apt and accurate quotations effectively. Clear expression and a convincing personal approach also contribute to the Grade A standard.

CLASS/HOMEWORK EXERCISES

1. In your opinion, does 'First Death in Nova Scotia' present a sentimental view of death? Support your argument with reference to the text of the poem.
2. Copy the table below into your own notes and use the blank spaces to fill in the missing critical comments about the last two quotations.

Key Quotes

In the cold, cold parlor/my mother laid out Arthur	The atmosphere in the 'parlor' is icy and formal, emphasised by repetition and assonance.
he hadn't said a word./He kept his own counsel	In her confusion, the child narrator personifies the stuffed bird and assumes that the loon refuses to reveal the truth about how it died.
But how could Arthur go,/clutching his tiny lily	The child's final, poignant concern is for her dead cousin. Are her feelings sincere or sentimental?
Arthur's coffin was/a little frosted cake	
Arthur was very small./He was all white, like a doll	

• Poetry Focus •

Filling Station

Oh, but it is dirty!
– this little filling station,
oil-soaked, oil-permeated
to a disturbing, over-all
black translucency.　　　　　　　　　　　　　　5
Be careful with that match!

Father wears a dirty,
oil-soaked monkey suit
that cuts him under the arms,
and several quick and saucy　　　　　　　　　10
and greasy sons assist him
(it's a family filling station),
all quite thoroughly dirty.

Do they live in the station?
It has a cement porch　　　　　　　　　　　　15
behind the pumps, and on it
a set of crushed and grease-
impregnated wickerwork;
on the wicker sofa
a dirty dog, quite comfy.　　　　　　　　　　20

Some comic books provide
the only note of color –
of certain color. They lie
upon a big dim doily
draping a taboret　　　　　　　　　　　　　　25
(part of the set), beside
a big hirsute begonia.

Why the extraneous plant?
Why the taboret?
Why, oh, why, the doily?　　　　　　　　　　30
(Embroidered in daisy stitch
with marguerites, I think,
and heavy with gray crochet.)

Somebody embroidered the doily.
Somebody waters the plant, 35
or oils it, maybe. Somebody
arranges the rows of cans
so that they softly say:
ESSO—SO—SO—SO
to high-strung automobiles. 40
Somebody loves us all.

'it's a family filling station'

GLOSSARY

3 *oil-permeated*: soaked through with oil.
5 *translucency*: shine, glow.
8 *monkey suit*: dungarees; all-in-one working clothes.
10 *saucy*: cheeky, insolent.
18 *impregnated*: saturated.
24 *doily*: ornamental napkin.
25 *taboret*: drum-shaped low seat; a stool.
27 *hirsute*: hairy.

27 *begonia*: house plant with large multicoloured leaves.
28 *extraneous*: unnecessary, inappropriate.
31 *daisy stitch*: stitch pattern used in embroidery.
32 *marguerites*: daisies.
33 *crochet*: intricate knitting patterns.
39 *ESSO—SO—SO*: Esso is a brand of oil; reference to the careful arrangement of oil cans.

• Poetry Focus •

EXPLORATIONS

1. In your opinion, how does Bishop make the opening of this poem dynamic and interesting? Comment on her use of punctuation, direct speech and compound words which draw us into the world of the poem. Support your response with quotation from the text.
2. Trace the development of the poet's attitude to the filling station throughout the poem. Does it change from being critical and patronising to being more positive? Illustrate your answer with close reference to the text.
3. Comment on the effectiveness of Bishop's use of repetition in lines 34–41. Refer to the text in your response.

STUDY NOTES

Elizabeth Bishop was strongly influenced by a poetic movement called imagism, which was concerned with the accurate description of a particular thing. In this poem, she gives us an iconic description of a familiar American scene, the small-town gas station. Bishop found the new culture in 1960s California bewildering and it is noteworthy that the voice in this poem is that of an outsider trying to make sense of what is observed.

The prosaic title of the poem sets the mood for this commonplace scene. The poem **opens** with a **highly strung comment, disparaging the lack of hygiene** at the little station: 'Oh, but it is dirty!' The compound words ('oil-soaked', 'oil-permeated') suggest that everything is covered in a fine film of grease. This 'black translucency' has its own particular glow. Bishop's tense, dismissive tone creates a volatile, brittle atmosphere. Another voice interrupts her reverie: 'Be careful with that match!' In a few deft lines, the poet has set the scene, established the mood and introduced her characters. She uses a series of intensely descriptive lines that gives the poem a cinematic quality as we observe the details, like close-ups on a big screen.

The busy little station is captured in the **second stanza** through the poet's critical observations as she watches the family bustle about their business. The father is wearing a 'dirty,/oil-soaked monkey suit' that is too small for him ('cuts him under the arms'). The sons are described using alliteration of the letter 's', which suggests their fluid movements as well as their oily appearance ('several quick and saucy/and greasy sons assist'). Like the poet, we also become fascinated by this unremarkable place. Bishop's critical tone becomes more strident as she comments on the sons' insolence ('saucy') and their lack of hygiene ('all quite thoroughly dirty'). **We can hear the contempt in her voice.**

The third stanza questions, in a disbelieving tone, whether anyone could actually reside in such an awful place: 'Do they live in the station?' The poet's eye seems to pan around her surroundings **like a film camera, picking up on small details** as she tries to piece the scene into some kind of order. She lingers on the porch and its set of 'crushed and grease-/impregnated wickerwork'. Her disdain is obvious to the reader. The dog is described as a 'dirty dog' – it is almost as if it, too, has been smeared in oil. The repetition of the dead 'd' sound emphasises the unkempt appearance of everything. Then, suddenly, the poem pivots and turns on the homely word 'comfy'. The poet is surprised to note that the dog is quite content in this place. We are reminded that because of the harrowing circumstances of her own childhood, Bishop never fully knew what home was; we are left wondering if she longed to be 'comfy' too.

In stanzas four and five, she begins to notice evidence of a woman's hand in this place, particularly 'a big dim doily' on the 'taboret'. She notes the colourful 'comic books' and her eye is caught by the incongruous sight of 'a big hirsute begonia'. Even the plant has masculine qualities, being big and hairy. Bishop is observing the extraordinary in the ordinary; **in the most unlikely places, there is beauty and love.** We understand her bemusement as she reflects, almost in exasperation: 'Why, oh why, the doily?' We, like the narrator, have to reassess our initial view of this cluttered gas station. On closer observation, there is care and attention to detail, including artistic embroidery. We are brought right up close to examine this marvellous 'daisy stitch'. The critical, conversational tone of the poem clearly belongs to someone who is the observer, someone who does not belong. Is this the role Bishop was forced to adopt in her own life?

The poet's disturbed tone gives way in the final stanza to one of comfort. The lines whisper softly with sibilant 's' sounds. 'Somebody' cares for things, arranging the cans in order 'so that they softly say:/'ESSO-SO-SO-SO'. Bishop commented that 'so-so-so' was a phrase used to calm highly strung horses. It is used here to calm herself, just as the oil in the cans is used to make the engines of 'high-strung automobiles' run smoothly. The tone relaxes and a touch of humour creeps in: she notes that 'Somebody waters the plant,/or oils it, maybe'. The use of repetition is also soothing as we, like Bishop, come to realise that there is 'Somebody' who cares. **The poem concludes on a quiet note of assurance that everybody gets love from somewhere: 'Somebody loves us all'.** This is a particularly poignant ending when we consider that Elizabeth Bishop's parents were both absent from her childhood. The wonderfully comforting conclusion soothes the reader, just as a mother might quieten a cranky child.

ANALYSIS

'Elizabeth Bishop's poems are often described as deceptively casual'. Discuss this view of the poet's work, with particular reference to 'Filling Station'. Support your response with close reference to the text.

SAMPLE PARAGRAPH

'Filling Station' deals with a central concern of all human beings, the need to feel wanted and cared for, the need to belong. Instead of a heavy, moralising tone, Bishop adopts a deceptively casual tone in this poem from the start, with its almost colloquial, conversational opening: 'Oh, but it is dirty!' However, the carefully selected compound phrases ('oil-soaked, oil-permeated') show a carefully crafted poem. The subtle use of repetition of 'why' to suggest the increasing puzzlement of the poet as she tries to make sense of this scene also convinces me that Bishop is a master craftsperson at work, whose art conceals her effort. Similarly, the repetition of 'Somebody' at the end of the poem leaves a lasting sense of reassurance not only for the high-strung cars and their drivers, but also for us, as the poet states with deliberate calm that 'Somebody loves us all'. The tone is that of a loving parent soothing a contrary child who won't go to sleep. Here is a first-class poet skilfully communicating her message of quiet optimism. The word 'comfy' is also deceptively casual as, suddenly, the critical tone of the poem changes when the poet realises that the dog is content to be living there. Now the realisation dawns that even in the most outlandish places there is comfort and caring. I thought it was clever of the poet to use such a homely word as 'comfy' to totally change the mood of the poem. Finally, I think that Bishop shows her skill with a beautiful use of quiet, soothing music in the use of the sibilant 's' at the conclusion of the poem. Just as the oil stops the gears in a car from making noise and grating, the carefully arranged oil cans in the filling station send their message of comfort to the narrator and to us: 'Somebody loves us all'.

EXAMINER'S COMMENT

This is a competent answer, which addresses the question throughout. There is some very good engagement with the poem and effective use is made of apt references. The expression is reasonably well-controlled, although slightly repetitive at times. Grade B.

CLASS/HOMEWORK EXERCISES

1 A sense of homelessness pervades Bishop's poetry. Comment on this statement, referring to both the content and stylistic techniques used in 'Filling Station'. Support your discussion with reference to the poem.
2 Copy the table below into your own notes and fill in critical comments about the last two quotations.

Key Quotes

Be careful with that match!	We overhear this exchange on the forecourt. Bishop draws us into the dramatic world of this small family station.
a set of crushed and grease-/impregnated wickerwork	Precise detail helps us to visualise the grubby little station and to hear the disdainful tone of the poet's observations as she surveys the unappealing surroundings.
Why the extraneous plant?	A feeling of disbelief is captured in the question, as Bishop tries to make sense of what she sees as an incongruous detail.
so that they softly say: ESSO–SO–SO–SO	
Somebody loves us all	

• Poetry Focus •

In the Waiting Room

In Worcester, Massachusetts,
I went with Aunt Consuelo
to keep her dentist's appointment
and sat and waited for her
in the dentist's waiting room. 5
It was winter. It got dark
early. The waiting room
was full of grown-up people,
arctics and overcoats,
lamps and magazines. 10
My aunt was inside
what seemed like a long time
and while I waited and read
the *National Geographic*
(I could read) and carefully 15
studied the photographs:
the inside of a volcano,
black, and full of ashes;
then it was spilling over
in rivulets of fire. 20
Osa and Martin Johnson
dressed in riding breeches,
laced boots, and pith helmets.
A dead man slung on a pole
– 'Long Pig', the caption said. 25
Babies with pointed heads
wound round and round with string;
black, naked women with necks
wound round and round with wire
like the necks of light bulbs. 30
Their breasts were horrifying.
I read it right straight through.
I was too shy to stop.
And then I looked at the cover:
the yellow margins, the date. 35

Suddenly, from inside,
came an *oh!* of pain

– Aunt Consuelo's voice –
not very loud or long.
I wasn't at all surprised;
even then I knew she was
a foolish, timid woman.
I might have been embarrassed,
but wasn't. What took me
completely by surprise
was that it was *me*:
my voice, in my mouth.
Without thinking at all
I was my foolish aunt,
I – we – were falling, falling,
our eyes glued to the cover
of the *National Geographic*,
February, 1918.

I said to myself: three days
and you'll be seven years old.
I was saying it to stop
the sensation of falling off
the round, turning world
into cold, blue-black space.
But I felt: you are an *I*,
you are an *Elizabeth*,
you are one of *them*.
Why should you be one, too?
I scarcely dared to look
to see what it was I was.
I gave a sidelong glance
– I couldn't look any higher –
at shadowy gray knees,
trousers and skirts and boots
and different pairs of hands
lying under the lamps.
I knew that nothing stranger
had ever happened, that nothing
stranger could ever happen.
Why should I be my aunt,
or me, or anyone?
What similarities –

• Poetry Focus •

boots, hands, the family voice
I felt in my throat, or even
the *National Geographic*   80
and those awful hanging breasts –
held us all together
or made us all just one?
How – I didn't know any
word for it – how 'unlikely' …   85
How had I come to be here,
like them, and overhear
a cry of pain that could have
got loud and worse but hadn't?

The waiting room was bright   90
and too hot. It was sliding
beneath a big black wave,
another, and another.

Then I was back in it.
The War was on. Outside,   95
in Worcester, Massachusetts,
were night and slush and cold,
and it was still the fifth
of February, 1918.

'then it was spilling over'

GLOSSARY

1 *Worcester*: much of the poet's childhood was spent here.
9 *arctics*: waterproof overshoes.
14 *National Geographic*: international geography magazine.
21 *Osa and Martin Johnson*: well-known American explorers.
23 *pith helmets*: sun helmets made from dried jungle plants.
25 *'Long Pig'*: term used by Polynesian cannibals for human flesh.
61 *Elizabeth*: the poet is addressing herself.
95 *The War*: First World War (1914–18).

EXPLORATIONS

1. In your view, what image of women is presented in the poem? Support your answer with reference to the text.
2. Select two images that have a surreal or dreamlike impact in the poem. Comment on the effectiveness of each image.
3. Write your personal response to the poem, using textual reference.

STUDY NOTES

'In the Waiting Room' describes a defining coming-of-age experience for the poet when she was just six years old. While her aunt receives dental treatment, the child narrator browses through the pages of a *National Geographic* magazine and observes what is happening around her. In the powerful and provocative moments that follow, she begins to acknowledge her individual sense of being female.

The poem opens with a specific setting recalled in vivid detail by the child narrator. She flicks through a *National Geographic* magazine in the dentist's office while her aunt is in the patients' surgery. Familiar images of 'grown-up people,/arctics and overcoats' seem to convey a sense of wellbeing. It is the winter of 1918 in Worcester, Massachusetts. **The language is direct and uncomplicated, mirroring the candid observations of a young girl** as filtered through the adult poet's mature interpretation. Short sentences establish the fragmented flashback, allowing the reader to identify immediately with the narrative: 'It was winter. It got dark/early'. In addition to the unguarded tone, Bishop's short lines give the poem a visual simplicity, even though the **first stanza** is composed of 35 lines.

The mood changes from **line 18** onwards, as the young girl studies the dramatic magazine photographs of an active volcano 'spilling over/in rivulets of fire'. For the first time, **she recognises the earth's destructive force**. In contrast to the earlier feeling of security in the waiting room, the atmosphere becomes uneasy. Disturbing pictures ('A dead man slung on a pole' and 'Babies with pointed heads') are as intriguing as they are shocking. The child is drawn further into an astonishingly exotic world of cannibalism and violence. Graphic images of ornamental disfigurement seem horrifying: 'naked women with necks/wound round and round with wire'. The repetition of 'round and round' emphasises the young girl's spiralling descent into an enthralling world. Caught between fascination, repulsion and embarrassment ('too shy to stop'), she concentrates on the magazine's cover in an effort to regain control of her feelings.

Elizabeth Bishop

The child is unexpectedly startled by a voice 'from inside' (**line 36**). At first, she presumes that the sound ('an *oh!* of pain') has been made by her aunt. But then something extraordinary happens and she realises that she has made the sound herself: 'it was *me*'. This sudden awareness that the cry has come from within herself prompts a **strange, visionary experience** in which she identifies closely with her 'foolish aunt'. The scene is dramatic and dreamlike: 'I – we – were falling, falling'.

In the surreal sequence that follows, the child focuses on her approaching birthday as she tries hard to resist the sensation of fainting: 'three days/and you'll be seven years old' (**line 54**). Ironically, it is at this crucial point (on the edge of 'cold, blue-black space') that she gains an astonishing insight into her own sense of self: 'you are an *Elizabeth,*/you are one of *them*'. The idea of sharing a common female identity with her aunt and the unfamiliar women in the magazine pictures is almost overwhelming: 'nothing stranger/had ever happened' (**line 72**). To the distraught child, it seems as though **all women have lost their individuality and have merged into a single female identity**. Although she attempts to stay calm, she is plagued by recurring questions and confusion: 'Why should I be my aunt,/or me, or anyone?' The young Elizabeth's awakening to adulthood is obviously painful. In attempting to come to terms with her destiny as both an individual and also as part of a unified female gender, she makes this hesitant statement: 'How – I didn't know any/word for it – how "unlikely" …'.

Before she can return to everyday reality, the young girl must endure further discomfort. Her surroundings feel 'bright/and too hot' (**line 90**) and she imagines being repeatedly submerged 'beneath a big black wave', a metaphor for helplessness and disorientation. In the **final stanza**, she regains her composure in the waiting room's apparent safety, where she lists the certainties of place and time. But there is a distinct sense of life's harshness: 'The War was on' and Massachusetts is encountering 'slush and cold' (**line 97**). Such **symbols are central to our understanding of this deeply personal poem**. Just as the image of the erupting volcano seemed to signify Bishop's development, the waiting room itself is a significant location as a transition point in her self-awareness.

ANALYSIS

'An unsettling sense of not being fully in control is a central theme in the poetry of Elizabeth Bishop.' To what extent is this true of 'In the Waiting Room'? Support your answer with reference to the text of the poem.

SAMPLE PARAGRAPH

The theme of the trauma of growing up is central to 'In the Waiting Room'. It's unlike many nostalgic poems. They often describe childhood experiences in a sentimental way. But this one's very disturbing. It's set in a dentist's where the poet remembers waiting for 'Aunt Consuelo' who is having treatment. The atmosphere at the start is quite relaxed as the child passes the time by reading an old copy of the *National Geographic*. However, the photographs of a black volcano 'full of ashes' and of cannibals carrying a dead man ('Long Pig') are extremely upsetting. The mood becomes nervous. Photographs of African native women terrify the child as some of them wear wire necklaces. The poet compares them to 'light bulbs' – an image which immediately frightens her. The outside world is so violent and unexpected that she then goes into a trance-like state and cries out in agony. Her experience is more and more unsettled as she struggles to keep a grip on reality. Instead, she faints into 'cold, blue-black space'. The image suggests how out of control she is. However, what really unsettles her is the discovery for the very first time that she herself is a young woman and she shares this with every other female. The unusual photos of the naked African women suggest her own future and she becomes terrified. Her uneasy feelings are summed up at the end when she describes being overcome by the heat in the crowded waiting room, 'beneath a big black wave'. This leaves me feeling sympathy for this traumatised girl who is very unsure about her life and future role as a woman.

EXAMINER'S COMMENT

A reasonably well-focused and sustained response, which addresses the question competently. Good use is made of quotations. The expression could be more controlled in places, particularly in the opening section. Grade B.

CLASS/HOMEWORK EXERCISES

1. 'Bishop's reflective poems combine precise observation with striking imagery.' Discuss this view with reference to 'In the Waiting Room'. Refer to the poem in your answer.
2. Copy the table below into your own notes and fill in critical comments about the last two quotations.

Key Quotes

the inside of a volcano,/black, and full of ashes	The dramatic image suggests danger and the unknown. It might also symbolise the child's coming of age.
naked women with necks/wound round and round with wire	Graphic imagery illustrates the child's introduction to a disconcerting world. The alliteration and insistent rhythm emphasise her sense of shock.
you are an **Elizabeth**,*/you are one of* them	The alarming insight that her secure sense of uniqueness is being absorbed into a greater female identity is a moment of epiphany for the child.
It was sliding/beneath a big black wave	
Then I was back in it./The War was on	

LEAVING CERT SAMPLE ESSAY

Q **'Reading the poetry of Elizabeth Bishop.'**

Write out the text of a talk that you would give to your class in response to the title above. Your talk should include the following:
- **Your reactions to her themes or subject matters.**
- **What you personally find interesting in her style of writing.**
- **Refer to the Elizabeth Bishop poems that you have studied.**

MARKING SCHEME GUIDELINES

Note the instruction ('should') to candidates to deal with **both** elements of the question. Expect discussion, though not necessarily equal, of both elements. Reward achievement of an appropriate register. Answers must contain clear evidence of engagement with the poetry of Elizabeth Bishop on the course.

Some of the following areas might provide material for candidates:

- Travel and sense of place.
- Celebration of the ordinary.
- Childhood, nature, death.
- Range of moods in her poems.
- Freshness of her viewpoint.
- Vivid, detailed description.
- Energy and intensity of her language.
- Variety of poetic forms, etc.

SAMPLE ESSAY
(Reading the poetry of Elizabeth Bishop)

1 *Fellow students, a poet who travelled widely and asks, 'But surely it would have been a pity not to have seen this road?' is worth reading. Even more so when she follows this up by the cryptic, 'Should we have stayed at home – wherever that may be?' Bishop's tragic early childhood resonates sadly in this question. She did not have the advantage of a stable home life. This loss is a dominant feature in her poetry. She is an outsider, an observer; someone who comments, but does not belong. I feel this is particularly evident in 'Sestina' and 'Filling Station'. These poems show a sense of exclusion, a feeling of insecurity, anxiety and tension. She feels different. Many teenagers can identify with these feelings.*

Elizabeth Bishop

② In 'Filling Station' the main character is looking at a scene that is complete. But the woman is not part of this. At first, this lady driver sits criticising the 'oil-soaked, oil-permeated' filling station in a condescending tone: 'Oh, but it is dirty'. She is critical of the family of male workers – the father in his 'dirty oil-soaked monkey suit' and his 'several quick and saucy/and greasy sons'. Her attitude towards the little station and its inhabitants is one of contemptuous superiority. Her focus is on the film of oil that permeates everything. She is revving at high speed, like the engines of the cars on the forecourt. She smokes and a terse voice shouts, 'Be careful with that match!' Not only does Bishop allow us to see this place, but also she enables us to hear its loud, rough sounds by the use of this conversational phrase.

③ But a detail stops the driver, and she begins to realise that this ordinary little place teaches a lesson: 'Somebody loves us all'. I found it interesting, and I hope you will too, that the poem turns on the line 'a dirty dog, quite comfy'. Animals and people are happy and secure in the filling station. This humble place is a caring environment, one where people look after each other. 'Somebody embroidered the doily', 'Somebody waters the plant', the highly strung lady driver relaxes enough to even crack a joke about the plant ('or oils it'). Just as the grating sound of the engine is lubricated to a silky purr by the oil, so the tense driver is soothed by the soft, sibilant sounds, 'ESSO–SO–SO–SO'. It suddenly becomes clear that love and happiness can be experienced in even the most dismal-looking environment. For me, a shadow hangs over this ending, as I wonder whether Bishop yearned for such comfort in her own life since she experienced, at a tender age, the death of her father and the institutionalisation of her mother. I wonder, when you read this poem, will you agree with me?

④ This incredible sadness is very intensely felt in 'Sestina'. The whole poem is filled with secret unhappiness as the older Bishop looks back at a domestic scene, a grandmother making tea and reading to her little granddaughter. An imaginative device is used by the poet – she adopts the role of observer, as she looks back at her own life. So, three pairs of eyes (the child's, the older Bishop's and the reader's) are on this intriguing scene. I thought it was poignant how the child tries to order her experiences by drawing 'rigid' houses. The older poet attempts to order the chaotic experiences of her early childhood by using the tightly knit form of the sestina, the 'song of sixes'. The child's unyielding house mirrors the uncompromising form of the poem, with its six highly charged words: grandmother, child, stove, tears, almanac and house. These words contain the meaning of the poem, unlike the house, which remains a puzzle. The older Bishop comprehends, the younger child is aware, but unknowing. The little girl feels, but does not understand the sadness in the atmosphere, so she draws 'a man with buttons likes tears'. Is this a reference to the absent father? The droplets of water 'dance like mad'. Is this a reference to the institutionalised mother? See what you think.

5. Often, when a person is dissatisfied with home, travel seems an option. Bishop certainly travelled. Nowadays we are all concerned with our global footprint and air travel is coming under scrutiny. In the poem 'Questions of Travel', Bishop examines this problem. The traveller could be seen as a greedy consumer: 'have we room for one more sunset?' Using a pleading, conversational tone, she seeks to justify this rushing around: 'But surely it would have been a pity/not to have seen … A pity not to have heard … a pity not to have pondered'. Her bleak tone ('Is it lack of imagination?') seeks to know why we have to travel instead of remaining at home, 'just sitting quietly in one's room'. I found this focus on home intriguing and sad. Had Bishop never filled the void left by her sad early experiences? I wondered had she found home in Florida where she caught her 'tremendous fish'? Or had she found it in Nova Scotia in 'the cold, cold parlor' where 'Arthur's coffin was/a little frosted cake'? Or was Bishop in a 'waiting room' all her life, standing apart, observing, recording: 'How had I come to be here?'

6. Thank you for your kind attention today. I hope you can see that Bishop has much to say to those of us who search to find meaning and long to belong. I urge you to travel with Elizabeth Bishop and hope that you find home, 'wherever that may be'.

(approx. 930 words)

GRADE: A1		
P	=	15/15
C	=	15/15
L	=	15/15
M	=	5/5
Total	=	50/50

EXAMINER'S COMMENT

This personal response shows a close reading of the question. The register of a talk is well-established and sustained and the student has given thoughtful opinions on Bishop's themes and offered interesting analysis on her writing style, particularly the use of point of view.

SAMPLE LEAVING CERT QUESTIONS ON BISHOP'S POETRY (45–50 MINUTES)

1. 'I enjoyed (**or** did not enjoy) the poetry of Elizabeth Bishop.' Respond to this statement, referring to the poetry of Elizabeth Bishop on your course. Explain why you enjoyed (**or** did not enjoy) her poetry. Support your views with reference to the poems of Bishop on your course.
2. What impact did the poetry of Elizabeth Bishop make on you as a reader? In shaping your answer, you might like to consider the following:
   - The poet's themes and subject matter.
   - The poet's use of language and imagery.
   - Your favourite poem or poems.
3. 'The poetry of Elizabeth Bishop appeals to the modern reader for many reasons.' Write an essay in which you outline the reasons why poems by Elizabeth Bishop have this appeal. Refer closely to the poems by Bishop on your course.

SAMPLE ESSAY PLAN (Q3)

'The poetry of Elizabeth Bishop appeals to the modern reader for many reasons'. Write an essay in which you outline the reasons why poems by Elizabeth Bishop have this appeal. Refer closely to the poems by Bishop on your course.

- *Intro*: Poet takes ordinary, everyday experiences and shows us the drama and wonder there. Detailed, imaginative descriptions fill her poetry so that the reader journeys to self-discovery with her. The modern reader does not like to be lectured; instead, the quiet voice of Bishop shows. Clever use of form and viewpoint intrigue today's reader, as the themes are examined honestly and sympathetically.

Elizabeth Bishop

- *Point 1:* Based on an actual event, 'The Fish' describes a day spent alone when the poet caught a 'tremendous fish'. Precise details allow us to examine the fish: similes ('hanging like wallpaper', 'packed in like feathers'). Bravery of the old fish is shown ('five big hooks', 'Like medals'). Wonder ('rainbow, rainbow, rainbow').

- *Point 2:* Modern reader enjoys documentary-style background information on a character. 'First Death in Nova Scotia' deals with the young Bishop's first experience of death ('Come and say goodbye/to your little cousin'). Childhood viewpoint enchants and fills reader with sadness (coffin like a 'frosted cake'). Uses unexpected, startling imagery to make the reader see the event through the eyes of a child.

- *Point 3:* Sense of alienation is a phenomenon of today ('falling off/the round, turning world/into cold, blue-black space') and is shown effectively in 'In the Waiting Room'. Reader experiences with the young Bishop the dawning that everybody is a separate individual ('you are an I'), yet all are connected ('I was my foolish aunt').

- *Point 4:* Form of 'Sestina' increases depth of poet's feeling as she strains to hold in order a feeling of chaos. Six key end-words in each of six stanzas, all contained in final rhyming triplet.

- *Point 5:* Viewpoint of high-strung voice in 'Filling Station'. Cinematic quality of description: camera panning ('plant', 'taboret', 'doily') and camera close-up ('Embroidered in daisy stitch/with marguerites'). Sympathetic conclusion: 'Somebody loves us all'.

- *Conclusion:* Bishop's honesty in showing her struggle with life and her honesty in confronting the awful side of life endears her to the modern reader: 'When you write my epitaph, you must say I was the loneliest person who ever lived.'

EXERCISE

Develop one of the above points into a paragraph.

POINT 2 – SAMPLE PARAGRAPH

Bishop's poetry deals with the memory of specific occurrences in her life. The modern reader is familiar with this type of writing in magazines and documentaries. 'First Death in Nova Scotia' is about her little cousin Arthur's death when he was five. It is the young Bishop's first experience of death and it is clear she does not understand the concept. The poet enables us to see the event through the eyes of the child and also allows us to see the workings of the child's mind. The setting frightens her: a stuffed loon 'hadn't said a word' since 'Uncle Arthur fired/a bullet in him'. The 'red glass' eyes were 'much to be desired'. The poignancy of the description of the little dead boy as a 'doll/that hadn't been painted yet' is heartbreaking as we see the young girl apply a childish understanding to an adult event, death. 'Jack Frost had started to paint him': this is the child referencing her nursery rhyme store of knowledge as she tries to comprehend what is happening. She continues this storybook line of thought as she looks at the royal pictures on the walls and imagines the 'gracious royal couples' having her dead cousin as their 'smallest page at court'. However, the awfulness of death is shown in the final question, as the young Bishop wonders: 'how could Arthur go … with his eyes shut up so tight/and the roads deep in snow?' Yet again, we see Bishop, the outsider.

EXAMINER'S COMMENT

This paragraph engages very closely with the poem – but in a general sense. There is little direct analysis of its appeal for the modern reader. While it focuses well on the child's point of view, with judicious use of quotations, the original essay question could be addressed more explicitly. Grade C.

Last Words

'Elizabeth Bishop is spectacular in being unspectacular.'

Marianne Moore

'Bishop disliked the swagger and visibility of literary life.'

Eavan Boland

'The sun set in the sea ... and there was one of it and one of me.'

Elizabeth Bishop

'Forever is composed of nows.'

Emily Dickinson (1830–86)

Emily Dickinson was born on 10 December 1830 in Amherst, Massachusetts. Widely regarded as one of America's greatest poets, she is also known for her unusual life of self-imposed social seclusion. An enigmatic figure with a fondness for the macabre, Dickinson never married. She was a prolific letter-writer and private poet, though fewer than a dozen of her poems were published during her lifetime. It was only after her death in 1886 that her work was discovered. It is estimated that she wrote about 1,770 poems, many of which explore the nature of immortality and death, with an almost mantric quality at times. Ultimately, however, she is remembered for her distinctive style, which was unique for the era in which she wrote. Her poems contain short lines, typically lack titles and often ignore the rules of grammar, syntax and punctuation, yet she expressed far-reaching ideas within compact phrases. Amidst paradox and uncertainty, her poetry has an undeniable capacity to move and provoke.

• Poetry Focus •

PRESCRIBED POEMS (HIGHER LEVEL)

Emily Dickinson

1 '"Hope" is the thing with feathers' (p. 76)

In this upbeat poem, Dickinson addresses the experience of hope and imagines it as having some of the characteristics of a small bird.

2 'There's a certain Slant of light' (p. 80)

A particular beam of winter light puts the poet into a depressed mood in which she reflects on human mortality and our relationship with God.

3 'I felt a Funeral, in my Brain' (p. 84)

Dickinson imagines the experience of death from the perspective of a person who is about to be buried.

4 'A Bird came down the Walk' (p. 89)

The poet observes a bird and tries to establish contact with it, revealing both the beauty and danger of nature.

5 'I Heard a Fly buzz—when I died' (p. 93)

Another illustration of Dickinson's obsession with the transition of the soul from life into eternity.

6 'The Soul had Bandaged moments' (p. 97)

This intricate poem explores the soul's changing moods, from terrified depression to delirious joy.

7 'I could bring You Jewels—had I a mind to' (p. 102)

In this short love poem, Dickinson celebrates nature's simple delights and contrasts the beauty of an everyday flower with more exotic precious gifts.

8 'A narrow Fellow in the Grass' (p. 106)

Using a male perspective, the poet details the fascination and terror experienced in confronting a snake.

9 'I taste a liquor never brewed' (p. 110)

Dickinson uses an extended metaphor of intoxication in this exuberant celebration of nature in summertime.

10 **'After great pain, a formal feeling comes' (p. 114)**

A disturbing examination of the after-effects of suffering and anguish on the individual. Dickinson's comparisons highlight the experience of deadly numbness.

• Poetry Focus •

'Hope' is the thing with feathers

'Hope' is the thing with feathers—
That perches in the soul—
And sings the tune without the words—
And never stops—at all—

And sweetest—in the Gale—is heard—   5
And sore must be the storm—
That could abash the little Bird
That kept so many warm—

I've heard it in the chillest land—
And on the strangest Sea—   10
Yet, never, in Extremity,
It asked a crumb—of Me.

Emily Dickinson

'And sweetest—in the Gale—is heard—'

GLOSSARY

5 *And sweetest—in the Gale—is heard*: hope is most comforting in times of trouble.
7 *abash*: embarrass; defeat.
11 *in Extremity*: in terrible times.

EXPLORATIONS

1 What are the main characteristics of the bird admired by Dickinson? Does the image help to or hinder your understanding of the meaning of hope? Refer to the poem in support of your opinions.
2 Would you consider Dickinson to be an optimist or pessimist? How does the poem contribute to your view?
3 In your view, what is the purpose of the poem – to instruct, to explain, to express a feeling? Support your response by reference to the text.

STUDY NOTES

> Few of Emily Dickinson's poems were published during her lifetime and it was not until 1955, 69 years after her death, that an accurate edition of her poems was published, with the original punctuation and words. This didactic poem explores the abstraction, hope. It is one of her 'definition' poems, wherein she likens hope to a little bird, offering comfort to all.

The dictionary definition of hope is an expectation of something desired. The Bible refers to hope, saying, 'Hope deferred maketh the heart sick', while the poet Alexander Pope (1688-1744) declares that 'Hope springs eternal in the human breast'. In **stanza one**, Dickinson explores hope by using the **metaphor of a little bird** whose qualities are similar to those of hope: non-threatening, calm and powerful. Just like the bird, hope can rise above the earth with all its troubles and desperate times. Raised in the Puritan tradition, Dickinson, although rejecting formal religion, would have been aware of the religious symbolism of the dove and its connection with divine inspiration and the Spirit or Holy Ghost, as well as the reference to doves in the story of Noah's Ark and the Flood. Hope appears against all odds and 'perches in the soul'. But this hope is not easily defined, so she refers to it as 'the thing', an inanimate object. This silent presence is able to **communicate** beyond reason and logic and far **beyond the limitations of language**: 'sings the tune without the words'. Hope's permanence is highlighted by the unusual use of dashes in the punctuation: 'never stops—at all—'. This effective use of punctuation suggests the ongoing process of hope.

Stanza two focuses on the tangible qualities of hope (sweetness and warmth) and shows the spiritual, emotional and psychological **comfort found in hope**. The 'Gale' could refer to the inner state of confusion felt in the agony of despair. The little bird that comforts and shelters its young offers protection to 'so many'. The vigour of the word 'abash' suggests the buffeting wind of the storm against which the little bird survives. The last two lines, which run on, convey the welcoming, protective circle of the little bird's wing.

A **personal experience of hope in times of anguish** ('I've heard') is referred to in **stanza three**. Extreme circumstances are deftly sketched in the phrases 'chillest land' and 'strangest Sea'. This reclusive poet, who spent most of her life indoors in her father's house, deftly catches an alien, foreign element. She then explains that hope is not demanding in bad times; it is generous, giving rather than taking: 'Yet, never, in Extremity,/It asked a crumb—of Me'. The central paradox of hope is expressed in the metaphor of the bird, delicate and fragile, yet strong and indomitable. The tiny bird is an effective image for the first stirring of hope in a time of despair. In the solemn ending, the poet gives hope the dignified celebration it deserves.

Dickinson is a unique and original talent. She used the metre of hymns. She also uses their form of the four-line verse. Yet this is not conventional poetry, due to Dickinson's use of the dash to slow the line and make the reader pause and consider. Ordinary words like 'at all' and 'is heard' assume a tremendous importance and their position is to be considered and savoured. **Her unusual punctuation has the same effect, as it highlights the dangers ('Gale', 'Sea').** The alliteration of 's' in 'strangest Sea' and the run-on line to suggest the circling comfort of the little bird all add to the curious music of Dickinson's poems. The buoyant, self-confident tone of the poem is in direct contrast to the strict Puritanical tradition of a severe, righteous God, with which she would have been familiar in her youth and which she rejected, preferring to keep her Sabbath 'staying at home'.

ANALYSIS

'Emily Dickinson's poetry contains an intense awareness of the private, inner self.' Discuss how Dickinson gives expression to this interior world in her poetry. Support your exploration with quotations from her prescribed poems.

SAMPLE PARAGRAPH

Everyone has experienced the 'dark night of the soul' when it seems nothing is ever going to go right again. Dickinson, with her simple image of the bird singing in the soul, derived from psalms, provides the perfect optimistic antidote to this dark interior state of mind, 'Hope is the thing with feathers'. She then develops this metaphor throughout the poem, comforting us with the thought that the bird/hope can communicate with us without the need for the restrictions of language, 'sings the tune without words'. There is no end to hope 'And never stops at all'. She understands the darkness of despair, 'in the Gale', 'the strangest Sea'. The use of capitalisation by the poet seems to me to point out the terror of the individual struggling to survive. But the bird of hope provides comfort and warmth, 'And sweetest'. I like the poet's use of enjambment in the lines 'That could abash the little Bird/That kept so many warm'. It is as if the protection of hope encircles the individual, just as the wing of the little bird protects her young in the nest. This is an optimistic, buoyant poem in which Dickinson appears to be instructing the reader that one should never despair. The phrase 'perches in the soul' suggests to me that the poet regards hope as coming of its own volition, it just appears, there is a sense of otherworldliness about it. Hope, she tells us, is generous, never demanding, always giving, 'Yet, never, in Extremity,/It asked a crumb—of Me'. I think the use of the capital for 'Me' shows the heightened concern of someone for him/herself when the feeling of despair envelops.

EXAMINER'S COMMENT

This response shows an awareness of the poet's style and content. It is a solid B grade response. However, it lacks the in-depth analysis required for an A grade answer.

CLASS/HOMEWORK EXERCISES

1. 'Dickinson is a wholly new and original poetic genius.' Do you agree or disagree with this statement? Support your response with reference to the poems on your course.
2. Copy the table below into your own notes and fill in critical comments about the last two quotations.

Key Quotes

'Hope' is the thing with feathers	The image of the bird is used to represent hope.
And sweetest—in the Gale	Hope is needed most in times of trouble.
And sore must be the storm	The danger must be very great.
I've heard it in the chillest land	
Yet, never, in Extremity,/It asked a crumb —of Me	

• Poetry Focus •

There's a certain Slant of light

Emily Dickinson

There's a certain Slant of light,
Winter Afternoons—
That oppresses, like the Heft
Of Cathedral Tunes—

Heavenly Hurt, it gives us—   5
We can find no scar,
But internal difference,
Where the Meanings, are—

None may teach it—Any—
'Tis the Seal Despair—   10
An imperial affliction
Sent us of the Air—

When it comes, the Landscape listens—
Shadows—hold their breath—
When it goes, 'tis like the Distance   15
On the look of Death—

'Heavenly Hurt, it gives us'

GLOSSARY

1 *Slant*: incline; fall; interpretation.
3 *oppresses*: feels heavy; overwhelms.
3 *Heft*: strength; weight.
9 *Any*: anything.
10 *Seal Despair*: sign or symbol of hopelessness.
11 *imperial affliction*: God's will for mortal human beings.

EXPLORATIONS

1. Describe the mood and atmosphere created by the poet in the opening stanza.
2. Comment on Dickinson's use of personification within the poem.
3. Write your own personal response to the poem, supporting your views with reference or quotation.

STUDY NOTES

> Dickinson was a keen observer of her environment, often dramatising her observations in poems. In this case, a particular beam of winter light puts the poet into a mood of depression as the slanting sunlight communicates a sense of despair. The poem typifies her creeping fascination with mortality. But although the poet's subject matter is intricate and disturbing, her own views are more difficult to determine. Ironically, this exploration of light and its effects seems to suggest a great deal about Dickinson's own dark consciousness.

From the outset, Dickinson creates an uneasy atmosphere. The setting ('Winter Afternoons') is dreary and desultory. Throughout stanza one, there is an underlying sense of time weighing heavily, especially when the light is compared to solemn cathedral music ('Cathedral Tunes'). We usually expect church music to be inspirational and uplifting, but in this case, its 'Heft' has a burdensome effect which simply 'oppresses' and adds to the **downcast mood**.

In stanza two, the poet considers the significance of the sunlight. For her, its effects are negative, causing pain to the world: 'Heavenly Hurt, it gives us'. The paradoxical language appears to reflect Dickinson's ironic attitude that **human beings live in great fear of God's power**. Is there a sense that deep down in their souls ('Where the Meanings, are'), people struggle under the weight of God's will, fearing death and judgement?

This feeling of humanity's helplessness is highlighted in stanza three: 'None may teach it' sums up the predicament of our limitations. Life and death can never be fully understood. Perhaps this is our tragic fate – our 'Seal Despair'. Dickinson presents **God as an all-powerful royal figure** associated with suffering and punishment ('An imperial affliction'). Is the poet's tone critical and accusatory? Or is she simply expressing the reality of human experience?

Stanza four is highly dramatic. **Dickinson personifies a terrified world** where 'the Landscape listens'. The earlier sombre light is now replaced by 'Shadows' that 'hold their breath' in the silence. The poet imagines the shocking moment of death and the mystery of time ('the Distance'). While the poem's ending is open to speculation, it seems clear that Dickinson is exploring the transition from life into eternity, a subject that is central to her writing. The only certain conclusion is an obvious one – that death is an inescapable reality beyond human understanding, as mysterious as it is natural. The poet's final tone is resigned, almost relieved. The 'Slant of light' offers no definitive answers to life's questions and the human condition is as inexplicable as death itself.

Throughout the poem, Dickinson's fragmented style is characterised by her **erratic punctuation and repeated use of capital letters**. She uses the dash at every opportunity to create suspense and drama. For the poet, the winter light is seen as an important sign from God, disturbing the inner 'Landscape' of her soul. In the end, the light (a likely metaphor for truth) causes Dickinson to experience an inner sadness and a deep sense of spiritual longing.

ANALYSIS

In your view, what is the central theme in this poem? Support the points you make with suitable reference to the text.

SAMPLE PARAGRAPH

I think that death is the main theme in all of Emily Dickinson's poems, including this one. The poem is very atmospheric, but the light coming through the church window can be interpreted as a symbol of God, hope for the world. However, Dickinson's language is quite negative and it could be argued that our human lives are under pressure and that fear of eternal damnation is also part of life. The phrases 'Heavenly Hurt' and 'imperial affliction' suggest that we are God's subjects, trying to avoid sin in this life in order to find salvation after death. One of the central points in the poem is the fear of dying that people have. It is outside of our control. All humans can do is 'hold their breath'. I believe that the central message of Dickinson's poem is that death comes to us all and we must accept it. The mood throughout the poem is oppressive, just like the sunlight coming in through the church window and the depressing 'Cathedral Tunes' the poet hears. The poet's distinctive punctuation, using dashes and abrupt stops and starts, is part of the tense mood of the poem. Dickinson's theme is quite distressing and the broken rhythms and disturbing images such as 'scar', 'Seal Despair' and 'Shadows' add to the uneasiness of the theme that death is unavoidable.

EXAMINER'S COMMENT

A well-sustained response which attempted to stay focused throughout. In the main, references and quotations were used effectively and there were some worthwhile attempts to show how features of the poet's style enhanced the presentation of her central theme. Grade A.

CLASS/HOMEWORK EXERCISES

1. How would you describe the dominant mood of the poem? Is it positive in any way? Explain your response, supporting the points you make with suitable reference to the text.
2. Copy the table below into your own notes and fill in critical comments about the last two quotations.

Key Quotes

Winter Afternoons	The oppressive mood is reinforced through the setting itself and suggested by the use of this assonant phrase.
But internal difference	Dickinson believes that the pain of being mortal is an inner one, both psychological and spiritual.
'Tis the Seal Despair	This rich metaphor suggests that because people are subject to God's will, their spiritual fate is sealed.
Heavenly Hurt	
Shadows—hold their breath	

• Poetry Focus •

I felt a Funeral, in my Brain

I felt a Funeral, in my Brain,
And Mourners to and fro
Kept treading—treading—till it seemed
That Sense was breaking through—

And when they all were seated, 5
A Service, like a Drum—
Kept beating—beating—till I thought
My Mind was going numb—

And then I heard them lift a Box
And creak across my Soul 10
With those same Boots of Lead, again,
Then Space—began to toll,

As all the Heavens were a Bell,
And Being, but an Ear,
And I, and Silence, some strange Race 15
Wrecked, solitary, here—

And then a Plank in Reason, broke,
And I dropped down, and down—
And hit a World, at every plunge,
And Finished knowing—then— 20

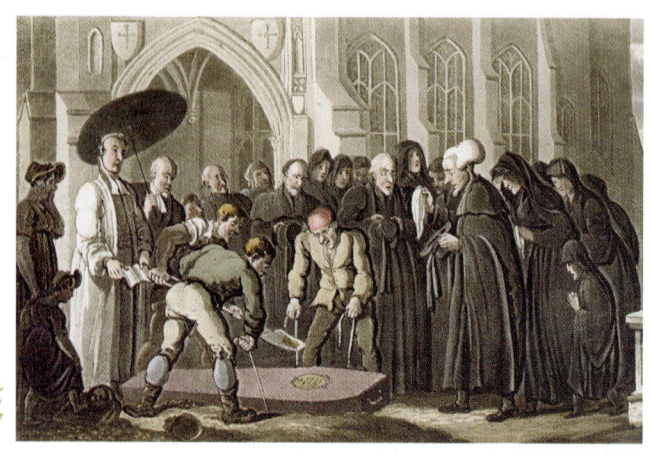

'And then a Plank in Reason, broke'

GLOSSARY

3 *treading*: crush by walking on.
4 *Sense*: faculty of perception; the senses (seeing, hearing, touching, tasting, smelling); sound, practical judgement.
12 *toll*: ring slowly and steadily, especially to announce a death.
13 *As all*: as if all.
14 *And Being, but an Ear*: all senses, except hearing, are now useless.

EXPLORATIONS

1 Do you find the pictures in this poem frightening, macabre or coldly realistic? Give reasons for your answer, supported by textual reference.
2 What is the dominant tone in the poem? Where is the climax of the poem, in your opinion? Refer to the text in your answer.
3 Consider the rhyme scheme of the poem. In your view, why does the poet rhyme words like 'Drum'/'numb' and 'Soul'/'toll'? In your opinion, why does the rhyme scheme break down in the last stanza?

STUDY NOTES

This poem is thought to have been written in 1861 at a time of turbulence in Dickinson's life. She was having religious and artistic doubts and had experienced an unhappy time in a personal relationship. This interior landscape paints a dark picture of something falling apart. It is for the reader to decide whether it is a fainting spell, a mental breakdown or a funeral. That is the enigma of Dickinson.

The startling perspective of this poem in **stanza one** can be seen as the view experienced by a person in a coffin, if the poem is read as an **account of the poet imagining her death**. Alternatively, it could refer to the suffocating feeling of the breakdown of consciousness, either through fainting or a mental breakdown. Perhaps it is the dearth of artistic activity. Whichever reading is chosen, and maybe all co-exist, the **interior landscape of awareness is being explored**. The use of the personal pronoun 'I' shows that this is a unique experience, although it has relevance for all. The relentless pounding of the mourners walking is reminiscent of a blinding migraine headache. The repetition of the hard-sounding 't' in the verb 'treading—treading' evocatively describes this terrible experience. The 'I' is undergoing an intense trauma beyond understanding: 'Sense was breaking through'. This repetition and disorientation are synonymous with psychological breakdown.

Stanza two gives a **first-person account of a funeral**. The mourners are seated and the service has begun. Hearing ('an Ear') is the only sense able to perceive the surroundings. All the verbs refer to sound: 'tread', 'beat', 'heard', 'creak', 'toll'. The passive 'I' receives the experience, hearing, not listening, which is an active process. The experience is so overwhelming that 'I' thought the 'Mind was going numb', unable to endure any more. The use of the past tense reminds the reader that the experience is over, so is the first-person narrative told from beyond the grave? Is this the voice of someone who has died? Or is it the voice of someone in the throes of a desperate personal experience? The reader must decide.

The reference to 'Soul' in **stanza three** suggests a **spiritual dimension** to the experience. The 'I' has begun to become disoriented as the line dividing an external experience and an internal one is breaking. The mourners 'creak across my Soul'. The oppressive, almost suffocating experience is captured in the onomatopoeic phrase 'Boots of Lead' and space becomes filled with the tolling bell. Existence in **stanza four** is reduced totally to hearing. The fearful transitory experience of crossing from awareness to unconsciousness, from life to death, is being imagined. The 'I' in stanza four is now stranded, 'Wrecked', cut off from life. The person is in a comatose state, able to comprehend but unable to communicate: 'solitary, here'. The word 'here' makes the reader feel present at this awful drama.

Finally, in **stanza five**, a new sensation takes over, the **sense of falling uncontrollably**. The 'I' has finished knowing and is now no longer aware of surroundings. Is this the descent into the hell of the angels in *Paradise Lost*? Is it the descent of the coffin into the grave? Or is it the descent into madness or oblivion? The 'I' has learned something, but it is not revealed. The repetition of 'And' advances the movement of the poem in an almost uncontrollable way, mimicking the final descent. The 'I' is powerless under the repetitive verbs and the incessant rhythm punctuated by the ever-present dash. This poem is extraordinary, because before the study of psychology had defined it, it is a step-by-step description of mental collapse. Here is 'the drama of process'.

ANALYSIS

'This poem is a detailed exploration of the experience of death.' Discuss this statement, using references from the text to support your views.

SAMPLE PARAGRAPH

When I first read Emily Dickinson's poem 'I felt A Funeral, in my Brain', I was reminded of the macabre pictures of Salvador Dali, where everything is real, but not quite right. It also reminded me of the films of Tim Burton, such as *The Nightmare Before Christmas*. All the elements are there, but nothing is totally right, it is surreal. This imagined funeral in the poem suggests to me the losing of the grip on life by the individual 'I'. The incessant noise, 'treading', 'beating', induces an almost trance-like state as the brain cannot function any more, and so becomes numb. In death, the senses are supposed to shut down, sight is one of the first to go, so I think it is very clever of the poet to suggest that being is just reduced to the one sense hearing – 'an Ear'. I also find the perspective of the poem chilling, the idea that this is the view of someone lying in the coffin observing their funeral is macabre in the extreme. But the most compelling line in the poem is 'And then a Plank in Reason, broke'. This graphically conveys the snap of reason as the 'I' finally loses a grip on consciousness and slips away, hurtling uncontrollably into another dimension. Even the punctuation, with the use of the two commas, conveys this divided reality. But the most unnerving word is yet to come, 'then'. Does the poet know now? What does the poet know, is it about the existence or non-existence of an afterlife? Where is the poet standing now – here or there, alive or dead?

EXAMINER'S COMMENT

An unusual, individual reading of the poem, and generally well supported by reference to the text. There are some weaknesses in expression and the paragraph is not fully focused on the question. Overall, a B grade response.

CLASS/HOMEWORK EXERCISES

1. 'She seems as close to touching bottom here as she ever got.' Discuss this view of Emily Dickinson with reference to the poem 'I felt a Funeral, in my Brain'.
2. Copy the table below into your own notes and fill in critical comments about the last two quotations.

• Poetry Focus •

Emily Dickinson

Key Quotes

That Sense was breaking through	This enigmatic line could refer to the breakdown of the five senses, or that reason was collapsing or coming.
My Mind was going numb	The narrator in the poem is presented as a passive recipient who can no longer endure this traumatic experience. This is enhanced by assonance.
As all the heavens were a Bell	All the universe had turned into this great pealing of the bell; nothing else existed for the narrator.
And creak across my Soul	
And then a Plank in Reason, broke	

A Bird came down the Walk

Emily Dickinson

A Bird came down the Walk—
He did not know I saw—
He bit an Angleworm in halves
And ate the fellow, raw,

And then he drank a Dew 5
From a convenient Grass—
And then hopped sidewise to the Wall
To let a Beetle pass—

He glanced with rapid eyes
That hurried all around— 10
They looked like frightened Beads, I thought—
He stirred his Velvet Head

Like one in danger, Cautious,
I offered him a Crumb
And he unrolled his feathers 15
And rowed him softer home—

Than Oars divide the Ocean,
Too silver for a seam—
Or Butterflies, off Banks of Noon
Leap, plashless as they swim. 20

'He glanced with rapid eyes'

GLOSSARY

3 *Angleworm*: small worm used as fish bait by anglers.
17 *the Ocean*: Dickinson compares the blue sky to the sea.
18 *silver*: the sea's surface looks like solid silver.
18 *a seam*: opening; division.
20 *plashless*: splashless; undisturbed.

EXPLORATIONS

1 In your view, what does the poem suggest about the relationship between human beings and nature?
2 What effect does Dickinson's use of humour in the poem have? Does it let you see nature in a different way? Support the points you make with reference to the text.
3 From your reading of the poem, what impression of Emily Dickinson herself is conveyed? Refer to the text in your answer.

STUDY NOTES

In this short descriptive poem, Dickinson celebrates the beauty and wonder of animals. While the bird is seen as a wild creature at times, other details present its behaviour and appearance in human terms. The poem also illustrates Dickinson's quirky sense of humour as well as offering interesting insights into nature and the exclusion of human beings from that world.

The poem begins with an everyday scene. Because the bird is unaware of the poet's presence, it behaves naturally. **Stanza one** demonstrates the **competition and danger of nature**: 'He bit an Angleworm in halves'. Although Dickinson imagines the bird within a human context, casually coming 'down the Walk' and suddenly eating 'the fellow, raw', she is amused by the uncivilised reality of the animal kingdom. The word 'raw' echoes her self-deprecating sense of shock. Despite its initial elegance, the predatory bird could hardly have been expected to cook the worm.

The poet's comic portrayal continues in **stanza two**. She gives the bird certain social qualities, drinking from a 'Grass' and politely allowing a hurrying beetle to pass. The tone is relaxed and playful. The slender vowel sounds ('convenient') and soft sibilance ('sidewise', 'pass') add to the seemingly refined atmosphere. However, the mood changes in **stanza three**, reflecting the bird's cautious fear. Dickinson observes the rapid eye movement, 'like frightened Beads'. Such **precise detail increases the drama** of the moment. The details of the bird's prim movement and beautiful texture are wonderfully accurate: 'He stirred his Velvet Head'. The simile is highly effective, suggesting the animal's natural grace.

The danger becomes more explicit in **stanza four**. Both the spectator and the observed bird are 'Cautious'. The crumb offered to the bird by the poet is rejected, highlighting the **gulf between their two separate worlds**. The description of the bird taking flight evokes the delicacy and fluidity of its movement: 'And he unrolled his feathers/And rowed him softer home'. The confident rhythm and emphatic alliteration enrich our understanding of the harmony between the creature and its natural environment. The sensual imagery captures the magnificence of the bird, compared to a rower moving with ease across placid water.

Stanza five develops the metaphorical description further, conveying the bird's poise and mystery: 'Too silver for a seam'. Not only was its flying seamless, it was smoother than that of butterflies leaping 'off Banks of Noon' and splashlessly swimming through the sky. The **breathtaking image and onomatopoeic language** remind us of Dickinson's admiration for nature in all its impressive beauty and is one of the most memorable descriptions in all of Dickinson's writing.

ANALYSIS

In your view, does Dickinson have a sense of empathy with the bird? Support your response with reference to the poem.

SAMPLE PARAGRAPH

It is clear from the start of the poem that Emily Dickinson is both fascinated and amused by the appearance of a small bird in her garden. She seems surprised and almost honoured that out of nowhere 'A Bird came down the Walk'. When it suddenly swallows a worm 'raw', she becomes even more interested. The fact that she admits 'He did not know I saw' tells me that she really has empathy for the bird. Her tone suggests that she feels privileged to watch and she certainly doesn't want to disturb it in its own world. The poet also finds the bird's antics funny. Although it devours the snail, it still behaves very mannerly towards the beetle. Towards the end, Dickinson shows her feelings for the bird when it becomes frightened and she notices its 'rapid eyes'. She sees that it is 'in danger'. The fact that she offered it a crumb also shows her empathy. At the very end, she shows her admiration for the beauty and agility of the bird as it flies off to freedom – to its 'softer home'. The descriptions of it like a rower or a butterfly also suggest that she admires its grace.

Poetry Focus

EXAMINER'S COMMENT

Apt references and short quotations are used very well to illustrate the poet's regard for the bird. The answer ranges well over much of the poem. Some further discussion on the poet's tone would have been welcome. A good grade B.

CLASS/HOMEWORK EXERCISES

1. Comment on Dickinson's use of imagery in 'A Bird came down the Walk'. Support the points you make with the aid of suitable reference.
2. Copy the table below into your own notes and fill in critical comments about the last two quotations.

Key Quotes

He did not know I saw	Dickinson is excited at the opportunity to view the bird in its natural element.
And then he drank a Dew	The poet's comic observation recognises signs of social etiquette in the bird's behaviour.
He stirred his Velvet Head	While the image conveys the bird's beauty and grandeur, 'stirred' suggests its hidden fear.
And rowed him softer home	
plashless as they swim	

I heard a Fly buzz—when I died

Emily Dickinson

I heard a Fly buzz—when I died—
The Stillness in the Room
Was like the Stillness in the Air—
Between the Heaves of Storm—

The Eyes around—had wrung them dry—   5
And Breaths were gathering firm
For that last Onset—when the King
Be witnessed—in the Room—

I willed my Keepsakes—Signed away
What portion of me be   10
Assignable—and then it was
There interposed a Fly—

With Blue—uncertain stumbling Buzz—
Between the light—and me—
And then the Windows failed—and then   15
I could not see to see—

'The Stillness in the Room/Was like the Stillness in the Air—'

GLOSSARY

4 *Heaves*: lift with effort.
7 *Onset*: beginning.
7 *the King*: God.
9 *Keepsakes*: gifts treasured for the sake of the giver.
12 *interposed*: inserted between or among things.

EXPLORATIONS

1. How would you describe the atmosphere in the poem? Pick out two phrases which, in your opinion, are especially descriptive and explain why you chose them.
2. Do you think Dickinson uses contrast effectively in this poem? Discuss one contrast you found particularly striking.
3. Look at the last line of the poem. What, in your view, is the poet suggesting to us about a person's fate after death?

STUDY NOTES

> Dickinson was fascinated with death. This poem examines the moment between life and death. At that time, it was common for family and friends to be present at deathbed vigils. It was thought that the way a person behaved or looked at the moment of death gave an indication of the soul's fate.

The last moment of a person's life is a solemn and often sad occasion. The perspective of the poem is that of the person dying and this significant moment is dominated by the buzzing of a fly in the room in the **first stanza**. This is **absurdly comic and strangely distorts** this moment into something grotesque. Surely the person dying should be concerned with more important matters than an insignificant fly: 'I heard a Fly buzz—when I died'. The room is still and expectant as the last breaths are drawn, a stillness like the moments before a storm. All are braced for what is to come. The word 'Heaves' suggests the force of the storm that is about to break.

The **second stanza** shows us that the mourners had now stopped crying and were holding their breath as they awaited the coming of the 'King' (God) into the room at the moment of death. The phrase 'Be witnessed' refers to the dying person and the mourners who are witnessing their faith, and it conjures up all the solemnity of a court. The word 'firm' also suggests these people's steadfast religious beliefs. The **third stanza** is concerned with putting matters right. The dying person has made a will – 'What portion of me be/Assignable' – and what is not assignable belongs to God. The person is awaiting the coming of his/her Maker, 'and then it was/There interposed a Fly' – the symbol of decay and corruption appeared. Human affairs cannot be managed; real life intervenes. The **fly comes between ('interposed') the dying person and the moment of death**, which **trivialises** the event.

The fractured syntax of the last stanza shows the **breakdown of the senses** at the moment of death: 'Between the light—and me'. Sight and sound are blurring. The presence of the fly is completely inappropriate, like a drunken person at a solemn ceremony, disturbing and embarrassing and interrupting proceedings. The fly is now between the dying person and the source of light. Does this suggest that the person has lost concentration on higher things, distracted by the buzzing fly? The sense of sight then fails: 'And then the Windows failed'. The moment of death had come and gone, dominated by the noisy fly. Has the fly prevented the person from reaching another dimension? Is death emptiness, just human decay, as signified by the presence of the fly, or is there something more? Do we need comic relief at overwhelming occasions? Is the poet signalling her own lack of belief in an afterlife with God? Dickinson, as usual, intrigues, **leaving the reader with more questions than answers**, so that the reader, like the dying person, is struggling to 'see to see'.

ANALYSIS

Dickinson's poems on mortality often lead to uncertainty or despair. Would you agree or disagree with this statement after reading the poem 'I heard a Fly buzz—when I died'? Discuss this statement, using references from the poem to support your views.

SAMPLE PARAGRAPH

This first-person, reminiscent narrative takes us through a series of images, inside and outside the head, showing us confused feelings and insurmountable problems, leading to an inconclusive ending. The view of this deathbed scene is from the dying person's perspective. The problem is that when all should be focused on the last drawing of breath, all are distracted by the inappropriate arrival of a noisy fly! Life won't be managed, nor death – both are lived and experienced. Life and death are not a play, a work of art; they are messy and disorganised, which goes against the human desire for order and control: 'Signed away/What portion of me be/Assignable'. I feel that the poet may be suggesting that the dying person, distracted by the silly fly, does not reach the understanding and knowledge appropriate at this great moment, and is therefore cheated in some way. The momentous moment has passed, dominated by a buzzing fly. This was no dress rehearsal; you can only die once. Life and death happen. Are we being told that we often lose concentration at important moments, for absurd reasons, and so lose valuable insight? Dickinson is not a reassuring poet in this poem. Instead, she coldly and dispassionately draws a deathbed scene and lets us 'see to see'. Can we? Or are we, like the dying person, distracted and unable to still ourselves at the appropriate time to achieve greater wisdom? The divided voice, that of the person dying and that of the person after death, leaves us with mysteries, and so this poem of Dickinson's on mortality leaves me with bleak uncertainties about the human condition and its ability to control and order.

EXAMINER'S COMMENT

This response is considered and shows a very good discursive treatment of the question. Expression is varied and fluent, and apt quotations are used effectively throughout the answer. Grade A.

CLASS/HOMEWORK EXERCISES

1. Comment on how Dickinson's style contributes to the theme or message in this poem. Quote from your prescribed poems to support your opinions.
2. Copy the table below into your own notes and fill in critical comments about the last two quotations.

Key Quotes

I heard a Fly buzz	The dying person is distracted from this significant moment by the noise made by a fly.
And Breaths were gathering firm/For that last Onset	The narrator is aware that those present are bracing themselves for the important moment of death, which for believers is associated with the coming of God.
and then it was/There interposed a Fly	All were disturbed by the dramatic arrival of the fly, disrupting the solemnity of the moment.
And then the Windows failed	
and then/I could not see to see	

The Soul has Bandaged moments

The Soul has Bandaged moments—
When too appalled to stir—
She feels some ghastly Fright come up
And stop to look at her—

Salute her—with long fingers— 5
Caress her freezing hair—
Sip, Goblin, from the very lips
The Lover—hovered—o'er—
Unworthy, that a thought so mean
Accost a Theme—so—fair— 10

The soul has moments of Escape—
When bursting all the doors—
She dances like a Bomb, abroad,
And swings upon the Hours,

As do the Bee—delirious borne— 15
Long Dungeoned from his Rose—
Touch Liberty—then know no more,
But Noon, and Paradise—

The Soul's retaken moments—
When, Felon led along, 20
With shackles on the plumed feet,
And staples, in the Song,

The Horror welcomes her, again,
These, are not brayed of Tongue—

'As do the Bee—delirious borne'

• Poetry Focus •

GLOSSARY

1 *Bandaged moments*: painful experiences.
2 *appalled*: shocked, horrified.
2 *stir*: act; retaliate.
10 *Accost*: address.
11 *Escape*: freedom.
13 *like a Bomb*: dramatically.
13 *abroad*: in unusual directions.
16 *Dungeoned*: imprisoned in the hive.
20 *Felon*: criminal.
21 *shackles*: chains, ropes.
21 *plumed*: decorated.
22 *staples*: fastenings.
24 *brayed*: inarticulate.

EXPLORATIONS

1 What details in the poem evoke the feelings of 'ghastly Fright' experienced by the soul? Support your answer with quotation or reference.
2 Choose one comparison from the poem that you find particularly effective. Explain your choice.
3 Comment on Dickinson's use of dashes in this poem, briefly explaining their effectiveness.

STUDY NOTES

Throughout much of her poetry, Dickinson focuses on the nature of consciousness and the experience of being alive. She was constantly searching for meaning, particularly of transient moments or changing moods. This search is central to 'The Soul has Bandaged moments', where the poet takes us through a series of dramatic images contrasting the extremes of the spirit and the conscious self.

Stanza one introduces the soul as being fearful and vulnerable, personified as a terrified female who 'feels some ghastly Fright', with the poem's stark opening line suggesting restriction and pain. Dickinson's language is extreme: 'Bandaged', 'appalled'. The **tone is one of helpless desperation and introspection**. Yet while the dominant mood reflects suffering and fear, the phrase 'Bandaged moments' indicates the resilient soul's ability to recover despite being wounded repeatedly.

Stanza two is unnervingly dramatic. The poet creates a mock-romantic scene between the victimised soul and the 'ghastly Fright' figure, now portrayed as a hideous goblin and her would-be lover, their encounter depicted in terms of gothic horror. The soul experiences terrifying fantasies as **the surreal sequence becomes increasingly menacing** and the goblin's long fingers 'Caress her freezing hair'. The appearance of an unidentified shadowy 'Lover' is unexpected. There is a sense of the indecisive soul being caught between two states, represented by the malevolent goblin and the deserving lover. It is unclear whether Dickinson is writing about the choices involved in romantic love or the relationship between herself and God.

The stanza ends inconclusively, juxtaposing two opposites: the 'Unworthy' or undeserving 'thought' and the 'fair' (worthy) 'Theme'. The latter might well refer to the ideal of romantic love. If so, it is confronted by erotic desire (the 'thought'). Dickinson's disjointed style, especially her frequent use of dashes within stanzas, isolates key words and intensifies the overwhelmingly **nightmarish atmosphere**.

The feeling of confused terror is replaced with ecstatic 'moments of Escape' in stanzas three and four. The soul recovers in triumph, 'bursting all the doors'. This **explosion of energy** ('She dances like a Bomb') evokes a rising mood of riotous freedom. Explosive verbs ('bursting', 'dances', 'swings') and robust rhythms add to the sense of uncontrollable excitement. Dickinson compares the soul to a 'Bee—delirious borne'. After being 'Long Dungeoned' in its hive, this bee can now enjoy the sensuous delights of 'his Rose'.

The mood is short lived, however, and in stanzas five and six, 'The Horror' returns. The soul becomes depressed again, feeling bound and shackled, like a 'Felon led along'. **Dickinson develops this criminal metaphor** – 'With shackles on the plumed feet' – leaving us with an ultimate sense of loss as 'The Horror welcomes her, again'. Is this the soul's inevitable fate? The final line is unsettling. Whatever horrible experiences confront the soul, they are simply unspeakable: 'not brayed of Tongue'.

As always, Dickinson's poem is **open to many interpretations**. Critics have suggested that the poet is dramatising the turmoil of dealing with the loss of creativity. Some view the poem's central conflict as the tension between romantic love and sexual desire. Others believe that the poet was exploring the theme of depression and mental instability. In the end, readers must find their own meaning and decide for themselves.

ANALYSIS

Comment on the dramatic elements that are present in the poem, supporting the points you make with reference to the text.

Emily Dickinson

SAMPLE PARAGRAPH

'The Soul has Bandaged moments' is built around a central conflict between two opposing forces, the 'Soul', or spirit, and its great enemy, 'Fright'. Emily Dickinson sets the dramatic scene with the Soul still recovering – presumably from the last battle. It is 'Bandaged' after the fight with its arch enemy. The descriptions of the soul's opponent are startling. Fright is 'ghastly', a 'Horror' and a sleazy 'Goblin' who is trying to seduce the innocent soul. Some of Dickinson's images add to the dramatic tension. In the seduction scene, the goblin is described as having 'long fingers'. His intended victim is seen as helpless, petrified with fear. The goblin uses its bony claws to 'Caress her freezing hair'. Both characters seem to have come out of an old black-and-white horror movie. I find the whole situation disturbing. The drama continues right to the end of the poem. The soul is compared to a 'Felon' who has just been recaptured and is being led away in 'shackles'. Such images have a distressing impact in explaining the pressures on the soul to be free. Finally, Dickinson's stop-and-start style is also unsettling. Broken rhythms and her condensed use of language increase the edgy atmosphere throughout this highly dramatic poem.

EXAMINER'S COMMENT

An assured and focused A-grade response, showing a clear understanding of the poem's dramatic elements. The answer addressed both subject matter and style, using back-up illustration very effectively. Expression throughout was also impressive.

CLASS/HOMEWORK EXERCISES

1. How would you describe the dominant tone of 'The Soul has Bandaged moments'? Use reference to the text to show how the tone is effectively conveyed.
2. Copy the table below into your own notes and fill in critical comments about the last two quotations.

Key Quotes

Bandaged moments	While the adjective suggests hurt and weakness, there is also a sense of healing and recovery.
The Lover—hovered—o'er	The verb suggests menace, typical of a poem where almost every image is tinged with fear and uncertainty.
She dances like a Bomb	Another of Dickinson's characteristics is her innovative and highly dramatic comparisons.
Caress her freezing hair	
The Horror welcomes her, again	

Emily Dickinson

I could bring You Jewels—had I a mind to

I could bring You Jewels—had I a mind to—
But You have enough—of those—
I could bring You Odors from St. Domingo—
Colors—from Vera Cruz—

Berries of the Bahamas—have I—   5
But this little Blaze
Flickering to itself—in the Meadow—
Suits Me—more than those—

Never a fellow matched this Topaz—
And his Emerald Swing—   10
Dower itself—for Bobadilo—
Better—Could I bring?

'Never a fellow matched this Topaz—'

GLOSSARY

3   *Odors*: fragrances, perfumes.
3   *St. Domingo*: Santo Domingo in the Caribbean.
4   *Vera Cruz*: city on the east coast of Mexico.
5   *Bahamas*: group of islands south-east of Florida.
6   *Blaze*: strong fire or flame; very bright light.
11 *Dower*: part of her husband's estate allotted to a widow by law.
11 *Bobadilo*: braggart; someone who speaks arrogantly or boastfully.

• Leaving Certificate English •

EXPLORATIONS

1. Does the poet value exotic or homely gifts? In your opinion, which phrases suggest this contrast most effectively?
2. Slant rhyme is when words almost rhyme, as in 'those' and 'Cruz'. Identify another example of slant rhyme in the poem and suggest why, in your opinion, the poet chooses to rhyme the words in this way. (Consider emphasis, order and music.)
3. What is the tone in this poem: arrogant, humble, gentle, strident, confident? Quote in support of your opinion.

STUDY NOTES

> Although described as a recluse, Dickinson had a wide circle of friends. She wrote letter-poems to them, often representing them as flowers, 'things of nature which had come with no practice at all'. This poem is one without shadows, celebratory and happy, focusing out rather than in as she concentrates on a relationship.

In the **first stanza,** the poem opens with the speaker **considering the gift she will give** her beloved, 'You'. The 'You' is very much admired, and is wealthy ('You have enough'), so the gift of jewels is dismissed. The phrase 'had I a mind to' playfully suggests that maybe the 'I' doesn't necessarily wish to present anything. There is a certain coquettish air evident here. A world of privilege and plenty is shown as, one after another, expensively exotic gifts are considered and dismissed. These include perfumes and vibrant colours from faraway locations, conjuring up images of romance and adventure: 'Odors from St. Domingo'.

The **second stanza** continues the list, with 'Berries of the Bahamas' being considered as an option for this special gift, but they are not quite right either. The tense changes to 'have I' and the laconic listing and dismissing stops. A small wildflower 'in the Meadow', 'this little Blaze', is chosen instead. This 'Suits Me'. Notice that it is not that this suits the other person. **This gift is a reflection of her own unshowy personality.** The long lines of considering exotic gifts have now given way to shorter, more decisive lines.

In the **third stanza,** the speaker has a definite note of conviction, as she confidently states that 'Never a fellow matched' this shining gift of hers. No alluring, foreign gemstone, be it a brilliant topaz or emerald, shines as this 'little Blaze' in the meadow. The gift glows with colour; it is natural, inexpensive and accessible. The reference to a dower might suggest a gift given by a woman

Emily Dickinson

• 103 •

to a prospective husband. This **gift is suitable** for a Spanish adventurer, a 'Bobadilo'. The assured tone is clear in the word 'Never' and the jaunty rhyme 'Swing' and 'bring'. The final rhetorical question suggests that this is the best gift she could give. The poem shows that **the true value of a present cannot be measured in a material way**.

ANALYSIS

'Dickinson is fascinated by moments of change.' Discuss this statement using the poem 'I could bring You Jewels—had I a mind to' as reference.

SAMPLE PARAGRAPH

Unlike many of Dickinson's poems on our course, this poem turns outwards, as the speaker considers what present would be suitable to give to her 'Bobadilo'. The happy, celebratory tone continues right through the poem. This is a confident, assured woman listing and dismissing exotic gifts in a world of privilege and wealth. The 'Odors' from St Domingo, the 'Colors' from Vera Cruz, the 'Berries' from the Bahamas are looked at and discarded by this knowing woman, 'had I a mind to'. The moment of change here is when the speaker chooses a gift that is natural and unassuming and, more importantly, which is to her liking: 'Suits Me'. It will convey something of her personality to the recipient, the swaggering 'Bobadilo'. This 'little Blaze/Flickering to itself' reflects the hidden qualities of the woman. Although it is not directly stated what this little shining gift is exactly, I think it is likely a meadow flower. It is free and easily picked, but how it shines! This is brighter than any precious stone of 'Topaz' or 'Emerald'. As the decision is reached, the long lines in which the speaker is considering her choice of gift change with her decision. Now short, crisp lines ring out with the self-belief of a woman who knows best. Even the rhyme changes from the slant rhyme where she is considering her options ('those'/'Cruz') in the first stanza to the more definite jaunty full rhyme of 'Swing' and 'bring' in the final stanza. I read that Dickinson's favourite chapter in the Book of Revelations was the description of Jerusalem as a jewel. In this poem, jewels are rejected for something more precious than material worth: beauty. I really enjoyed how Dickinson explored the very feminine trait of considering everything, and then finally deciding after humorous vacillating. This is the moment of change in the poem.

EXAMINER'S COMMENT

A lucid, fluent response to the question, backed up with a convincing use of quotation, ensures a grade A. The point about the change in line length was interesting. Varied vocabulary is impressive throughout.

CLASS/HOMEWORK EXERCISES

1. 'Dickinson disrupts and transforms our accepted view of things.' What is your opinion of this statement? Refer to 'I could bring You Jewels—had I a mind to' in support of your response.
2. Copy the table below into your own notes and fill in critical comments about the last two quotations.

Key Quotes

I could bring You Jewels—had I a mind to	The speaker is confidently considering her options.
But this little Blaze/Flickering to itself	The gift chosen is simple and natural, but it is warm, vivid and beautiful, as conveyed by the lively onomatopoeia.
Suits Me	The gift is appropriate for the speaker to give, as it reflects her confident personality, as shown by the capital 'M'.
Dower itself	
Better—Could I bring?	

Emily Dickinson

• Poetry Focus •

A narrow Fellow in the Grass

Emily Dickinson

A narrow Fellow in the Grass
Occasionally rides—
You may have met Him—did you not
His notice sudden is—

The Grass divides as with a Comb—			5
A spotted shaft is seen—
And then it closes at your feet
And opens further on—

He likes a Boggy Acre
A Floor too cool for Corn—			10
Yet when a Boy, and Barefoot—
I more than once at Noon
Have passed, I thought, a Whip lash
Unbraiding in the Sun
When stooping to secure it			15
It wrinkled, and was gone—

Several of Nature's People
I know, and they know me—
I feel for them a transport
Of cordiality—			20

But never met this Fellow
Attended, or alone
Without a tighter breathing
And Zero at the Bone—

'His notice sudden is—'

GLOSSARY

6 *a spotted shaft*: patterned skin of the darting snake.
13 *Whip lash*: sudden, violent movement.
14 *Unbraiding*: straightening out, uncoiling.
19 *transport*: heightened emotion.
20 *cordiality*: civility, welcome.
24 *Zero at the Bone*: cold terror.

Emily Dickinson

EXPLORATIONS

1 Select two images from the poem that suggest evil or menace. Comment briefly on the effectiveness of each.
2 How successful is the poet in conveying the snake's erratic sense of movement? Refer to the text in your answer.
3 Outline your own feelings in response to the poem.

STUDY NOTES

In this poem, one of the few published during her lifetime, Dickinson adopts a male persona remembering an incident from his boyhood. Snakes have traditionally been seen as symbols of evil. We still use the expression 'snake in the grass' to describe someone who cannot be trusted. Central to this poem is Dickinson's own portrayal of nature – beautiful, brutal and lyrical. She seems fascinated by the endless mystery, danger and unpredictability of the natural world.

The opening lines of stanza one casually introduce a 'Fellow in the Grass' (Dickinson never refers explicitly to the snake). **The conversational tone immediately involves readers** who may already 'have met Him'. However, there is more than a hint of warning in the postscript: 'His notice sudden is'. This underlying wariness now appears foreshadowed by the menacing adjective 'narrow' and by the disjointed rhythm and slightly awkward word order within the opening lines.

Dickinson focuses on the volatile snake's dramatic movements in stanza two. The verbs 'divide', 'closes' and 'opens' emphasise its dynamic energy. The snake suddenly emerges like a 'spotted shaft'. The poet's **comparisons are particularly effective**, suggesting a lightning bolt or a camouflaged weapon. Run-on lines, a forceful rhythm and the repetition of 'And' contribute to the vivid image of the snake as a powerful presence to be treated with caution.

Stanza three reveals even more about the snake's natural habitat: 'He likes a Boggy Acre'. It also divulges the speaker's identity – an adult male remembering

Emily Dickinson

his failed boyhood efforts to capture snakes. The memory conveys something of the intensity of childhood experiences, especially of dangerous encounters with nature. The boy's innocence and vulnerability ('Barefoot') contrasts with the 'Whip lash' violence of the wild snake. **Dickinson's attitude to nature is open to interpretation.** Does the threat come from the animal or the boy? Did the adult speaker regard the snake differently when he was young? The poet herself clearly appreciates the complexities found within the natural world and her precisely observed descriptions ('Unbraiding', 'It wrinkled') provide ample evidence of her interest.

From the speaker's viewpoint in stanza four, nature is generally benign. This positive image is conveyed by the affectionate tribute to 'Nature's People'. The familiar personification and personal tone underline the mutual 'cordiality' that exists between nature and human nature. Despite this, **divisions between the two worlds cannot be ignored**. Indeed, the focus in stanza five is on the sheer horror people experience when confronted by 'this Fellow'. The poet's sparse and chilling descriptions – 'tighter breathing', 'Zero at the Bone' – are startling expressions of stunned terror.

As in other poems, Dickinson attributes human characteristics to nature – the snake 'Occasionally rides', 'The Grass divides' and the bogland has a 'Floor'. One effect of this is to highlight the **variety and mystery of the natural environment**, which can only ever be glimpsed within limited human terms. The snake remains unknowable to the end, dependent on a chance encounter, a fleeting glance or a trick of light.

ANALYSIS

Comment on the effectiveness of Dickinson's use of the male persona voice in 'A Narrow Fellow in the Grass'. Support the points you make with reference to the poem.

SAMPLE PARAGRAPH

In some of her poems, Emily Dickinson chose to substitute her own voice with that of a persona, a fictional narrator. This is the case in 'A Narrow Fellow in the Grass', where she uses a country boy to tell the story of his experiences trying to catch snakes when he was young. It is obvious that he has a great love for nature, but neither is he blind to the cold fear he felt when he came face to face with the 'spotted shaft'. Dickinson's use of language emphasises his youthful terror. She lets him remember his encounter exactly as it happened. The images she uses are powerful and disturbing: 'a tighter breathing'. The boy remembers shuddering with uncontrollable fright, 'Zero at the Bone'. The description is dramatic and I found I could relate to the boy's sense of horror. The poem is all the more effective for being centred around one terrified character, the young boy. I can visualise the child in his bare feet trying to catch a frightened snake in the grass. It is only later that he realises the great danger he was in and this has taught him a lifelong lesson about nature. By using another speaker's persona, Dickinson explores the excitement and danger of nature in a wider way that allows readers to imagine it more clearly.

EXAMINER'S COMMENT

Although the answer drifts at times from the central question, there is good personal engagement and a great deal of insightful discussion. Quotations are well used throughout the answer to provide a very interesting response. Grade A.

CLASS/HOMEWORK EXERCISES

1. In your opinion, how does Dickinson portray nature in 'A Narrow Fellow in the Grass'? Support your points with reference to the poem.
2. Copy the table below into your own notes and fill in critical comments about the last two quotations.

Key Quotes

His notice sudden is	The awkward syntax used to describe the snake's jerky movements adds to our sense of unease.
And then it closes at your feet	Dickinson highlights the lethal unpredictability of the snake.
A Floor too cool for Corn	The cool sensation of the snake's boggy habitat is enhanced by the broad assonant sounds.
Nature's People	
And Zero at the Bone	

• Poetry Focus •

I taste a liquor never brewed

I taste a liquor never brewed—
From Tankards scooped in Pearl—
Not all the Vats upon the Rhine
Yield such an Alcohol!

Inebriate of Air—am I—   5
And Debauchee of Dew—
Reeling—thro endless summer days—
From inns of Molten Blue—

When 'Landlords' turn the drunken Bee
Out of the Foxglove's door—   10
When Butterflies—renounce their 'drams'—
I shall but drink the more!

Till Seraphs swing their snowy Hats—
And Saints—to windows run—
To see the little Tippler   15
Leaning against the—Sun—

'Not all the Vats upon the Rhine/
Yield such an Alcohol!'

GLOSSARY

2 *Tankards*: one-handled mugs, usually made of pewter, used for drinking beer.
3 *Vats*: large vessels used for making alcohol.
6 *Debauchee*: someone who has overindulged and neglected duty.
13 *Seraphs*: angels who are of the highest spiritual level.
15 *Tippler*: a person who drinks often, but does not get drunk.

EXPLORATIONS

1 What is the mood in this poem? Does it intensify or change? Use references from the text in your response.
2 Which stanza appeals to you? Discuss both the poet's style and content in your answer, using quotations from the poem as evidence for your views.
3 Look at the final dash in the poem. Why do you think the poet ended the poem with this punctuation? What is it suggesting about the little tippler? Does it add a sense of fun?

STUDY NOTES

This 'rapturous poem about summer' uses the metaphor of intoxication to capture the essence of this wonderful season. Dickinson's family were strict Calvinists, a religion that emphasised damnation as the consequence of sin. Her father supported an organisation that warned against the dangers of drink, the Temperance League.

This poem is written as **a joyful appreciation of this wonderful life**. The tone is playful and exaggerated from the beginning, as the poet declares this drink was never 'brewed'. The reference to 'scooped in Pearl' could refer to the great, white frothing heads of beer in the 'Tankards'. The poet certainly conveys the merriment of intoxication, as the poem reels along its happy way. The explanation for all this drunkenness is that the poet is drunk on life ('Inebriate', 'Debauchee'). The pubs are the inns of 'Molten Blue', i.e. the sky (stanza two). It is like a cartoon, with little drunken bees being shown the door by the pub owners as they lurch about in delirious ecstasy. The drinkers of the natural world are the bees and butterflies, but she can drink more than these: 'I shall but drink the more!' This roots the poem in reality, as drunken people always feel they can manage more.

But this has caused uproar in the heavens, as the angels and saints run to look out at this little drunk, 'the little Tippler'. She stands drunkenly leaning against the 'Sun', a celestial lamppost. The final dash suggests the crooked stance of the little drunken one. There is no heavy moral at the end of this poem. In fact, **there seems to be a slight note of envy for the freedom and happiness being experienced by the intoxicated poet**. Are the angels swinging their hats to cheer her on in her drunken rebellion? Is this poem celebrating the reckless indulgence of excess? Or is the final metaphor of the sun referring to Christ or to the poet's own arrival in heaven after she indulgently enjoys the beauty of the natural world?

Nature is seen as the spur for high jinks and good humour. The riddle of the first line starts it off: how was the alcohol 'never brewed'? The exaggerated imagery, such as the metaphor of the flower as a pub and the bee as the drunk, all add to the **fantasy-land atmosphere**. The words 'Inebriate', 'Debauchee' and 'renounce' are reminiscent of the language which those disapproving of the consumption of alcohol might use for those who do indulge. Is the poet having a sly laugh at the serious Temperance League to which her father belonged? The ridiculous costumes, 'snowy hats', and the uproar in heaven ('swing' and 'run') all add to the impression of this land of merriment. The juxtaposition of the sacred ('Seraphs') and the profane ('Tippler') in stanza four also adds to the comic effect. However, it is the verbs that carry the sense of mad fun most effectively: 'scooped', 'Reeling', 'drink', 'swing', 'run' and 'Leaning'. The poem lurches and flows in an almost uncontrollable way as the ecstasy of overindulging in the delirious pleasure of nature is vividly conveyed.

There are two different types of humour present in this irrepressible poem – the broad humour of farce and the more **subversive humour of irony**. She even uses the steady metre of a hymn, with eight syllables in lines one and three and six syllables in lines two and four. Dickinson seems to be standing at a distance, smiling wryly, as she gently deflates.

ANALYSIS

'Dickinson was always wary of excess, even of joy.' Discuss this statement in relation to the above poem, using references from the text to support your answer.

SAMPLE PARAGRAPH

I don't agree. I think this is a funny poem and the poet is enjoying herself getting very drunk. But she is not drunk on beer. She is drunk on nature. I think it is very funny when the angels are waving their white caps, egging her on. I think this is a good poem, the best poem I ever red, as it makes me want to red more of Dickinson's poems. There is a good metaphor for drinking all through. Some of it is definately full of joy EG the bee. The part on the tippler leaning against the paling post is also joyful. I think everyone should enjoy Emily's absolutely brilliant poem as it has many good joyful images such as the drinking bee and little tippler.

EXAMINER'S COMMENT

This short answer shows very little knowledge or engagement with the poem. There is no substantial referencing. The language used is repetitive, expression is flawed and there are mechanical mistakes. The over-enthusiastic ending is not convincing. A basic D grade standard.

CLASS/HOMEWORK EXERCISES

1. 'Hypersensitivity to natural beauty produced Dickinson's poetry.' Do you agree or disagree with this statement? Refer to the poem 'I taste a liquor never brewed' in your response.
2. Copy the table below into your own notes and fill in critical comments about the last two quotations.

Key Quotes

From tankards scooped in Pearl	This line, with its use of the descriptive verb, suggests the outlining of the tankard in white, foaming beer.
Inebriate of Air—am I	The narrator in the poem is confessing to drunkenness due to an excessive indulgence in the beauty of nature.
I shall but drink the more!	A reference to the narrator herself. Unlike the butterflies, who are going to stop drinking, she intends to continue.
Till Seraphs swing their snowy hats	
Leaning against the—Sun	

• Poetry Focus •

After great pain, a formal feeling comes

After great pain, a formal feeling comes—
The Nerves sit ceremonious, like Tombs—
The stiff Heart questions was it He, that bore,
And Yesterday, or Centuries before?

The Feet, mechanical, go round— 5
Of Ground, or Air, or Ought—
A Wooden way
Regardless grown,
A Quartz contentment, like a stone—

This is the Hour of Lead— 10
Remembered, if outlived,
As Freezing persons, recollect the Snow—
First—Chill—then Stupor—then the letting go—

'First—Chill—then Stupor'

GLOSSARY

1 *formal*: serious; exact.
2 *ceremonious*: on show.
3 *He*: the stiff Heart, or possibly Christ.
3 *bore*: endure; intrude.
6 *Ought*: anything.
9 *Quartz*: basic rock mineral.
10 *Hour of Lead*: traumatic experience.
13 *Stupor*: numbness; disorientation.

EXPLORATIONS

1. Comment on the poet's use of personification in the opening stanza.
2. How does the language used in the second stanza convey the condition of the victim in pain?
3. Write your own short personal response to the poem.

STUDY NOTES

> Dickinson wrote 'After great pain' in 1862, at a time when she was thought to have been experiencing severe psychological difficulties. The poet addresses the effects of isolation and anguish on the individual. Ironically, the absence of the personal pronoun 'I' gives the poem a universal significance. The 'great pain' itself is never fully explained and the final lines are ambiguous. Like so much of Dickinson's work, this dramatic poem raises many questions for consideration.

From the outset, Dickinson is concerned with the emotional numbness ('a formal feeling') that follows the experience of 'great pain'. The poet's authoritative tone in **stanza one** reflects a first-hand knowledge of trauma, with the adjective 'formal' suggesting self-conscious recovery from some earlier distress. Dickinson personifies the physical response as order returns to body and mind: 'The Nerves sit ceremonious, like Tombs'. The severe pain has also shocked the 'stiff Heart', which has become confused by the experience. Is the poet also drawing a parallel with the life and death of Jesus Christ (the Sacred Heart), crucified 'Centuries before'? The images certainly suggest timeless suffering and endurance. This **sombre sense of loss** is further enhanced by the broad vowel assonance of the opening lines.

The feeling of stunned inertia continues into **stanza two.** In reacting to intense pain, 'The Feet, mechanical, go round'. It is as if the response is unfocused and indifferent, lacking any real purpose. Dickinson uses two **analogies to emphasise the sense of pointless alienation**. The reference to the 'Wooden way' might be interpreted as a fragile bridge between reason and insanity, or this metaphor could be associated with Christ's suffering as he carried his cross to Calvary. The level of consciousness at such times is described as 'Regardless grown', or beyond caring. Dickinson's second comparison is equally innovative: 'A Quartz contentment' underpins the feeling of complete apathy that makes the victims of pain behave 'like a stone'. Is she being ironic by suggesting that the post-traumatic state is an escape, a 'contentment' of sorts?

There is a disturbing sense of resignation at the start of **stanza three**: 'This is the Hour of Lead'. The dull weight of depression is reinforced by the insistent monosyllables and solemn rhythm, but the devastating experience is not 'outlived' by everyone. Dickinson outlines the aftermath of suffering by using one final comparison: 'As Freezing persons'. This shocking simile evokes the unimaginable hopelessness of the victim stranded in a vast wasteland of snow. The poem's last line traces the tragic stages leading to oblivion: 'First—Chill—then Stupor—then the letting go—'. The inclusion of the dash at the end might indicate a possibility of relief, though whether it is through rescue or death is not revealed. In either case, **readers are left with an acute awareness of an extremely distraught voice**.

ANALYSIS

One of Dickinson's great achievements is her ability to explore the experience of deep depression. To what extent is this true of her poem 'After great pain, a formal feeling comes'? Refer closely to the text in your answer.

SAMPLE PARAGRAPH

'After great pain' is a very good example of Emily Dickinson's skill in addressing controversial and distressing subjects, such as mental breakdown. Although she never really explains what she means by the 'pain' referred to in the first line, she deals with the after-effects of suffering throughout the poem. The loss of a loved one can cause very great anguish. What Dickinson does very well is to explain how depression can lead to people becoming numb, beyond all emotion. I believe this is what she means by 'a formal feeling'. She uses an interesting image of a sufferer's nerves sitting quietly in a church at a funeral service. They 'sit ceremonious'. This same idea is used to describe the mourners following the hearse – 'Feet mechanical'. I get the impression that grief and mourning can destroy people's confidence and make them numb. They go beyond grief. Dickinson's images are compelling and suggest the coldness experienced by patients who have suffered depression. They are 'like a stone'. The best description is at the end, when she compares sufferers to being lost in the snow. They will slowly fade into a 'stupor' or death wish. I think Dickinson is very good at using images and moods to explore depression. She is very good at suggesting shock in this poem.

EXAMINER'S COMMENT

Although the expression is awkward in places, there are a number of worthwhile points in the paragraph. There is some good personal engagement with the poem and references are used well in support. A basic B grade standard.

CLASS/HOMEWORK EXERCISES

1. In your opinion, what is the dominant mood in 'After great pain, a formal feeling comes'? Is it one of depression, sadness or acceptance? Refer closely to the text in your answer.
2. Copy the table below into your own notes and fill in critical comments about the last two quotations.

Key Quotes

a formal feeling comes	Dickinson states that the reaction to the experience of intense suffering is stiff and self-conscious.
A Quartz contentment, like a stone	After experiencing trauma, sufferers retreat within themselves, feeling lifeless and inhuman.
This is the Hour of Lead	The metaphor sums up Dickinson's stark acknowledgement of the reality of depression. Broad vowel sounds add further depth to the feeling.
A Wooden way/Regardless grown	
First—Chill—then Stupor—then the letting go	

• Poetry Focus •

LEAVING CERT SAMPLE ESSAY

> **Q** Has the poetry of Emily Dickinson any relevance for young people today? Support the points you make in your answer by reference to the poems by Dickinson on your course.

MARKING SCHEME GUIDELINES

Some of the following areas might be addressed:

- Interesting personal themes.
- Engaging confessional style.
- Oblique imagery is appealing.
- Unusual/eccentric punctuation.
- Experimental use of language.
- Challenging/passionate voice.

SAMPLE ESSAY
(Dickinson's Relevance for Today's Youth)

1 *I feel the poetry of Emily Dickinson would recieve a very positive response from a young person today. I will discuss this with reference to the four poems:*

Hope is a thing with Feathers
There's a certain Slant of Light
I Felt a Funeral in my brain
A narrow Fellow in the Grass

Dickinson's appeal lies not only in the content of these poems – depression, altered consciousness and death. But also in her style, how she conveys her themes.

2 *The oddness of Dickinson's poetry would, I feel, appeal to young people. It has a different slant on things, it is odd. Young people like different, eccentric things. Look at the clothes we wear, we like to be different. In the poem Slant of Light Dickinson takes an odd slant. When one thinks of light, you think of bright, warm happiness. But in this poem, Dickinson is describing light which is cold, oppressive, dying. It is the end of the year so light is dying and it is the end of the afternoon so light is fading.*

3. In this poem she expresses religious doubts which in my opinion young people can relate to. When we were younger we looked at the concept of Heaven and God through 'rose-tinted glasses'. Anyone who dies belonging to us went to live with God in Heaven and everything was happy ever after. But in this poem, a portrayl of a merciless, vengeful God comes across. This is how many young people feel. 'Heavenly hurt' any young person who has lost someone close to them has felt this hurt. But there is no scar to prove this anguish.

4. Emily uses short four line stanza's in her poems which I feel young peple can definately relate to. In this fast, cosmopolitan world everyone enjoys reading a short poem. Her omission of words, articles and verbs is like a text message. Young people shorten words, leave them out in order to write a text. They therefor can relate to Emily's poetry as it is like one of the hundreds of texts they send.

5. She also has little regard for syntex, punctuation and formal grammer like young people in text messages. She uses capital letters for emphasis. 'I felt a Funeral in my Brain'. In text messages young people use capitals to emphasis something for example 'I saw JAMIE at the bus stop!'

6. Emily has two themes – Death and Nature. In her poem, 'I Felt a Funeral' she is describing the opression of her mental disorder. I feel young people can relate to this – not the mental disorder but the oppression Young people have tough lives. In Sixth year there are pre's, Leaving Cert, CAO points, the list is endless. We feel trapped, opressed like Emily. She describes the mourners as 'thuding – thuding'. This is like a bad headache. A headache students get from study and from CAO forms. The poet is lying in a coffin, she is powerless.

> 'And then they lifted the box
> And walked across my soul'.

7. Metaphorically speaking Sixth year and all the traumas that go with it is like being powerless in a coffin. Apparently prior to writing this poem, Emily was rejected by a man. All young girls can relate to this – being rejected by the love of your life.

8. In 'Hope is a thing with Feathers' she celebrates human resillance in the face of difficulty. Students can also relate to this poem with all that is going on in

their lives. She praises the power of hope to overcome the worst catastrophies, 'And hard must be the storm.' Hope lifts the human will to survive, hope is indomitable. Students can relate to this, they have to take what life throws at them. 'Yet never in extremnity, it asked a Crumb of Me'. The worst disaster imaginable leaves hope undaunted. Every young person needs hope and can relate to this poem.

9 Emily's other nature poem is 'A Narrow Fellow in the grass'. Dickinson is wary of nature in this poem. Instead of man and nature living in harmony she feels they have an acquaintance. She describes a snake 'a spotted shaft'. She is afraid of it but is curious to go after it. In my opinion, young people can relate to the curiosity in this poem. Young people are afraid to take drugs but take them out of curiosity. They would be feeling 'Zero at the bone' if they were caught but nevertheless human curiosity takes over. Like Emily going searching for the snake. She is afraid of it but intrigued by it.

10 Young people can respond to Emily Dickinson's poetry in a number of ways. The oddness of her poems entice young people to read them. They are unique. When she expresses religious doubts in her poem 'Slant of Light', in my opinion young people can relate to this. They too can harbour doubts. The compactness of her poems, her omission of words and use of capitals is like a text message which young people can definitaly relate to. Finally her themes suggesting opression relate to young people's student lives. The hardship, the studying. Her final theme of nature and curiosity can relate to young people also. The curiosity to dabble in drugs even with the fear of getting caught.

(approx. 880 words)

SPELLCHECKER	receive	extremity
	therefore	syntax
	portrayal	grammar
	resilience	oppression
	definitely	emphasis

GRADE: C2	
P	= 10/15
C	= 10/15
L	= 8/15
M	= 3/5
Total	= 31/50

EXAMINERS COMMENT

This is a reasonable response that tries hard to keep focused on the question. However, there is little detailed analysis of the poems themselves. For instance, although paragraph four makes a valid point about the poet's text-like style, no examples are given. The expression is awkward at times. Other distractions include spelling errors, careless punctuation and inaccurate quotations. As a convention of literary criticism, it is not usual to refer to authors by their first names.

SAMPLE LEAVING CERT QUESTIONS ON DICKINSON'S POETRY (45–50 MINUTES)

1. What impact did the poetry of Emily Dickinson make on you as a reader? Your answer should deal with the following:
   - Your overall sense of the personality of the poet.
   - The poet's use of language/imagery.

   Refer to the poems by Emily Dickinson you have studied.

2. Write about the feelings Emily Dickinson's poetry creates in you and the aspects of her poetry (content or style) that help to create those feelings. Support your points by reference to the poetry of Dickinson on your course.

3. 'Speaking of Emily Dickinson…'
   Write out the text of a public talk you might give on the poetry of Emily Dickinson. Your talk should make reference to the poetry on your course.

SAMPLE ESSAY PLAN (Q3)

'Speaking of Emily Dickinson…'

Write out the text of a talk you might give on the poetry of Emily Dickinson. Your talk should make reference to the poetry on your course.

•	Intro:	Original voice and expression of the poet has a broad appeal. Deals with the great themes.
•	Point 1:	'I heard a Fly buzz' – fascination with death shown by recreation of deathbed scene.
•	Point 2:	'"Hope" is the thing with feathers' – a celebration of human resilience in the face of constant difficulty.

- *Point 4:* Style – Dickinson's fondness for capitals and dashes.
- *Point 5:* Impact of reclusive life on themes and style of poetry.
- *Conclusion:* A poet who has much to say to the anxious modern reader coping with an ever-faster world.

EXERCISE

Develop one of the above points into a paragraph.

POINT 1 – SAMPLE PARAGRAPH

Dickinson's fascination with death is seen graphically in the poem 'I heard a Fly buzz'. She introduces a fly buzzing to the deathbed scene. She trivialises the solemn occasion as well as making it more realistic. In stanza one the 'Stillness' magnifies the sound of the buzzing fly. It is like the stillness at the centre of the storm. The storm is death, which is both powerful and destructive, just like the storm. The poet then startles us in stanza two. The reference to 'Eyes' shows the mourners who stand around the deathbed. They have stopped crying. They are waiting for the moment Death, 'King', appears. Then in stanza three we return to the narrator. She has made her last bequests and is ready to face her Maker when the fly makes its presence known. The word 'interposed' is deliberately used to show the fly interfering with the deathbed drama. The last stanza shows us the final moments of the narrator's life. Her sight goes. There is only darkness. 'And then the Windows failed'. Without the eyes and the other senses there can be no reality, as the person then has no means to perceive her surroundings. Here Dickinson is imagining her own death. She is passing comment on one of life's great moments which we must all face, yet succeeds through the introduction of the fly to show that even in the most solemn occasions there is always the trivial and unpredictable. This is what makes her poetry interesting to study.

EXAMINER'S COMMENT

The paragraph includes a number of interesting observations about the chosen poem and the discussion remains well focused on the question. The absence of the register of a talk prevents the student from attaining a higher grade, as the task is not fully completed. Otherwise, a solid B grade.

Last Words

'The Dickinson dashes are an integral part of her method and style ... and cannot be translated ... without deadening the wonderful naked voltage of the poems.'

Ted Hughes

'The Brain—is wider than the Sky—
The Brain is deeper than the sea—'

Emily Dickinson

(On her determination to hide secrets) 'The price she paid was that of appearing to posterity as perpetually unfinished and wilfully eccentric.'

Philip Larkin

'Walk on air against your better judgement.'

Seamus Heaney (1939–)

Seamus Heaney was born in 1939 in Co. Derry and was the eldest of nine children. He was accepted into Queen's University, Belfast in 1957 to study English Language and Literature. Heaney's poetry first came to public attention in the 1960s, when he and a number of other poets, including Michael Longley and Derek Mahon, came to prominence. They all shared the same fate of being born into a society that was deeply divided along religious grounds and was to become immersed in violence, intimidation and sectarianism. In 1966, his first poetry collection, *Death of a Naturalist*, was published. Heaney spent many years lecturing in Belfast, Dublin and America. Throughout this time he was publishing prolifically and giving public readings. He has also written several volumes of criticism. Widely regarded as the finest poet of his generation, he was awarded the Nobel Prize for Literature in 1995 'for works of lyrical beauty and ethical depth, which exalt everyday miracles and the living past'. In accepting the award, Heaney stated that his life had been 'a journey into the wideness of language, a journey where each point of arrival … turned out to be a stepping stone rather than a destination'.

• Poetry Focus •

PRESCRIBED POEMS (HIGHER LEVEL)

Seamus Heaney

1 'The Forge' (p. 128)

At one level, the poem celebrates a traditional craft. However, its central focus is on the mystery and beauty of the creative process itself. The blacksmith's work is used as an extended metaphor for the shaping of any work of art.

2 'Bogland' (p. 132)

The poet contrasts the expansive North American grasslands with the narrowly bounded landscape of Ireland's boglands. For Heaney, the bogs are a precious museum of the island's past.

3 'The Tollund Man' (p. 137)

Photographs of the preserved body of an Iron Age man found in the bogs of Jutland, Denmark, prompted Heaney to trace parallels between the imagined circumstances of the Tollund Man's death and more recent violence in the North of Ireland.

4 'Mossbawn: Sunlight' (p. 143)

This wonderfully atmospheric poem is a nostalgic celebration of the poet's childhood on the family farm in Co. Derry and his close relationship with his aunt. The importance of place, family and the simple joys of ordinary life are central themes in Heaney's poetry.

5 'A Constable Calls' (p. 148)

Based on another memory from his boyhood, the poet describes an uneasy encounter when his father was questioned by a local policeman. At a deeper level, the poet explores the complex relationship between the two communities in Northern Ireland.

6 'The Skunk' (p. 154)

Sensuous language and an edgy, romantic atmosphere enhance this unusual and playful love poem. Seeing his wife, Heaney is reminded of a lonely time he once spent in California, where he eagerly awaited the nightly visit of a skunk.

7 'The Harvest Bow' (p. 159)

A tightly wrought personal poem based on the central image of a decorative 'throwaway love-knot'. The straw bow provides a physical link between Heaney and his father, the present and the past, nature and art.

8 'The Underground' (p. 164)

The poem explores the enduring love between Heaney and his wife. Based on a memory from their honeymoon, the newlyweds are compared to Orpheus and Eurydice as they hurry through a London Underground Tube station.

9 'Postscript' (p. 169)

In this short lyric, the poet succeeds in conveying the extraordinary by way of an everyday experience – the memory of a vivid journey westward to the Flaggy Shore of the Co. Clare coastline.

10 'A Call' (p. 173)

Another poem dealing with one of Heaney's favourite themes: the father-son relationship and the passing of time. The setting is a routine domestic scene of a father weeding, a son visiting and a mother talking.

11 'Tate's Avenue' (p. 178)

In this beautifully discreet and understated love poem, Heaney recalls three car rugs that mark important stages in the changing relationship between himself and his wife.

12 'The Pitchfork' (p. 182)

Another typical Heaney poem, celebrating traditional rural life. The poet makes 'a journey back into the heartland of the ordinary', where he is both observer and visionary.

13 'Lightenings viii' (p. 187)

In his short account of how a mysterious floating airship appeared above the monks' oratory at Clonmacnoise monastery, Heaney blurs the lines between reality and illusion and challenges our ideas about life.

• Poetry Focus •

The Forge

Seamus Heaney

All I know is a door into the dark.
Outside, old axles and iron hoops rusting;
Inside, the hammered anvil's short-pitched ring,
The unpredictable fantail of sparks
Or hiss when a new shoe toughens in water.   5
The anvil must be somewhere in the centre,
Horned as a unicorn, at one end square,
Set there immoveable: an altar
Where he expends himself in shape and music.
Sometimes, leather-aproned, hairs in his nose,   10
He leans out on the jamb, recalls a clatter
Of hoofs where traffic is flashing in rows;
Then grunts and goes in, with a slam and a flick
To beat real iron out, to work the bellows.

'The unpredictable fantail of sparks'

GLOSSARY

The Forge: refers to a blacksmith's workshop, where iron implements are made and mended (in the poem, a smith is shaping horseshoes).
2 *axles*: bars or shafts on which wheels rotate.
3 *anvil*: iron block that the smith uses as a work surface.
7 *unicorn*: mythical animal (usually a white horse) with a spiralled horn growing from its forehead.
9 *expends*: burns up, expresses.
11 *jamb*: upright door support.
14 *bellows*: instrument for drawing air into a fire.

EXPLORATIONS

1 Describe the poet's attitude to the forge. Is he fascinated or fearful, or both? Support your answer with reference to the poem.
2 Based on your study of the poem, what is your impression of the blacksmith?
3 Comment on the effectiveness of the phrase 'The unpredictable fantail of sparks'.

STUDY NOTES

'The Forge' comes from Seamus Heaney's second collection, *Door into the Dark*, which was published in 1969. The sonnet form has a clear division of an octave (the first eight lines) and a sestet (the final six lines). While the octave, apart from its initial reference to the narrator, focuses on the inanimate objects and occurrences inside and outside the forge, the sestet describes the blacksmith and his work.

The poem's **opening line** ('All I know is a door into the dark') is both modest and assured. There is also a **mystical undertone** (a sense of otherworldliness) as Heaney revisits his childhood and his fascination with a local forge. The image, with its negative and mysterious connotations, incites our curiosity and invites us to find out what answers lie beyond. The poet recalls unwanted objects strewn outside, 'old axles and iron hoops rusting'. The irregular rhythm in **line 2** suggests the disorder of what has been discarded. He **contrasts** the lifeless exterior scene with the vigorous atmosphere ('the hammered anvil's short-pitched ring') inside the forge. The world outside is decrepit and old, a wasteland, whereas the noisy forge is a place of brilliant sparks where iron is beaten out and renewed.

Heaney's visual and aural images are characteristically striking. His vivid metaphor of 'The unpredictable fantail of sparks' (**line 4**) lets us see the glorious flurry of erratic, flashing light and hear the twang of reverberating iron. **Onomatopoeic effects** add to our sense of the physical activity taking place as the blacksmith works on a new horseshoe. Suddenly, the incandescent metal begins to 'hiss when a new shoe toughens in water'. The **tone is sympathetic** and attentive as the poet reimagines the smells, sounds and tactile impressions of the blacksmith's workshop.

Lines 6–9 contain the sonnet's central image of the smith's anvil: 'an altar/Where he expends himself in shape and music'. Interestingly, the transition from the octave to the sestet is a run-on (or enjambment) based around this key metaphor. One effect of this is to enable us to experience the anvil as a **sacred or magical point of transition** between the material and immovable world of everyday life and the fluid, imaginative world of human consciousness. Heaney stresses the **mystery of the creative process**, associating it with the mythical creature of medieval fiction, 'Horned as a unicorn'. Although the simile seems somewhat strained, the comparison with a legendary beast still serves to highlight the mysterious qualities ('shape and music') of poetry.

The **final lines** focus on the blacksmith's physical characteristics. **Heaney leaves us with a down-to-earth image of a gruff, hardworking man,** 'leather-aproned, hairs in his nose'. Is the poet suggesting that art – and poetry in particular – is independent of education and social class? Seemingly wary of the world at large, the smith remembers an earlier era of horse-drawn carriages, when his skills were fully appreciated. Contrasting images of 'a clatter/Of hoofs' and modern traffic 'flashing in rows' reflect the changes he has lived through. In the end, he grudgingly accepts that he must return 'into the dark' and resume doing what he does best: 'To beat real iron out, to work the bellows'.

Heaney's poem can immediately be read as an elegy to the past and a lament for the lost tradition of the blacksmith. Readers can also interpret the anvil as a metaphor of an unreachable heritage, a traditional craft made redundant by modernisation. Many critics have seen the blacksmith figure as a **symbol or construction of the role of the poet**, one who opens the 'door into the dark', the creative artist who ritually 'expends himself in shape and music' and who 'grunts' and flicks words and language, forging his poems. As with so much of Heaney's work, the poem attests to his ability to subtly evoke resonance by making us wonder.

ANALYSIS

'Heaney's poetry is populated with a variety of characters who have inspired him.' To what extent is this true of 'The Forge'? Refer to the poem in your answer.

SAMPLE PARAGRAPH

'The Forge' is a good example of a poem where Heaney's central character, the old blacksmith, represents a disappearing way of life. As a child, the poet was drawn to the rural blacksmith's shop which to his innocent mind was a place of excitement. The images in the poem evoke the realistic sights and sounds of the blacksmith's work in 'the dark' – such as 'the fantail of sparks' coming from the hammering of red-hot metal when horseshoes were being made. Heaney uses the unnamed blacksmith as a symbolic representation of all creative people who work at their artistic gifts. Much of this poem deals with the hard physical work involved. I can certainly imagine Heaney as a child wondering about what the blacksmith was doing, even wishing to try for himself. The poet paints a picture of a simple man who doesn't speak – he 'grunts and goes in' to his work. He certainly seems to be a simple loner, dedicated to the 'shape and music' of his craft. The whole poem reflects Heaney's own sense of wonder about this dedicated rural blacksmith – and about the inspiration for poetry. He compares the blacksmith at his anvil to a priest saying mass – but not fully understanding the mystery of it. The ending of the poem suggests that neither the blacksmith nor Heaney himself can ever fully understand the true nature of art and craft.

EXAMINER'S COMMENT

This is a reasonably good attempt at addressing the question. There is some welcome personal engagement and apt references are included to convey Heaney's use of the blacksmith as an exemplary figure. The expression is slightly repetitive in places. A basic B-grade standard overall.

CLASS/HOMEWORK EXERCISES

1. Comment on the poet's use of visual and aural images to create an overall picture of the blacksmith's forge.
2. Copy the table below into your own notes and fill in critical comments about the last two quotations.

Key Quotes

All I know is a door into the dark	The poem's opening line focuses on Heaney's fascination with the forge as an unknown and possibly frightening place of mystery.
the hammered anvil's short-pitched ring	Sound effects play an important part in recreating the reality of the forge and suggesting the deeper creative process. Note the sharp, shimmering effect of 'ring'.
he expends himself in shape and music	The artistry of the energetic work of the blacksmith – and of all creative people – is expressed in this memorable image. The verb 'expends' suggests the overwhelming effort involved in the smith's work.
recalls a clatter/Of hoofs where traffic is flashing in rows	
beat real iron out	

Bogland

for T.P. Flanagan

We have no prairies
To slice a big sun at evening –
Everywhere the eye concedes to
Encroaching horizon,

Is wooed into the cyclops' eye
Of a tarn. Our unfenced country
Is bog that keeps crusting
Between the sights of the sun.

They've taken the skeleton
Of the Great Irish Elk
Out of the peat, set it up,
An astounding crate full of air.

Butter sunk under
More than a hundred years
Was recovered salty and white.
The ground itself is kind, black butter

Melting and opening underfoot,
Missing its last definition
By millions of years.
They'll never dig coal here,

Only the waterlogged trunks
Of great firs, soft as pulp.
Our pioneers keep striking
Inwards and downwards,

Every layer they strip
Seems camped on before.
The bogholes might be Atlantic seepage.
The wet centre is bottomless.

'Encroaching horizon,/Is wooed into the cyclops' eye/Of a tarn'

Seamus Heaney

GLOSSARY

1 *prairies*: a large open area of grassland (in North America).
3 *concedes*: gives way to; admits defeat.
4 *Encroaching*: advancing gradually beyond acceptable limits.
5 *wooed*: courted, enticed.
5 *cyclops' eye*: in Greek mythology, a race of one-eyed giants.
6 *tarn*: small mountain lake.
10 *Great Irish Elk*: large northern deer found preserved in Irish bogland.
18 *definition*: transformation (into coal).
23 *pioneers*: adventurers, explorers.
27 *seepage*: the slow escape of liquid through a material.

EXPLORATIONS

1 In your opinion, what is Heaney's central theme or point? Briefly explain your response.
2 How does Heaney employ the senses to allow the reader to share in his experience of the bogland? Refer closely to the poem in your answer.
3 Trace the poet's tone throughout the poem. Comment on where, how and why, in your opinion, the tone changes. Support your views with reference to the text.

STUDY NOTES

'Bogland' (1969) is the result of a Halloween holiday Heaney spent with T.P. Flanagan (the artist to whom he dedicated the poem). Flanagan recalls that 'the bogland was burnt the colour of marmalade'. Heaney felt it was 'one of the most important poems' he had written because 'it was something like a symbol. I felt the poem was a promise of something else ... it represented a free place for me'. He thought the bogland was a 'landscape that remembered everything that happened in and to it'. Heaney recalled when they were children that they were told 'not to go near the bog because there was no bottom to it'.

• Poetry Focus •

Seamus Heaney

In the **opening stanza**, a **comparison** is drawn between the American prairies ('We have no prairies') and Ireland's bogs. Heaney said, 'At that time, I had … been reading about the frontier and the west as an important myth in the American consciousness, so I set up – or rather, laid down – the bog as an answering Irish myth.' The prairie in America represents the vastness of the country, its unfenced expanse a metaphor for the freedom of its people to pursue their dreams and express their beliefs. At first, Ireland's bog represents opposite values. It seems narrow, constricting and inward looking: 'the eye concedes', 'Encroaching horizon', 'cyclops' eye'. In America, the pioneers moved across the country. In Ireland, the pioneers looked 'Inwards and downwards', remembering, almost wallowing in, the past. Is the poet suggesting that Ireland is defined by the layers of its difficult history? Or is each set of pioneers on an adventure, one set discovering new places, the other set rediscovering forgotten places?

Stanza two captures **the bog's fluidity** in the onomatopoeic phrase 'keeps crusting/Between the sights of the sun'. Heaney draws the changing face of the bog, its element of mystery and danger, as it did not always remain exactly the same, but subtly fluctuates. The poet's sense of awe at this place is expressed in **stanza three** as he recounts the discovery of the Great Irish Elk as 'An astounding crate full of air'. Here the poet is referring to another aspect of the bog – its **ability to preserve the past**.

In **stanza four**, the bog's capacity to hold and preserve is emphasised when 'Butter sunk under/More than a hundred years' was recovered fit for use, 'salty and white'. This place is 'kind'. Stanza four runs into **stanza five** in a parallel reference to the bog's fluidity. The bog never becomes hard; 'its last definition' is 'Missing', so it will never yield coal. The squidgy nature of the bog is conveyed in **stanza six** in the phrase 'soft as pulp'. The phrases of the poem are opening and melting into each other in imitation of the bog. Is this in stark contrast to the hardening prejudices of the two communities in the North of Ireland? This poem was written in 1969. **The Irish explore their past**; to them, history is important as they 'keep striking/Inwards and downwards'.

Heaney leaves us with an **open-ended conclusion** in **stanza seven**. He remembers that the bog 'seemed to have some kind of wind blowing through it that could carry on'. The boglands are feminine, nurturing, welcoming. 'The wet centre is bottomless'. The poet is aware of the depth and complexity of the national consciousness. Should we, like the bog, embrace all aspects of our national identity? Is this how we should carry on? Is there a final truth? Is it unreachable? The poem is written in seven spare, unrhymed stanzas and uses casual, almost colloquial language.

ANALYSIS

'There is a quality of vivid sensuousness in the poetry of Heaney.' Discuss this statement, supporting your opinion with references to the poem.

SAMPLE PARAGRAPH

Heaney, for me, captures the essence of the bog in words like 'soft as pulp', 'melting', 'Missing'. The gentle consonants and broad vowels create the oozing fluid quality of the bog. The thin surface of the bog is vividly caught in the phrase 'keeps crusting'. The sound of the hard 'k' and 'c' suggest, to me, the brittle surface of the bog as it barely forms a thin skin under the rays of the sun. The rich sibilance of 'sights of the sun' suggests the quiet passing days out in the peaceful bog. The musical alliteration of the explosive 'b' in 'black butter' further emphasises the gloopy, muddy bog. I particularly like the references to sight in this poem. The opening stanza, with its reference to 'We have no prairies/To slice a big sun at evening', reminds me of cowboy films like *The Big Country* with their endless panoramic views of prairie and a huge half disc of flaming red sun disappearing over the horizon at evening time. I imagine the sense of freedom and excitement of the Wild West pioneers as they strike out to provide a better life for themselves and their families. We, instead, are represented by another visual reference, in a completely different way. We are almost deformed, 'cyclops' eye'. The image at the end of the poem, however, moves from this negative thought, as the bog is represented as 'bottomless'. The vivid quality of this image entices us, like the tarn wooed the horizon, into the dark mystery of the bog.

EXAMINER'S COMMENT

A well-sustained response to the question. Good examination of Heaney's appeal to the senses. Emphasis on style was maintained throughout, with effective references to sound effects. Interesting and well-illustrated points are made about the rich musicality of Heaney's language. Grade A.

• Poetry Focus •

Seamus Heaney

CLASS/HOMEWORK EXERCISES

1. 'The importance of tradition and a sense of place are recurring features of Heaney's poetry.' Discuss this statement, supporting your answer with reference to 'Bogland'.
2. Copy the table below into your own notes and fill in critical comments about the last two quotations.

Key Quotes

We have no prairies/To slice a big sun at evening	Heaney evocatively draws a picture of an American sunset in the vast grasslands there. The verb 'slice' gives the line sharpness.
Encroaching horizon,/Is wooed into the cyclops' eye/Of a tarn	This phrase sums up the inward outlook of Irish people, as it seems as if the vast sky is swallowed up into a small bog pool. The reference to the one-eyed race of giants suggests that this outlook could be regarded as deformed.
Missing its last definition	The bog never becomes hard enough to form coal. Is there a suggestion that the bog's soft, all-embracing approach is one that Irish people could adopt?
Every layer they strip/Seems camped on before	
The wet centre is bottomless	

The Tollund Man

I

Some day I will go to Aarhus
To see his peat-brown head,
The mild pods of his eyelids,
His pointed skin cap.

In the flat country nearby
Where they dug him out,
His last gruel of winter seeds
Caked in his stomach,

Naked except for
The cap, noose and girdle,
I will stand a long time.
Bridegroom to the goddess,

She tightened her torc on him
And opened her fen,
Those dark juices working
Him to a saint's kept body,

Trove of the turfcutters'
Honeycombed workings.
Now his stained face
Reposes at Aarhus.

II

I could risk blasphemy,
Consecrate the cauldron bog
Our holy ground and pray
Him to make germinate

The scattered, ambushed
Flesh of labourers,
Stockinged corpses
Laid out in the farmyards,

Tell-tale skin and teeth
Flecking the sleepers
Of four young brothers, trailed
For miles along the lines.

III

Something of his sad freedom
As he rode the tumbril
Should come to me, driving,
Saying the names

Tollund, Grauballe, Nebelgard,
Watching the pointing hands
Of country people,
Not knowing their tongue.

Out there in Jutland
In the old man-killing parishes
I will feel lost,
Unhappy and at home.

'Something of his sad freedom'

GLOSSARY

The Tollund Man: a reference to the well-preserved body found in 1950 by two turfcutters in Tollund, Denmark. The man had been hanged over 2,000 years earlier. One theory suggested that his death had been part of a ritualistic fertility sacrifice. The Tollund Man's head was put on display in a museum at Aarhus.

1 *Aarhus*: a city in Jutland, Denmark.
3 *pods*: dry seeds.
7 *gruel*: thin porridge.
10 *girdle*: belt.
13 *torc*: decorative metal collar.
14 *fen*: marsh or wet area.
16 *kept*: preserved.
17 *Trove*: valuable find.
18 *Honeycombed workings*: patterns made by the turfcutters on the peat.
21 *blasphemy*: irreverence.
22 *Consecrate*: declare sacred.
22 *cauldron bog*: basin-shaped bogland (some of which was associated with pagan rituals).
24 *germinate*: give new life to.
30 *sleepers*: wooden beams underneath railway lines.
31 *four young brothers*: refers to an infamous atrocity in the 1920s when four Catholic brothers were killed by the police.
34 *tumbril*: two-wheeled cart used to carry a condemned person to execution.
37 *Tollund, Grauballe, Nebelgard*: places in Jutland.

EXPLORATIONS

1 Comment on Heaney's tone in the first three stanzas of the poem.
2 Select one image from the poem that you find startling or disturbing and explain its effectiveness.
3 What is your understanding of the poem's final stanza? Refer closely to the text in your answer.

STUDY NOTES

Seamus Heaney was attracted to a book by P.V. Glob, *The Bog People*, that dealt with preserved Iron Age bodies of people who had been ritually killed. It offered him a particular frame of reference or set of symbols he could employ to engage with Ireland's historical conflict. The martyr image of the Tollund Man blended in the poet's mind with photographs of other atrocities, past and present, in the long rites of Irish political struggles. The poem comes from Heaney's third collection, *Wintering Out* (1972).

Part I opens quietly with **the promise of a pilgrimage**: 'Some day I will go to Aarhus'. The tone is expectant, determined. Yet there is also an element of detachment that is reinforced by the Danish place name, 'Aarhus'. Heaney's placid, almost reverential mood is matched by his economic use of language, dominated by simple monosyllables. The evocative description of the Tollund Man's 'peat-brown head' and 'The mild pods of his eyelids' conveys a sense of gentleness and passivity.

Lines 5–11 focus on the dead man's final hours in a much more realistic way. Heaney suggests that the Tollund Man's own journey begins when 'they dug him out', destroyed and elevated at the same time. The poet's meticulous observations ('His last gruel of winter seeds/Caked in his stomach') emphasise the dead man's **innocent vulnerability**. In the aftermath of a ritualistic hanging, we see him abandoned: 'Naked except for/The cap, noose and girdle'. While the poet identifies himself closely with the victim and makes a respectful promise to 'stand a long time', the action itself is passive.

Heaney imagines the natural boglands as the body of a fertility goddess. The revelation that the sacrificial victim was 'Bridegroom to the goddess' (**line 12**) conveys a more **ominous, forceful tone** as the bleak bog itself is also equated with Ireland, female and overwhelming: 'She tightened her torc on him'. Sensuous and energetic images in **lines 13–16** suggest the physical intimacy of the couple's deadly embrace. The Tollund Man becomes 'a saint's kept body', almost a surrogate Christ, buried underground so that new life would spring up. He is left to chance, 'Trove of the turfcutters', and finally resurrected so that 'his stained face/Reposes at Aarhus'. The delicate blend of sibilance and broad vowel sounds suggest tranquillity and a final peace.

Part II suddenly becomes more emphatic and is filled with references to religion. Heaney addresses the spirit of the Tollund Man, invoking him 'to make germinate' (**line 24**) and give life back to the casualties of more recent violence in Northern Ireland. Heaney acknowledges his own discomfort ('I could risk blasphemy') for suggesting that we should search for an alternative deity or religious symbol to unite people. But although it appears to be in contrast with the earlier violence, the poet's restrained style actually accentuates the horror of one infamous sectarian slaughter ('Of four young brothers'). The callous nature of their deaths – 'trailed/For miles along the lines' – is associated with the repulsive rituals in ancient Jutland. Heaney's **nightmarish images** ('Stockinged corpses') are powerful and create a surreal effect. However, the paradoxical 'survival' and repose of the Tollund Man should, the poet implies, give him the power to raise others.

Part III returns to the mellow beginning, but instead of anticipation, there is sorrow and a sense of isolation. Heaney insists that the 'sad freedom' (**line 33**) of the Tollund Man 'Should come to me'. Along with religion and a sense of history and myth, evocative language is central to Heaney's poetry, and here the idea of isolation is brought sharply to the reader through the sense of being 'lost' in a foreign land. Yet ultimately the paradoxical nature of exile is realised: the poet feels at home in a state of homelessness, and welcomes the feeling of not belonging to society which he shares with the Tollund Man, who is no longer tied to religious forces. This estrangement from society is emphasised by the list of foreign names ('Tollund, Grauballe, Nebelgard'). **The poem ends on a note of pessimistic resignation** which describes both the familiar sense of isolation and hopelessness Heaney experiences: 'I will feel lost,/Unhappy and at home'.

Heaney's imaginary pilgrimage to Aarhus has led to **a kind of revelation**. By comparing modern Ulster to the 'old man-killing parishes' (**line 42**) of remote Jutland, the poet places the Northern Irish conflict in a timeless, mythological context. It is as though the only way Heaney can fully express the horrific scenes he has seen in Ireland is to associate them with the exhumed bodies of ancient bog corpses.

ANALYSIS

'Heaney's poetry manages to evoke passion and pain through language that is both simple and dignified.' In your opinion, is this true of 'The Tollund Man'? Refer to the poem in your response.

> **SAMPLE PARAGRAPH**
>
> Of all the Heaney poems I have studied, I find 'The Tollund Man' the most moving. Heaney imagines the short life and death of this sacrificial martyr who was executed sometime during the Iron Age and whose body was preserved in a Jutland bogland for over 2,000 years. The story is narrated in simple, colloquial language – 'I will go to Aarhus/To see his peat-brown head'. The poet is captivated by the man's gentle features – 'The mild pods of his eyelids' – as he reposes in death. While Heaney's tone of voice is always measured and respectful, there is also a passionate admiration for what the dead man has endured, only achieving a 'sad freedom' in being executed. He compares the Tollund Man to Irish people who have lost their lives here in sectarian violence. Again the language is direct but powerful – 'ambushed/Flesh of labourers'. For me, the poem sums up the lonely

terror of innocent victims, past and present. What I really admire is Heaney's quiet strength of language – his realistic images and sincere tone in empathising with all those who are victims of conflict in our 'man-killing parishes'.

EXAMINER'S COMMENT

This is a clearly focused response which shows genuine interaction with the poem. Relevant points are supported with accurate illustrations, showing a very good knowledge of the text. Expression is fluent, varied and controlled throughout. An assured A grade.

CLASS/HOMEWORK EXERCISES

1 'Seamus Heaney presents us with a contradictory world that is both familiar and unnerving.' Discuss 'The Tollund Man' in light of this view, supporting your answer with reference to the poem.
2 Copy the table below into your own notes and fill in critical comments about the last two quotations.

Key Quotes

Some day I will go to Aarhus	Heaney's firm sense of a religious pilgrimage is central to the poem. The diction is simple and the tone is one of hushed reverence.
Bridegroom to the goddess	The bog itself is personified as an ancient fertility goddess and the killing is described as a ritual marriage.
Tell-tale skin and teeth/Flecking the sleepers	Typically well-crafted phrasing, graphic imagery, short lines and a fragmented rhythm emphasise the disturbing reality of violent death.
Something of his sad freedom	
I will feel lost,/Unhappy and at home	

Mossbawn: Sunlight

for Mary Heaney

      Sunlight

There was a sunlit absence.
The helmeted pump in the yard
heated its iron,
water honeyed

in the slung bucket   5
and the sun stood
like a griddle cooling
against the wall

of each long afternoon.
So, her hands scuffled   10
over the bakeboard,
the reddening stove

sent its plaque of heat
against her where she stood
in a floury apron   15
by the window.

Now she dusts the board
with a goose's wing,
now sits, broad-lapped,
with whitened nails   20

and measling shins:
here is a space
again, the scone rising
to the tick of two clocks.

And here is love   25
like a tinsmith's scoop
sunk past its gleam
in the meal-bin.

• Poetry Focus •

Seamus Heaney

'to the tick of two clocks'

GLOSSARY

Mossbawn was Heaney's birthplace. 'Bawn' refers to the name the English planters gave to their fortified farmhouses. 'Ban' is Gaelic for 'white'. Heaney wonders if the name could be 'white moss' and has commented, 'In the syllables of my home, I see a metaphor of the split culture of Ulster.'
Dedication: The poem is dedicated to the poet's aunt, Mary Heaney, who lived with the family throughout Heaney's childhood. He shared a special relationship with her, 'a woman with a huge well of affection and a very experienced, dry-eyed sense of the world'.

7 *griddle*: circular iron plate used for cooking food.
10 *scuffled*: moving quickly, making a scraping noise.
13 *plaque*: area of intense heat, originally a hot plate.
21 *measling*: red spots on legs made by standing close to heat.
24 *the tick of two clocks*: the two time sequences in the poem, past and present.
26 *tinsmith*: person who made pots and pans from tin.
28 *meal-bin*: a container used to hold flour, etc.

EXPLORATIONS

1 Describe the atmosphere in the poem 'Mossbawn', with particular reference to Heaney's treatment of time.
2 What image of Mary Heaney, the aunt, is drawn? Do you find the picture appealing or unappealing? Quote from the poem in support of your views.
3 Choose one image or phrase from the poem that you found particularly effective, and say why you found it so.

STUDY NOTES

'Sunlight' appeared in the collection *North* (1975) and was the first of two poems under the title 'Mossbawn', the name of Heaney's family home. To the poet, this farm was 'the first place', an idyllic Garden of Eden, full of sunlight and feminine grace, a contrast to the brute reality of the outside world. At this time, terrible atrocities were being committed by both Catholics and Protestants in the sectarian struggle which was taking place in the North of Ireland.

This poem opens with a **vivid, atmospheric portrayal of the silent sunlit yard**, a beautiful, tranquil scene from Heaney's boyhood in the 1940s. The pump marked the centre of this private world, which was untroubled by the activities outside. American soldiers had bases in Northern Ireland during the Second World War. For the impressionable Heaney growing up, the water pump was a symbol of purity and life. This guardian of domestic life is described as 'helmeted', a sentry soldier on duty, ready to protect. The phrase 'water honeyed' (line 4) emphasises this slender iron idol as an image of deep and hidden goodness, the centre of another world. The poet creates a nostalgic picture of a timeless zone of slow, deep, domestic ritual and human warmth. Here are childhood days of golden innocence and security. The repetition of 'h' (in 'helmeted', 'heated' and 'honeyed') portrays the heating process as the reader exhales breath. The sun is described in the striking simile 'like a griddle cooling/against the wall'. This homely image of the iron dish of the home-baked flat cake evokes a view of a serene place.

Line 10 moves readers from the place to the person. 'So' introduces us to a **warm, tender portrait of Heaney's beloved Aunt Mary at work**. She is a symbol of the old secure way of life, when a sense of community was firm and traditional rural values were held in high esteem. We are shown the unspectacular routine of work; she 'dusts the board' for baking. We see her domestic skill, her hands 'scuffled' as she kneads the dough. Visual detail paints this picture as if it were a Dutch still life from the artist Vermeer: 'floury apron', 'whitened nails'. There is an almost religious simplicity on the essentials of life: bread, water, love (water 'honeyed', 'scone rising', 'here is love'). The people in this scene are not glamorous. Realistic details remind us of their ordinariness: 'broad-lapped', 'measling shins'.

The **closing simile** in lines 26–8, 'like a tinsmith's scoop/sunk past its gleam/in the meal-bin', **shows how the ordinary is transformed into the extraordinary** by the power of love. The hidden shine of love is present in the ordinary ritual of baking. Remembering the past, the poet makes it present, 'here is love'. The two time zones of passing time and a timeless moment are held in the alliterative phrase 'to the tick of two clocks'. We are invited to listen to the steady rhythm of the repetitive 't'. As the life-giving water lies unseen beneath the cold earth, the aunt's love is hidden, but constant, ready to be drawn on, like the water in the pump. The radiant glow of love is hidden like a buried light. The change of tenses at the word 'Now' brings the moment closer as the abstract becomes concrete, and the outside becomes inside. The short four-line stanzas run on, achieving their own momentum of contained energy in this still scene, which reaches its climax in the elevating last stanza.

ANALYSIS

Heaney explores local history, communicating the experience of his own place with customs, rituals, atmosphere and characters. Discuss this view of Heaney's poetry, with particular reference to the poem 'Mossbawn: Sunlight'.

SAMPLE PARAGRAPH

In Heaney's poem 'Sunlight', the pump stands squarely at the centre of this tranquil, magical place. Although American troops were on manoeuvres in the nearby fields, this place is untouched by outside forces. The pump seems to stand guard, 'helmeted', on this oasis of feminine grace. The custom of baking bread is referred to in the simile 'the sun stood/like a griddle cooling', and in the visual and aural details of the aunt, Mary Heaney, 'her hands scuffled/over the bakeboard'. I can almost hear the rasping of her nails as they hit the surface as she kneads the baking mixture. Even the last simile, 'like a tinsmith's scoop/sunk past its gleam/in the meal-bin', is a further reference to this custom of home baking, as it tells of the wonderful source of hidden love which exists between the aunt and the young boy. These rural references, 'the reddening stove', 'a goose's wing', reach back to a time which is pre-modern. It shows us a picture of an ideal way of living. The silence and peace of Mossbawn are portrayed in the phrases 'each long afternoon' and 'the tick of two clocks'. Time stands still in this idyllic place. Heaney makes the reader feel as if they have visited Mossbawn, seen the pump, tasted the 'honeyed water', saw and heard the aunt baking and savoured the peace and tranquillity of this traditional way of life.

EXAMINER'S COMMENT

A well-developed, focused answer displaying a clear appreciation of Heaney's poem. Quotations range widely over the entire text. Expression is varied and well controlled throughout. Grade A.

CLASS/HOMEWORK EXERCISES

1. The Royal Swedish Academy announced that Seamus Heaney's Nobel Prize for Literature was for 'lyrical beauty ... which brings out the miracles of the ordinary day and the living past'. Discuss this statement, referring closely to the text.
2. Copy the table below into your own notes and fill in critical comments about the last two quotations.

Key Quotes

There was a sunlit absence	This short line creates the still atmosphere of Heaney's home place. It also intrigues us – what exactly is absent?
her hands scuffled	Onomatopoeia suggests the repeated movement of his aunt's hands and lets the reader become part of the loving domestic scene.
and measling shins	The poet uses graphic, realistic details to show the ordinariness of this extraordinary person.
the scone rising/to the tick of two clocks	
like a tinsmith's scoop/sunk past its gleam/in the meal-bin	

A Constable Calls

His bicycle stood at the window-sill,
The rubber cowl of a mud-splasher
Skirting the front mudguard,
Its fat black handlegrips

Heating in sunlight, the 'spud'　　　　　　　　　　　5
Of the dynamo gleaming and cocked back,
The pedal treads hanging relieved
Of the boot of the law.

His cap was upside down
On the floor, next his chair.　　　　　　　　　　　　10
The line of its pressure ran like a bevel
In his slightly sweating hair.

He had unstrapped
The heavy ledger, and my father
Was making tillage returns　　　　　　　　　　　　15
In acres, roods, and perches.

Arithmetic and fear.
I sat staring at the polished holster
With its buttoned flap, the braid cord
Looped into the revolver butt.　　　　　　　　　　　20

'Any other root crops?
Mangolds? Marrowstems? Anything like that?'
'No.' But was there not a line
 Of turnips where the seed ran out

In the potato field? I assumed　　　　　　　　　　　25
Small guilts and sat
Imagining the black hole in the barracks.
He stood up, shifted the baton-case

Further round on his belt,
Closed the domesday book,　　　　　　　　　　　　30
Fitted his cap back with two hands,
And looked at me as he said goodbye.

A shadow bobbed in the window.
He was snapping the carrier spring
Over the ledger. His boot pushed off   35
And the bicycle ticked, ticked, ticked.

*'The pedal treads hanging relieved/
Of the boot of the law'*

GLOSSARY

2 *cowl*: covering shaped like a hood.
5 *'spud'*: potato-like shape.
8 *the boot of the law*: heavy footwear of policeman; power and control of the law.
11 *bevel*: marked line on policeman's forehead made by his cap.
14 *ledger*: book containing records of farm accounts.
15 *tillage returns*: amount harvested from cultivated land.
19 *braid*: threads woven into a decorative band.
22 *Mangolds*: beets grown for animal feed.
22 *Marrowstems*: long green vegetables.
30 *domesday book*: William the Conqueror, the English king, had ordered a survey to be carried out of all the land and its value in England; also refers to Judgement Day, when all will be brought to account.
33 *bobbed*: moved up and down.
34 *carrier spring*: spiral metal coil on the back of a bike used to secure a bag, etc.

EXPLORATIONS

1 How does the poet create an atmosphere of tension in this poem? Support your response with reference to the text.
2 What type of relationship do you think the young boy has with his father? Refer closely to the text in your response.
3 Critics disagree about the ending of the poem. Some find it 'false', others 'stunning'. How would you describe the ending? Give reasons for your conclusions.

• Poetry Focus •

STUDY NOTES

> 'A Constable Calls' was written in 1975 and forms the second part of the poem sequence 'Singing School'. The Heaneys were a Catholic family. The constable would have been a member of the Royal Ulster Constabulary and probably a Protestant. This poem was written when the tensions between the two communities in Northern Ireland were at their height. Heaney's 'country of community … was a place of division'.

'A Constable Calls' is written from the **viewpoint of a young boy** caught in the epicentre of the Troubles, a time of recent sectarian violence in Northern Ireland. The poem explores fear and power from the perspective of the Nationalist community. The Catholics did not trust or like the RUC (Royal Ulster Constabulary). In the opening stanzas, crude strength, power and violence are all inherent in the cold, precise language used to describe the constable's bicycle. The 'handlegrips' suggest handcuffs, while the 'cocked back' dynamo hints at a gun ready to explode, its trigger ready for action. It also signifies confidence and cockiness. The oppression of the local authorities is contained in the phrase 'the boot of the law'. Heaney personifies the bicycle, which he describes as being 'relieved' of the pressure of the weight of the constable. This poem was written during the civil rights protest marches, when Nationalists were sometimes treated very severely by the RUC. This is evoked in the ugly sound of 'ow' in the word 'cowl', the assonance of the broad vowels in 'fat black' and the harsh-sounding repetition of 'ck' in the phrase 'cocked back'. Here are the observations of the child of a divided community. The character (and symbolic significance) of the constable is implicit in the description of his bicycle.

In stanzas three to five, Heaney gives us an explicit **description of the constable**. His uniform and equipment are all symbols of power, which the young boy notes in detail: 'the polished holster/With its buttoned flap, the braid cord/Looped into the revolver butt'. Here is no friendly community police officer. The repetition of 'his' tells us that the possession of power belongs to him and what he represents. He is not a welcome visitor. His hat lies on the ground. He is not offered refreshment, although he is presumably thirsty from his work. Even the one human detail ('slightly sweating hair') revolts us. Is he as tense as the Catholic family in this time of sectarian conflict? The print of his great authority is stamped on him like a 'bevel', but does his power weigh heavily on him?

The policeman's function was to oblige the boy's father to give an account of his farm crop returns. Their terse exchange underlines the **tension in this troubled community**. The interrogation by the constable consists of four questions: 'Any other root crops?/Mangolds? Marrowstems? Anything like that?' This is met by the father's short, clipped, monosyllabic reply: 'No'. The encounter is summed up succinctly in the line 'Arithmetic and fear'. In the seventh stanza, the young boy becomes alarmed as he realises that his father has omitted to account for 'a line/Of turnips'. He 'assumed/Small guilts'. His Catholic inferiority is graphically shown in the reference to the 'domesday book', or 'ledger', belonging to the constable. The child imagines a day of reckoning, almost like Judgement Day, when God calls every individual to account for past sins. He imagines the immediate punishment of 'the black hole in the barracks', the notorious police cell where offenders were held. This terror of being incarcerated by the law ran deep in the Catholic psyche throughout the Troubles.

In the end, the constable takes his leave (stanzas seven and eight), formally fitting 'his cap back with two hands'. We can empathise with the young boy as he 'looked at me'. In the final stanza, the oppressive presence of the visitor ('A shadow') is wryly described as 'bobbed', an ironic reference to the friendly English bobby – which this particular constable was not. The verbs in this stanza continue the underlying ominous mood: 'snapping', 'pushed off'. The **poem concludes** with an intimidating reference to the sound of the departing bicycle as a slowly ticking time bomb: 'And the bicycle ticked, ticked, ticked'. Does this suggest that the tension in this divided community was always on the verge of exploding? Do you consider this an effective image or do you think the symbolism is too obvious?

ANALYSIS

'Heaney has written a poem of childhood unease and fear.' Do you agree or disagree with this statement? Support your opinion with references from the poem.

SAMPLE PARAGRAPH

Seamus Heaney was born in Derry and won a Nobel Prize for Literature in 1995. I think Heaney has written a good poem about a young childs unease and fear. I especially liked the last line with the ticking bomb. It was really good. I really think Heaneys poems are especially good. I think I will read lots of Heaneys poems in my lifetime. I could see the sweaty cap of the constable. I thought it was gross enough to scare any child. I thought the father stood up to the police man well, and in a convincing way. 'No' he said. I thought well done, the child must have been proud of him. I also thought the discription of the holster was good. 'Polished' means shining. The 'rubber cowl' of the 'mud-slasher' on the front mud-guard is fairly sinister, rather like hoodies on teenagers. The identity of the person cannot be seen. This threatens. This is a very good poem that really sums up childhood unease and fear.

SPELLCHECKER
child's
Heaney's
description

EXAMINER'S COMMENT

An under-developed response, repetitive and lacking in depth of knowledge of the poem. Punctuation errors and repetition also mar the answer. The autobiographical detail is extraneous to the task required. Limited vocabulary. A basic grade D.

CLASS/HOMEWORK EXERCISES

1. Heaney has written a memory poem filled with lyrical beauty which brings out the miracles of the ordinary day. Having read 'A Constable Calls', would you agree or disagree with this view? Support your answer with reference to the text.
2. Copy the table below into your own notes and fill in critical comments about the last two quotations.

Key Qoutes

Its fat black handlegrips/Heating in sunlight	The run-on line and assonance in this phrase suggest the oppressive atmosphere experienced by the Nationalist minority in Northern Ireland at this time.
Arithmetic and fear	This succinct phrase sums up the tension. Many Catholics were being held to account and feared they would be subject to punishment if found guilty.
Closed the domesday book	In the young boy's imagination, the account book of tillage returns is associated with the Book of Accounts of the King of England, or the Book of Judgement used by God on the Last Day.
A shadow bobbed in the window	
And the bicycle ticked, ticked, ticked	

Seamus Heaney

• Poetry Focus •

The Skunk

Seamus Heaney

Up, black, striped and damasked like the chasuble
At a funeral Mass, the skunk's tail
Paraded the skunk. Night after night
I expected her like a visitor.

The refrigerator whinnied into silence. 5
My desk light softened beyond the verandah.
Small oranges loomed in the orange tree.
I began to be tense as a voyeur.

After eleven years I was composing
Love-letters again, broaching the word 'wife' 10
Like a stored cask, as if its slender vowel
Had mutated into the night earth and air

Of California. The beautiful, useless
Tang of eucalyptus spelt your absence.
The aftermath of a mouthful of wine 15
Was like inhaling you off a cold pillow.

And there she was, the intent and glamorous,
Ordinary, mysterious skunk,
Mythologized, demythologized,
Snuffing the boards five feet beyond me. 20

It all came back to me last night, stirred
By the sootfall of your things at bedtime,
Your head-down, tail-up hunt in a bottom drawer
For the black plunge-line nightdress.

'the skunk's tail/Paraded the skunk'

GLOSSARY

Skunks are small black and white striped American mammals, capable of spraying foul-smelling liquid on attackers.
1 *damasked*: patterned; rich, heavy damask fabric.
1 *chasuble*: garment worn by a priest saying Mass.
5 *whinnied*: sound a horse makes.
6 *verandah*: roofed platform along the outside of a house.
8 *voyeur*: a person who watches others when they are being intimate.
10 *broaching*: raising a subject for discussion.
12 *mutated*: changed shape or form.
14 *eucalyptus*: common tree with scented leaves found in California.
15 *aftermath*: consequences of an unpleasant event.
19 *Mythologized*: related to or found in myth.
22 *sootfall*: soft sound (like soot falling from a chimney).
24 *plunge-line*: low-cut.

EXPLORATIONS

1. In your opinion, how effective is Heaney in creating the particular sense of place in this poem? Refer closely to the text in your answer.
2. The poet compares his wife to a skunk. Does this image work, in your view? Quote from the poem in support of your response.
3. Comment on the poem's dramatic qualities. Refer to setting, characters, action and sense of tension/climax, particularly in the first and last stanzas.

STUDY NOTES

'The Skunk' comes from Heaney's 1979 collection, **Field Work**. The poet called it a 'marriage poem'. While spending an academic year (1971–2) teaching in America, he had been reading the work of Robert Lowell, an American poet. Lowell's poem, 'Skunk Hour', describes how isolation drives a man to become a voyeur of lovers in cars. Heaney's reaction to his own loneliness is very different; he rediscovers the art of writing love letters to his wife, who is living 6,000 miles away in Ireland. This separation culminated in an intimate, humorous, erotic love poem which speaks volumes for the deep love and trust between husband and wife.

In the **opening stanza**, the reader is presented with four words describing the skunk's tail, 'Up, black, striped and damasked'. The punctuation separates the different aspects of the animal's tail for the reader's observation. An unusual simile occurs in **line 1**. In a **playfully irreverent tone**, Heaney likens the skunk's tail to the black and white vestments worn by a priest at a funeral. He then gives us an almost cartoon-like visual image of the animal's tail leading the skunk. The self-importance of the little animal is effectively captured in the verb 'Paraded'. All the ceremony of marching is evoked. The poet eagerly awaits his nightly visitor: 'Night after night/I expected her like a visitor'.

Seamus Heaney

In **stanza two**, the poet's senses are heightened. The verbs 'whinnied', 'softened' and 'loomed' vividly capture **the atmosphere of the soft, exotic California night**. The bright colours of orange and green are synonymous with the Sunshine State. The anticipation of stanza one now sharpens: 'I began to be tense'. He regards himself as a 'voyeur', but here there is no violation. He is staring into darkness, getting ready to communicate with his wife. In **stanza three**, the poet, after a break of 11 years, is penning love letters to his wife again. In this separation period, he realises how much he misses her. His wife's presence, although she is absent, fills his consciousness. He is totally preoccupied with her. He uses the simile 'Like a stored cask' to show how he values her as something precious. The word 'wife' is savoured like fine wine and his affection is shown in his appreciation of 'its slender vowel', which reminds him of her feminine grace. She is present to him in the air he breathes, 'mutated into the night earth and air/Of California'.

Heaney's depth of longing is captured in the **sensuous language** of **stanza four**. The smell of the eucalyptus 'spelt your absence'. The word 'Tang' precisely notes the penetrating sensation of loneliness. Even a drink of wine, 'a mouthful of wine', does not dull this ache. Instead it intensifies his longing, 'like inhaling you off a cold pillow'. Now, the skunk, long awaited, appears. It is full of contradictions: 'glamorous', 'Ordinary'. We hear in **stanza five** the sound the little animal makes in the onomatopoeic phrase 'Snuffing the boards'.

Only in **stanza six** is the comparison between the wife and the skunk finally drawn: 'It all came back to me last night'. Heaney is now back home. His wife is rummaging in the bottom drawer for a nightdress. She adopts a slightly comic pose, 'head-down, tail-up', reminding him of the skunk as she 'hunt[s]'. The sibilance of the line 'stirred/By the sootfall of your things' suggests the tender intimacy between the married couple. The word 'sootfall' conveys the gentle rustle of clothes falling. The reader's reaction is also 'stirred' to amused surprise as the realisation dawns that the adjectives 'intent and glamorous,/Ordinary, mysterious ... Mythologized, demythologized' also apply to his wife. A **mature, trusting relationship** exists between the couple.

Longer lines suggest ease. The poet is relaxed and playful, his language conversational and sensuous. All our senses are 'stirred'. The light is romantic ('softened') and the colour black is alluring. The touch of the 'cold pillow' will now be replaced by the warm, shared bed. The sounds of California and the couple's bedroom echo: 'Snuffing', 'sootfall'. The smell of the eucalyptus's

'Tang' hangs in the air. The 'aftermath of a mouthful of wine' lingers on the tongue. Here is a rarity, **a successful love poem about marriage**, tender but not cosy, personal but not embarrassingly self-revealing.

ANALYSIS

Heaney stated that 'poetry verifies our singularity'. How does this poem establish the unique relationship between husband and wife? Refer closely to the text in your answer.

SAMPLE PARAGRAPH

In the poem 'The Skunk', Seamus Heaney dares to compare his wife to a skunk. He must have known and trusted his wife's sense of humour and generosity of spirit to a great degree to chance such a risky comparison. But Heaney is writing about a long-established mature relationship which, unusually, recognises the 'Ordinary' qualities of his wife, 'head-down, tail-up' and also her mysterious qualities, 'spelt your absence', 'glamorous', 'black plunge-line nightdress'. His year spent teaching in California sharpened his appreciation of his wife. He realised how valuable she was, 'Like a stored cask'. The phrase 'cold pillow' really made me realise how much Heaney wanted the shared intimacy of their relationship. I thought his wife must indeed be singular to inspire such feeling. In the last stanza, the onomatopoeia of 'the sootfall of your things', the soft whisper of silky garments slipping to the floor, showed me how the poet was still fascinated by this woman. The unique relationship between these two individuals is both ordinary and routine, 'demythologized', and also extraordinary and tender, 'Mythologized'. This poem's exploration of the relationship between the poet and his wife does indeed show the truth of human uniqueness.

EXAMINER'S COMMENT

A confident and focused treatment of the poem in relation to the task of this challenging question. A well-structured personal response and judicious use of quotation merits a grade A.

• Poetry Focus •

Seamus Heaney

CLASS/HOMEWORK EXERCISE

1. 'Relationships, personal or otherwise, lie at the heart of Seamus Heaney's poetry.' Discuss this statement and support your answer with reference to the text.
2. Copy the table below into your own notes and fill in critical comments about the last two quotations.

Key Quotes

damasked like the chasuble/ At a funeral Mass	In this cheeky simile, the skunk's appearance is compared to the rich patterned clothes worn by a priest officiating at a solemn occasion, a funeral.
The refrigerator whinnied into silence	The noise of the fridge is captured in the onomatopoeic verb 'whinnied' as Heaney personifies this object.
Mythologized, demythologized	As wonderful as an exotic myth or legend, as ordinary and familiar as everyday routine.
broaching the word 'wife'/Like a stored cask	
Your head-down, tail-up hunt in a bottom drawer	

The Harvest Bow

As you plaited the harvest bow
You implicated the mellowed silence in you
In wheat that does not rust
But brightens as it tightens twist by twist
Into a knowable corona,   5
A throwaway love-knot of straw.

Hands that aged round ashplants and cane sticks
And lapped the spurs on a lifetime of gamecocks
Harked to their gift and worked with fine intent
Until your fingers moved somnambulant: 10
I tell and finger it like braille,
Gleaning the unsaid off the palpable,

And if I spy into its golden loops
I see us walk between the railway slopes
Into an evening of long grass and midges,   15
Blue smoke straight up, old beds and ploughs in hedges,
An auction notice on an outhouse wall –
You with a harvest bow in your lapel,

Me with the fishing rod, already homesick
For the big lift of these evenings, as your stick   20
Whacking the tips off weeds and bushes
Beats out of time, and beats, but flushes
Nothing: that original townland
Still tongue-tied in the straw tied by your hand.

The end of art is peace   25
Could be the motto of this frail device
That I have pinned up on our deal dresser –
Like a drawn snare
Slipped lately by the spirit of the corn
Yet burnished by its passage, and still warm.   30

Seamus Heaney

• Poetry Focus •

Seamus Heaney

'A throwaway love-knot of straw'

GLOSSARY

The harvest bow, an emblem of traditional rural crafts, was made from straw and often worn in the lapel to celebrate the end of harvesting. Sometimes it was given as a love-token or kept in the farmhouse until the next year's harvest.

2 *implicated*: intertwined; revealed indirectly.
2 *mellowed*: matured, placid.
5 *corona*: circle of light, halo.
8 *lapped the spurs*: tied the back claws of fighting birds.
8 *gamecocks*: male fowl reared to take part in cock-fighting.
9 *Harked*: listened, attuned.
10 *somnambulant*: automatically, as if sleepwalking.
11 *braille*: system of reading and writing by touching raised dots.
12 *Gleaning*: gathering, grasping; understanding.
12 *palpable*: what can be handled or understood.
15 *midges*: small biting insects that usually swarm near water.
22 *flushes*: rouses, reveals.
25 *The end of art is peace*: art brings contentment (a quotation from the English poet Coventry Patmore, 1823–96). It was also used by W.B. Yeats.
26 *device*: object, artefact.
27 *deal*: pine wood.
28 *snare*: trap.
30 *burnished*: shining.

EXPLPORATIONS

1 Based on your reading of the poem, what impression do you get of Heaney's father? Refer to the text in your answer.
2 In your view, is the harvest bow a symbol of love? Give reasons for your answer, using reference to the poem.
3 What do you understand by the line *'The end of art is peace'*? Briefly explain your answer.

STUDY NOTES

'The Harvest Bow' (from the 1972 collection **Field Work**) is an elegiac poem in which Heaney pays tribute to his father and the work he did with his hands, weaving a traditional harvest emblem out of stalks of wheat. Remembering his boyhood, watching his father create the corn-dolly, he already knew that the moment could not last. The recognition of his father's artistic talents leads the poet to a consideration of his own creative work.

The poem begins with a measured description of Heaney's reticent father as he twists stalks of wheat into decorative love-knots. The delicate phrasing in **stanza one** ('You implicated the mellowed silence in you') reflects the poet's awareness of how **the harvest bow symbolised the intricate bond between father and son**. The poet conveys a subdued but satisfied mood as another farm year draws to a close. Autumnal images ('wheat that does not rust') add to the sense of accomplishment. Heaney highlights the practised techniques involved in creating this 'throwaway love-knot of straw'. The harvest bow 'brightens as it tightens twist by twist'. Emphatic alliteration and internal rhyme enliven the image, almost becoming a metaphor for the father's expertise. The bow is likened to 'a knowable corona', a reassuring light circle representing the year's natural cycle.

In **stanza two**, the intricate beauty of the straw knot prompts Heaney to recall some of the other manual skills his father once demonstrated 'round ashplants and cane sticks'. He acknowledges the older man's 'gift' of concentration and 'fine intent' as he fashioned the harvest bow ('your fingers moved somnambulant') **without conscious effort towards artistic achievement**. Is Heaney also suggesting that poets should work that way? Carefully handling the bow 'like braille', the poet clearly values it as an expression of undeclared love: 'Gleaning the unsaid off the palpable'.

The pleasurable sentiments of Heaney's childhood memories are realised by the strength of detailed imagery in **stanza three**: 'I see us walk between the railway slopes'. Such **ordinary scenes are enhanced by sensuous details** of 1940s rural life: 'Blue smoke straight up, old beds and ploughs in hedges'. Many of the sounds have a plaintive, musical quality ('loops', 'slopes', 'midges', 'hedges'). The poet seems haunted by his father's ghost, and the silence that once seemed to define their relationship is now recognised as a secret code of mutual understanding.

Stanza four focuses on the relentless passing of time. The **tone is particularly elegiac** as Heaney recalls his father 'Whacking the tips off weeds' with his stick.

In retrospect, he seems to interpret such pointless actions as evidence of how every individual 'Beats out of time' – but to no avail. The poet extends this notion of time's mystery by suggesting that it is through art alone ('the straw tied by your hand') that 'tongue-tied' communities can explore life's wonder.

At the start of stanza five, Heaney tries to make sense of the corn-dolly, now a treasured part of his own household 'on our deal dresser'. It mellows in its new setting and gives out heat. While 'the spirit of the corn' may have disappeared from the knot, the power of the poet's imagination can still recreate it there. So rather than being merely a nostalgic recollection of childhood, the poem takes on universal meaning in the intertwining of artistic forces. We are left with a deep sense of lost rural heritage, the unspoken joy of a shared relationship and the rich potential of the poet's art. For Heaney, **artistic achievements produce warm feelings of lasting contentment**. Whatever 'frail device' is created, be it a harvest bow or a formal elegy, *'The end of art is peace'*.

ANALYSIS

What is your personal response to Heaney's treatment of the relationship between himself and his father in 'The Harvest Bow'? Support the points you make with reference to the poem.

SAMPLE PARAGRAPH

'The Harvest Bow' is a good example of where Seamus Heaney shows his emotional side. He begins by describing his aged father at work. It is clear that he admires him very much even though the old man is totally immersed in weaving the stalks of wheat into a bow. There is a very moving 'mellow silence' between them, but the bow or 'love-knot' symbolises their feelings. For most of the poem Heaney treats his father with deep respect, admiring his artistic fingers which 'moved somnambulant' without effort. He even imitates his father as he fingers the love-knot – or 'frail device' – which he displays on his kitchen dresser. I liked the way Heaney was prepared to express his emotions for his father by including memories of times they shared together – 'I see us walking along the railway lines'. What was also interesting was the fact that Heaney did not glorify his father in a sentimental or false way. In some ways, the older man seems morose 'whacking the weeds', but this would be typical of Irish farmers. The relationship is presented in a realistic way, but I still get the feeling that Heaney really loved his father and models his own work as a poet – to 'work with fine intent' – on his mentor.

EXAMINER'S COMMENT

This is a reasonably well-focused response that addresses the given question in a sustained way. There is genuine personal engagement with the poem and the answer includes several interesting points. However, some of the quotations are imprecise. A basic B grade.

CLASS/HOMEWORK EXERCISES

1. 'The Harvest Bow' is essentially a poem of celebration. To what extent do you agree? Give reasons for your response, using close reference to the text.
2. Copy the table below into your own notes and fill in critical comments about the last two quotations.

Key Quotes

A throwaway love-knot of straw	The colloquial description of the harvest bow is highly ironic, since Heaney greatly values the corn-dolly.
worked with fine intent	Just as his father used dedicated artistry to fashion the bow, the poet's self-acknowledged task is to knot his visions into language.
if I spy into its golden loops	The verb 'spy' has undertones of a secretive childhood game. The loops of the harvest bow open out into visions.
Gleaning the unsaid off the palpable	
The end of art is peace	

• Poetry Focus •

The Underground

Seamus Heaney

There we were in the vaulted tunnel running,
You in your going-away coat speeding ahead
And me, me then like a fleet god gaining
Upon you before you turned to a reed

Or some new white flower japped with crimson   5
As the coat flapped wild and button after button
Sprang off and fell in a trail
Between the Underground and the Albert Hall.

Honeymooning, mooning around, late for the Proms,
Our echoes die in that corridor and now   10
I come as Hansel came on the moonlit stones
Retracing the path back, lifting the buttons

To end up in a draughty lamplit station
After the trains have gone, the wet track
Bared and tensed as I am, all attention   15
For your step following and damned if I look back.

'Our echoes die in that corridor'

• Leaving Certificate English •

GLOSSARY

In Greek mythology, Eurydice, the beloved wife of Orpheus, was killed by a venomous snake. Orpheus travelled to the Underworld (Hades) to retrieve her. It was granted that Eurydice could return to the world of the living, but on condition that Orpheus should walk in front of her and not look back until he had reached the upper world. In his anxiety, he broke his promise, and Eurydice vanished again – but this time forever.

1 *vaulted*: domed, arched.
2 *going-away coat*: new coat worn by the bride leaving on honeymoon.
3 *fleet*: fast; momentary.
4 *reed*: slender plant; part of a musical instrument.
5 *japped*: tinged, layered.
8 *the Albert Hall*: famous London landmark and concert venue.
9 *the Proms*: short for promenade concerts, a summer season of classical music.
11 *Hansel*: fairytale character who, along with his sister Gretel, retraced his way home using a trail of white pebbles.

Seamus Heaney

EXPLORATIONS

1 Comment on the atmosphere created in the first two stanzas. Refer to the text in your answer.
2 From your reading of this poem, what do you learn about the relationship between the poet and his wife? Refer to the text in your answer.
3 Write a short personal response to 'The Underground', highlighting the impact it made on you.

STUDY NOTES

'The Underground' is the first poem in *Station Island* (1984). It recounts a memory from Heaney's honeymoon when he and his wife (like a modern Orpheus and Eurydice) were rushing through a London Underground Tube station on their way to a BBC Promenade Concert in the Albert Hall. In Dennis O'Driscoll's book, *Stepping Stones*, Heaney has said, 'In this version of the story, Eurydice and much else gets saved by the sheer cussedness of the poet up ahead just keeping going.'

The poem's title is infused with a piercing sense of threat. Underground journeys are shadowed with a certain menace. Not only is there a mythical association with crossing into the land of the dead, but there is also the actuality of accidents and terrorist outrages. The **first stanza** of Heaney's personal narrative uses everyday colloquial speech ('There we were in the vaulted tunnel running') to introduce his **dramatic account**. Broad vowel sounds ('vau', 'tun' and 'run') dominate the opening line with a guttural quality. The oppressively

• 165 •

'vaulted' setting and urgent verbs ('speeding', 'gaining') increase this sense of subterranean disquiet. For the poet, it is a psychic and mythic underground where he imagines his own heroic quest ('like a fleet god'). What he seems to dread most is the possibility of change and that, like a latter-day Orpheus, he might somehow lose his soulmate.

Cinematic images and run-on lines propel the second stanza forward. This **fast-paced rhythm is in keeping with the restless diction** – 'the coat flapped wild'. The poet's wife is wearing her going-away wedding outfit and in the course of her sprint, the buttons start popping off. Internal rhyme adds to the tension; 'japped' and 'flapped' play into each other, giving the impression that whatever is occurring is happening with great intensity.

The poem changes at the beginning of the third stanza and this is evident in the language, which is much more playful, reflecting Heaney's assessment of the occasion in hindsight. He now recognises the youthful insecurity of the time: 'Honeymooning, mooning around'. The wry reference to the fictional Hansel and Gretel hints at the immaturity of their relationship as newlyweds and emphasises the couple's initial fretfulness. But recalling how he carefully gathered up the buttons, like Hansel returning from the wilderness, **Heaney appears to have now come to terms with his uneasy past**: 'Our echoes die in that corridor'.

This latent confidence underscores the poet's recollections in the fourth stanza. The action and speed have now ceased. After the uncertainty of the 'draughty lamplit station', he has learned to trust his wife and his own destiny. Unlike Orpheus, the tragic Greek hero, Heaney has emerged from his personal descent into Hades, 'Bared and tense'. Although **he can never forget the desolation of being threatened with loss**, the poet has been well served by the experience, having realised that it will always be him – and not his wife – who will be damned if he dares to look back.

The ending of the poem is characteristically compelling. Commenting on it in *Stepping Stones*, Heaney has said, 'But in the end, the "damned if I look back" line takes us well beyond the honeymoon.' Although some critics feel that the final outlook is more regretful, it is difficult to miss the sheer determination that is present in the poem's last line. **The poet's stubborn tone leaves us with overwhelming evidence of his enduring devotion to love**, an emotional commitment which seems to be even more precious with the passing of time.

ANALYSIS

'Heaney's poems are capable of capturing moments of insight in a strikingly memorable fashion.' Discuss this view, with particular reference to 'The Underground'.

SAMPLE PARAGRAPH

'The Underground' is really a love poem, written about the time Seamus Heaney and his wife were in London on honeymoon. They got delayed at a Tube station and Heaney had a panic attack. He imagined the legend of Orpheus rescuing Eurydice from the underworld, the next world. The comparison gave him a deeper insight into the love he felt for his new wife. Firstly, he was frightened that she would disappear among the crowd, but he eventually had faith in her (and himself) and refused to look back to find her in case he suffered the same bad luck as Orpheus. What I found of interest was the way Heaney suggested the nervousness he felt 'running' in the 'vaulted tunnel'. The uninterrupted rhythm of the young couple rushing through the station vividly captures their anxiety. His vivid imagery of the 'draughty lamplit station' brought home to me the loneliness he experienced. In the end, he learned from what happened to believe in the power of love and his final words reflect his strength of love – 'damned if I look back'. For me, Heaney really communicates the way true love grows stronger in this short dramatic poem. The insight came from his belief in the relationship with his wife. They made a promise to each other and had the courage to keep it.

EXAMINER'S COMMENT

This is a focused and sustained approach that addresses both aspects of the question. There is good personal interaction and evidence of close reading of the poem. Quotations are integrated effectively. Grade-A standard.

CLASS/HOMEWORK EXERCISES

1. In Heaney's poem 'The Underground', the poet compares his wife and himself to the legend of Eurydice and Orpheus. In your opinion, how effective is this comparison? Refer to the text in your answer.
2. Copy the table below into your own notes and fill in critical comments about the last two quotations.

• Poetry Focus •

Seamus Heaney

Key Quotes

There we were in the vaulted tunnel running	This strong, visual image invites the reader into a fast-moving drama. The underground setting increases the uneasy atmosphere.
before you turned to a reed/Or some new white flower	An underlying fear of change and loss of love is central to the early part of the poem.
Honeymooning, mooning around	Recalling the experience in the Underground station, Heaney's mood is more reflective and he acknowledges his earlier immaturity.
Our echoes die in that corridor	
and damned if I look back	

Postscript

Seamus Heaney

And some time make the time to drive out west
Into County Clare, along the Flaggy Shore,
In September or October, when the wind
And the light are working off each other
So that the ocean on one side is wild   5
With foam and glitter, and inland among stones
The surface of a slate-grey lake is lit
By the earthed lightning of a flock of swans,
Their feathers roughed and ruffling, white on white,
Their fully grown headstrong-looking heads   10
Tucked or cresting or busy underwater.
Useless to think you'll park and capture it
More thoroughly. You are neither here nor there,
A hurry through which known and strange things pass
As big soft buffetings come at the car sideways   15
And catch the heart off guard and blow it open.

'along the Flaggy Shore'

GLOSSARY

2 *the Flaggy Shore*: stretch of coastal limestone slabs in the Burren, Co. Clare.
4 *working off*: playing against.
11 *cresting*: stretching, posing.
15 *buffetings*: vibrations, shudderings.

EXPLORATIONS

1. Choose one image from the poem that you find particularly effective. Briefly explain your choice.
2. What is your understanding of the poem's final line?
3. In your opinion, is the advice given by Heaney in 'Postscript' relevant to our modern world? Give reasons to support your response.

• Poetry Focus •

STUDY NOTES

This beautiful pastoral lyric comes at the end of Seamus Heaney's 1996 collection, *The Spirit Level*. The title suggests an afterthought, something that was missed out earlier. As so often in his poetry, Heaney succeeds in conveying the extraordinary by way of an everyday experience – in this case, the vivid memory of a journey westwards. The poem resonates with readers, particularly those who have also shared moments when life caught them by surprise.

Line 1 is relaxed and conversational. The poet invites others (or promises himself, perhaps) to 'make the time to drive out west'. The phrase 'out west' has connotations both of adventurous opportunity and dismal failure. By placing 'And' at the start of the poem, Heaney indicates a link with something earlier, some unfinished business. **Keen to ensure that the journey will be worthwhile**, he recommends a definite destination ('the Flaggy Shore') and time ('September or October').

The untamed beauty of the Co. Clare coastline is described in some detail: 'when the wind/And the light are working off each other' (lines 3–4). The phrase 'working off' is especially striking in conveying the **tension and balance between two of nature's greatest complementary forces: wind and light**. Together, they create an effect that neither could produce singly.

Close awareness of place is a familiar feature of the poet's writing, but in this instance he includes another dimension – the notion of in-betweeness. The road Heaney describes runs between the ocean and an inland lake. Carefully chosen images **contrast** the unruly beauty of the open sea's 'foam and glitter' with the still 'slate-grey lake' (line 7). In both descriptions, the sounds of the words echo their sense precisely.

The introduction of the swans in line 8 brings unexpected drama. Heaney captures their seemingly effortless movement between air and water. The poet's **vigorous skill with language** can be seen in his appreciation of the swans' transforming presence, which he highlights in the extraordinary image of 'earthed lightning'. His expertly crafted sketches are both tactile ('feathers roughed and ruffling') and visual ('white on white'). Tossed by the wind, their neck feathers resemble ruffled collars. To Heaney, these exquisite birds signify an otherworldly force that is rarely earthed or restrained. In response, he is momentarily absorbed by the swans' purposeful gestures and powerful flight.

In **line 12**, the poet cautiously accepts that such elemental beauty can never be fully grasped: 'Useless to think you'll park and capture it'. Because we are 'neither here nor there', we can only occasionally glimpse 'known and strange things'. Despite this, the poem concludes on a redemptive note, acknowledging those special times when we edge close to the miraculous. **These experiences transcend our mundane lives** and we are shaken by revelation, just as unexpected gusts of winds ('soft buffetings') can rock a car.

Heaney's journey has been both **physical and mystical**. It is brought to a crescendo in **line 16**, where it ends in the articulation of an important truth. He has found meaning between the tangible and intangible. The startling possibility of discovering the ephemeral quality of spiritual awareness is unnerving enough to 'catch the heart off guard and blow it open'. The seemingly contradictory elements of comfort and danger add to the intensity of this final image. Heaney has spoken about the illumination he felt during his visit to the Flaggy Shore as a 'glorious exultation of air and sea and swans'. For him, the experience was obviously inspirational, and the poem that it produced might well provide a similar opportunity for readers to experience life beyond the material.

ANALYSIS

'Seamus Heaney involves himself in finding inspiration for the creation of poetry.' Using reference to his poem 'Postscript', give your opinion of this assessment of Heaney's work.

SAMPLE PARAGRAPH

'Postscript' is a typical Heaney poem in that it begins with a simple description of an unforgettable occasion which truly inspired him. Many of his poems entice readers to be open to marvellous moments of enlightenment in everyday life. His advice is to go to the windswept West of Ireland and experience the beauty and wonder of the coastline at the Flaggy Shore. It's clear that he has had something like a religious experience there as he felt 'the wind/And the light ... working off each other'. His simple description of the swans – 'white on white' – seems to have lifted his spirits and transported him to a world where 'strange things pass'. I have read some nature poems by Hopkins and Yeats, and the same fascination with nature can be seen. In his poem 'Lightenings', Heaney used the experience of the monks being taken to a higher level of consciousness through prayer and chanting. Much the same happened in 'Postscript', where the poet was at one with nature and his spiritual self for a moment – 'neither here nor there'. I liked the last line of this poem where Heaney is simply saying that if we stop rushing around and stop to admire nature's beauty once in a while, anybody can have their heart 'caught off guard' and blown open. Such inspiration will not make everyone write poetry – as Heaney did – but it will have a similar spiritual effect.

EXAMINER'S COMMENT

A good personal response to a challenging question, focusing well on the idea of inspiration – both for the poet and the reader. References and quotations are used effectively. Grade A.

CLASS/HOMEWORK EXERCISES

1 'The response to his experience of vivid scenery is a central feature of Seamus Heaney's poetry.' Discuss this view with reference to 'Postscript'.
2 Copy the table below into your own notes and fill in critical comments about the last two quotations.

Key Quotes

And some time make the time to drive out west	Heaney's advice is quietly insistent, emphasising the need to make good use of time. Later on in the poem, he is more critical of our hurried, modern lifestyle.
the wind/And the light are working off each other	In this subtle image, the phrase 'working off' captures the interplay between the natural elements.
the earthed lightning of a flock of swans	The shock of the swans' sudden appearance is conveyed in this sharp metaphor. For Heaney, it is an inspirational moment of magic.
A hurry through which known and strange things pass	
And catch the heart off guard and blow it open	

A Call

'Hold on,' she said, 'I'll just run out and get him.
The weather here's so good, he took the chance
To do a bit of weeding.'
                        So I saw him
Down on his hands and knees beside the leek rig,   5
Touching, inspecting, separating one
Stalk from the other, gently pulling up
Everything not tapered, frail and leafless,
Pleased to feel each little weed-root break,
But rueful also...   10
                    Then found myself listening to
The amplified grave ticking of hall clocks
Where the phone lay unattended in a calm
Of mirror glass and sunstruck pendulums...

And found myself then thinking: if it were nowadays,   15
This is how Death would summon Everyman.

Next thing he spoke and I nearly said I loved him.

Seamus Heaney

'Pleased to feel each little weed-root break'

GLOSSARY

8 *tapered*: slender; reducing in thickness towards the end.
8 *frail*: weak.
10 *rueful*: expressing regret.
12 *amplified*: increased the strength of the sound.
14 *pendulums*: weights that hang from a fixed point and swing freely, used to regulate the mechanism of a clock.

Seamus Heaney

• Poetry Focus •

EXPLORATIONS

1. How does Heaney dramatise this event? Refer to setting, mood, dialogue, action and climax in your response. Support your answer with reference to the text.
2. How would you describe the tone of this poem? Does it change? Quote to support the points you make.
3. One critic said that the 'celebration of people and relationships in Heaney's poetry is characterised by honesty and tenderness'. Do you agree or disagree? Refer to the text in your response.

STUDY NOTES

'A Call' comes from Heaney's collection *The Spirit Level* (1996) and deals with two of the poet's favourite themes: the father–son relationship and the passing of time. The setting is a routine domestic scene of a father weeding, a son visiting and a mother talking. *The Spirit Level* suggests balance, getting the level right, measuring. It also suggests poetry, which is on another plane, free-floating above the confines of the earth. In his Nobel Prize speech, Heaney said he was 'permitting myself the luxury of walking on air'.

This personal narrative opens with a conversational directness, as Heaney is told to 'Hold on' while his father is contacted. He is busy weeding the garden: 'The weather here's so good, he took the chance/To do a bit of weeding'. The rhythm of colloquial dialogue is realistically caught by the use of commonplace language. **The simple scene of domesticity is set.** In line 4, the poet now becomes the observer on the fringes of the scene, 'So I saw him'. The detail of 'Down on his hands and knees beside the leek rig' invites the reader to observe alongside the poet. The broken lines show the care and skill of the gardener's activity, 'Touching, inspecting, separating', as the father tends his vegetable patch. All farming tradition is associated with decay and growth, and for both animals and plants, the weakest is discarded, 'gently pulling up/Everything not tapered'. What is not a leek is removed. The onomatopoeia of the word 'break', with its sharp 'k' sound, suggests the snap of the root as it is pulled from the earth. The father takes pleasure ('Pleased to feel') in his work ('each little weed-root break') but he is, perhaps, regretful too ('rueful') that a form of life is ending, snapped from the nurturing earth. Or is he just sorry that he has not removed all of the weed's root and so it will grow again, giving him more work to do?

In **line 11**, the **visual imagery is replaced by aural imagery**. The focus changes from the father to the poet as he finds himself 'listening'. Time is passing in this little scene, not just for the weeds but also for man, measured by the 'grave ticking of hall clocks'. Here the poem begins to move between earthbound reality and airiness, as an almost surreal image of ticking clocks in a sea ('calm') of 'mirror glass and sunstruck pendulums' is presented. The broad vowel sounds create an air of serenity and otherworldliness. The echo of the clocks is vividly conveyed in the sound 'amplified'; we can imagine the loud ticking of the clocks as the sound increases in intensity, the 'ticking' filling this space. Is the sound increasing as time starts to end for man? Why is the phone unattended? Is a 'call' expected? From whom, to whom? Is communication no longer possible in this place?

In **line 15**, Heaney moves from observation to meditation, walking on air, 'And found myself then thinking'. He decides that Death would call ('summon') man to his final destination using this modern means, the telephone. The poet is pushing at the boundaries of what is real. The father, like the weeds, will be uprooted, spirited away to some afterlife. Here Heaney is 'seeing things'; he is mediating between states of awareness. **A sense of mortality informs the poem**. The **last line** stands apart, as he is jolted out of his reverie by: 'Next thing he spoke'. Family love is important to Heaney. Here it is the uncommunicated closeness of the father–son relationship. Here are the frustrating attempts at communication between father and son, 'and I nearly said I loved him'. Was it an awareness of his father's mortality, like the weeds, which prompts this reaction from the poet? The diction, relaxed and casual, holds the powerful love between these silent men, and the heartbreaking tension of the impossibility of articulating that love. In that final line – 'Next thing he spoke and I nearly said I loved him' – father and son are both joined and separated.

The title of this poem is intriguing. It could signal the visit of the son to the family home, or the wife calling her husband to let him know his son has arrived. Or might it refer to a telephone call, or even the final summons 'Everyman' will receive from Death?

ANALYSIS

'Heaney habitually finds mystery and significance behind ordinary objects and events.' Discuss this statement in relation to the poem 'A Call' and support your response with reference to the text.

SAMPLE PARAGRAPH

I thought this poem was very deep, as Heaney describes a common event, his father weeding, and turns it into a reflection on mortality. The ordinary event is effectively set by the casual, conversational dialogue, as the wife tells the poet to 'Hold on'. The father's activity is vividly described in the verbs 'Touching, inspecting, separating'. For Heaney, creativity was held in the hands. But another layer of meaning suggests itself. Is Death, the final caller, checking us? I especially liked the word 'rueful'. The father is sorry that he is ending life, 'each little weed-root break'. Is this in contrast to the cold, dispassionate hand of death, who calls all men? This examination of the simple, ordinary growth in the garden gives way to an examination of death. A weird picture of loud ticking clocks in a fantastical hall of mirrors and sun is painted. The ominous ticking of passing time is given due respect, 'The amplified grave ticking'. I liked the pun on 'grave'. The glass mirrors suggest to me the different states of reality, of life and death, what is real, what is reflected. The broad vowel sounds of 'sunstruck pendulums' again emphasise the unstoppable passing of time, as the weights swing to and fro. Now from the physical detail of his father weeding, the poet moves to another level, Heaney said, 'One gains the air'. The 'unattended' phone makes him imagine that this is how Death would 'call' man to his inevitable fate. Here, Heaney is finding significance behind an ordinary object.

EXAMINER'S COMMENT

A sustained exploratory response, subtly addressing all aspects of the question in a personal way, and referring to both 'objects' and 'events'. Expression is varied throughout and points are aptly supported with integrated quotes. Grade A.

CLASS/HOMEWORK EXERCISES

1. 'Heaney's poetry, whether explicit or implicit, is autobiographical in the main.' Would you agree or disagree with this view? Support your answer with reference to the poem 'A Call'.
2. Copy the table below into your own notes and fill in critical comments about the last two quotations.

Key Quotes

'Hold on'	The colloquial phrase communicates what is often said in telephone conversations. This dense use of language is a feature of Heaney's writing.
I'll just run out and get him	The conversational, colloquial tone sets the ordinariness of this little scene. It also reverberates at the end as a contrast to the difficulty the poet has in communicating with his father.
separating one/Stalk from the other	Sibilance suggests the endurance of the father as he carefully tends his garden. The line arrangement mirrors the organisation of his weeding.
Where the phone lay unattended	
and I nearly said I loved him	

• Poetry Focus •

Tate's Avenue

Seamus Heaney

Not the brown and fawn car rug, that first one
Spread on sand by the sea but breathing land-breaths,
Its vestal folds unfolded, its comfort zone
Edged with a fringe of sepia-coloured wool tails.

Not the one scraggy with crusts and eggshells   5
And olive stones and cheese and salami rinds
Laid out by the torrents of the Guadalquivir
Where we got drunk before the corrida.

Instead, again, it's locked-park Sunday Belfast,
A walled back yard, the dust-bins high and silent   10
As a page is turned, a finger twirls warm hair
And nothing gives on the rug or the ground beneath it.

I lay at my length and felt the lumpy earth,
Keen-sensed more than ever through discomfort,
But never shifted off the plaid square once.   15
When we moved I had your measure and you had mine.

GLOSSARY

Tate's Avenue is located in South Belfast, a popular student area. Heaney's girlfriend (later his wife) lived there in the late 1960s.
3 *vestal*: innocent, untouched (Heaney is comparing the crumpled rug to the modest dresses of vestal virgins in ancient Rome).
4 *sepia-coloured*: faded brownish colour; old looking.
7 *Guadalquivir*: river in Andalusia, Spain.
8 *corrida*: bullfight.
9 *locked-park*: Belfast's public parks were closed on Sundays in the 1960s.
15 *plaid*: checked, tartan.

EXPLORATIONS

1 Comment on the poet's use of sound effects in the first two stanzas.
2 'I had your measure and you had mine.' Briefly explain what you think Heaney means by this statement.
3 Write your own personal response to the poem,

STUDY NOTES

'Tate's Avenue' (from the 2006 collection *District and Circle*) is another celebration of Heaney's love for Marie Devlin. They married in 1965 and lived off Tate's Avenue in South Belfast during the late 1960s. Here, the poet reviews their relationship by linking three separate occasions involving a collection of car rugs spread on the ground by the couple over the years.

Stanza one invites us to eavesdrop on a seemingly mundane scene of everyday domesticity. It appears that the poet and his wife have been reminiscing – presumably about their love life over the years. Although the negative opening tone is emphatic ('Not the brown and fawn car rug'), we are left guessing about the exact nature of the couple's discussion. A few tantalising details are given about 'that first' rug, connecting it with an early seaside visit. Heaney can still recall the tension of a time when the couple were **caught between their own desire and strong social restrictions**. He describes the rug in terms of its texture and colours: 'Its vestal folds unfolded' (suggesting their youthful sexuality) contrasting with the 'sepia-coloured wool tails' (symbolising caution and old-fashioned inhibitions). As usual, Heaney's tone is edged with irony as he recalls the 'comfort zone' between himself and Marie.

The repetition of 'Not' at the start of stanza two clearly indicates that the second rug is also rejected, even though it can be traced back to a more exotic Spanish holiday location. Sharp onomatopoeic effects ('scraggy with crusts and eggshells') and the list of Mediterranean foods ('olive stones and cheese and salami rinds') convey **a sense of freedom and indulgence**. Although the couple's hedonistic life is communicated in obviously excessive terms ('Laid out by the torrents of the Guadalquivir'), Heaney's tone is somewhat dismissive. Is he suggesting that their relationship was mostly sensual back then?

'Instead' – the first word in stanza three – signals a turning point in the poet's thinking. Back in his familiar home surroundings, he recalls the rug that mattered most and should answer whatever doubts he had about the past. He has measured the development of their relationship in stages associated with special moments he and Marie shared. The line 'it's locked-park Sunday Belfast' conjures up memories of their early married life in the Tate's Avenue district. The sectarian 1960s are marked by dour Protestant domination, a time when weekend pleasures were frowned upon and even the public parks were closed.

Despite such routine repression and the unromantic setting ('A walled back yard, the dust-bins high and silent'), **the atmosphere is sexually charged**. Heaney is aware of the scene's underlying drama; the seconds tick by 'As a page is turned, a finger twirls warm hair'. The unfaltering nature of the couple's intimacy is evident in the resounding declaration: 'nothing gives on the rug or the ground beneath it'.

This notion of confidence in their relationship is carried through into **stanza four** and accentuated by the alliterative 'I lay at my length and felt the lumpy earth'. The resolute rhythm is strengthened by the robust adjectival phrase 'Keen-sensed' and the insistent statement: 'But never shifted off the plaid square once'. Heaney builds to a discreet and understated climax in the finely balanced last line: 'When we moved I had your measure and you had mine'. While there are erotic undertones throughout, the poet presents us with restrained realism in place of expansive sensuality. 'Tate's Avenue' is **a beautiful, unembarrassed poem of romantic and sexual love within a committed relationship**. Characteristically, when Heaney touches on personal relationships, he produces the most tender and passionate emotions.

ANALYSIS

How effective is Seamus Heaney's use of images in 'Tate's Avenue'? Refer to the poem in your answer.

> **SAMPLE PARAGRAPH**
>
> I was very impressed by Seamus Heaney's use of effective images in his poem 'Tate's Avenue'. He uses three separate settings to show how his lifetime love affair with his wife changed from their early courtship to a mature married relationship. The first image of them sharing a brown and fawn rug by the sea suggests the distant past – 'sepia-coloured'. The rug is personified – 'breathing' to symbolise their feelings for each other. But the memory of their first date is almost like a faded picture. The second scene Heaney remembers is vividly described – during a summer sun holiday as students going to a Spanish bullfight – 'we were drinking before the corrida'. The details also add to my understanding of the scene – 'eating our scraggy crusts and eggshells'. I thought the best images were used at the end of the poem when Heaney described his memories of lying with his wife on a blanket in their back garden in Belfast. The details of the mutual attraction were very true-to-life – 'a finger twirls warm hair'. I could sense

their eye contact and body language in these images – 'We felt the lumpy earth'. Heaney has the ability to bring the reader into a scene and this is largely due to the precise images which he used to create a romantic mood between himself with his wife. Overall, I thought his use of clear images was very effective in 'Tate's Avenue'.

EXAMINER'S COMMENT

This is a reasonably successful personal response to the question, showing some familiarity with the images in the poem and how Heaney uses these to explore the theme of love. The point about the faded photograph was interesting. However, the incorrect quotes and slightly awkward expression reduce the standard to an average grade B.

CLASS/HOMEWORK EXERCISES

1. '"Tate's Avenue" has the drama and immediacy of feeling that is the hallmark of good love poetry.' Discuss this view, using reference to the poem.
2. Copy the table below into your own notes and fill in critical comments about the last two quotations.

Key Quotes

Spread on sand by the sea but breathing land-breaths	Sibilance and personification suggest the strong physical attraction between Heaney and his wife.
its comfort zone	As he remembers the importance of the rug in the couple's committed relationship, the poet's description is wry and sardonic.
it's locked-park Sunday Belfast	The image highlights an era of sectarian rule in Northern Ireland when Protestant-controlled councils insisted that parks and other amenities were closed on Sundays.
As a page is turned, a finger twirls warm hair	
When we moved I had your measure and you had mine	

• Poetry Focus •

The Pitchfork

Of all implements, the pitchfork was the one
That came near to an imagined perfection:
When he tightened his raised hand and aimed with it,
It felt like a javelin, accurate and light.

So whether he played the warrior or the athlete   5
Or worked in earnest in the chaff and sweat,
He loved its grain of tapering, dark-flecked ash
Grown satiny from its own natural polish.

Riveted steel, turned timber, burnish, grain,
Smoothness, straightness, roundness, length and sheen.   10
Sweat-cured, sharpened, balanced, tested, fitted.
The springiness, the clip and dart of it.

And then when he thought of the probes that reached the farthest,
He would see the shaft of a pitchfork sailing past
Evenly, imperturbably through space,   15
Its prongs starlit and absolutely soundless –

But has learned at last to follow that simple lead
Past its own aim, out to an other side
Where perfection – or nearness to it – is imagined
Not in the aiming but the opening hand.   20

'When he tightened his raised hand and aimed with it'

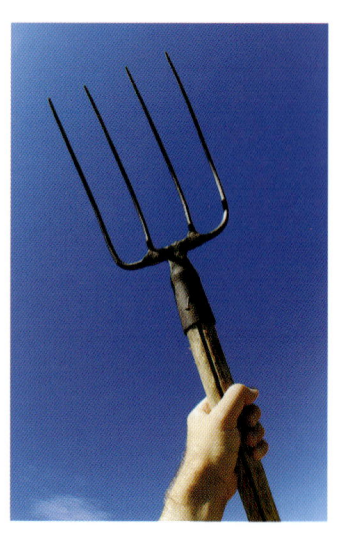

GLOSSARY

4 *javelin*: long spear thrown in a competitive sport as used as a weapon.
6 *chaff*: husks of grain separated from the seed.
7 *grain*: wheat.
7 *tapering*: reducing in thickness towards one end.
9 *Riveted*: fastened.
9 *burnish*: the shine on a polished surface.
12 *clip*: clasp; smack (colloquial).
12 *dart*: follow-on movement; small pointed missile thrown as a weapon.
13 *probes*: unmanned, exploratory spacecraft; a small measuring or testing device.
15 *imperturbably*: calmly, smoothly; unable to be upset.
16 *prongs*: two or more projecting points on a fork.

EXPLORATIONS

1 What is the tone of this poem? Does it change or not? Refer closely to the text in your response.
2 Select one image (or one line) that you find particularly interesting. Briefly explain your choice.
3 What do you think about the ending of this poem? Do you consider it visionary or far-fetched? Give reasons for your answer.

STUDY NOTES

'The Pitchfork' was published in Heaney's 1991 collection, *Seeing Things*. These poems turn to the earlier concerns of the poet. Craft and natural skill, the innate ability to make art out of work, is seen in many of his poems, such as 'The Forge'. Heaney is going back, making 'a journey back into the heartland of the ordinary'. The poet is now both observer and visionary.

In **stanza one**, Heaney describes a pitchfork, an ordinary farming 'implement'. Through **looking at an ordinary object with intense concentration**, the result is a fresh 'seeing', where the ordinary and mundane become marvellous, 'imagined perfection'. For Heaney, the creative impulse was held in the hand, in the skill of the labourer ('tightened his raised hand and aimed with it'). This skill was similar to the skill of the poet. They both practise and hone their particular ability. The pitchfork is now transformed into a sporting piece of equipment, 'a javelin'. The heaviness of physical work falls away as it becomes 'accurate and light' due to the practised capability of the worker. This is similar to the lightness of being and the **freeing of the poet's spirit** that Heaney allows himself to experience in this collection of poetry.

The worker is described as sometimes playing 'the warrior or the athlete' (**stanza two**). **Both professions command respect** and both occupations require courage and skill. But the worker's real work is also described realistically, 'worked in earnest in the chaff and sweat'. This is heavy manual labour, and Heaney does not shirk from its unpleasant side. However, the worker is not ground down by it because he 'loved' the beauty of the pitchfork. Here we see both the poet and the worker dazzled, as the intent observation of the humble pitchfork unleashes its beauty, its slender 'dark-flecked ash'. The shine of the handle is conveyed in the word 'satiny'. The tactile language allows the reader to feel the smooth, polished wooden handle. Now three pairs of eyes (the worker's, the poet's and our own) observe the pitchfork.

Close observation of the pitchfork in **stanza three** continues with a virtuoso display of description, as **each detail is lovingly depicted**, almost like a slow sequence of close-ups in a film. The meeting of the handle and fork is caught in the phrase 'Riveted steel'. The beauty of the wood is evoked in the alliteration of 'turned timber'. The marvellous qualities of the wood are itemised with growing wonder: its shine ('burnish'), its pattern ('grain'). It is as if the worker and the poet are twirling the pitchfork round as they exclaim over its 'Smoothness, straightness, roundness, length and sheen'. This is more like the description one would give to a work of art or a thoroughbred animal than to a farm implement. The skill that went into the making of the pitchfork is now explored in a list of verbs beginning with the compound word 'Sweat-cured'. This **graphically shows the sheer physical exertion that went into making this instrument**, as it was 'sharpened, balanced, tested, fitted'. The tactile quality of the pitchfork is praised: 'The springiness, the clip and dart of it'. The worker, just like the athlete or warrior, tests his equipment. The feel of the pitchfork in the hand is given to the reader, due to the 'Sweat-cured' poet's sensitive and accurate observation and description.

In **stanza four**, the labourer imagines space 'probes' searching the galaxy, 'reached the farthest'. The long line stretches out in imitation of space, which pushes out to infinity. The pitchfork now becomes transformed into a spaceship, 'sailing past/Evenly, imperturbably through space'. This ordinary pitchfork now shines like the metal casing of a spaceship, 'starlit', and moves, like the spaceship, through the vastness of outer space, 'absolutely soundless'. **Stanza five** shows the poet becoming a mediator between different states, actual and imagined, ordinary and fantastical. He stands on a threshold, exploring and philosophising about the nature of his observation as a familiar thing grows stranger. Together (poet, worker and reader), all follow the line of the pitchfork to 'an other side', a place where 'perfection' is 'imagined'. Perfection does not exist in our world. But it is not the 'tightened' hand, which was 'aiming' at the beginning of the poem, which will achieve this ideal state, but the 'opening hand' of the last stanza. Is the poet suggesting we must be open and ready to receive in order to achieve 'perfection'? Heaney states: 'look at the familiar things you know. **Look at them with ... a quality of concentration ... you will be rewarded with insights and visions**.' The poet has become a seer.

ANALYSIS

'Heaney's poetry celebrates traditional crafts. Heaney himself is also a master craftsman of poetry.' Discuss this view of the poet using close reference to the poems of Heaney on your course.

SAMPLE PARAGRAPH

I read the description of the humble pitchfork, which became like some other strange item, as the poet Heaney lovingly described this farm implement in close detail: 'Riveted steel, turned timber'. The hard 't' sound emphasised the fact that this was no pretty ornament, but a man's working instrument which did serious manual work in the 'chaff and sweat'. I was impressed at how the poet gave due respect to the skill not only of the farm labourer who played 'the warrior or the athlete' with his pitchfork as a 'javelin', but also to the craftsman who made this pitchfork. He was the man whose skill 'sharpened, balanced, tested, fitted' it. It seems to me that Heaney is suggesting that the craftsman is producing wonderful items honed by his skill. This is similar to the poet who is producing a wonderful poem which reaches beyond to another plane, 'imagined perfection'. The poet, it seems to me, is achieving this through the vision of the pitchfork as a spaceship probing the huge sky, as it moves 'starlit and absolutely soundless'. Here indeed poetry is translating the ordinary into mystery, as the poet moves from detailed observation and description into the visionary state. The skilled craft of the poet transforms the pitchfork into the spacecraft. We experience its appearance ('Its prongs starlit') and its silence ('absolutely soundless'). The poet makes us see and hear this vision. The master craftsman is at work as both he and we soar 'imperturbably through space'.

• Poetry Focus •

Seamus Heaney

EXAMINER'S COMMENT

The student shows a real personal engagement in this sustained response. There is a clear focus on the task and a succinct conclusion to the paragraph. Good use of well-integrated quotations. Grade A.

CLASS/HOMEWORK EXERCISES

1. 'Heaney's language is both realistic and mystical.' Discuss this view of the poet's work, referring particularly to 'The Pitchfork'.
2. Copy the table below into your own notes and fill in critical comments about the last two quotations.

Key Quotes

It felt like a javelin, accurate and light	This simile effectively transforms the pitchfork into a powerful piece of sporting or fighting equipment.
tapering, dark-flecked ash	The vivid description of the pitchfork's slim handle appeals to our sense of sight. The compound word 'dark-flecked' is particularly evocative, as the repetition of 'k' suggests the small, intricate pattern of the wood.
The springiness, the clip and dart of it	In this tactile description, the poet enables the reader to feel the sensation of holding the pitchfork in his or her hand.
when he thought of probes	
Not in the aiming but the opening hand	

Lightenings viii

The annals say: when the monks of Clonmacnoise
Were all at prayers inside the oratory
A ship appeared above them in the air.

The anchor dragged along behind so deep
It hooked itself into the altar rails   5
And then, as the big hull rocked to a standstill,

A crewman shinned and grappled down the rope
And struggled to release it. But in vain.
'This man can't bear our life here and will drown,'

The abbot said, 'unless we help him.' So   10
They did, the freed ship sailed, and the man climbed back
Out of the marvellous as he had known it.

'Out of the marvellous'

GLOSSARY

1 *annals*: monastic records.
1 *Clonmacnoise*: established in the sixth century, the monastery at Clonmacnoise was renowned as a centre of scholarship and spirituality.
2 *oratory*: place of prayer, small chapel.
7 *shinned*: climbed down, clambered.
10 *abbot*: head of the monastery.

• Poetry Focus •

EXPLORATIONS

1. How is the surreal atmosphere conveyed in this poem? Quote in support of your response.
2. Choose one striking image from the poem and comment on its effectiveness.
3. In your view, what does the air-ship symbolise? Refer to the text in your answer.

STUDY NOTES

> Written in four tercets (three-line stanzas), 'Lightenings viii' (from Seamus Heaney's 1991 collection, *Seeing Things*), tells a legendary story of a miraculous air-ship which once appeared to the monks at Clonmacnoise, Co. Offaly. Heaney has said: 'I was devoted to this poem because the crewman who appears is situated where every poet should be situated: between the ground of everyday experience and the airier realm of an imagined world.'

Heaney's matter-of-fact approach at the start of **stanza one** leads readers to expect a straightforward retelling of an incident recorded in the 'annals' of the monastery. The story's apparently scholarly source seems highly reliable. While they were at prayers, the monks looked up: 'A ship appeared above them in the air'. We assume that the oratory is open to the sky. The simplicity of the colloquial language, restrained tone and run-through lines all ease us into a **dreamlike world** where anything can happen. But as with all good narratives, the magic ship's sudden appearance raises many questions: Why is it there? Where has it come from? Is this strange story all a dream?

Then out of the air-ship came a massive anchor, which 'dragged along behind so deep' (**stanza two**) before lodging itself in the altar rails. The poet makes **effective choices in syntax (word order) and punctuation**, e.g. placing 'so deep' at the end of the line helps to emphasise the meaning. The moment when the ship shudders to a halt is skilfully caught in a carefully wrought image: 'as the big hull rocked to a standstill'.

A crewman clambered down the rope to try to release the anchor, but he is unsuccessful. Heaney chooses his words carefully: 'shinned', 'grappled', 'struggled' (**stanza three**) are all powerful verbs, helping to create a clear picture of the sailor's physical effort. The phrase 'But in vain' is separated from the rest of the line to emphasise the man's hopelessness. The contrasting worlds of magic and reality seem incompatible. Ironically, the story's turning point is the abbot's instant recognition that **the human, earthly atmosphere will be fatal to the visitor**: 'This man can't bear our life here and will drown'.

But a solution is at hand: 'unless we help him' (stanza four). The unconditional generosity of the monks comes naturally to them: 'So/They did'. The word 'So' creates a pause and uncertainty before the prompt, brief opening of the next line: 'They did'. When the anchor is eventually disentangled and 'the freed ship sailed', **the crewman will surely tell his travel companions about the strange beings he encountered** after he 'climbed back out of the marvellous as he had known it'. This last line is somewhat surprising and leaves the reader wondering – marvelling, even.

Heaney's poem certainly raises interesting questions, blurring the lines between reality and illusion, and challenging our ideas about human consciousness. **The story itself can be widely interpreted**. Is the ship a symbol of inspiration while the monks represent commitment and dedication? Presumably, as chroniclers of the annals (preserving texts on paper for posterity), they were not aware of the miracle of their own labours – crossing the barrier from the oral tradition to written records – which was to astonish the world in the forthcoming centuries and help spread human knowledge.

'Lightenings viii' is a beautiful poem that highlights the fact that **the ordinary and the miraculous are categories defined only by human perception**. For many readers, the boat serves as an abstract mirror image, reversing our usual way of seeing things. In Heaney's rich text, we discover that from the outsider's perspective, the truly marvellous consists not of the visionary or mystical experience, but of the seemingly ordinary experience.

ANALYSIS

What aspects of 'Lightenings viii' are typical of Heaney's distinctive poetry? Refer closely to the text in your answer.

SAMPLE PARAGRAPH

I found many parallels between 'Lightenings' and some of the other Heaney poems we studied. His writing style is direct and colloquial – and this is typical of him. His poetry is dramatic – populated with memorable characters – and this is also true of 'Lightenings'. He used simple images to describe the surreal scene where the monks imagine a vision of a flying ship hovering over their altar – 'the big hull rocked to a standstill'. 'The Forge' also deals with an imaginary vision – 'the dark' interior of the blacksmith's workshed. The religious references are present here as well in the image of the 'altar' where the blacksmith 'expends himself in shape and music'. I have also noticed how Heaney contrasts completely different moods in his poetry. In both 'A Constable Calls' and 'The Harvest Bow', he is inspired by moments of unspoken tension. Firstly, the poet is aware through 'small guilts' that his father might be arrested for breaking the law. In the second poem, the nervous silence between himself as a boy and his non-communicative father becomes the basis of poetry later on in his adult life. In 'Lightenings', the theme also centres around two distinct worlds – the mundane monks and the magical sailors. By contrasting the two, Heaney made me think about the way ordinary life, which we take for granted, could be seen from a very different point of view. In my opinion, 'Lightenings' is an unmistakable Heaney poem.

EXAMINER'S COMMENT

This is a fresh and focused response that addresses the question directly. A range of interesting comparisons is made with several other Heaney poems. References show good knowledge and personal engagement. Ideas are handled very effectively throughout. Grade A.

CLASS/HOMEWORK EXERCISES

1. In much of his poetry, Heaney quietly disturbs our complacent distinction between the visionary and the real. Discuss this view based on your study of 'Lightenings viii'. Support the points you make with reference to the text.
2. Copy the table below into your own notes and fill in critical comments about the last two quotations.

Key Quotes

The annals say	The poem begins on a scholarly note, establishing a serious, authoritative tone in advance of the fanciful story that follows. Is Heaney being playful?
A ship appeared above them in the air	Detached in prayer from the ordinary world, the monks live curious, visionary lives and would not be strangers to miracles.
the big hull rocked to a standstill	Broad assonant sounds suggest the enormous bulk of the ship, while the verb 'rocked' reflects its cumbersome movement as it settles 'in the air'.
A crewman shinned and grappled down the rope	
the man climbed back/ Out of the marvellous	

• Poetry Focus •

LEAVING CERT SAMPLE ESSAY

Q 'Dear Seamus Heaney ...'

Write a letter to Seamus Heaney telling him how you responded to some of his poems on your course. Support the points you make by detailed reference to the poems you choose to write about.

MARKING SCHEME GUIDELINES

Reward responses that show clear evidence of engagement with the poems and/or the poet. While a conversational approach is suggested by the question, expect and allow for a wide variety of approaches in candidates' answering. Candidates are obviously free to challenge and 'confront' the poet. Accept treatment of positive and negative aspects of Heaney's poetry.

Some of the following areas might be addressed:
- Powerful use of everyday language.
- Vividly detailed imagery.
- Poet's focus on memory, especially memories of childhood.
- Personal character of the writing.
- Political and social perspectives of the poems.
- Striking love poetry, etc.

SAMPLE ESSAY
(Letter to Seamus Heaney)

1 *Dear Seamus Heaney,*

I have been studying a selection of your poems for my Leaving Certificate, and I wanted to write to tell you what impact your poems had on a 17-year-old teenager.

2 *I was particularly struck by 'The Tollund Man'. It made me think about humanity and the stupid things we do. Using the man found in the bogland, you showed that humankind is still committing acts of needless violence. The graphic imagery and fragmented rhythm of the lines 'Tell-tale skin and teeth/Flecking the sleepers/Of four young brothers, trailed/For miles along the rails' contribute* to the shocking deed. You show how the innocent are affected by violence. You made the Tollund Man look like a martyr by creating a holy atmosphere: 'risk blasphemy', 'consecrate', 'pray'. I thought it was interesting how you told us that the bog (the Mother Goddess of the ground who needed bridegrooms) preserved him, 'Those dark juices working', as if he were a saint, 'a saint's kept body'.

3. I could really relate to this man's experience as a foreigner in a strange country. I was on an exchange to Germany, and I couldn't speak the language and so the phrase 'Watching the pointing hands/Of country people,/Not knowing their tongue' summed up the ordeal of 'them' and 'us'. I can imagine you driving along ('Saying the names'), as the Tollund Man was driven, calling out all the foreign names of places you both pass, almost like a litany of holy names, 'Tollund, Grabaulle, Nebelgard'. I can also understand how you, a Northern Irishman, would feel 'at home' in the 'man-killing parishes'. Both in Jutland and in Ireland, you remind us that man was sacrificed for a cause, a need of the community, whether it was the search for fertility or freedom.

4. Another poem that deals with the tensions in the North is 'A Constable Calls'. I found it interesting how you gave us the sketch of the character of the policeman from the details of his bicycle. The perception of an almost sinister hidden force of the Royal Ulster Constabulary is contained in the word 'cowl', a hood. It reminds me of the hoods of the Ku Klux Klan, or the hood worn by a hangman, or even some young teenagers, up to no good, in their 'hoodies'. The image of the 'boot of the law' reinforces this. The dynamo light 'cocked back' was the most threatening image of all for me. This was a tense society, as at any moment sectarian violence could erupt. The hard 'c' sounds reflect this.

5. I could see the awkwardness of his visit. He is not made welcome, as his cap was 'upside down/On the floor'. No one offered to take it. His 'slightly sweating hair' suggests the effort he is making, but there is no mention of anything to drink. You show the tense interrogation very effectively, in my opinion, as he snaps out four questions and what was the terse response? A curt, monosyllabic 'No' is the response from the father. You convey the full majesty of the law through the details of the policeman's equipment; 'the polished holster/With its buttoned flap' shows that the law was enforced, if need be, with violence.

6. The love poems are original and fresh. In 'The Skunk', I liked your descriptions of sounds ('Snuffing', 'whinnied'), smells ('Tang of eucalyptus'), and colour

('Small oranges loomed in the orange tree') of an exotic California. But in this paradise there is a flaw, the pain of loneliness, the elements of California merely pointing out what the poet is missing, 'spelt your absence'. Your powerful longing cannot even be dulled by drink, 'The aftermath of a mouthful of wine/Was like inhaling you off a cold pillow'. But love is rewarded, as you recall the 'sootfall' of your wife's things at bedtime. Usually love poetry is associated with young lovers, but you dared to talk about mature love's attractions, 'the black plunge-line nightdress'. The soft 's' and long vowel sound in 'sootfall' make me hear the whisper of silky garments sliding to the floor. I must say I think your wife has some sense of humour, and you are a very lucky man that she is not offended by the comparison of herself to a skunk, 'head-down, tail-up'. She is indeed a 'stored cask', as I think a sense of humour helps a person through the darkest times.

7. I found your poems honest, thought provoking, original and direct. Your choices of unusual associations made me look at some things in a new light. Thank you for the experience.

Yours sincerely,
Paul

(approx. 770 words)

GRADE: A1
P   = 15/15
C   = 15/15
L   = 15/15
M   = 5/5
Total = 50/50

EXAMINER'S COMMENT

A personal response that is focused and well supported. The candidate displays a clear knowledge of Heaney's work. In-depth discussion on a single poem is rewarded, as it fulfils the task set in the question. There is a good sense of appreciation of sound. Quotations are accurate and successfully integrated into the general commentary. Grade A.

SAMPLE LEAVING CERT QUESTIONS ON HEANEY'S POETRY
(45–50 MINUTES)

1. 'The subjects of Heaney's poems are treated with great love and sympathy together with a keen eye for significant detail.'
   How true is this statement of the poems by Seamus Heaney that you have studied? Support your discussion with relevant references from the poems on your course.

2. 'Sensuously evocative and rich in imagery' is a phrase used to describe the language of Seamus Heaney's poetry. Would you agree or disagree? Quote in support of your views from the prescribed poetry on your course.

3. 'Heaney's poetry appeals to the modern reader for many reasons.' Write an essay in which you outline the reasons why the poems by Seamus Heaney you have studied have this wide appeal. Support your reasons with detailed references from your prescribed poems.

SAMPLE ESSAY PLAN (Q3)

'Heaney's poetry appeals to the modern reader for many reasons.' Write an essay in which you outline the reasons why the poems by Seamus Heaney you have studied have this wide appeal. Support your reasons with detailed references from your prescribed poems.

• Intro:	Heaney's use of vivid imagery, realistic detail, use of memory, universality of theme all appeal to the modern reader.
• Point 1:	'The Forge' – magical quality of blacksmith's work contained in appealing imagery; 'fantail of sparks', 'unicorn'. Today's reader enjoys the 'otherworld' quality.
• Point 2:	'Sunlight' – realistic detail conveys beloved Aunt Mary to the reader; 'measling shins', 'broad-lapped', etc. Homely image of scoop shows the depth of love, which is appealing.
• Point 3:	'A Constable Calls' – imagery conveys power and tension in this divided community. Interesting perspective given of recent Troubles in Northern Ireland.

- *Point 4:* 'The Harvest Bow' – Heaney's silent father is remembered in this intricately structured poem, which mirrors the skill used by his father in making the harvest bow. All readers are intrigued by family relationships.

- *Point 5:* 'Bogland' – Heaney shows us through his treatment of the bog the limitations and possibilities of dealing with our fractured past. History has never been so important as in the modern world. We run the risk that those who cannot remember the past are doomed to repeat it.

- *Conclusion:* Heaney is a great observer of ordinary lives/places, but he also forces his reader to consider wider issues that impact on their lives. This is the appeal of Heaney's poetry.

EXERCISE

Develop one of the above points into a paragraph.

CONCLUSION – SAMPLE PARAGRAPGH

I feel that Seamus Heaney speaks eloquently to the modern reader when he is drawing a picture of the wonderful serenity of the Mossbawn farmyard in the poem 'Sunlight', with its two ticking clocks of past and present time, his realistic imagery conveying the wonderful, modest love warming this place as the oven warms and bakes the bread. He clearly shows us the magic in homely skills such as those of the blacksmith ('The Forge'), or indeed of his father ('The Harvest Bow'), as he uses memory to get us to consider the present and the future. He bravely confronts the unpleasant in 'A Constable Calls'. The tension of the Catholic community is palpable in the description of the policeman's bicycle, appearance and behaviour. In 'Bogland' he uncovers the essence of the fluid bog, which holds and embraces the past. Here is a lesson for all of us, both from Heaney and the bog. How could Heaney, therefore, not appeal to the modern reader, as he conveys, remembers, reminds and teaches us with such skill?

EXAMINER'S COMMENT

As part of a full essay answer, the student has written a B-grade paragraph and gives a summary of what has been dealt with in the main body of the essay. The concluding paragraph could have been improved with a quotation from either Heaney or a critic which makes a statement about poetry in general or Heaney's poetry in particular.

Last Words

'Heaney has an uncanny capacity to transform basic intuitions into universal insights'.
John McGurk

'He [Heaney] is proposing an idea of poetry which combines psychic investigation with historical inquiry.'
Elmer Andrews

'The best moments are those when your mind seems to implode and words and images rush of their own accord into the vortex.'
Seamus Heaney

'The Ideal exists not in our achievement of it but in our aspiration toward it.'

Thomas Kinsella (1928–)

Thomas Kinsella was born in Inchicore, Dublin in 1928 and educated through the medium of Irish at the local Model School and the O'Connells Christian Brothers School. He attended University College Dublin in 1946, initially to study science. After a few terms in college, he went to work in the Irish Civil Service and continued his studies at night, having switched to Humanities. His earliest poems were printed in university magazines and in *Poetry Ireland.* He began publishing short collections in 1952. Influenced by W.H. Auden and dealing with a primarily urban landscape and with questions of identity and relationships, Kinsella's early work marked him out as distinct from the mainstream Irish poets of the 1950s. While his earlier poems tended to be introspective and soul searching, he was increasingly drawn to mythology and tradition. During the 1970s, his work was influenced by contemporary American writers, such as Robert Lowell and Ezra Pound. In later years, his themes included political and historical trends. This developed into a sometimes darkly satirical focus throughout the late 1980s and 1990s, when he was Professor of English at Philadelphia's Temple University. Kinsella has said that his poetry is largely concerned with love and death. An acclaimed translator and editor, he received the Honorary Freedom of the City of Dublin in May 2007. Thomas Kinsella has been credited with bringing modernism to Irish poetry and is regarded by many as one of the leading Irish poets of his generation.

• Poetry Focus •

Thomas Kinsella

PRESCRIBED POEMS (HIGHER LEVEL)

1 'Thinking of Mr D.' (p. 202)

In this early poem, Kinsella recalls a memorable Dublin character from his past. But Mr D.'s animated personality masks a darker, more troubled self as he struggles to turn 'aside from pain'.

2 'Dick King' (p. 206)

The poet considers the significance of an elderly neighbour who was an important presence in his childhood. Love, loss and memory are central to Kinsella's assessment of Dick King's life and its essential goodness.

3 'Mirror in February' (p. 212)

Ageing and lost youth are key themes in the poem. While casually shaving on a damp February morning, the sudden realisation of time's erosive impact has a dramatic effect on Kinsella.

4 'Chrysalides' (p. 217)

The poet tells the story of a youthful summer cycling trip through the countryside, a memory that he has come to understand as marking the end of youth. Familiar themes include the effects of time as well as life's beauty and horror.

5 *from* 'Glenmacnass: VI Littlebody' (p. 222)

Kinsella's imagined encounter with a demonic music-making leprechaun provides the basis for expressing his own belief that creativity should never be sacrificed for notoriety or financial gain.

6 'Tear' (p. 228)

This detailed memory of visiting his grandmother as she lay dying allows Kinsella to examine people's attitudes to suffering and death. The poem also contrasts fearful innocence with the wisdom that comes with old age.

7 'Hen Woman' (p. 235)

The poem's opening description of a hen laying an egg becomes a symbol for all of life's mystery and possibilities. In the dreamlike scenes that follow, Kinsella addresses the processes of poetry and memory, prominent themes throughout his work.

8 'His Father's Hands' (p. 243)

A moment of conflict between father and son moves to memories of the poet's grandfather at his work and playing the fiddle. Family history, community and the creative tradition are recurring themes in the poem.

9 *from* 'Settings: Model School, Inchicore' (p. 252)

Kinsella's nostalgic look at his early schooldays evokes the innocence and enthusiasm of young minds. However, time changes everything, as the poet reflects on how he became more introspective and alienated in adult life.

10 *from* 'The Familiar: VII' (p. 258)

The poem examines the complex nature of one couple's relationship and how it changes over the years. Kinsella uses sensual details and draws on religious images to suggest love's subtle dimensions.

11 *from* 'Belief and Unbelief: Echo' (p. 263)

This short poem also explores the themes of love, transience and death. Characteristically realistic, Kinsella acknowledges that honesty is an essential requirement of a successful relationship.

• Poetry Focus •

Thinking of Mr D.

A man still light of foot, but ageing, took
An hour to drink his glass, his quiet tongue
Danced to such cheerful slander.

He sipped and swallowed with a scathing smile,
Tapping a polished toe.   5
His sober nod withheld assent.

When he died I saw him twice.
Once as he used retire
On one last murmured stabbing little tale
From the right company, tucking in his scarf.   10

And once down by the river, under wharf-
Lamps that plunged him in and out of light,
A priestlike figure turning, wolfish-slim,
Quickly aside from pain, in a bodily plight,
To note the oiled reflections chime and swim.   15

'still light of foot, but ageing'

GLOSSARY

3 *slander*: insult, slur.
4 *scathing*: mocking, derisive.
6 *assent*: agreement.
11 *wharf*: riverside, quayside.
15 *chime*: ring.

EXPLORATIONS

1. Based on your reading of the first two stanzas, what do you learn of Mr D.'s character?
2. Choose one interesting image from the poem and comment on its effectiveness.
3. In your opinion, what is the central theme or message of this poem? Refer to the text in support of your answer.

STUDY NOTES

Through much of his poetic career, Thomas Kinsella has been concerned with human disappointment and people's engagement with the presence of uncertainty in their lives. 'Thinking of Mr D.' (published in 1958) focuses on Dublin's nocturnal pub society. While the poem typifies Kinsella's bleak suspicion of a distasteful world, his dry, compassionate irony is also present.

The poet introduces Mr D. as a well-groomed man of contradictions, 'still light of foot, but ageing'. In his local public house, he gives the appearance of being happy enough, drinking slowly, delighting in ridicule and malicious gossip. The **tone is circumspect** and guarded from the start. What seems to interest Kinsella is Mr D.'s contrasting 'cheerful slander'. Beneath the genial appearance lies a more calculating nature, emphasised by the sharp reference to his 'scathing smile' (line 4). The underlying image conveyed is of a cynical character with a deeply resentful side to his personality.

Pent-up frustration adds to Mr D.'s inscrutability. Is he finding it hard to accept that he cannot escape the inevitability of ageing? Or is he struggling with the reality of an unfulfilled existence? The poet goes on to review Mr D.'s **seemingly dissatisfied life** ('When he died I saw him twice') and locates him in two telling moments. The first memory focuses on his habit of leaving a social gathering after 'one last murmured stabbing little tale' (line 9). This revealing gesture, with its hint of petty violence, is further evidence of Mr D.'s small-minded disaffection. Is Kinsella suggesting that he is typical of those who lack the courage of their convictions and who will only express their views where it is safe to do so in 'the right company'?

The poet's second recollection is darker still. In the shadowy riverside setting 'that plunged him in and out of light', Mr D. is depicted as a 'priestlike figure', becoming increasingly predatory ('wolfish-slim'). Surrounded by **desolate urban images**, Kinsella imagines him 'turning' away from reality ('pain') as though 'in a bodily plight' (line 14). The poem's final image is of this silhouetted character staring at the river (presumably the Liffey), seeking some meaning – or escape – in its 'oiled reflections'. We are left wondering about the poet's attitude to this man. Does he have any sympathy for him? Does he identify with him? It is characteristic of Kinsella to combine compassion and criticism at the same time.

But **Mr D. seems incapable of action**, as indecisive as a latter-day Hamlet. We do not know exactly what he is running away from – an unhappy life, old age, death? Is he on the verge of ending his misery? Although he is severely troubled, he can still find some respite in the river's enticing beauty. But while the phrase 'chime and swim' indicates hope, it is inconclusive. It's hardly surprising that critics have seen Mr D. as an ageing Stephen Dedalus, the cynical hero of James Joyce's novel, A Portrait of the Artist as a Young Man. Stephen struggled to find fulfilment and took perverse pleasure in his increasing alienation. Mr D. has also been associated with the embittered Italian writer Dante Alighieri and with the sceptical Irish poet Austin Clarke.

ANALYSIS

'Kinsella uses effective contrasts to unveil his portrait of Mr D.' Discuss this view, referring to the poem in your answer.

SAMPLE PARAGRAPH

Kinsella describes Mr D in a series of contradictions – 'cheerful slander' suggests that he ridiculed other people, but did so in a quite good-natured way. I thought this added mystery to the old man's paradoxical charachter. It was never clear whether he was simply malicious or not. His 'scathing smile' added to his puzzling charachter. The most intresting use of contrast comes at the end of the poem where Kinsella protrays Mr D as a man 'in and out of light'. This brightness and darkness suggests the good and evil balance in his charachter, the tension inside him. He describes him as 'priestlike' but also as 'wolfish'. These are disturbing images to me which make Mr D seem unpredactable. I got the distinct impression that Kinsella wanted us to see Mr D as a typical flawed human being – a mixture of good and evil, happiness and depression. I didn't think it was a very positive picture in the end, as if Kinsella himself believed that Mr D's life was a bitter disappointment – 'bodily plight'. The contrasts helped to show his inner struggle very well.

SPELLCHECKER
character
interesting
portrays
unpredictable

EXAMINER'S COMMENT
This average C-grade response includes one or two good points that address the poet's use of contrast to reveal a complex character. References are reasonably effective and there is some personal interaction with the poem. Language is poorly controlled in places and there are a number of spelling errors.

CLASS/HOMEWORK EXERCISES
1. In your opinion, what is the dominant mood in 'Thinking of Mr D.'? Refer closely to the text of the poem in your answer.
2. Copy the table below into your own notes and fill in critical comments about the last two quotations.

Key Quotes

still light of foot, but ageing	Contrasts play an important part in uncovering Mr D.'s complex and somewhat regretful personality.
one last murmured stabbing little tale	The character's deeply rooted anger and frustration are revealed in this slightly violent and cowardly gesture.
A priestlike figure turning	Mr D.'s behaviour beside the river, whether actual or imagined, suggests someone who is intensely uneasy within himself.
wolfish-slim	
the oiled reflections chime and swim	

• Poetry Focus •

Dick King

Thomas Kinsella

In your ghost, Dick King, in your phantom vowels I read
That death roves our memories igniting
Love. Kind plague, low voice in a stubbled throat,
You haunt with the taint of age and of vanished good,
Fouling my thought with losses.   5

Clearly now I remember rain on the cobbles,
Ripples in the iron trough, and the horses' dipped
Faces under the Fountain in James's Street,
When I sheltered my nine years against your buttons
And your own dread years were to come: 10

And your voice, in a pause of softness, named the dead,
Hushed as though the city had died by fire,
Bemused, discovering ... discovering
A gate to enter temperate ghosthood by;
And I squeezed your fingers till you found again   15
My hand hidden in yours.

                I squeeze your fingers:

    Dick King was an upright man.
    Sixty years he trod
    The dull stations underfoot.   20
    Fifteen he lies with God.

    By the salt seaboard he grew up
    But left its rock and rain
    To bring a dying language east
    And dwell in Basin Lane.   25

    By the Southern Railway he increased:
    His second soul was born
    In the clangour of the iron sheds,
    The hush of the late horn.

    An invalid he took to wife.   30
    She prayed her life away;

Her whisper filled the whitewashed yard
Until her dying day.

And season in, season out,
He made his wintry bed.   35
He took the path to the turnstile
Morning and night till he was dead.

He clasped his hands in a Union ward
To hear St James's bell.
I searched his eyes though I was young,   40
The last to wish him well.

'Clearly now I remember rain on the cobbles'

GLOSSARY

1 *phantom*: slight, ghostly.
2 *roves*: wanders through.
3 *plague*: bother, trouble.
3 *stubbled*: unshaven, spiky.
5 *Fouling*: upsetting, tainting.
6 *cobbles*: cobblestones (used for paving streets).
13 *Bemused*: puzzled, preoccupied.
14 *temperate*: gentle, mild.
20 *stations*: railway stations.
22 *salt seaboard*: west coast of Ireland.
28 *clangour*: noise, ringing.
29 *late horn*: sound of the factory horn in the evening.
36 *turnstile*: entrance gate; mechanical barrier.
38 *clasped*: joined hands (in prayer).
38 *Union ward*: trade union retirement home.
39 *St James's*: local church.

EXPLORATIONS

1 Based on the evidence of the poem's opening stanza, what are Kinsella's feelings towards Dick King?
2 In your opinion, what does this poem tell you about Thomas Kinsella's own attitude to life? Refer to the text in your answer.
3 Write a short personal response to the poem, supporting the points you make with reference to the text.

STUDY NOTES

> Thomas Kinsella has emphasised the importance of 'personal places' in his writing. Many of his early poems are set in the small courtyard at Dublin's Basin Lane. It was here that he spent his childhood near the canal and the brewery. For Kinsella, it was a 'separate world', a place of 'selfless kindness'. Dick King had come from the west coast of Ireland to live there. He worked on the Great Southern Railway and became a close friend of the Kinsella family. The poem is another example of Kinsella's fondness for the meditative sequence.

Lines 1–5 have the plaintive quality of a conventional elegy. Dick King's name ('your phantom vowels') has revived **conflicting memories of love and loss** in the poet. Kinsella addresses his former neighbour directly, recalling his 'low voice in a stubbled throat'. The poet's sentiments are couched in resentful terms: 'You haunt with the taint of age and of vanished good'. Prominent assonant sounds add to the underlying sense of aggrieved sorrow as Kinsella accuses the old man's restless spirit of 'Fouling my thought with losses'.

Lines 6–10 take the poet back to a time when he felt especially close to the old man: 'When I sheltered my nine years against your buttons'. A series of **nostalgic images** ('rain on the cobbles', 'the horses' dipped/Faces under the Fountain in James's Street') are particularly evocative, reflecting Kinsella's fondness for this former life. But the reflection is abruptly checked from lapsing into sentimentality as the poet acknowledges the destructive effects of time and the inevitability of death ('your own dread years').

The flashback is extended into **lines 11–16**, where effective sibilance ('your voice, in a pause of softness') echoes the poet's own poignant feelings. The past was clearly important to the old man, who – like many elderly people – must have frequently 'named the dead'. It seems evident that Dick King's death has made an astonishing impact on Kinsella, leaving him 'Bemused, discovering ... discovering'. **This early bereavement marks a critical stage in his self-awareness**, encompassing both personal grief and a much wider understanding of human mortality. However, the repeated references to death ('named the dead', 'the city had died', 'temperate ghosthood') are balanced by a more positive view, celebrating the powerful friendship between Dick King and the young Kinsella: 'I squeezed your fingers till you found again/My hand hidden in yours'. The natural spontaneity of the gesture defines the warmth of a companionship that has never been forgotten. This enduring connection – based on the sensation of physical contact – has transcended time, allowing the poet to continue experiencing love at will.

Line 17 ('I squeeze your fingers') represents a turning point in the poem. Isolated and out of time, the poet's imaginary act, described in the present tense, allows him to use the lively rhymes and jaunty rhythms of childhood street games to suggest Dick King's austere life. The second half of the poem is distinctive for its **portrayal of Dublin's working class** in the 1930s. The ironic quality of line 18 ('Dick King was an upright man') combines both respect and pity for this virtuous man who struggled ('trod') through a long lifetime of hardship. Details from King's relentless routine emphasise the tragic history of this dependable rail worker (the reference to 'stations' even has associations with Christ's Way of Sorrows towards Calvary).

It is ironic that images of sacrifice and death define Dick King's solitary life. The 'dying language' (line 24) he had brought from his West of Ireland birthplace was of little use in Dublin's Basin Lane, where daily life was measured by 'the clangour of the iron sheds' and factory sirens. But at least 'he increased' and found **some self-worth in honest labour**: 'His second soul was born'. At times, Kinsella's depiction edges close to droll bleakness, particularly in his description of King's dependent wife, who 'prayed her life away'. An equally sardonic voice sums up the old man's entire existence as working 'Morning and night till he was dead'.

The poem's final lines focus on Dick King's initial impact on the poet: 'I searched his eyes though I was young'. **We can only wonder about the child's questions**, but they may well have touched on the fragile mystery of existence itself. Although Kinsella later described life as 'a given ordeal', there is no doubt about his enduring affection for his elderly neighbour. But while the poet seems heartened that he was the 'last to wish him well', readers will not be unaware of the tragic reality that Dick King's lonely life was neither happy nor fulfilled. Nevertheless, this unusual elegy has immortalised an ordinary person from this ordinary community. In his own way, King was at one with the world, and his simple acceptance of life seems to characterise an entire generation's resilience.

ANALYSIS

'Thomas Kinsella's poems reveal a great deal about the poet himself.' Discuss this view, using reference to Kinsella's poem 'Dick King'.

SAMPLE PARAGRAPH

In my opinion, 'Dick King' tells us much about the man who wrote the poem. Kinsella is a highly introspective poet, always trying to come to terms with the past and to make sense of things. He is very clearly obsessed with death – and images of ghosts and dying are found throughout the poem. Many of his poems are based on and around his youthful experiences around St James's Street. Names of people, such as 'Dick King', and places, e.g. 'Basin Lane', give his poetry a strong sense of realism. I thought Kinsella revealed himself as someone with a genuine sense of belonging for the buildings and local community in Dublin. His childhood seems to have been a happy one – 'I squeezed your fingers' and his genuine friendship with Mr King is something which is central to the poem. Kinsella seems to have been a great observer and the poem is filled with detailed images – 'Ripples in the iron trough' as he describes the horses dipping their heads to drink in the street fountain. He also has a dry sense of humour, describing Dick almost killing himself with work on the railway – 'He took the path to the turnstile'. The second half of the poem recalls Kinsella's own childhood games and the happy times he had growing up. Overall, I thought that Kinsella's poem showed him as proud of his past and the hard-working community he grew up in, so 'Dick King' is revealing.

EXAMINER'S COMMENT

This is a reasonably good personal response to the poem and includes a number of well-supported points. There is a sustained attempt to remain focused throughout and references are supportive. However, the expression is awkward in places. Grade B.

CLASS/HOMEWORK EXERCISES

1. 'Love, death and the artistic process are Kinsella's most prominent themes.' To what extent is this true of 'Dick King'? Refer to the text of the poem in your answer.
2. Copy the table below into your own notes and fill in critical comments about the last two quotations.

Key Quotes

death roves our memories	Kinsella's memories of Dick King are constantly diverted into meditations about the passing of time and the inevitability of death. The verb 'roves' even suggests a ghost haunting him.
Kind plague	This apparent contradiction reminds us that the poet's tender love for his childhood friend is inseparable from the grief and sense of loss he feels.
My hand hidden in yours	The simplicity of the image conveys the trust and naturalness of the friendship between the elderly neighbour and the young child.
I squeeze your fingers	
The last to wish him well	

• Poetry Focus •

Mirror in February

The day dawns with scent of must and rain,
Of opened soil, dark trees, dry bedroom air.
Under the fading lamp, half dressed – my brain
Idling on some compulsive fantasy –
I towel my shaven jaw and stop, and stare,   5
Riveted by a dark exhausted eye,
A dry downturning mouth.

It seems again that it is time to learn,
In this untiring, crumbling place of growth
To which, for the time being, I return.   10
Now plainly in the mirror of my soul
I read that I have looked my last on youth
And little more; for they are not made whole
That reach the age of Christ.

Below my window the awakening trees,   15
Hacked clean for better bearing, stand defaced
Suffering their brute necessities,
And how should the flesh not quail that span for span
Is mutilated more? In slow distaste
I fold my towel with what grace I can,   20
Not young and not renewable, but man.

'Hacked clean for better bearing'

GLOSSARY

1 *must*: staleness.
2 *opened soil*: ploughed ground.
4 *compulsive*: compelling, obsessive.
6 *Riveted*: fixed, fascinated.
14 *age of Christ*: 33 years (the age Christ lived to).
16 *Hacked*: cut down, pruned.
18 *quail*: recoil, flinch.
18 *span*: stage, phase.
19 *mutilated*: disfigured, maimed.

EXPLORATIONS

1 Based on your reading of the poem, comment on the effectiveness of the title 'Mirror in February'.
2 In your view, does the poet find nature uplifting or depressing, or both? Give reasons for your answer.
3 Select one line (or image) from the poem to show the poet's keen eye for rich description. Comment briefly on the effectiveness of Kinsella's language.

STUDY NOTES

> The sudden awareness of lost youth is a recurring theme for many poets. 'Mirror in February' was written when Kinsella was in his early thirties. It is a haunting, disturbing yet beautiful reflection on the experience of growing older and on the dawning realisation that perfection evades everyone. Nature provides a background for the development of his soul-searching and his examination of life's great mysteries. Thomas Kinsella used mirrors in his poetry as a means of exploring inner and outward reflections of self.

The poem opens dramatically as Kinsella locates himself in a particular time and place. From the start of **stanza one**, his **elegantly sonorous tone defines the physical setting**: 'opened soil, dark trees, dry bedroom air'. A deep feeling of dejection is suggested by such **sensuous detail** and clashing vowels. Readers can clearly imagine the mouldy 'scent of must and rain'. In the mechanical routine of an early morning shave, the poet suddenly catches sight of his 'dark exhausted eye', the carefully chosen adjectives defining Kinsella's unflattering imagery. The poet's return to the familiar surroundings of an awakening orchard prompts him to consider the cycle of growth and decay. He seems caught between the world of dreams and reality ('Under the fading lamp, half dressed'), his world-weary voice emphasised by a laboured rhythm: 'I towel my shaven jaw and stop, and stare'. However, Kinsella is soon wrenched from his 'compulsive fantasy' to face the reality of ageing. His mood of **startled sullenness** is heightened by the repetition of 'dark' and 'dry', and more particularly by the alliterative sound of the deadening letter 'd'.

In **stanza two**, the poet's mood becomes more reflective as he contrasts himself with the natural world outside his window. Unlike the ploughed garden in springtime, he must accept that 'I have looked my last on youth'. While nature is paradoxically a 'crumbling place of growth', **his own decaying life will not be renewed**. Imagining a spiritual mirror in his soul, he is immediately disheartened by an inherent sense of failure. In contrast to Christ (who fulfilled his destiny on earth at the age of 33), Kinsella feels that he has achieved nothing. Instead, he recognises his own mortality and insignificance: 'I have looked my last on youth/And little more'. The **dismissive tone of this central image reveals an acute awareness of loss**. As in the first stanza, the final unrhymed line is strikingly abrupt, enhancing our understanding of his inner disorder.

Stanza three introduces another paradox, reminding the poet of his inescapable decline: 'the awakening trees,/Hacked clean for better bearing'. This vivid image illustrates the irony of natural regeneration and reflects Kinsella's own deep-rooted frustration. His **graphic diction** has underlying associations with Christ's suffering ('brute necessities', 'mutilated') and reflects a distasteful view of human existence. The rhetorical question 'And how should the flesh not quail that span for span/Is mutilated more?' is intensely dramatic and emphasises his revulsion.

There is a definite air of finality in the grudging gesture as Kinsella folds his towel 'with what grace I can'. The pun on 'grace' (referring to both God's blessing and his own unconvincing attempt to retain some dignity) is a reminder of the poet's droll humour. The poem concludes on a realistic note of stoical acceptance, with a dignified acknowledgement that he is 'Not young and not renewable, but man'. Kinsella's response to the realisation that he has looked his 'last on youth' is **open to several interpretations**, ranging from bitterness and self-mockery to courage and resignation. Whether we see the ending as triumph or defeat, there seems to be some hint of purpose as the poet comes to terms with the challenge of getting on with life.

ANALYSIS

'Mirror in February' provides a good example of Kinsella's sense of the dramatic. Discuss this view of the poem, supporting the points you make with reference to the text.

SAMPLE PARAGRAPH

There are many dramatic features in 'Mirror in February'. The poem has a distinctive setting – dawn in the bedroom of a country retreat where Kinsella has returned 'for the time being'. He himself is the central figure in the drama as he stares into the mirror and tries to make sense of his life. The present tense adds to the dramatic effect – 'The day dawns with scent of must and rain'. To me, Kinsella is experiencing a mid-life crisis, comparing himself with the orchard outside which is ironically coming to life again in springtime. The opening reminds me of a movie scene where a character confronts himself – 'I towel my shaven jaw and stop, and stare'. Kinsella's language is also highly compelling – especially his use of specific adjectives, such as 'dark', 'compulsive' and 'brute'. He is forced to accept that life is slipping by and he can do nothing about it. In a final dramatic action, he slowly folds the towel he is using and concludes that he has little choice but to make the most of his remaining years because like everyone else, he is 'not renewable, but man'. I thought that the mood and atmosphere were edgy throughout the poem – and a striking example of psychological drama.

EXAMINER'S COMMENT

A well-illustrated personal response that is firmly focused on the poem's dramatic qualities. Points about setting and style are made effectively and are nicely rounded off by the confident final sentence. Expression throughout the paragraph is clear and controlled. A-grade standard.

CLASS/HOMEWORK EXERCISES

1. Contrasts play an important part in the poetry of Thomas Kinsella. To what extent is this true of 'Mirror in February'? Refer to the poem in your answer.
2. Copy the table below into your own notes and fill in critical comments about the last two quotations.

• Poetry Focus •

Thomas Kinsella

Key Quotes

The day dawns with scent of must and rain	The early morning setting marks a blurred transition from sleep to waking in which Kinsella is poised dramatically between dreams and reality.
for they are not made whole/ That reach the age of Christ	Unlike Christ, the poet is mortal and imperfect and feels like a failure. Does this also mean that Kinsella feels Christianity has let him down?
the awakening trees	The personification of nature suggests spring's renewal and contrasts sharply with Kinsella's own sense of physical and spiritual decay.
this untiring, crumbling place of growth	
Not young and not renewable, but man	

Chrysalides

Our last free summer we mooned about at odd hours
Pedalling slowly through country towns, stopping to eat
Chocolate and fruit, tracing our vagaries on the map.

At night we watched in the barn, to the lurch of melodeon music,
The crunching boots of countrymen – huge and weightless
As their shadows – twirling and leaping over the yellow concrete.

Sleeping too little or too much, we awoke at noon
And were received with womanly mockery into the kitchen,
Like calves poking our faces in with enormous hunger.

Daily we strapped our saddlebags and went to experience
A tolerance we shall never know again, confusing
For the last time, for example, the licit and the familiar.

Our instincts blurred with change; a strange wakefulness
Sapped our energies and dulled our slow-beating hearts
To the extremes of feeling – insensitive alike

To the unique succession of our youthful midnights,
When by a window ablaze softly with the virgin moon
Dry scones and jugs of milk awaited us in the dark,

Or to lasting horror: a wedding flight of ants
Spawning to its death: a mute perspiration
Glistening like drops of copper, agonised, in our path.

'flight of ants/ Spawning to its death'

> **GLOSSARY**
>
> *Chrysalides* (plural of chrysalis): insect pupae, especially of moths or butterflies; the hard case enclosing this.
>
> 3 *vagaries*: unexpected and mysterious changes.
> 20 *Spawning*: releasing or depositing eggs.

EXPLORATIONS

1. The title of this poem is intriguing. What is unusual or interesting about the word 'chrysalides'? Does the word have any links with the rest of the poem? Support your response with reference to the text.
2. Which image in this poem appeals to you most? Give reasons for your choice.
3. In your opinion, where does the tone of the poem change? Why does this change take place? Refer closely to the text in your answer.

STUDY NOTES

> 'Chrysalides' first appeared in *Downstream*, published in 1962. In this collection, Kinsella developed ways of feeling and seeing that coped with his constrained universe. The book begins with an idealised portrait of domestic happiness, but then examines the destructive aspects of this world. The poet finds his own words and imagery for exploring the aggressive elements of his inner and outer world. Neither his struggles with himself nor his struggles with his poetry have been much affected by the examples of other writers.

The poem opens with a **celebration of young love**, tinged with melancholy, precisely because love itself and the lovers are subject to change ('Our last free summer'). The long vowel sounds in the phrase 'mooned about at odd hours' suggest the seemingly never-ending time of youthful love. Kinsella often associates love with eating, a satisfying of the senses, 'stopping to eat/Chocolate and fruit'. The lovers' early journeys were on a whim; there was no pre-planning or purpose; the world and time were theirs ('vagaries on the map')'. **Lines 1–3** vividly illustrate this idyllic time. **Lines 4–6** show the couple as observers, somewhat isolated as they watched the countrymen dancing. The lilting music is conveyed in the onomatopoeic verb 'lurch' and the soft alliterative 'm' sound in 'melodeon music'. The hard rasping of the big farmers' footsteps on cement is heard in the onomatopoeic phrase, 'The crunching boots'. An almost grotesque tableau now unfolds as the shadows of these men are described as 'twirling and leaping over yellow concrete'. There is no mention of the young couple joining in this strange dance.

Lines 7–9 also add to the **dreamy mood of the young couple**, 'Sleeping too little or too much'. They are greeted with 'womanly mockery' as they come looking for food. The simile 'Like calves poking our faces in with enormous hunger' reinforces the innocence and simplicity of the passionate young couple in contrast with the knowing women ('womanly mockery'). The couple are joined with the fundamental rhythms of the natural world as they strapped saddlebags on and 'went to experience/A tolerance we shall never know again'. Everything seemed right then, 'licit and ... familiar' (**line 12**), but that period of unthinking existence was coming swiftly to a close.

Lines 13–15 speak of a world when **humanity is placed within the perspective of time and space** and this calls attention to human littleness and impermanence. The verbs 'blurred', 'Sapped' and 'dulled' all show the destructive passage of time. The run-on line from **stanza five** to **six** shows how heedless the young were of their special time, 'insensitive alike/To the unique succession of our youthful midnights'. **Lines 16–18** give a magical picture of a romantic night, 'ablaze softly with the virgin moon'. The reference to 'virgin' further suggests the innocence of the young couple. The Irish scene of 'Dry scones and jugs of milk' awaiting the couple shows a world far removed from present-day Irish society. Does the adjective 'dry' point to more than the scones? Is it implying decay or death?

Lines 19–21 bring the poem to a **chilling state** as a flight of ants appear, 'Spawning to its death'. This is a favourite theme of Kinsella's, the recognition that there is life in death and death in life. Again, a detailed simile, 'Glistening like drops of copper', describes the hard shells of the ants as they journey on. They, too, like us, are agonised by the ordeal of life. The poem is open ended, as it does not reach a definite conclusion. Kinsella has examined an unendurable reality. Out of waste, he has tried to create beauty. By shaping experience into lyric form, he achieves a victory over mutability. The poet sees the world as flawed because his perception never allows him to forget the forces that take away innocence. The title of the poem refers to the little egg of an insect before it hatches, so the egg itself contains life, as does the young couple and even the ants. In the midst of life, there is death. Kinsella has remarked: 'I believe now, with a certain nervousness, that you simply go back from where you came from – which is nowhere.'

ANALYSIS

'Kinsella's work dramatises one man's varied relationship with a desolate universe in which there are great, if precarious, consolations.' Discuss this statement in relation to the poem 'Chrysalides'. Support your view with quotation and reference.

SAMPLE PARAGRAPH

This poem certainly contains the elements of a mini-drama. The scene is set firmly in the countryside in summer. The main characters are established as a young couple head-over-heels in love, 'Our last free summer we mooned about at odd hours'. Time nor place have touched this pair. The slow action is caught in the verbs 'mooned', 'Pedalling slowly' and 'tracing'. A leisurely pace is described. The desolation comes in the fifth stanza, although there have been warnings earlier, 'last', 'confusing … the licit and the familiar'. The reality of the transient nature of man is forensically described: 'blurred', 'Sapped'. They are unaware of the 'succession', time is passing. They are unaware also of the horror of this human existence which contains death in every breath we take. However, love is the consolation for Kinsella in this cold, unwelcoming world. But this consolation does not last. He uses the symbol of the ants breeding and dying on their wedding march as an effective illustration of the precarious nature of the consolation of love. It does not last.

EXAMINER'S COMMENT

This is a competent answer to a challenging question that focuses on the dramatic tension between the poet and his loved one as well as the relationship between the poet and the world. Although the lack of length does not allow for much development, expression is very good throughout. Grade B.

CLASS/HOMEWORK EXERCISES

1. 'To be able to write exploratory narratives that absorb particular surroundings is to clarify Kinsella's relationship with the outside world.' Discuss this statement in relation to 'Chrysalides'. Support your answer with reference to the text.
2. Copy the table below into your own notes and fill in critical comments about the last two quotations.

Key Quotes

tracing our vagaries on the map	The young lovers are leisurely exploring the countryside in a haphazard fashion.
Like calves poking our faces in with enormous hunger	This simile suggests youthful innocence and a natural desire to enjoy life to the full.
Our instincts blurred with change	The couple no longer live by their senses. Time has passed and they have changed.
insensitive alike/To the unique succession of our youthful midnights	
a wedding flight of ants/Spawning to its death	

• Poetry Focus •

from Glenmacnass: VI Littlebody

Thomas Kinsella

Up on the high road, as far as the sheepfold
into the wind, and back. The sides of the black bog channels
dug down in the water. The white cottonheads
on the old cuttings nodding everywhere.
Around one more bend, toward the car shining in the distance.   5

From a stony slope half way, behind a rock prow
with the stones on top for an old mark,
the music of pipes, distant and clear.

                    *

I was climbing up, making no noise
and getting close, when the music stopped,   10
leaving a pagan shape in the air.

There was a hard inhale,
a base growl,
and it started again, in a guttural dance.

I looked around the edge   15
– and it was Littlebody. Hugging his bag
under his left arm, with his eyes closed.

I slipped. Our eyes met.
He started scuttling up the slope with his gear
and his hump, elbows out and neck back.   20

But I shouted:
            'Stop, Littlebody!
I found you fair and I want my due.'

He stopped and dropped his pipes,
and spread his arms out, waiting for the next move.   25
I heard myself reciting:

'Demon dwarf
with the German jaw,
surrender your purse
with the ghostly gold.'   30

• 222 •

He took out a fat purse,
put it down on a stone
and recited in reply, in a voice too big for his body:

'You found me fair,
and I grant your wishes. 35
But we'll meet again,
when I dance in your ashes.'

He settled himself down once more
and bent over the bag,
                looking off to one side. 40

'I thought I was safe up here.
You have to give the music a while to itself sometimes,
up out of the huckstering

– jumping around in your green top hat
and showing your skills 45
with your eye on your income.'

He ran his fingers up and down the stops,
then gave the bag a last squeeze.
His face went solemn,

his fingertips fondled all the right places, 50
and he started a slow air
                out across the valley.

        *

I left him to himself.
And left the purse where it was.
I have all I need for the while I have left 55

without taking unnecessary risks.
And made my way down to the main road
with my mind on our next meeting.

• Poetry Focus •

Thomas Kinsella

'You have to give the music a while to itself sometimes'

GLOSSARY

1 *sheepfold*: enclosure or shelter for sheep.
3 *cottonheads*: bog cotton, hillside weeds.
6 *prow*: projecting area of land.
8 *pipes*: uilleann (elbow) pipes, traditional Irish instrument.
14 *guttural*: rough, rasping.
16 *his bag*: it was believed that a leprechaun carried a purse full of gold coins.
27 *Demon*: devil, mischievous sprite.
28 *German jaw*: square featured, obstinate.
37 *your ashes*: dead bones.
43 *huckstering*: selling cheap goods.
47 *stops*: stop keys on uilleann pipes.

EXPLORATIONS

1 What does the poem suggest to you about Thomas Kinsella's attitude to music and music-making? Refer to the text in your response.
2 Select one distinctly vivid or unusual image from the poem. Comment on its effectiveness.
3 Write a short personal response to the poem, highlighting its impact on you.

STUDY NOTES

Published in 2000, 'Littlebody' makes up one part of a longer sequence, 'Glenmacnass' (a scenic valley in Co. Wicklow). Kinsella is keen to celebrate both the beauty of the natural Irish landscape and to argue the importance of art for its own sake. The poem has a vibrant, dreamlike quality and is driven by what the poet Gerald Dawe called 'the complex accidental moment of the here and now'.

Kinsella's narrative opening – itself a tribute to Ireland's storytelling tradition – is set amid the remote windswept hillsides, 'Up on the high road'. The poet is drawn to this remote Irish landscape, a setting often associated with Celtic mythology, with its distinctive 'black bog channels' and 'white cottonheads' (lines 2 and 3). **He is attracted by the ruggedness of the terrain and the natural freedom it offers.** This is suggested by the broad vowel assonance ('rock prow', 'stones on top') and the many references to the barren terrain. Increasingly aware of the haunting atmosphere around him, Kinsella encounters another sound: 'the music of pipes, distant and clear' (line 8).

In his visionary experience, he is confronted with 'a pagan shape', a dancing leprechaun – 'it was Littlebody'. The roguish sprite ('eyes closed') is caught up in his own merry-making and seems intent on 'scuttling up the slope'. But Kinsella is tempted by the leprechaun's purse of gold and immediately tries to claim it: 'Stop, Littlebody!/I found you fair and I want my due' (lines 22–3). **The mood is both playful and antagonistic.** The music stops dramatically as the poet challenges the 'Demon dwarf' to hand over his 'ghostly gold'. The leprechaun surrenders the 'fat purse', but issues a sobering warning of the inevitable consequences: 'we'll meet again,/when I dance in your ashes'.

Littlebody goes on to explain himself further, criticising the poet for intruding on his music-making: 'I thought I was safe up here'. At this point, Kinsella's didactic voice takes over and he uses the exchange to illustrate an age-old conflict about art for art's sake. Music does not need an audience. **The leprechaun articulates the voice of the purist – 'You have to give the music a while to itself sometimes'** (line 42) – and takes Kinsella to task for his money-grabbing 'huckstering'. The tone here is particularly contemptuous. Littlebody also reprimands the poet for seeking affirmation among his own people and showing off in public: 'jumping around in your green top hat'. Clearly disgusted by such egotism and greed, the 'solemn' leprechaun takes refuge in his own music and plays a 'slow air' that reaches 'out across the valley' (lines 51 and 52).

While self-deprecation marks Kinsella's sardonic tone throughout this whimsical tale, he ends on a serious note, leaving Littlebody 'to himself' and 'the purse where it was'. Clearly recognising that **genuine art should not be compromised**, neither for fame nor fortune, he comes to an important conclusion: 'I have all I need for the while I have left' (line 55). This realisation brings a deep feeling of contentment, allowing the poet to return to his ordinary life 'without taking unnecessary risks', but wondering about the 'next meeting' – after death – when he is likely to come face to face with Littlebody again.

Having committed most of his adult life to his own art as poet and translator, Kinsella's views are as clear as they are predictable. For him, the pursuit of 'income' and publicity are false rewards that are untrue to himself. The poem's final lines are heartfelt, a gentle reminder that death is always closer than we think – and that **the artist should therefore make the most of the creative impulse**, just as Littlebody's 'fingertips fondled all the right places'.

ANALYSIS

'Kinsella's poetry is primarily concerned with the artistic experience.' Discuss this view with particular reference to 'Littlebody'.

SAMPLE PARAGRAPH

I enjoyed reading Kinsella's fairytale poem, 'Littlebody'. The poem was really a moral story, making the point that music is a reward in itself. Kinsella is often said to be obscure and difficult to understand, but in this poem, the meaning is clear enough. To my mind, Littlebody represents the real artist, totally into his music – 'the music of pipes, distant and clear'. The gold under his arm is of no interest to him, except to warn him of false musicians who are only interested in payment or cheap notoriety – 'huckstering'. To my mind, the main theme is that such an interest in 'ghostly gold' will be the end of any true artist. Luckily, the speaker who is almost fooled by the attraction of the fairy's 'fat purse' gets sense in the end and realises that he will have wasted his creative and imaginative talent. Fortunately, he reconsiders his situation and saves himself just in time – 'And left the purse where it was'. This is Kinsella's key point – the real artist must put his or her work first – this is the process that is most important. Littlebody himself is a good example of this – he works hard playing the pipes – 'eyes closed'. To my mind, this concentration and commitment represent Kinsella's own philosophy and his fairy story demonstrates this very well for the ordinary reader.

EXAMINER'S COMMENT

A good attempt at addressing the question directly. Apt references and quotations are used effectively in supporting the poet's central point about the importance of the artistic process. The language lacks control in places and there is some repetition. Grade B.

CLASS/HOMEWORK EXERCISES

1. 'Conflict between opposing forces is central to much of Kinsella's writing.' To what extent is this true of 'Littlebody'? Support the points you make with reference to the poem.
2. Copy the table below into your own notes and fill in critical comments about the last two quotations.

Key Quotes

the music of pipes, distant and clear	Slender vowels and soft sibilance give a special musical quality, creating a pleasant mood.
There was a hard inhale,/a base growl	Playing the pipes takes great effort and Littlebody works hard to make music. The harsh onomatopoeic effects suggest the labour involved in the artistic process.
I have all I need for the while I have left	The speaker in the poem (presumably Kinsella himself) resists the temptation to 'sell' his artistic soul.
You have to give the music a while to itself sometimes	
my mind on our next meeting	

• Poetry Focus •

Tear

Thomas Kinsella

I was sent in to see her.
A fringe of jet drops
chattered at my ear
as I went in through the hangings.

I was swallowed in chambery dusk.　　　　　　　5
My heart shrank
at the smell of disused
organs and sour kidney.

The black aprons I used to
bury my face in　　　　　　　　　　　　　　　　10
were folded at the foot of the bed
in the last watery light from the window

(Go in and say goodbye to her)
and I was carried off
to unfathomable depths.　　　　　　　　　　　　15
I turned to look at her.

She stared at the ceiling
and puffed her cheek, distracted,
propped high in the bed
resting for the next attack.　　　　　　　　　　　20

The covers were gathered close
up to her mouth,
that the lines of ill-temper still
marked. Her grey hair

was loosened out like a young woman's　　　　　25
all over the pillow,
mixed with the shadows
criss-crossing her forehead

and at her mouth and eyes,
like a web of strands tying down her head　　　30
and tangling down toward the shadow
eating away the floor at my feet.

I couldn't stir at first, nor wished to,
for fear she might turn and tempt me
(my own father's mother) 35
with open mouth

– with some fierce wheedling whisper –
to hide myself one last time
against her, and bury my
self in her drying mud. 40

Was I to kiss her? As soon
kiss the damp that crept
in the flowered walls
of this pit.

Yet I had to kiss. 45
I knelt by the bulk of the death bed
and sank my face in the chill
and smell of her black aprons.

Snuff and musk, the folds against my eyelids,
carried me into a derelict place 50
smelling of ash: unseen walls and roofs
rustled like breathing.

I found myself disturbing
dead ashes for any trace
of warmth, when far off 55
in the vaults a single drop

splashed. And I found
what I was looking for
– not heat nor fire,
not any comfort, 60

but her voice, soft, talking to someone
about my father: 'God help him, he cried
big tears over there by the machine
for the poor little thing.' Bright

drops on the wooden lid
for my infant sister.
My own wail of child-animal grief
was soon done, with any early guess

at sad dullness and tedious pain
and lives bitter with hard bondage.
How I tasted it now –
her heart beating in my mouth!

She drew an uncertain breath
and pushed at the clothes
and shuddered tiredly.
I broke free

and left the room
promising myself
when she was really dead
I would really kiss.

My grandfather half looked up
from the fireplace as I came out,
and shrugged and turned back
with a deaf stare to the heat.

I fidgeted beside him for a minute
and went out to the shop.
It was still bright there
and I felt better able to breathe.

Old age can digest
anything: the commotion
at Heaven's gate – the struggle
in store for you all your life.

How long and hard it is
before you get to Heaven,
unless like little Agnes
you vanish with early tears.

• Leaving Certificate English •

Thomas Kinsella

'She drew an uncertain breath'

GLOSSARY

- 5 *chambery*: closeted, enclosed.
- 15 *unfathomable*: immeasurable, unknowable.
- 19 *propped*: raised, supported.
- 20 *attack*: sickness, coughing fit.
- 30 *strands*: stray hair, tresses.
- 37 *wheedling*: coaxing, demanding.
- 49 *Snuff*: powdered tobacco.
- 49 *musk*: greasy odour.
- 50 *derelict*: neglected, dilapidated.
- 70 *bondage*: suffering, hardship.
- 90 *commotion*: fuss, turmoil.

EXPLORATIONS

1. Select one image from the poem that evokes the boy's sense of discomfort in the presence of his dying grandmother. Comment on its effectiveness.
2. From your reading of the poem, what do you understand by the phrase 'her heart beating in my mouth' (line 72)?
3. Comment on the ending of the poem. In your opinion, what is Kinsella's attitude to the cycle of life and death? Refer to the text in your answer.

STUDY NOTES

Kinsella has written that his grandparents 'seemed very dark in themselves'. He described his grandmother as a 'formidable' woman who managed a small shop in Dublin. 'Tear' is taken from his 1973 collection, *New Poems,* in which he explored some of his earliest 'awarenesses' and absorbed 'the textures of life'. For a very young observer, some random details were hard to grasp fully, but were equally hard to forget. This collection marked a striking change in the poet's style, especially a preference for writing in free verse.

• Poetry Focus •

Thomas Kinsella

The poet begins his childhood memory of visiting his grandmother as she lay dying in the 'chambery dusk' (line 5). From the outset, we are plunged into a suffocating household environment, **a world of urgent unease**: 'My heart shrank'. The scene is recalled with intense clarity, with Kinsella's detailed recollection of fearful reluctance bordering on revulsion. Time is subtly and sensitively suspended. Feeling out of place and powerless ('I was sent', 'I was swallowed', 'I was carried off'), he recalls being overwhelmed by the experience and focuses on such 'unfathomable' sensations as 'the smell of disused/organs'.

Already confused by the order to 'say goodbye to her' (line 13), he is shocked by the appearance of the 'distracted' old lady who seems strangely unfamiliar. The young boy narrator is particularly **startled by her age and decrepitude**. He notices her 'puffed' cheek and her grey hair 'loosened out like a young woman's'. The onset of death is suggested by images of wrinkled skin, wayward strands of hair 'tying down her head' and 'shadows/criss-crossing her forehead'. Kinsella dramatises the scene: 'I couldn't stir at first'. The grandmother figure lies on her deathbed in the half-light that threatens to engulf the young boy. He is horrified at the prospect of having to draw close to the dying woman, who has suddenly become 'fierce', her skin resembling 'drying mud' (line 40).

The poet exaggerates the eerie atmosphere. His childish dilemma over what he should do ('Was I to kiss her?') is eventually resolved when the boy finds strength ('any trace/of warmth') in another memory ('a derelict place/smelling of ash'), where he can again relate to the grandmother he once loved. For the first time, we hear the old lady's voice commenting on an earlier tragedy – the death of the poet's infant sister. For the poet, **the traumatic occasion is marked by the tears of three generations**, unified in helpless sorrow. Kinsella is deeply moved by the grandmother's compassion for his distraught father: 'God help him, he cried/big tears' (lines 62–3). In retrospect, the poet is able to understand how this life-shaping occurrence made sense of his own 'wail of child-animal grief' and strengthened his awareness of family history, identified by 'lives bitter with hard bondage' (line 70).

The experience is a turning point for Kinsella, propelling him into the past and offering him a clearer grasp of his own identity. It is no longer the grandmother who is the centre of attention, but the child poet's awed perception of her: 'How I tasted it now –/her heart beating in my mouth'. This is a **coming of age episode** that he recollects as a moment of liberation: 'I broke free' (line 76). Characteristically, for a poet associated with self-preoccupation,

Kinsella's writing style is often fragmentary, with multiple voices jostling for attention.

The closing section of the poem records his exit from the bedroom in a precise series of friezes. Although there is no direct communication with his grandfather ('I fidgeted beside him for a minute'), the earlier sense of terror has disappeared. Retreating to the small family shop, Kinsella remembers feeling 'better able to breathe' (line 88). But **he now acknowledges the resilience and wisdom of his grandparents**: 'Old age can digest/anything'. The poet concludes by paying tribute to all the previous generations who were never far removed from death ('the commotion/at Heaven's gate'). Kinsella's final thoughts are a poignant reminder of his personal heartache at the loss of his young sister. Ironically, unlike her grandmother, who endured a long life of hardship, 'little Agnes' was destined to 'vanish with early tears'.

ANALYSIS

'Although Thomas Kinsella is associated with obscure introspection, his poetry has a universal significance.' Discuss this statement with particular reference to 'Tear'. Refer to the text of the poem in your answer.

SAMPLE PARAGRAPH

I thought 'Tear' was obscure and hard to understand in places, but the main narrative of the poem was very moving and did have some significance for me. Kinsella describes two deaths in his family, his grandmother and his infant sister. As a boy, he was terrified by the dying figure of his sick grandmother. The images he recalls fill him with fear and revulsion – 'the smell of disused/organs', 'black aprons'. Young children are still terrified of the unknown. Kinsella was totally unaware of how changed his grandmother had become as she drew close to death. Yet by remembering a time when the old woman had been sympathetic to his father during the funeral of 'little Agnes', the poet's sister, Kinsella is able to see a more human side to his grandmother. The whole experience helped him to develop and learn about the reality of death. I found the poem interesting because it was really a sequence of dramatic moments. These reflected the intensity of what the poet had experienced and it felt almost timeless. I think we all store memories in this way – almost like dramatic fragments, and that is why the poem does have a wider relevance. All of us are faced with time passing and the reality of death.

EXAMINER'S COMMENT

This is a competent response to a challenging question. The answer takes a personal approach and attempts to remain focused, although more discussion of Kinsella's soul-searching would have been useful. The expression is reasonably well controlled overall. Grade-B standard.

CLASS/HOMEWORK EXERCISES

1. Kinsella has said that his three themes are love, death and the poetic process. To what extent is this true of 'Tear'? Support your answer with reference to the poem.
2. Copy the table below into your own notes and fill in critical comments about the last two quotations.

Key Quotes

I was swallowed in chambery dusk	The metaphor highlights the young boy's traumatic sense of foreboding and dread as he entered his dying grandmother's darkened room.
the shadows/criss-crossing her forehead	Symbols of darkness are used throughout the poem to suggest fear and menace.
'God help him, he cried/big tears over there by the machine/for the poor little thing.'	Complex personal relationships are at the heart of the poem. The grandmother's sensitivity towards his grieving father humanises her again in Kinsella's eyes.
I broke free	
Old age can digest/anything: the commotion/at Heaven's gate	

Hen Woman

The noon heat in the yard
smelled of stillness and coming thunder.
A hen scratched and picked at the shore.
It stopped, its body crouched and puffed out.
The brooding silence seemed to say 'Hush...'

The cottage door opened,
a black hole
in a whitewashed wall so bright
the eyes narrowed.
Inside, a clock murmured 'Gong...'

(I had felt all this before.)

She hurried out in her slippers
muttering, her face dark with anger,
and gathered the hen up jerking
languidly. Her hand fumbled.
Too late. Too late.

It fixed me with its pebble eyes
(seeing what mad blur).
A white egg showed in the sphincter;
mouth and beak opened together;
and time stood still.

Nothing moved: bird or woman,
fumbled or fumbling – locked there
(as I must have been) gaping.

*

There was a tiny movement at my feet,
tiny and mechanical; I looked down.
A beetle like a bronze leaf
was inching across the cement,
clasping with small tarsi
a ball of dung bigger than its body.

The serrated brow pressed the ground humbly,
lifted in a short stare, bowed again;
the dung-ball advanced minutely,
losing a few fragments,
specks of staleness and freshness.   35

*

A mutter of thunder far off
– time not quite stopped.
I saw the egg had moved a fraction:
a tender blank brain
under torsion, a clean new world.   40

As I watched, the mystery completed.
The black zero of the orifice
closed to a point
and the white zero of the egg hung free,
flecked with greenish brown oils.   45

It fell and turned over slowly.
Dreamlike, fussed by her splayed fingers,
it floated outward, moon-white,
leaving no trace in the air,
and began its drop to the shore.   50

*

I feed upon it still, as you see;
there is no end to that which, not understood,
may yet be hoarded in the imagination,
in the yolk of one's being, so to speak,
there to undergo its (quite animal) growth,   55

dividing blindly, twitching, packed with will,
searching in its own tissue
for the structure in which it may wake.
Something that had – clenched in its cave –
not been now as was: an egg of being.   60

Through what seemed a whole year it fell
– as it still falls, for me, solid and light,
the red gold beating in its silvery womb,
alive as the yolk and white of my eye.
As it will continue to fall, probably, until I die,   65
through the vast indifferent spaces
with which I am empty.

*

It smashed against the grating
and slipped down quickly out of sight.
It was over in a comical flash.   70
The soft mucous shell clung a little longer,
then drained down.

She stood staring, in blank anger.
Then her eyes came to life, and she laughed
and let the bird flap away.   75

    'It's all the one.
There's plenty more where that came from!'

'fussed by her splayed fingers'

GLOSSARY

19 *sphincter*: a ring of muscle that surrounds an opening.
29 *tarsi*: groups of small bones in the ankle or foot.
31 *serrated*: having a jagged edge like the tooth of a saw.
40 *torsion*: the action of twisting or being twisted.
42 *orifice*: an opening in a body.
47 *splayed*: spread out.
71 *mucous*: slimy substance used for lubrication or protection.

EXPLORATIONS

1. The opening of this poem is a mini-drama. Comment on the poet's use of setting, atmosphere, characters and action. Support your response with reference from the poem.
2. The poet reflects on the motion of the falling egg. What, in your opinion, does this symbolise for Kinsella? Quote from the poem to support your views.
3. Two lines of dialogue end the poem. Is this an effective conclusion to this open-ended work? Refer closely to the text in your answer.

STUDY NOTES

'Hen Woman' comes from Thomas Kinsella's collection *New Poems*, published in 1973. He is among the most innovative poets in modern Ireland. He regularly touches on one of the most difficult aspects of contemporary life, isolation, which is very much part of the human condition. This, together with the theme of disappointment, pervades much of Kinsella's writing. He is experimental, bringing touches of international modernism to Irish verse.

In his short memoir, *A Dublin Documentary*, Thomas Kinsella spoke of a 'world dominated' by people, some of whom were 'formidable women', both family and neighbours: 'I remember many things of importance happening to me for the first time. And it is in their world that I came to terms with these things as best I could, and later set my attempts at understanding.' He speaks of 'taking in the textures of life in their random detail'. Kinsella is a poet of place, 'the yard outside, a silent square courtyard at the back, off Basin Lane, with a couple of white-washed cottages in the corners, with half-doors. A separate world, with a few other people. And cats and hens and a feel of the country. A whole place that has long disappeared.' **This place becomes a mindscape as well as a real place,** with the poet using it as a vehicle for understanding his own identity, separate from yet part of a whole community.

Readers are presented with an extraordinarily **detailed recollection of Kinsella's childhood** 'with a deliberate troubled intensity of focus that slows time down and creates a series of friezes'. Immediately, urgently, we are part of this world without introduction or preamble. The scene is set in a hot backyard, with the threat of thunder in the background. A hen scratches the ground. A woman appears in a doorway. A clock strikes. Kinsella himself comments on the poem as a 'scene ridiculous in its content, but of early awareness of self and process: of details insisting on their survival, regardless of any immediate significance'. One approach to this poem would be to divide it into four sections: **lines 1–24**, the opening drama; **lines 25–50**, the moment of birth/being; **lines 51–67**, furious rumination in an urge to know; and **lines 68–77**, the open-ended conclusion. This fragmentary poem falls within a defined structural design.

In this poem, the 'I', **a watchful attender**, tells the story as a witness. The tone is serious, brooding, alert and perceptive. The small event of the falling egg is noted and the trivial scene is packed with significance. In **lines 1–24**, the narrative freezes the moment: the woman hurries out, the egg falls and breaks in slow motion ('time stood still'). All three characters (poet, woman and hen) are caught: 'locked there … gaping'. The **dramatic tension** is caught in the brooding atmosphere, conveyed vividly by the sensuous sibilant 's' ('stillness', 'silence'). This is the calm before the storm. The setting is shown as a series of contrasts between the blinding white of the walls and the mysterious darkness of the 'black hole' shown when the cottage door opens. Time present and past is referenced: 'a clock murmured' and 'I had felt all this before'. Suddenly a storm erupts in the form of an irate woman, 'her face dark with anger'. The theme of disappointment is emphasised: 'Too late. Too late'. The **dynamic detail** is described when the hen 'fixed me with its pebble eyes'. The effort of creation, 'mouth and beak opened together', is conveyed as the hen tried to lay the egg. The white spaces between the solitary and conclusive asterisks seem to be as much a part of the drama as the written text is. Readers are being invited to remain within that silence before proceeding to the next moment that has grown out of it.

In **lines 25–50**, **the tiny movement suggests life**. The poet's mind is arrested by the detail of 'A beetle like a bronze leaf'. The verbs 'inching' and 'clasping' show that even the smallest creature contains the impulse of life. The minute observation of the poet, 'clasping with small tarsi/a ball of dung bigger than its body', draws the reader to look closely at the little insect. Even its brow is noted: 'serrated'. Kinsella's child/poet is fascinated by the dignity of the insect as it goes about its business ('pressed the ground humbly'). The **sharply focused attention on detail contrasts with the blurred narrative**. The back-stories are not told. Another asterisk leads us gently into the next section.

Poetry Focus

Thomas Kinsella

The **tension grows** as the silence of the first section gives way to the 'mutter of thunder', an effective personification of the grumbling sky. Time is passing, 'not quite stopped'. The child/poet sees that the egg is moving, ready to be released. Forceful onomatopoeia in the word 'torsion' conveys the twisting movement as the egg struggles to escape. Now the egg hangs free, a 'white zero'. Is Kinsella describing its shape? Or saying that it is nothing, as it has not yet experienced the world? Is it 'a tender blank'? The **movement of the falling egg is dreamlike** as it floats through space, making its bid for a separate identity. Do you think this detail references Kinsella's own bid for separate identity?

Lines 51–67 show **detail becoming a single impulse to find 'structure'** for the poet's 'mess of angers'. 'I feed upon it still, as you see'. Kinsella's poems are experienced rather than understood. This relentless urge to know, the 'yolk of one's being', is the poet's inward journey and its impetus is graphically caught in the description 'twitching, packed with will,/searching in its own tissue/for the structure in which it may wake'. This searching into the substance is presented as part of the way in which the imagination seizes experience and takes it in. The egg, before release, was 'clenched in its cave'. Then it was not – but now it is – 'an egg of being'. Kinsella felt that after each new beginning we are 'penetrating our context to know ourselves'. But this is doomed to disappointment. Is it the fate of the watchful to be disappointed? Is this poem **a progress towards exhaustion and disillusionment**? Does the process continue until we fail? Echoes of T.S. Eliot's 'The Waste Land' resonate in the final lines of this section: 'through the vast indifferent spaces/with which I am empty'. The terror of modern alienation is exposed.

The final section, **lines 68–77**, deals with the **inevitability of destruction** in this existence: 'It smashed against the grating'. Life's brief experience is depicted as being almost funny: 'over in a comical flash'. Now the woman's anger evaporates as the poem concludes with her comment that nothing matters, 'It's all the one'. She comforts herself with the thought that there will be more eggs: 'There's plenty more where that came from'. Is Kinsella also consoling himself that life continues despite its endings? Is there anything more to come? Is there no end to discovering oneself?

The vibrant and dynamic **use of colourful imagery** shimmers through this fragmented narrative. Stark black and white (the mystery of 'a black hole', the blinding brightness of 'a whitewashed wall') moves to the dull glow of bronze, 'A beetle like a bronze leaf'. The black and white contrast emerges again in the description of the laying of the egg: a 'white zero' from the 'black zero'. It attains an almost surreal existence of opposites as the egg floats 'moon-white'. The mucous slime of nature clinging to the egg is evoked in the phrase 'greenish brown oils'. The life within the egg, 'the red gold beating', glows warmly in contrast to the cool paleness of the egg's 'silvery womb'. Kinsella's adept use of colour to clearly etch detail resonates in our consciousness long after the poem is read. So where is the end? Does Kinsella's poem confound the usual expectation of resolution?

ANALYSIS

'The energy of Kinsella's poetry comes from the mind arrested by detail.' Discuss this statement in relation to the poem 'Hen Woman'. Support your views with reference and quotation.

SAMPLE PARAGRAPH

I totally agree with this statement, because I think that Kinsella, through his minute observation and cinematic detail, draws the eye of the reader down to observe the minutiae of life almost as if looking through a powerful magnifying glass. One detail which captured my attention was his energetic description of the 'tiny and mechanical' beetle carrying the ball of dung. To me it represents the potential of life as well as the waste of death. I liked the simile 'A beetle like a bronze leaf'. The hard 'b' sound reminded me of the hard scaly outer casing of the little beetle, and the adjective 'bronze' suggested the flat shimmer of its little body. Kinsella carefully describes the delicate movement of the insect, 'inching across the cement' as it goes methodically and carefully about its business, 'clasping with small tarsi'. There seems to be a note of admiration for the hard-working insect as we are told it carried a ball of dung 'bigger than its body'. The strange beauty of the beetle is captured in the adjective 'serrated', which is used to describe the jagged appearance of its brow. The dignity of the insect is shown by its polite actions, 'pressed the ground humbly', 'bowed again'. The child/poet is fascinated by its efforts, 'the dung-ball advanced minutely'. In this hushed moment, time slows down, as reader, poet and beetle are 'locked' into the effort of this activity. The energy of Kinsella's poetry comes from the clarity of its detail.

EXAMINER'S COMMENT

This paragraph shows a sensitive reading of Kinsella's poetry. A clear focus on the task is maintained throughout in this fluent response, which comments well on the effectiveness of style features such as similes and adjectives. Grade A.

CLASS/HOMEWORK EXERCISES

1 'For poets, place is always as much a mindscape as it is a landscape.' Discuss this statement in relation to 'Hen Woman' by Thomas Kinsella. Support your answer with close reference to the poem.
2 Copy the table below into your own notes and fill in critical comments about the last two quotations.

Key Quotes

A hen scratched and picked at the shore	The onomatopoeic verbs 'scratched' and 'picked' allow the reader to hear the minute scraping sound of the action of the hen in this tense little drama.
(I had felt all this before.)	Time fades out from its chronological line as the poet experiences the same thoughts and sensations again.
clasping with small tarsi	The unusual word 'tarsi', describing the little feet of the insect, emphasises the strangeness of familiar objects when examined in detail.
an egg of being	
'It's all the one./There's plenty more where that came from!'	

His Father's Hands

Thomas Kinsella

I drank firmly
and set the glass down between us firmly.
You were saying.

My father
Was saying. 5

His finger prodded and prodded,
marring his point. Emphas-
emphasemphasis.

I have watched
his father's hands before him 10

      cupped, and tightening the black Plug
between knife and thumb,
carving off little curlicues
to rub them in the dark of his palms,

or cutting into new leather at his bench, 15
levering a groove open with his thumb,
insinuating wet sprigs for the hammer.

He kept the sprigs in mouthfuls
and brought them out in silvery
units between his lips. 20

I took a pinch out of their hole
and knocked them one by one into the wood,
bright points among hundreds gone black,
other children's – cousins and others, grown up.

      Or his bow hand scarcely moving, 25
scraping in the dark corner near the fire,
his plump fingers shifting on the strings.

To his deaf, inclined head
he hugged the fiddle's body

whispering with the tune
with breaking heart
whene'er I hear
in privacy, across a blocked void,

the wind that shakes the barley.
The wind...
round her grave...

on my breast in blood she died...
But blood for blood without remorse
I've ta'en...

Beyond that.

*

Your family, Thomas, met with and helped
many of the Croppies in hiding from the Yeos
or on their way home after the defeat
in south Wexford. They sheltered the Laceys
who were later hanged on the Bridge in Ballinglen
between Tinahely and Anacorra.

From hearsay, as far as I can tell
the Men Folk were either Stone Cutters
or masons or probably both.
                    In the 18
and late 1700s even the farmers
had some other trade to make a living.

They lived in Farnese among a Colony
of North of Ireland or Scotch settlers left there
in some of the dispersions or migrations
which occurred in this Area of Wicklow and Wexford
and Carlow. And some years before that time
the Family came from somewhere around Tullow.

Beyond that.

*

Littered uplands. Dense grass. Rocks everywhere,　　60
wet underneath, retaining memory of the long cold.
First, a prow of land
chosen, and wedged with tracks;
then boulders chosen
and sloped together, stabilized in menace.　　65

I do not like this place.
I do not think the people who lived here
were ever happy. It feels evil.
Terrible things happened.
I feel afraid here when I am on my own.　　70

　　　　　　　*

Dispersals or migrations.
Through what evolutions or accidents
toward that peace and patience
by the fireside, that blocked gentleness...

That serene pause, with the slashing knife,　　75
in kindly mockery,
as I busy myself with my little nails
at the rude block, his bench.

The blood advancing
– gorging vessel after vessel –　　80
and altering in them
one by one.

Behold, that gentleness already
modulated twice, in others:
to earnestness and iteration;　　85
to an offhandedness, repressing various impulses.

　　　　　　　*

Extraordinary... The big block – I found it
years afterward in a corner of the yard
in sunlight after rain

and stood it up, wet and black: 90
it turned under my hands, an axis
of light flashing down its length,
and the wood's soft flesh broke open,
countless little nails
squirming and dropping out of it. 95

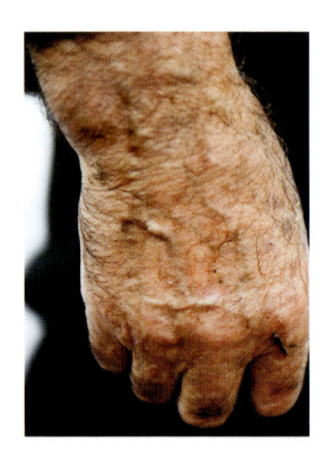

'his father's hands'

GLOSSARY

11 *Plug*: piece of solid tobacco.
13 *curlicues*: decorative curls or twists.
17 *sprigs*: wedge-shaped nails often used for mending shoes.
21 *pinch*: a number of nails that can be held between finger and thumb.
42 *Croppies*: name of Irish rebels in 1798 Rebellion.
42 *Yeos*: yeomen, a volunteer force in the British army, composed mainly of wealthy farmers.
62 *prow*: pointed front part of land or a ship.
85 *iteration*: to do or say repeatedly.

EXPLORATIONS

1 The repetition in lines 1–8 contribute to a mood of confrontation and masculine posturing. How does Kinsella's language convey this? Support your response with reference to the poem.

2 How many generations of the Kinsella family are mentioned in the poem? How does this illustrate the poet's theme of continuity? Pay particular attention to the action of the hands, which helps to illustrate this. Refer closely to the text in your answer.

3 Write a personal response to this poem, using reference and quotation to illustrate your views.

• Leaving Certificate English •

STUDY NOTES

'His Father's Hands' comes from Thomas Kinsella's collection *New Poems*, published in 1973. Kinsella contextualised the poem in his memoir, *A Dublin Documentary*: 'The details absorb their own order. It was later in life, when I was on equal terms with my father, that something else important out of that early time became clear: the dignity and quiet of his own father, remembered as we talked about him. With an awareness of the generations as they succeed each other. That process, with the accompanying awareness, recorded and understood, is a vital element in life as I see it now.'

Thomas Kinsella

Kinsella **remembers an occasion he shared with his father**. The atmosphere in **lines 1–24** is tense. This is emphasised by the repetition of the adverb 'firmly' to describe the action of the poet as he drank and set down his glass. Father and son mirror each other's obstinacy. 'You were saying' is a common phrase used between men socialising in pubs. The poet shows the forceful presence of his father by the repetition of 'saying'; there is also a sense of family pride in 'My father'. Repetition is used to describe the earnest conversation as his father seeks to drive home his point, 'His fingers prodded and prodded'. A new compound word adds to the very serious conversation: 'Emphas-/emphasemphasis'. The scene changes in **line 9**; the poet is now watching his grandfather. Has the conversation ignited this picture? The grandfather is cutting slivers off a hard piece of solid tobacco, 'the black Plug'.

Then the poet remembers another action, of his grandfather cutting 'new leather' (**line 15**). Again, tiny pieces are shaved off. Although this refers to mending shoes, which many people used to do at home in this period in Dublin, the poet's grandfather was a barge-pilot on the tugs that ran between Guinness's brewery and the sea-going vessels in Dublin Port. This was regarded in the community as a steady job. Kinsella is coaxing the reader to follow him in search of understanding, as he has said, 'back to the dark/and the depth that I came from'. He is arrested by detail as he tells stories, each of which is minutely particularised. The timeline becomes blurred, as the poet recalls his action that repeats his grandfather's action as he mended the family shoes: 'I took a pinch'. Kinsella also knocked in the nails ('sprigs'), as others in his family had done before him.

This **is a poem of 'blood and family'** with sharply focused attention on details of damp places and people, and yet at the same time it is slightly blurred, like

• 247 •

Poetry Focus

Thomas Kinsella

old sepia photographs. Kinsella has said, 'I always remembered/who and what I am'. In **lines 25–40**, the poet recalls another action of his grandfather, playing the violin, 'his plump fingers shifting on the strings'. The onomatopoeic 'scraping' allows the reader to hear the shrill tone of the old fiddle as the grandfather gives a rendition of a traditional Irish tune, 'the wind that shakes the barley'. This song is written from the perspective of a young Wexford rebel who is about to sacrifice his relationship with his loved one and plunge into the cauldron of violence associated with the 1798 rebellion in Ireland. The reference to barley in the song also alludes to the fact that barley often marked the 'croppy-holes', mass unmarked graves into which the slain rebels were thrown. This symbolised the regenerative nature of Irish resistance to British rule. Kinsella adopts **the lyrics of the song as a metaphor for Ireland's tragic past**. In contrast to the sharp tone of the fiddle, the grandfather is 'whispering', almost like the soft surge of the wind through the crops. Both poet and grandfather are brought back 'with breaking heart' by the words of the song to another time, 'Beyond that'.

An asterisk leads us into the family's past. Kinsella places asterisks in this poem almost like pinpricks of light to lead the way into his past. The poet is keen to share his thinking process through the different, strongly defined subsections. An uncle of Kinsella's, Jack Brophy, **recorded part of the family's history** as follows: 'The Men Folk were either Stone Cutters or Masons, or probably both. In the 17 and late 1800s, even the Farmers had some other trade to make a living. The Kinsellas lived in Farnese … among a colony of North of Ireland or Scotch settlers left there in some of the dispersals, or migrations which occurred in this Area of Wicklow, Wexford and Carlow, even after the '98 Rebellion of which this part was a centre, between two big Battles, Hacketstown and Ballyrahan … The Kinsellas met with and helped many of the Croppies in hiding from the Yeos or on their way home after the defeat in south Wexford. And some years before that time the Family came from somewhere round Tullow.'

Most of this passage (**lines 41–59**) is an almost verbatim account of the family history written by Kinsella's uncle. The horror of the sacrifice of these people is couched in **simple, unadorned language**: 'They sheltered the Laceys/who were later hanged on the Bridge in Ballinglen/between Tinahely and Anacorra'. This reinforces the terror of these times, but the lines have their own music due to the lilting polysyllables of the Irish place names: 'Ballinglen', 'Tinahely', 'Anacorra'. Is Kinsella asking us to consider whether the land was worth this sacrifice? Again, we are invited to travel back, 'Beyond that', as the second asterisk beckons us to observe closely the actuality of this place.

Lines 60–70 describe **a landscape that is 'Littered'**. Does it contain more than the rocks strewn 'everywhere'? Is it holding the stories of the past and its people as it retains the 'memory of the long cold'? Does this refer to the cold of the 'wet' ground or the cold dead bodies of those 'hanged' and defeated? The verbs 'wedged' and 'stabilized' suggest persistence. Who was persisting, the Yeos or the Croppies, or both? There is a sense of threat ('menace') and the poet admits, 'I do not like this place'. Kinsella felt that an individual must engage with evil, absorb it and transmute it. He believes the people were never happy here. 'It feels evil'. He is scared: 'I feel afraid here when I am on my own'.

Lines 71–86 echo an earlier part of the poem, 'Dispersals or migrations'. This ground from where Kinsella's family emerged was **a place of flux and change**, as people moved here and there. But the 'blocked void' of the earlier section of the poem changes to 'blocked gentleness', and calm returns, 'That serene pause'. This is a welcome respite from the savagery of the past contained in the detail of 'the slashing knife'. In the present day, this knife does not murder as it did in the past; now the poet's hands re-enact his grandfather's actions, 'as I busy myself with my little nails/at the rude block, his bench'. The scene melts at the edges as the stagger and recovery of the spirit is described in the metaphor of 'The blood advancing/– gorging vessel after vessel –/and altering in them/one by one'. Evil is being transmuted to gentleness as the blood passes through the generations, 'modulated twice'. Successively, they perform the same action, 'iteration'. Blood, a link with primal sources, is part of both an impersonal biological and a personal social inheritance. These **disturbing images lift the transitory into the never-ending**. They transform our individual destiny into the destiny of mankind.

The final asterisk introduces us to **lines 87–95** and a wonderfully **clear moment of insight**. A last metaphor concludes the poem. The abandoned **block of wood**, surviving through the years, gives birth, beautifully, to its legacy, 'an axis/of light flashing down its length'. The disintegration of the rotting block reveals the energy and effort of Kinsella's ancestors. Does the insight reveal the possibilities of source, the availability of redemption? Growth and renewal or continuity are shown in the interaction of past and present, in the heritage of time, in the very nature of things: 'the wood's soft flesh broke open,/countless little nails/squirming and dropping out of it', almost like woodlice. The language of change and movement ('squirming', 'dropping', 'flashing') enacts the dynamic of possibility. Ghostly presences and ancestors emerging from the wood permeate barriers of time, space and matter. Hoarded cumulative images, represented by the 'countless little nails', are now released in a burst of imaginative vitality. Kinsella undergoes, yet again, **the mythical experience of death and rebirth**. Here is a sense of death in the midst of life, which resonates in the wet, black Irish landscape.

The block of wood is a visible symbol of the poem itself, tracing the line of the Kinsella family from son to father to grandfather, and back to the previous generations who lived at a time of great strife. This poem does indeed capture an awareness of the generations as they succeed one another and it becomes part of their record.

ANALYSIS

Kinsella stated that 'there are established personal places that receive our lives' heat and adapt in their mass, like stone'. Discuss this statement in relation to the poem 'His Father's Hands'. Support your response with illustrations from the text.

SAMPLE PARAGRAPH

Kinsella's poem 'His Father's Hands' echoes through time and place, and in my opinion, this area around Farnese in Co. Wicklow particularly resonates with Kinsella's 'blood and family'. I liked the section in the sequence lines 41–59, when he quotes his uncle's writings about the family: 'They lived in Farnese among a Colony/of North of Ireland or Scotch settlers'. In the third sequence, he describes this land where bitter battles between the Croppies and the Yeos raged, this 'prow of land' certainly received 'lives' heat'. He shows, through strong verbs, the physical effort expended, as things were 'wedged', 'sloped together' and 'stabilized in menace'. We wonder who had done this, the Yeos or the Croppies? Or both in their effort to lay claim to this ground? This was a frightful place, as he says, 'It feels evil'. Even the use of the present tense brings home to the reader how this human evil transformed the physical shape of the land. The land was shaped by the mass graves of the rebels, as well as by the barriers erected by both sides. This evil reverberates to this day, 'I feel afraid here when I am on my own'. The 'dispersals or migrations' had shaped these 'Littered uplands'. I wonder are they strewn just with rocks, or also with the suffering of those who lived there? I feel the dreadful events which occurred in this place did indeed make the land adapt in its mass, like stone.

EXAMINER'S COMMENT

This paragraph shows a close reading of Kinsella's poem. A well-controlled response to a challenging question, developing relevant points and confidently using pertinent quotation from the poem. Grade A.

CLASS/HOMEWORK EXERCISES

1. 'The beginning must be inward. Turn inward.' How does Kinsella's poem 'His Father's Hands' illustrate this statement? Support your answer with reference to the text.
2. Copy the table below into your own notes and fill in critical comments about the last two quotations.

Key Quotes

carving off little curlicues/to rub them in the dark of his palms	Kinsella's private, microscopic memory details the action of his grandfather's hands. The hard 'c' alliteration clearly conveys the graceful action of the hands as they form the small curling shavings of the tobacco.
the wind that shakes the barley	A reference to the Irish ballad by Robert Dwyer Joyce (1836–83), which refers to the rebellion of 1798. It also alludes to a force of nature, as time passes through the generations.
stabilized in menace	The very land was shaped into a threat. The issues for the reader to consider are by whom and for whom was this landscape changed.
The blood advancing	
the wood's soft flesh broke open,/ countless little nails/squirming and dropping out of it	

Poetry Focus

from Settings: Model School, Inchicore

Miss Carney handed us out blank paper and marla,
old plasticine with the colours
all rolled together into brown.

You started with a ball of it
and rolled it into a snake curling   5
around your hand, and kept rolling it
in one place until it wore down into two
with a stain on the paper.

We always tittered at each other
when we said the adding-up table in Irish   10
and came to her name.

                    *

In the second school we had Mr Browne.
He had white teeth in his brown man's face.

He stood in front of the blackboard
and chalked a white dot.   15

            'We are going to start
                  decimals.'

            I am going to know
                  everything.

                    *

One day he said: 20
'Out into the sun!'
We settled his chair under a tree
and sat ourselves down delighted
in two rows in the greeny gold shade.

A fat bee floated around   25
shining amongst us

Thomas Kinsella

and the flickering sun
warmed our folded coats
and he said: 'History...!'

*

When the Autumn came
and the big chestnut leaves
fell all over the playground
we piled them in heaps
between the wall and the tree trunks
and the boys ran races
jumping over the heaps
and tumbled into them shouting.

*

I sat by myself in the shed
and watched the draught
blowing the papers
around the wheels of the bicycles.

Will God judge
    our most secret thoughts and actions?
God will judge
    our most secret thoughts and actions
and every idle word that man shall speak
he shall render an account of it
on the Day of Judgment.

*

The taste
of ink off
the nib shrank your
mouth.

GLOSSARY

1 *marla*: plasticine (soft modelling material).
48 *Day of Judgment*: Catholic schools taught that every person's soul would eventually be judged by God. Depending on the state of the soul, it would go to Heaven or Hell.

• Poetry Focus •

'I am going to know/everything'

EXPLORATIONS

1. How does the poet convey a sense of childhood innocence in lines 1–19? Refer to the text in your answer.
2. Select one image from the poem that demonstrates the young Kinsella's feeling of closeness to nature. Comment on its effectiveness.
3. How would you describe the tone of lines 38–48? In your opinion, is it confused? Dismissive? Frightened?

STUDY NOTES

> Kinsella received his primary education through the medium of Irish at The Model School in Inchicore from 1932 until 1940. This poem is taken from the 1985 pamphlet *Songs of the Psyche*, published by his own Peppercanister Press. It is a mixture of memory and stream of consciousness, exploring the roots of his inspiration as a poet.

Unlike so many of his poems, which begin on a note of weariness or mental exhaustion, 'Model School, Inchicore' opens with a series of **precise and powerful details evoking the intense wonder of Kinsella's schooldays**: 'Miss Carney handed us out blank paper and marla'. The poet addresses his youthful sense of being immersed in an early classroom activity, modelling plasticine: 'You started with a ball of it/and rolled it into a snake' (**lines 4–5**). Tactile imagery ('curling', 'rolling it') emphasises the concentration involved in the exercise. Kinsella's interest in identifying people and places is evident throughout. Miss Carney's name provided innocent amusement in class when the children chanted their arithmetic tables in Irish (the word for four, *ceathair*, is not unlike the Irish for Carney, *Cathnirnigh*).

This childish delight in words and associations is also evident in the playful description of another of the poet's primary teachers, Mr Browne: 'He had white teeth in his brown man's face' (line 13). Although the language used in the poem has an accessible prose sense that largely avoids metaphors and symbolism, there is **an implicit impression of 'blank' young minds about to discover new worlds**. Kinsella draws on voices from the past to dramatise the excitement of learning as he mimics the teacher's introduction to studying decimals with his self-assured response: 'I am going to know/everything.' The child's statement is both touching and ironic, particularly as this initial confidence seems to have been so disappointed by the adult poet's retrospective awareness of how much he does not know.

Lines 20–37 continue to explore the poet's formative years through vividly realised images and incidents. Presumably his teachers are remembered because they made sense of things for him. Kinsella's recollection of Mr Browne's enthusiasm and spontaneity are particularly nostalgic: 'One day he said:/"Out into the sun!"' The delights of shared pleasures having lessons in the open air are expressed through **vigorous run-on rhythms and colourful descriptions** of nature's 'greeny gold shade'. The natural world has always provided a background against which Kinsella carries out his examination of life. But references to the 'flickering sun' and 'big chestnut leaves' are a stark reminder of life's transience.

The contrast between the carefree childhood games ('boys ran races') and the lonely image of Kinsella's introspective development ('I sat by myself in the shed') illustrates the **origins of his poetic imagination**. At the end of the poem, he considers the deep fears raised by early religion lessons from the Catholic school catechism: 'God will judge/our most secret thoughts and actions' (**lines 44–5**). As the lines grow shorter, they become sharper. Kinsella concludes by returning to an unforgettable sensuous detail: 'The taste/of ink off/the nib shrank your/mouth'. The sensation marked his youth in several ways, allowing him to experience everyday self-awareness while suggesting a growing consciousness of the decaying process. This engagement with inner self is present in much of Kinsella's poetry and is characterised by a bittersweet preoccupation with earthly decay and human mortality.

ANALYSIS

'Kinsella's poetry is primarily concerned with tensions of one kind or another.' Discuss this statement with reference to 'Model School, Inchicore'.

SAMPLE PARAGRAPH

Thomas Kinsella's poems are usually edgy and dramatic. To some extent, he is a brooding pessimist whose ideas are difficult to understand, but this is not so in his poem 'Model School, Inchicore', where he looks back on his national schooling in a sentimental way. The first section of the poem is filled with pleasant memories of using play-dough in the classroom with his friends – 'We always tittered at each other'. The poet uses positive images of nature and its 'greeny gold shade'. One teacher took the children outside to study history, and Kinsella remembers that the class 'sat ourselves down delighted'. However, by contrast, there are personal tensions in the second half of the poem where he recalls being alone and frightened of the religious teaching he had learned – especially about the Last Judgment – 'Will God judge/our most secret thoughts and actions?' Feelings of guilt gripped him at that stage, taking away his childish delights and making him terrified of Hell. The language in this part of the poem is condensed and repetitive, suggesting his troubled thoughts. I thought that the tensions related mainly to fear of death and the fact that as a child, he was very impressionable.

EXAMINER'S COMMENT

A good personal response, demonstrating solid engagement with the poem in the second half of the poem. Quotations are well used here to highlight Kinsella's ability to create contrasting atmospheres. The reference to the poet's use of language is interesting, but might have been developed more. Grade-B standard.

CLASS/HOMEWORK EXERCISES

1 'What distinguishes Thomas Kinsella's writing is a tragic sense of lost youth and lost innocence.' Write a response to this view of Kinsella's poetry, with particular reference to 'Model School, Inchicore'.
2 Copy the table below into your own notes and fill in critical comments about the last two quotations.

Key Quotes

old plasticine with the colours/ all rolled together into brown	Kinsella's precise description and intense tone reflect his childhood fascination with everyday experiences.
A fat bee floated around/shining amongst us	The poet's sense of self-awareness is expressed through his early acknowledgement of nature's wonder.
When the Autumn came	The sobering effect of time (bringing change and decay) is an important feature of the poem.
I am going to know/everything	
The taste/of ink off/the nib shrank your/mouth	

• Poetry Focus •

from **The Familiar: VII**

Thomas Kinsella

I was downstairs at first light,
looking out through the frost on the window
at the hill opposite and the sheets of frost
scattered down among the rocks.

The cat back in the kitchen.   5
Folded on herself. Torn and watchful.

*

A chilled grapefruit
– thin-skinned, with that little gloss.
I took a mouthful, looking up along the edge of the wood

at the two hooded crows high in the cold   10
talking to each other,
flying up toward the tundra, beyond the waterfall.

*

I sliced the tomatoes in thin discs
in damp sequence into their dish;
scalded the kettle; made the tea,   15

and rang the little brazen bell.
And saved the toast.
                Arranged the pieces

in slight disorder around the basket.
Fixed our places, one with the fruit   20
and one with the plate of sharp cheese.

*

And stood in my dressing gown
with arms extended
over the sweetness of the sacrifice.

Her shade showed in the door. 25
Her voice responded:
'You are very good. You always made it nice.'

'I sliced the tomatoes in thin discs / in damp sequence into their dish'

GLOSSARY

12 *tundra*: vast, flat, treeless Arctic region, whose subsoil is permanently frozen.
14 *sequence*: particular order in which related things follow each other.
16 *brazen*: made of brass; bold, shameless, defiant.
21 *sharp*: tapering to a point; strong and slightly bitter.

EXPLORATIONS

1. Comment on the title of the poem, 'The Familiar'. Do you think it suggests being bored with routine or drawing comfort from the well-known? Refer closely to the poem in your response.
2. In your opinion, which aspects of the woman are evoked in the poem? Is she lover, judge, goddess, companion, friend? Illustrate your response with references to the text.
3. The poem concludes with two spoken sentences from the woman beloved. Are they positive and affirming comments? Or are they patronising and almost belittling? Support your views with close reference to the poem.

STUDY NOTES

Thomas Kinsella wrote this seven-part narrative poem, 'The Familiar', in 1999. The poet believes in the importance and enabling power of love. Here he is examining his relationship with his lover. Love is seen as a countermeasure to human isolation. The full poem sequence explores his lonely condition before they met, the intricate feelings experienced as they began their shared life together and finally their intimacy. The seventh section details an ordinary daily ritual: the poet has risen early and is preparing their breakfast.

Thomas Kinsella

The **cinematic opening of the first sequence** of the poem (**lines 1–6**) shows the poet 'downstairs at first light'. Kinsella believes that these transitional moments between night and day are important times when real insightful truth can be glimpsed. The scene outside is cold and forbidding: 'frost on the window', 'sheets of frost/scattered'. Is this a metaphor for the coldness and isolation of modern relationships? Inside the kitchen, the atmosphere seems warm and cosily domestic: 'The cat ... Folded on herself'. However, a note of tension creeps in as the cat is described as 'Torn'. Has it been fighting? The cat also scrutinises the poet's movements, 'watchful'.

In the second section (**lines 7–12**), a close-up of the citric 'chilled grapefruit' is visually striking, 'thin-skinned, with that little gloss'. The slight bitterness of the fruit and the adjective 'chilled' both hint at **a certain discomfort being experienced**. Kinsella often uses the metaphor of eating when speaking of relationships. The phrase 'I took a mouthful' could relate to Kinsella's wholehearted engagement with this attachment. He now looks out again and notices two crows flying 'high in the cold/talking to each other'. They symbolise the coming together of the poet and his loved one as they go through this forbidding life in companionship and close communication. The crow is a symbol from Celtic mythology of Morrigan, the Goddess of War. The turbulent nature of love is hinted at again.

In the third section (**lines 13–21**), the poet carefully and methodically prepares their breakfast with great solemnity. He 'sliced the tomatoes in thin discs'. Assonance of the slender vowel 'i' suggests the wafer thinness of the slices. Again, Kinsella's eye for detail draws the reader firmly into the narrative, as the feel of the tomatoes is shown in the adjective 'damp'. The **imposition of order**, another Kinsella preoccupation, is stressed through the word 'sequence'. This ritual continues as he 'scalded the kettle; made the tea'. A careful preparation now takes on the overtones of a religious ceremony, the Mass. The breaking of bread is mirrored in saving 'the toast'. The disorder of the toast slices is cleverly imitated by the slight disorder in **lines 18–19**. The tang of the 'sharp cheese' also hints that the relationship could at times hurt.

In the final section (**lines 22–7**), the poet now assumes the gesture of the priest at the moment of consecration, 'And stood in my dressing gown/with arms extended'. The preparation of the breakfast that is about to be shared is seen as 'the sweetness of the sacrifice'. Do people in a relationship have to surrender their individuality and personal preferences in compromise for the good of the relationship? The breakfast has been offered to his beloved. Now she appears, 'Her shade showed in the door'. **The soft alliterative 'sh' evokes a hushed, almost spiritual dimension to the woman**, as if she were a goddess who will accept or reject the poet's 'sacrifice', the carefully prepared breakfast. She affirms his effort in measured tones: 'You are very good. You always made it nice.' Does this response show an equal relationship or does it suggest that the poet is 'always' trying to please/appease this woman and waits slightly in fear of her judgment? Through his sensitive use of imagery, the poet has involved the reader in the intricate entanglement of human emotions.

The poem resonates with uneasiness and a veiled tension. This is conveyed in the **detailed imagery** through words like 'Torn', 'watchful', 'thin-skinned', 'disorder', 'sharp', 'sacrifice'. The hesitant rhythm ('scalded the kettle; made the tea') adds to the fraught atmosphere. At the conclusion of the poem, the woman's comment underlines why the poet is on edge. Does the familiar inspire dread?

ANALYSIS

'The enduring strength of love is a recurring theme in the poetry of Thomas Kinsella.' Discuss this statement, referring to the poem 'The Familiar: VII'. Quote from the text in support of your views.

SAMPLE PARAGRAPH

I found this poem of Kinsella's slightly unnerving. I thought the contrast between the frozen scene outside, 'sheets of frost/scattered', and the cosy scene inside, 'The cat ... Folded on herself', very comforting at first. But soon, it appeared to me that cracks began to show in the relationship. The cat was 'Torn and watchful', as it lay scrutinising the poet. There had obviously been a fight the night before. All the fruit is acidic and slightly bitter, 'chilled grapefruit', 'tomatoes', 'sharp cheese'. I thought the poet was making a tremendous effort in getting the breakfast prepared 'just right'; he even had got up 'at first light'. There is a suggestion of previous criticism in the phrase 'And saved the toast'. He called the breakfast a 'sacrifice'. Was this a making-up gesture after a row? The strength in this relationship, seems to me, to belong to the woman, as she appeared when all was ready, and delivered her judgment, 'You are very good. You always made it nice.' I feel this man spends a lot of time trying to please this woman. I found a slight hint of condescension in her comment, 'You are very good'. I think Kinsella is very honest in his portrayal of 'enduring love'. Love is an effort, it is something to be suffered and endured if it is to exist in the long term. Kinsella portrays this idea very effectively in the poem, although I do think the relationship is rather one-sided.

EXAMINER'S COMMENT

The second half of the paragraph shows some good engagement with the question. However, the first section is off task. The emphasis should be on Kinsella's attitude to love. While the expression is very good, the lack of focus reduces the standard to a grade C.

CLASS/HOMEWORK EXERCISES

1 'A troubled intensity of focus is the hallmark of much of Thomas Kinsella's poetry.' Discuss this view, with particular reference to 'The Familiar: VII'. Support your answer with reference to the text.
2 Copy the table below into your own notes and fill in critical comments about the last two quotations.

Key Quotes

Torn and watchful	The adjectives suggest that the cat has been in a scrap and is carefully following the poet's movements. Is this also relating to the woman in his life?
thin-skinned, with that little gloss	The description of the sour grapefruit is evocative of more than just the fruit; it can also refer to the poet's bittersweet relationship.
with arms extended	This gesture is the traditional pose adopted by the priest at the moment of Consecration in the Catholic Mass. Is Kinsella being slightly ironic?
the sweetness of the sacrifice	
'You are very good. You always made it nice.'	

from Belief and Unbelief: Echo

Thomas Kinsella

He cleared the thorns
from the broken gate,
and held her hand
through the heart of the wood
to the holy well.   5

They revealed their names
and told their tales
as they said that they would
on that distant day
when their love began.   10

And hand in hand
they turned to leave.
When she stopped and whispered
a final secret
down to the water.   15

'He cleared the thorns/from the broken gate'

GLOSSARY

In Greek mythology, Echo was a nymph who loved her own voice. She was punished for telling tales and had her voice taken away, except to repeat another's words. She fell in love with Narcissus, a vain young man who rejected her. Echo fled to lonely places where she mourned her lost love and wasted away until only her voice remained.

EXPLORATIONS

1. This poem has the feel of a fairytale. What details in the text support this view? Use quotation from the poem to illustrate your response.
2. Having read the glossary concerning the myth of Echo, why do you think Kinsella chose this as his title for the poem? Support your answer with references from the text.
3. This poem reveals and conceals. Paying particular attention to the final stanza, what, in your view, is being hidden and what is being shared?

STUDY NOTES

'Echo' is part of the collection *Belief and Unbelief,* published in 2007 by Thomas Kinsella. Kinsella returns, again, to one of his particular themes, the examination of love, relationships and death. He is examining process, how we discover and how we understand.

In the **first stanza, the lovers embark on a pilgrimage**, a journey with a religious purpose. They travel as a result of a promise they made when they fell in love. The man is strong as he 'cleared the thorns', pushing away obstacles and problems. The thorns suggest suffering, reminiscent of Christ on the cross. The man assumes a protective role in relation to the woman ('held her hand'). He acts as a guide. The 'holy well' is a place sanctified by a blessing from the Irish saints, where people went to be healed and comforted and to receive reassurance in times of sickness or trouble. The Celts thought these places were access points to another world. Woods ('the heart of the wood') and magic wells are the stuff of legend and fairytale. The mood in this stanza is similar to the hushed atmosphere of the children's story of Sleeping Beauty. The stanza flows smoothly in a single sentence as the couple enter by the 'broken gate'. This is an interesting image. A gate, if locked, bars access, but if broken, it permits entrance, as it is no longer a barrier. It becomes useless.

Stanza two is full of **self-revelation**, as the couple declare 'their names'. They told their stories ('tales') to fulfil a promise made at the beginning of their relationship. The simple language reinforces this impression of an ancient legend or fairytale, 'as they said that they would'. They have been together a long time, 'on that distant day/when their love began'. A sense of union and harmony has been created in this second fluid sentence. The pledge has been honoured.

The **third stanza** begins with a clear picture of the lovers as equals, who leave 'hand in hand'. But now the punctuation (a full stop) halts the flowing movement of the poem. The reader is made to pause in synchronisation with the couple. The woman 'stopped and whispered'. **Relationships require openness and honesty** if they are to succeed, yet most relationships have some secrets. There is always something withheld. But this is the 'final secret' to be disclosed. Is everything now open between the couple? The steady rhythm of the two-beat line would suggest this. The relationship seems to go on. Yet the longer third line, with its sibilant 's' ('stopped', 'whispered'), seems to suggest that all is not as it might appear. Is she mimicking the action of Narcissus, the beloved of Echo, as he lay speaking to his own reflection in the water? Is she still self-absorbed? Is she sharing the 'final secret' with the man or her reflection in the water? Is this action an image of openness or concealment?

This poem reveals and hides. It ends, yet it is not concluded – what will happen next? Are the couple more united now that they have fulfilled their promise and come to this place, or is there still some distance between them, private thoughts which they have not shared with each other? Is this the true nature of relationships, that someone always holds something back? Does anyone ever really know everything about another person?

ANALYSIS

'Happiness is qualified in this life.' Discuss how this statement could refer to the poem 'Echo' by Thomas Kinsella. Refer closely to the poem in your response.

SAMPLE PARAGRAPH

This poem has a fairytale feel to it with the details of the 'broken gate' and the 'heart of the wood' and the 'holy well'. So I thought that this poem would be describing a happy-ever-after scene. I was therefore rather surprised in the third stanza when I realised that Kinsella was exploring a great truth about all human relationships, that none of them are perfect, there is always something hidden, the 'final secret'. It is not clear to me that the man in the poem hears what the 'final secret' is. The woman 'whispered/a final secret/down to the water', not to him. I thought she was like the character in the story of Echo, Narcissus. He had fallen in love with his own reflection and so ignored the loving Echo who pined away until only the sound of her voice remained. I think this woman is mostly concerned with herself, as all people are. So now the fairytale element of the story, the happy ending, goes, and we are given a portrait of happiness in life which is not the picture perfect image in stories, as it says, 'And hand in hand'. Nobody tells another person everything. Secrets are always there between people, total honesty is not possible. The punctuation in this third stanza, the full stop after the word 'leave' mirrors this insight. The smooth flow of the poem is interrupted by the action of the woman. I think that the verb 'whispered' suggests that the poet has not heard the 'final secret' between them and so a distance still remains in their relationship. 'Happiness is qualified in this life.'

EXAMINER'S COMMENT

This paragraph shows a personal engagement with the theme of Kinsella's poem. A competent answer, though at times the syntax is awkward and the expression can be repetitive. Some points, e.g. about the punctuation in the third stanza, are not developed. Grade B.

CLASS/HOMEWORK EXERCISES

1. 'The expression of love is central to Kinsella's work.' How does the poem 'Echo' illustrate this statement? Support your answer with reference to the text.
2. Copy the table below into your own notes and fill in critical comments about the last two quotations.

Key Quotes

He cleared the thorns	This simple, tender image suggests that the man is sweeping aside problems to allow clear access. Is a metaphorical sense also intended?
the holy well	A reference to the Irish tradition of visiting holy springs to seek favours or cures. People often leave a token, a coin or a piece of cloth tied on a branch nearby.
And hand in hand	The phrase suggests an idyllic relationship between the couple, one of perfect unity and equality.
told their tales	
When she stopped and whispered/ a final secret	

LEAVING CERT SAMPLE ESSAY

> **Q** 'Kinsella is a poet drowning in a sea of disappointment.'
>
> Using the above statement as your title, write an essay on the poetry of Thomas Kinsella. Support the points you make by reference to the poetry of Kinsella on your course.

MARKING SCHEME GUIDELINES

Expect candidates to agree and/or disagree with the given statement. The poet's treatment of themes, subjects, attitudes and issues should be discussed, as well as his individual style, manner, phraseology, appropriate vocabulary, imagery, etc.

The candidate should show a clear sense of personal engagement with the poetry.

Some of the following areas might provide material for candidates:
- Poet's disillusioned views on life/relationships.
- Recurring despondent themes: transience, death.
- Fragmented rhythm, disjointed detail.
- Patterns of bleak and disturbing imagery/language.
- Melancholy, morose tone in the texts.
- Kinsella celebrates the past.
- A realistic approach to themes.
- Energetic, varied, innovative style, etc.

SAMPLE ESSAY
(Kinsella Is a Poet Drowning in a Sea of Disappointment)

1 One criticism that has been hurtled at Kinsella's work is that it is 'good in parts' as he seems to have an 'uncertainty where to stop'. Kinsella responded to this by stating that 'others read what I do ... disappointment is the invariable outcome of that'. But while others may be 'disappointed', because his poems, as he remarked, didn't come to 'an end with the last line', he is not disappointed and neither am I.

He, in my opinion, intended his poetry to reflect the sifting process through details of memory stored in the depths of his mind. He persistently self-analyses, and as he recognises imperfections he is dissatisfied, and yet, he gives us an insight into the very processes of life itself. He gives the ordinary 'profound significance'.

2 *In the poem 'His Father's Hands', Kinsella remembers a moment he shared with his father. Both son and father share the same obstinacy, emphasised by the repetition of the adverb 'firmly' and the verbs 'saying' and 'prodded'. Here were two strong men squaring up to each other. But this remembered detail becomes transformed into a meditation on family connections, as he recalls in cinematic detail his grandfather paring 'curlicues' from a piece of solid tobacco, 'the black Plug'. The scene is drawn in such concrete terms that the reader shares the memory as intensely as the poet remembered it. Kinsella and the reader travel 'back to the dark/and the depth' that he came from. This is not 'drowning in a sea of disappointment', rather it is a tender recall of a cherished memory, as his grandfather plays the violin. The onomatopoeic 'scraping' allows the reader to hear the rasping noise of the violin as the 'wind that shakes the barley' is played 'with breaking heart'.*

3 *The ending of the poem is a similar moment of clear and positive insight, as the block of 'wood's soft flesh broke open', and 'countless little nails' came 'squirming and dropping out of it'. It is as if Kinsella's ancestors were pushing through the barriers of time and space. The dynamic image of continuing life is captured in the active verbs 'squirming and dropping'. The block of wood is a symbol that stands for Kinsella's family, from son to father, to grandfather and beyond. It remains firmly rooted in the real world of the dark, Irish landscape.*

4 *This realism permeates the poem 'The Familiar: VII', which deals with a taut relationship between a man and a woman. Although the details here, 'Torn' cat, the 'chilled grapefruit', the acidic 'thin discs' of tomatoes and the 'sharp cheese', suggest a brittle, tense relationship, nevertheless the energy and devotion of the man is what we remember and uplifts us. He 'scalded the kettle; made the tea', ordinary actions which are transformed into the 'sweetness of the sacrifice' as the action takes on the resonance of the sacrifice of the Mass, as he stood 'with arms extended'. The poem concludes with two sentences of dialogue from the woman. She speaks in measured terms, accepting the gift offered, 'You always made it very nice'. This brittle type of relationship is also examined in the poem 'Echo'.*

5 In 'Echo', a fairytale poem of a couple renewing a pledge, the man, again, is shown working hard at the relationship, 'cleared the thorns', 'held her hand'. They both 'revealed their names/and told their tales'. But this poem pauses with the woman who 'stopped and whispered'. The soft sibilant 's' lets us hear the quiet confession of 'a final secret'. Yet it is not to the man the woman confesses, but 'down to the water'. Is this disappointment? I do not think so, as the couple are described as 'hand in hand'. I believe it is Kinsella stating the truth of human relationships, that none are perfect, always something is held back and that a couple have to take time to nurture their relationship, 'as they said they would/on that distant day/when their love began'. The simple language used in this poem conceals the depth and profundity of insight hidden in this dreamlike poem.

6 The poem 'Chrysalides' also examines through remembered details the truth of a relationship, beginning with a celebration of young love, as they moon 'about at odd hours'. The disregard for time is emphasised by the long vowel sounds used. The lovers felt that they were at the centre of the universe, all revolved around them. They satisfied their senses, 'stopping to eat/Chocolate and fruit'. The magical mood of young love is conveyed in the picture of the moonlit night as 'ablaze softly with the virgin moon'. This is also another poem that concludes open-ended with an image that is very similar to the block of wood at the conclusion of 'His Father's Hands'. In 'Chrysalides', a flock of ants, 'Spawning to its death', appears. Kinsella may see the world as flawed, but he is not disenchanted or upset. The title of the poem refers to the egg that contains the insect before it hatches, the egg contains life, as do the young couple and the ants. I believe Kinsella saw love as a consolation in this cold, bitter world. He may recognise the reality of transience, but it is the sweet image of young love that remains with the reader. Out of waste the poet has fashioned beauty as we are invited to share the 'unique succession' of 'youthful midnights'. The lyric transcends mutability.

7 So, Kinsella's poetry, although lacking a clear narrative, instead allows us to experience the 'complex, accidental moment of the here and now'. Instead of story, the poet presents us with detail. Instead of conclusion, we are asked to experience the pursuit of the real. Kinsella sails, but does not drown, in the sea of disappointment of life guided unerringly by his almost forensic attention to detail.

(approx. 1,000 words)

Thomas Kinsella

GRADE: A1
P = 15/15
C = 13/15
L = 14/15
M = 5/5
Total = 47/50

EXAMINER'S COMMENT

This well-prepared, focused response takes a positive view of Kinsella. It shows real personal engagement with the poetry. There is a slight drift away from the question in paragraph 3. The expression is formal and mature and well-interwoven quotations are evident.

SAMPLE LEAVING CERT QUESTIONS ON KINSELLA'S POETRY (45–50 MINUTES)

1. Thomas Kinsella has said, 'We simply go back from where you came from – which is nowhere.' Discuss this statement, focusing particular attention on Kinsella's themes and how he expresses them. Support the points you make by reference to the poetry of Thomas Kinsella on your course.

2. What impact did the poetry of Thomas Kinsella make on you as a reader? In shaping your answer, you might like to consider the following:
   - Your overall sense or outlook of the poet.
   - The poet's use of language and/or imagery.
   - Your favourite poem or poems.

3. 'Kinsella is the quintessential Dublin poet' (Andrew Fitzsimons). Discuss this view, referring both to the subject matter, themes and style of the poetry of Thomas Kinsella on your course.

SAMPLE ESSAY PLAN (Q3)

'Kinsella is the quintessential Dublin poet' (Andrew Fitzsimons). Discuss this view, referring both to the subject matter, themes and style of the poetry of Thomas Kinsella on your course.

- *Intro*: 'His Dublin will sell few beers.' Kinsella is battered and baffled by the actual. Dublin provides a background to his poetry, which is cumulative and fragmented.

- *Point 1*: City of his childhood – narrow streets, dark yards. 'Thinking of Mr D.' – 'lamps that plunged him in and out of light'. 'Hen Woman' – 'The noon heat in the yard'.

- *Point 2*: Family history is a central feature. 'His Father's Hands' – traces Kinsella's family back to his father, grandfather and his ancestors. 'I have watched his father's hands before him/cupped, and tightening the black Plug', 'Beyond that'. Detailed memories that are the essence of old Dublin.

- *Point 3*: Community history details the ghostly failures that stagger and recover. 'Dick King' – 'You haunt with the taint of age and vanished good/Fouling my thoughts with losses'. 'Thinking of Mr D.' – 'under wharf-/Lamps that plunged him in and out of light,/A priestlike figure turning'.

- *Point 4*: A record of established personal places that mark our lives. 'Model School, Inchicore' – 'I sat by myself in the shed/and watched the draught/blowing the papers/around the wheels of the bicycles'.

- *Point 5*: Captures the authentic sound of Dublin speech. 'You were saying', 'We are going to start/decimals, 'Out into the sun', 'scalding the kettle'.

- *Conclusion*: A difficult, provocative, stubborn poet in the tradition of Yeats and Joyce, capturing the essence of 'old, dirty Dublin'. A unique voice in contrast to the traditional rural Irish poets, Kavanagh and Heaney.

EXERCISE

Develop one of the above points into a paragraph.

CONCLUSION – SAMPLE PARAGRAPH

In his book *The Poetry of Thomas Kinsella*, the critic Maurice Harmon states, 'There are no final conclusions' in the poetry of Kinsella. This difficult, provocative poet gives us a dry view of 'dirty Dublin' in the 1930s and 1940s in the tradition of Joyce and Yeats. The old city is brought to a dim glow as railway, brewery, backyard and old schoolrooms are brought to life from the microscopic precision of Kinsella's memory. Ghostly figures emerge from the city background as the universal processes of growth, maturing and extinction take their inevitable course. The stultifying atmosphere of this time in the city, a place of silent pints and hushed backyards, emerges from Kinsella's poetry in black and white, just like old grainy photographs. A unique Irish city voice is now heard in marked contrast to the traditional rural voice of Kavanagh and Heaney. As Kinsella says, 'I have devoted my life to the avoidance of affectation.' So Kinsella continues writing his poetry in the manner of 'A beetle like a bronze leaf ... inching across the cement,/clasping with small tarsi'. This is the dull glow of a marginalised poet sifting through his quintessential Dublin, 'noted and hoarded in the imagination'.

EXAMINER'S COMMENT

As the conclusion of a full essay answer, this is a thoughtful summary that shows a real understanding of the aims of Kinsella. The paragraph focuses successfully on the essence of the poet. The response also benefits greatly from well-integrated quotations. Grade A.

Last Words

'*Writing for most of my life has been a solitary matter – trying to respond as precisely as I could to mostly private impulses.*'

Thomas Kinsella *(on being honoured as a Freeman of Dublin)*

'*The interruption of the immediate by the mediative and meditative is a constant in Kinsella's work.*'

Peter Sirr

'*All of these poems, whatever their differences, have a feature in common: a tendency to look inward for material – into family or self.*'

Thomas Kinsella

'An event provides a lead into a poem.'

Philip Larkin (1922–85)

Philip Larkin was born in 1922 in Coventry, England. He did not enjoy his childhood: 'Get out as early as you can/And don't have any kids yourself'. Nor did he like school. He had a stammer and was short-sighted, although he read widely and contributed to the school magazine. After graduating from Oxford, he went on to become a librarian. Larkin became a great admirer of Thomas Hardy's poetry, learning from Hardy how to make the commonplace and often dreary details of his life the basis for extremely tough, unsparing and memorable poems. He published several collections of poetry, much of which reflected ordinary English life. His searing, often mocking wit rarely concealed the poet's dark vision and underlying obsession with universal themes of mortality, love and human solitude. Yet Larkin's poems face the trials of living and dying with an orderly elegance that always moves the reader. Philip Larkin believed poetry should come from personal experience: 'I write about experiences ... simple everyday experiences ... I hope other people will come upon this ... pickled in verse ... and it will mean something to them.'

• Poetry Focus •

Philip Larkin

PRESCRIBED POEMS (HIGHER LEVEL)

1 'Wedding-Wind' (p. 278)

A celebration of the healing power of love and marriage. The speaker is a young bride who is looking forward to a life of happiness.

2 'At Grass' (p. 283)

A nostalgic narrative poem describing retired racehorses, in which the poet reflects on the changes brought about by time and the contentment of old age.

3 'Church Going' (p. 288)

Conversational and self-mocking, Larkin meditates on the role and significance of churches and religious practice in people's lives.

4 'An Arundel Tomb' (p. 295)

This bittersweet exploration of the power of love to transcend time was written after the poet visited the tomb of the medieval Earl and Countess of Arundel.

5 'The Whitsun Weddings' (p. 301)

The central theme is marriage in all its complexity and its importance within an increasingly urbanised society.

6 'MCMXIV' (p. 308)

The Roman numeral title stands for 1914, the start of World War I. For Larkin, the date marked the end of innocence for the young soldiers and their families.

7 'Ambulances' (p. 313)

This poem uses the symbol of an ambulance to outline Larkin's views on the futility of life and the inevitable reality of death.

8 'The Trees' (p. 318)

This short poem, contrasting nature (the trees) and the lives of human beings, is another review of the theme of transience.

9 'The Explosion' (p. 322)

An affirmative poem based on a tragic coal mine accident. There were reports that at the time of the explosion, some of the miners' wives saw visions of their husbands.

10 'Cut Grass' (p. 327)

Another short lyric about the cycle of life and death. The poem's title image suggests how life and natural growth can be abruptly ended.

Wedding-Wind

Philip Larkin

The wind blew all my wedding-day,
And my wedding-night was the night of the high wind;
And a stable door was banging, again and again,
That he must go and shut it, leaving me
Stupid in candlelight, hearing rain,   5
Seeing my face in the twisted candlestick,
Yet seeing nothing. When he came back
He said the horses were restless, and I was sad
That any man or beast that night should lack
The happiness I had.   10

                Now in the day
All's ravelled under the sun by the wind's blowing.
He has gone to look at the floods, and I
Carry a chipped pail to the chicken-run,
Set it down, and stare. All is the wind   15
Hunting through clouds and forests, thrashing
My apron and the hanging cloths on the line.
Can it be borne, this bodying-forth by wind
Of joy my actions turn on, like a thread
Carrying beads? Shall I be let to sleep   20
Now this perpetual morning shares my bed?
Can even death dry up
These new delighted lakes, conclude
Our kneeling as cattle by all-generous waters?

'and the hanging cloths on the line'

• Leaving Certificate English •

GLOSSARY
12 *ravelled*: pulled apart and untangled.
16 *thrashing*: moving; beating violently.
18 *borne*: carried by, endured.

EXPLORATIONS

1   How realistic do you think Larkin's portrayal of marriage is? Support your views with reference to the text.
2   Trace the tone in this poem. Does it change? What is different in the attitude of the speaker in the second section?
3   In your opinion, why does the poem end with three questions?

STUDY NOTES

> 'Wedding-Wind' was published in 1946. This narrative poem (Larkin was also a novelist) records details of a wedding day, night and the morning after. Larkin adopts the persona of a young bride to tell the story. He said, 'I can imagine ... the emotions of a bride ... without ever having been a woman or married.' This poem is a celebration of the joy of passionate love.

This direct, personal poem's **opening section** begins with the young bride stating that 'The wind blew all my wedding-day'. This 'high wind' blew throughout her day and the wedding night. Is it a **symbol for passion and change**? Is the poem linking the energy of the natural world with the force of human love? The adjective 'high' for Larkin meant elevated and elevating experiences. People rise above the ordinary to experience a spiritual feeling. The restless atmosphere of the day and night is caught in the description of the stable door 'banging, again and again'. This mundane detail shows Larkin's ear for the ordinary. The young woman relates how her husband has to 'go and shut' the banging door. Larkin believed that life as it was lived by ordinary people should and could provide the subject for poetry. The young bride feels inadequate, 'Stupid in candlelight', 'seeing nothing'. Her new husband returns, saying 'the horses were restless'. She feels compassion for all living things that are not experiencing the happiness 'I had'.

The **second section** of the poem is an interior monologue by the bride as she observes the destruction caused by the 'wind's blowing'. 'All's ravelled under the sun': the debris of the storm is clear for everyone to see. Both the world and

Philip Larkin

the bride have been changed by some huge elemental force. She is now a **woman of responsibilities**. She recognises the practicalities of farming. There is no honeymoon. 'He has gone to look at the floods' and she has gone to feed the chickens. The detail of her 'chipped pail' lends a human, imperfect note to the scene. She sets the pail down and begins to reflect ('stare').

Now, unlike last night, **she is seeing**. The wind, this powerful force of nature, was a predator, 'Hunting through clouds and forests' (**line 16**). The violent force of the wind is contained in the verb 'thrashing'. Does this have connotations of the violent passion of love? Again, an ordinary sight, clothes hanging on a washing line ('My apron and the hanging cloths on the line'), makes the poem accessible to all, academic and non-academic. There is no exclusive reference to classical mythology, but the common stuff of life. The poem concludes with three questions. The young woman wonders if she will survive the 'joy my actions turn on'. The compound word 'bodying-forth' and the verb 'borne' suggest pregnancy. The simile 'like a thread/Carrying beads' implies praying and the sacredness of the holy state of matrimony. Or this thread could refer to a necklace, a gift or symbol of love given between the young couple.

The second question poses the problem of sleep: 'Shall I be let to sleep' (**line 20**). The bride now feels that every day is 'perpetual morning', as life seems full of exciting possibilities, so it is impossible to rest. She feels so blessed by love that she has almost been made immortal: 'Can even death dry up' her joy? She believes that these 'new delighted lakes' can never be 'dry', even though the wind dries water from the land. She is compelled to make a sign, 'conclude/Our kneeling as cattle'. The biblical tones of the compound word 'all-generous' show **an optimistic view that joy can outlive death**.

Larkin wanted his readers to experience his poetry and say, 'I've never thought of it that way before, but that's how it is.' **He believed poetry should come from personal experience**. Larkin disliked the idea that poetry should come from other poems. He was opposed to Modernism, a poetry movement that is allusory and inaccessible to the ordinary person. It is interesting to note that this poem takes a private, human experience and links it with nature. Does this lend a note of danger to the experience of young, passionate love? Parallel to the poem, dramatic changes were taking place in English society. The Second World War had just ended, followed by the depression of the 1950s, the affluence and student unrest of the 1960s and the emergence of socialism and multiculturalism. This rural English experience of young love is preserved by Larkin, 'pickled as it were in verse', despite all the changes taking place.

ANALYSIS

Larkin believed that poetry should help us 'enjoy and endure'. Do you agree or disagree with this statement? Support your view with references from the poem.

SAMPLE PARAGRAPH

I believe that this poem helps us enjoy life, thanks to the beautiful, passionate narrative of this young bride. The wind represents change and dynamism in the natural world, as well as in the world of the young woman. It is 'sacred', a 'high wind', which both scatters and cleans, 'All's ravelled under the sun by the wind's blowing'. The human details of ordinary life shine under the craftsmanship of Larkin, 'chipped pail', 'stable door … banging, again and again', 'hanging cloths on the line'. The ordinary, somewhat irksome chores which we all must endure become the basis of passionate poetry as the young bride wonders whether all this 'joy of action' can be 'borne'. We are elevated, as the woman is, by the optimistic, mystical vision that love cannot be dimmed by death. We kneel at the 'all-generous waters'. Larkin has helped us to enjoy and endure.

EXAMINER'S COMMENT

This short paragraph addresses both aspects of the question (enjoy and endure). The response shows a real appreciation of Larkin's poetic beliefs. More detailed analysis and comment on the key quotations would have resulted in a higher grade. However, the style throughout is assured and vocabulary and expression are very good. Grade B.

CLASS/HOMEWORK EXERCISES

1. Write a paragraph on how effectively Larkin uses metaphors to communicate his message in this poem. Support your answer with reference to the text.
2. Copy the table below into your own notes and fill in critical comments about the last two quotations.

• Poetry Focus •

Philip Larkin

Key Quotes

And my wedding-night was the night of the high wind	The reflective tone and adjective 'high' suggest that the wind is a sacred force for change.
All is the wind/ Hunting through clouds and forests	The entire scene is pervaded by the personification of the wind as a hunter, on its lookout for prey.
this bodying-forth by wind/ Of joy my actions turn on	This terse line conveys the swelling motion of the wind enmeshed in the happiness experienced by the young bride.
Now this perpetual morning shares my bed	
Our kneeling as cattle by all-generous waters	

At Grass

Philip Larkin

The eye can hardly pick them out
From the cold shade they shelter in,
Till wind distresses tail and mane;
Then one crops grass, and moves about
– The other seeming to look on –　　　　　5
And stands anonymous again.

Yet fifteen years ago, perhaps
Two dozen distances sufficed
To fable them: faint afternoons
Of Cups and Stakes and Handicaps,　　　10
Whereby their names were artificed
To inlay faded, classic Junes –

Silks at the start: against the sky
Numbers and parasols: outside,
Squadrons of empty cars, and heat,　　　15
And littered grass: then the long cry
Hanging unhushed till it subside
To stop-press columns on the street.

Do memories plague their ears like flies?
They shake their heads. Dusk brims the shadows.　20
Summer by summer all stole away,
The starting-gates, the crowds and cries –
All but the unmolesting meadows.
Almanacked, their names live; they

Have slipped their names, and stand at ease,　25
Or gallop for what must be joy,
And not a fieldglass sees them home,
Or curious stop-watch prophesies:
Only the groom, and the groom's boy,
With bridles in the evening come.　　　30

• Poetry Focus •

Philip Larkin

'The starting-gates, the crowds and cries'

GLOSSARY

At Grass: a reference to the retirement of old racehorses.
3 *mane*: the hair on the back of a horse's neck.
4 *crops*: eats, chews.
8 *Two dozen distances sufficed*: 24 races were enough.
9 *To fable*: to make famous.
10 *Cups and Stakes and Handicaps*: various types of horse races.
11 *artificed*: displayed (on trophies, etc.).
12 *inlay*: ornamental fabric.
12 *classic*: traditional, important June races.
13 *Silks*: shirts ('colours') worn by jockeys.
14 *Numbers*: betting numbers displayed by bookies.
14 *parasols*: ladies' umbrellas.
15 *Squadrons*: long lines (of parked cars).
18 *stop-press*: news update (latest racing results).
19 *plague*: irritate.
23 *unmolesting*: harmless, gentle.
24 *Almanacked*: listed in the racing records.
29 *groom*: worker who looks after the horses.
30 *bridles*: restraints placed on the heads of horses.

EXPLORATIONS

1 Using close reference to the text, describe the atmosphere/mood in the opening stanza.
2 How does Larkin convey the excitement of the racecourse in stanza three? Refer to the text in your answer.
3 Choose two memorable images from the poem and briefly explain their effectiveness.

STUDY NOTES

'At Grass' was written in 1950 after the poet had seen a documentary film about a retired racehorse. Larkin, himself a lover of horses, saw them as exploited during their racing careers. This strikingly reflective poem, exploring the changes brought about by the passage of time, has been interpreted as a criticism of the passing fashion of celebrity and as a requiem for a bygone age.

Stanza one begins with a short description of two horses sheltering in the distance. Larkin remarks that 'The eye can hardly pick them out' before he has even explained what there is to pick out. It is only when a slight breeze 'distresses tail and mane' that the horses come to life. Even then, the 'cold shade' setting has a vague suggestion that these forgotten ('anonymous') animals are close to death. There is an **evocative visual quality** within these early lines and a **mood of wistful sadness** dominates.

In contrast to this feeling of stillness, Larkin begins to imagine the racehorses in their prime 'fifteen years ago'. The **nostalgic flashback** in the second and third stanzas recalls their triumphs in 'Cups and Stakes and Handicaps', enough 'To fable them' and ensure their reputation in racing history. The thrill and glamour of 'classic Junes' is recreated through vibrant images of the jockeys' colours ('Silks') and the 'Numbers and parasols'. Cinematic details ('empty cars', 'littered grass') and the excited cheering ('the long cry') of the crowds all convey the joy of unforgettable race meetings.

Stanza four returns to the present as Larkin considers the conscious experiences of the horses themselves. The line 'They shake their heads' is playfully ambiguous, both a negative response to the earlier question ('Do memories plague their ears like flies?') and an actual movement which horses carry out naturally. Larkin's elegant imagery communicates the subtle advance of time: 'Summer by summer' as 'Dusk brims the shadows'. There is a strong sense that at the end of their lives, these once-famous horses deserve to take their ease in 'unmolesting meadows'. Interestingly, the most remarkable verbs in the poem – 'fabled', 'artificed', 'inlay', 'Almanacked' – are all concerned with the way people have seen and recorded these horses. They have become racecourse stories, names engraved into trophies and recorded in official histories.

The **dignified language and slow rhythm** of stanza five suggest both the tranquil freedom of these retired horses and the reality that they are nearing the end of their long lives. For the moment, though, they 'gallop for what must be joy' – a typical Larkin comment which throws doubt onto an assertion even while in the process of making it. The poem ends on a consolatory note. Now that the horses have 'slipped their names' and are no longer chasing fame or glory, they can 'stand at ease', enjoying the peace and quiet. Broad assonant effects emphasise their sense of quiet fulfilment: 'Only the groom, and the groom's boy,/With bridles in the evening come'. The inverted syntax and mellow tone add to the sense of finality. In completing the natural cycle of their lives, Larkin's racehorses offer a model for the human condition of youth, achievement and old age. Characteristically, the development of thought in the poem moves from observation to reflection, leaving us to appreciate the blend of celebration and sadness that mark this beautiful poem.

ANALYSIS

Using close reference to the text, comment on the poet's use of contrast in 'At Grass'.

SAMPLE PARAGRAPH

Philip Larkin uses two distinct settings in 'At Grass'. This is a very effective device to highlight the past and present lives of the racehorses. At the start of the poem, he describes two horses grazing – but they are 'anonymous'. There is a dreamy, timeless feeling to the picture Larkin paints. I thought that even the title of the poem was similar to the title used of a painting of racehorses. There is very little movement involved in the description of the retired horses – in complete contrast with the middle section of the poem, where Larkin brings us back to their glory days, winning 'Cups, Stakes and Handicaps'. The hustle and bustle of the busy racetracks is seen in the colourful images and lively rhythms – 'Silks at the start against the blue sky'. The scene is noisy, with race goers shouting and reporters rushing to write their 'stop-press columns' after the winners are announced. The two contrasting atmospheres are very different. At the end of the poem, we see the two old horses 'stand at ease' – even the gentle sibilant sounds are in contrast with the hectic description of 'littered grass' at the race meetings. The tone in the last lines of the poem as the grooms 'in the late evening come' is gentle and subdued, highlighting the final days of these champion horses. Overall, Larkin uses contrasts very effectively to show the dramatic changes in the lives of these great horses, who have swapped their past glory for a well-earned rest.

EXAMINER'S COMMENT

This is a well-sustained and focused response that examines the poet's use of contrasting settings, moods and sound effects in some detail. The commentary is informed and interesting. However, the answer is less successful due to the inaccurate quotations. A basic grade B.

CLASS/HOMEWORK EXERCISES

1 Describe the tone of the poem. Is it celebratory, sorrowful, resigned or realistic, or a combination of these? Refer to the text in your answer.
2 Copy the table below into your own notes and fill in critical comments about the last two quotations.

Key Quotes

From the cold shade they shelter in	The description of sheltering horses in the shadows suggests the inevitability of impending death.
Two dozen distances sufficed/ To fable them	Alliteration echoes the energy and triumph of these great horses in their prime.
Summer by summer all stole away	The passing of time is a central theme in the poem, evoked in the bittersweet sibilance and fluent rhythm of this memorable image.
Almanacked, their names live	
Only the groom, and the groom's boy,/ With bridles in the evening come	

• Poetry Focus •

Church Going

Philip Larkin

Once I am sure there's nothing going on
I step inside, letting the door thud shut.
Another church: matting, seats, and stone,
And little books; sprawlings of flowers, cut
For Sunday, brownish now; some brass and stuff   5
Up at the holy end; the small neat organ;
And a tense, musty, unignorable silence,
Brewed God knows how long. Hatless, I take off
My cycle-clips in awkward reverence,

Move forward, run my hand around the font.   10
From where I stand, the roof looks almost new –
Cleaned, or restored? Someone would know: I don't.
Mounting the lectern, I peruse a few
Hectoring large-scale verses, and pronounce
'Here endeth' much more loudly than I'd meant.   15
The echoes snigger briefly. Back at the door
I sign the book, donate an Irish sixpence,
Reflect the place was not worth stopping for.

Yet stop I did: in fact I often do,
And always end much at a loss like this,   20
Wondering what to look for; wondering, too,
When churches fall completely out of use
What we shall turn them into, if we shall keep
A few cathedrals chronically on show,
Their parchment, plate and pyx in locked cases,   25
And let the rest rent-free to rain and sheep.
Shall we avoid them as unlucky places?

Or, after dark, will dubious women come
To make their children touch a particular stone;
Pick simples for a cancer; or on some   30
Advised night see walking a dead one?
Power of some sort or other will go on
In games, in riddles, seemingly at random;
But superstition, like belief, must die,
And what remains when disbelief has gone?   35
Grass, weedy pavement, brambles, buttress, sky,

A shape less recognisable each week,
A purpose more obscure. I wonder who
Will be the last, the very last, to seek
This place for what it was; one of the crew   40
That tap and jot and know what rood-lofts were?
Some ruin-bibber, randy for antique,
Or Christmas-addict, counting on a whiff
Of gowns-and-bands and organ-pipes and myrrh?
Or will he be my representative,   45

Bored, uninformed, knowing the ghostly silt
Dispersed, yet tending to this cross of ground
Through suburb scrub because it held unspilt
So long and equably what since is found
Only in separation – marriage, and birth,   50
And death, and thoughts of these – for which was built
This special shell? For, though I've no idea
What this accoutred frowsty barn is worth,
It pleases me to stand in silence here;

A serious house on serious earth it is,   55
In whose blent air all our compulsions meet,
Are recognised, and robed as destinies.
And that much never can be obsolete,
Since someone will forever be surprising
A hunger in himself to be more serious,   60
And gravitating with it to this ground,
Which, he once heard, was proper to grow wise in,
If only that so many dead lie round.

'Which, he once heard, was proper to grow wise in,/If only that so many dead lie round'

Philip Larkin

GLOSSARY

9 *cycle-clips*: old-fashioned clips that fasten a cyclist's trouser leg.
10 *font*: stone bowl in a church used to store holy water.
13 *lectern*: a tall stand from which a speaker can read.
13 *peruse*: read carefully.
14 *Hectoring*: bullying, blustering.
15 *'Here endeth'*: Church of England services end each reading with the phrase 'Here endeth the lesson'.
24 *chronically*: lasting a long time; very badly.
25 *parchment*: animal skin formerly used for writing on.
25 *plate*: bowls, cups, etc. made of gold or silver and used for religious ceremonies.
25 *pyx*: container in which the blessed bread of the Eucharist is kept.
28 *dubious*: doubtful.
30 *simples*: medicinal herbs.
30 *cancer*: malignant growth.
31 *Advised*: recommended.
36 *buttress*: support for a wall.
41 *rood-lofts*: galleries in the shape of a cross.
42 *ruin-bibber*: someone fond of old buildings.
42 *randy*: excited.
44 *gowns-and-bands*: clerical dress.
44 *myrrh*: sweet-smelling resin used in incense at a religious ceremony.
46 *silt*: deposit left behind.
49 *equably*: calm and even-tempered.
53 *accoutred*: dressed; equipped.
53 *frowsty*: stale smelling; musty.
56 *blent*: blended, mixed.
56 *compulsions*: irresistible urges to do something.
58 *obsolete*: out of date.
61 *gravitating*: attracted towards.

EXPLORATIONS

1 What impression do you have of the speaker in the first two stanzas of this poem? Support your answer with reference to the text.
2 List two images that you consider to be spiritual in 'Church Going'. Comment on their effectiveness.
3 How does this poem change after the first two stanzas? What are the main considerations of the poet? Refer closely to the poem in your response.

STUDY NOTES

'Church Going' was written in 1954 as part of Larkin's poetry collection *The Less Deceived*. He adopts his famous persona of the self-deprecating, observant, conversational outsider. Larkin said he felt the need to be on 'the periphery of things'. The title is a pun, suggesting both the attendance of religious ceremonies (church-going) and also suggesting that religious practice/religion itself was on the way out, passé. The inspiration for the poem came from an actual event experienced by Larkin when he stopped to look at a church while on a cycling trip.

In the **first stanza**, Larkin is an interloper/intruder who only enters the church when he's sure it's empty ('nothing going on'). The run-on line movement mirrors the poet popping inside ('I step inside'). The onomatopoeic closing of the door echoes in 'thud shut'. We hear what is happening. A jaded tone of one who has seen and done it all before sounds from the phrase 'Another church'. He now gives us a general view of the church from floor to wall: matting, wooden seats, stone walls. He then closes in for a detailed view: 'little books', flowers that are 'brownish now'. This telling detail suggests something is not fresh; it's dying. Is this similar to church-going? Larkin felt strongly that when you go into church, you get **a feeling that something is over, derelict**.

He now becomes dismissive as he describes the sacred objects as 'some brass and stuff'. He says it is 'Up at the holy end'. **He is indifferent rather than ignorant**: 'I don't bother about that kind of thing,' he once declared. The atmosphere is 'tense', not serene; the church is 'musty', stale-smelling. The silence is all-pervasive, 'unignorable'. The atmosphere has been stewing or fermenting a long time, like tea or beer – only 'God knows how long'. This fact makes him anxious to show respect. He had already removed his hat, but now he cuts a slightly ridiculous figure as he removes his cycle-clips 'in awkward reverence'.

He moves around in the **second stanza**, like an **uninformed tourist**, randomly touching things ('run my hand around the font'). The use of the present tense in the first two stanzas gives an immediacy to the description. A telling question, 'Cleaned, or restored?', shows the poet's mind at work. It also shows that there is a community at work, and therefore continuity. The roof is being preserved, just as Larkin is preserving the church in his poem. Yet the dismissive, casual, conversational tone returns when he says that he thinks 'the place was not worth stopping for'.

A more **formal, serious voice now is heard** as the poet's inner self comes into focus. He begins to meditate in **stanza three** on the importance of churches ('wondering, too,/When churches fall completely out of use/What we shall turn them into'). This knowledgeable voice knows the ecclesiastical vocabulary: 'parchment', 'pyx'. In the future, these will no longer be used for ceremonies, but stored 'in locked cases'. Larkin was fond of the traditions of the Anglican Church, but now the old world is fading. He imagines the future of these churches as 'rent-free', worth nothing, housing only 'rain and sheep'. Here is a desolate outlook. The use of the plural first person pronoun 'we' suggests that Larkin thinks we will all be confronted with what to do with these large empty buildings. The negative view continues as the churches are described as 'unlucky places'.

In **stanza four**, **superstition is overtaking belief**. This is 'dark', 'dubious'; Larkin doesn't approve. However, he feels the power will remain ('Power of some sort'), and eventually, as always happens, nature will reclaim it: 'Grass ... brambles ... sky'. This landscape recalls the opening view of the interior of the church. Now, in Larkin's imaginings, it lies open to the elements. The long sentence shows the ruminative mood of the poet, as he wonders, in **stanza five**, who will be the last to seek out this place for what it once was, a dynamic church. He dismisses the learned academics ('ruin-bibber'), someone mad for old buildings.

In **stanza six**, Larkin wonders if his 'representative', 'Bored', will be one who understood the church's role in marking the great human landmarks of a life: birth, marriage and death. The poet is happy to be part of this space: 'It pleases me to stand in silence here'. In the **seventh stanza**, the contemplative voice states, 'A serious house on serious earth it is'. He realises he will be someone who is drawn to this place, as it is a place 'to grow wise in' as he experiences the **essence of life, being alone** ('dead lie around').

Larkin uses a **traditional form of English poetry**, a formal stanza pattern of seven nine-line stanzas. The rhythm is iambic pentameter, the traditional rhythm of English verse. The large, spacious form of the poem echoes the cavernous space of the church. The regular rhyme scheme punctuates this ordered but disappearing world. This poem is reminiscent of Shakespeare's sonnet recording the ruins of England's monasteries: 'Bare ruined choirs, where late the sweet birds sang'. Both poems are shot through with melancholy for a disappeared world.

ANALYSIS

After reading 'Church Going', do you feel a sense of disappointment and depression or a feeling of optimism? Support your view with references from the poem.

SAMPLE PARAGRAPH

I feel I have gained insight from this poem, as the poet, although he is dismissive in the first stanzas, when he flippantly remarks that the place was 'not worth stopping for', and that he donated an 'Irish sixpence' (inferior coinage?). Nevertheless, he feels that this place merits reverence, however 'awkward'. This place has a 'Power of some sort'. When his more serious side emerges, at the end of the poem, he acknowledges, rather like the Communists, that people need religion/belief, 'A hunger in himself'. We cannot exist totally on the level of animals, or in the shallow state of the cynical, critical sneer. He uses the word, 'gravitating', as if he/we are pulled by an irresistible force 'to this ground'. He has been told, 'he once heard', that there is a 'proper' place 'to grow wise in'. 'If only that so many dead lie round' shows us that this place marks the reality and finality of life-death. We live our lives in the shadow of our death, our loved ones' deaths, and the death of all living things. The poem has given me a real insight into the pessimistic reality of human affairs.

EXAMINER'S COMMENT

This general response does not focus directly on the question. While expression and vocabulary are good, a treatment of stylistic effects, such as tone, would have improved the answer. Grade C.

CLASS/HOMEWORK EXERCISES

1. Larkin stated that the 'impulse to preserve lies at the bottom of all art'. What is Larkin trying to preserve in the poem 'Church Going'? In your opinion, does he succeed or fail? Support your answer with reference to the text.
2. Copy the table below into your own notes and fill in critical comments about the last two quotations.

• Poetry Focus •

Philip Larkin

Key Quotes

Brewed God knows how long	The metaphor of brewing emphatically underlines the length of time the church has been here.
Yet stop I did: in fact I often do	The casual tone of this line shows the first voice of the poem, that of the disinterested tourist.
Pick simples for a cancer	Superstition will replace belief as the churches die. People are looking for miracle cures for their ailments.
knowing the ghostly silt/Dispersed	
In whose blent air all our compulsions meet	

An Arundel Tomb

Side by side, their faces blurred,
The earl and countess lie in stone,
Their proper habits vaguely shown
As jointed armour, stiffened pleat,
And that faint hint of the absurd –   5
The little dogs under their feet.

Such plainness of the pre-baroque
Hardly involves the eye, until
It meets his left-hand gauntlet, still
Clasped empty in the other; and   10
One sees, with a sharp tender shock,
His hand withdrawn, holding her hand.

They would not think to lie so long.
Such faithfulness in effigy
Was just a detail friends would see: 15
A sculptor's sweet commissioned grace
Thrown off in helping to prolong
The Latin names around the base.

They would not guess how early in
Their supine stationary voyage   20
The air would change to soundless damage,
Turn the old tenantry away;
How soon succeeding eyes begin
To look, not read. Rigidly they

Persisted, linked, through lengths and breadths   25
Of time. Snow fell, undated. Light
Each summer thronged the glass. A bright
Litter of birdcalls strewed the same
Bone-riddled ground. And up the paths
The endless altered people came,   30

Washing at their identity.
Now, helpless in the hollow of
An unarmorial age, a trough

• Poetry Focus •

Philip Larkin

Of smoke in slow suspended skeins
Above their scrap of history,   35
Only an attitude remains:

Time has transfigured them into
Untruth. The stone fidelity
They hardly meant has come to be
Their final blazon, and to prove   40
Our almost-instinct almost true:
What will survive of us is love.

'What will survive of us is love'

GLOSSARY

The title refers to a 14th-century monument of the Earl of Arundel and his wife in Chichester Cathedral, West Sussex, England.
3 *proper habits*: appropriate burial clothes.
4 *pleat*: fold.
7 *pre-baroque*: plain, simple design (before the elaborate 17th-century baroque style).
9 *gauntlet*: glove.
14 *effigy*: figure, sculpted likeness.
20 *supine*: lying down.
22 *tenantry*: tenants living on a landlord's estate.
27 *thronged*: crowded.
28 *strewed*: spread across.
29 *Bone-riddled ground*: buried human remains.
33 *unarmorial*: unheroic.
33 *trough*: channel.
34 *skeins*: threads or coils (of smoke).
37 *transfigured*: transformed.
40 *blazon*: sign, symbol.

EXPLORATIONS

1 How would you describe the tone in the first stanza? Reverential? Intrigued? Superior?

2. Select two illustrations from the poem to show Larkin's keen eye for detail. Comment briefly on the effectiveness of each example.
3. Write a short personal response to this poem, highlighting the impact it made on you.

STUDY NOTES

'An Arundel Tomb' was written in 1956 after Larkin had visited Chichester Cathedral. He said that the effigies were unlike any he had ever seen before and that he found them 'extremely affecting'. The poem can be viewed in many ways – as a meditation on love and death, a tribute to the power of art or even as a celebration of English history. Despite differences of interpretation, 'An Arundel Tomb' has always been a favourite of Larkin readers. It was read aloud at his memorial service held in London's Westminster Abbey in 1986.

In **stanza one**, we are immediately located before the stone statue of the Earl and Countess of Arundel. Larkin's description of the couple seems detached, the **tone one of ironic hesitation**. The couple's 'blurred' faces (eroded by time) are indistinct. Indeed, the earl's outdated armour and the 'little dogs under their feet' add a ludicrous dimension (a 'faint hint of the absurd') to the commemorative monument.

The poet continues to criticise the 'plainness' of the lifeless sculpture in **stanza two**. It is etched in an unappealingly dull 'pre-baroque' style. But he is suddenly taken by one particular detail. The earl's left hand has been withdrawn from its 'gauntlet' and is 'holding her hand'. This affectionate gesture between husband and wife has an immediate **impact on Larkin – 'a sharp tender shock'**. The image of 'His hand withdrawn, holding her hand' stops the poet in his tracks. We can sense Larkin's concentration in the slow rhythm and emphatic 'h' alliteration of **line 12**. Do the joined hands represent the triumph of love over time, or is that just wishful thinking?

In **stanza three**, Larkin reflects on the relationship between the earl and countess. **Line 13 is puzzling**: 'They would not think to lie so long'. Is this an obvious reference to the couple's long rest in the tomb? Or have they failed to find a heavenly afterlife? Might there be a pun on the word 'lie'? Perhaps the loving hand-holding is an untrue representation? Larkin wonders if the sculptor invented this demonstrative touch to make the statue more interesting to the general public and to 'prolong' the earl's family name long after the Latin inscription would be understood.

Stanzas four and **five** focus particularly on the **passing of time**, a central theme in the poem. The earl and countess could not have imagined the effects of the damp cathedral air ('soundless damage') eroding their tomb. Great social change has also happened over the centuries; 'the old tenantry' and the use of Latin – and the importance of Christianity, presumably – have disappeared. Larkin's strikingly sensory images evoke the changing seasons: 'Snow fell, undated. Light/Each summer thronged the glass'. The signs of natural vitality and rejuvenation are in stark contrast to the 'Bone-riddled ground' over which modern-day visitors to the cathedral ('endless altered people') arrive to view the monument.

The countless tourists to the medieval couple's tomb have long been 'Washing at their identity' (**stanza six**). There is a suggestion of erosion (the earl and countess are no longer understood as they once were) and purification (the couple are idealised as romantic and artistic symbols). Larkin asserts that the effigies are 'helpless' in this 'unarmorial age'. The **poet's cynical tone** reflects his distaste for the vulgarity and ignorance around him. Today's generation has a shallow appreciation of love – 'Only an attitude remains'.

This idea is developed in **stanza seven**, where **Larkin questions the public's misguided response to the statue**. For him, the sentimental yearning to see the couple's 'fidelity' as a triumph of love over death is an 'Untruth', and something the earl and countess probably never intended. Nonetheless, the instinctual desire for enduring love may well be another admirable aspect of human behaviour. Many commentators view the **final lines** ('Our almost-instinct almost true:/What will survive of us is love') as a positive affirmation by Larkin. Others see in it a typically despondent statement of the opposite (namely, self-deluding hope in the face of reality). Like the rest of the poem, the ending is typically paradoxical and thought provoking, allowing us to decide for ourselves about Larkin's attitude concerning the power of love to transcend time.

ANALYSIS

Comment on Larkin's use of ambiguous language in 'An Arundel Tomb'.

SAMPLE PARAGRAPH

Philip Larkin's poem 'An Arundel Tomb' is noted for its ambiguity. The opening description of the rigid figures carved in stone is both sympathetic and satirical at the same time. Their expressions are described as 'blurred', suggesting that they are faceless and unreal. Larkin adds that there are 'little dogs under their feet'. He finds this ridiculous and might be hinting that this privileged earl and countess were used to being spoiled and pampered. On the other hand, the image makes the elderly pair seem human. The word 'lie' is used a number of times. The couple 'lie in stone'. This might simply refer to the position of the bodies, but it could also mean that they are sending out a false message that they are a loving couple whose love has conquered death. Yet the earl and his wife 'would not think to lie so long', suggesting that they never planned to give this false impression. Although Larkin's ambivalent approach engaged my interest in the poem, I am still not exactly sure about his own point of view as to the true relationship between the earl and countess. However, the effect of his wordplay is to produce a poem which is very rich and suggestive in meaning, encouraging us to think twice before judging by appearances.

EXAMINER'S COMMENT

A well-illustrated personal response that examines Larkin's subtle use of language at various points in the poem. The expression throughout the paragraph is clear and varied. Grade-A standard.

CLASS/HOMEWORK EXERCISES

1. Outline the main theme presented in 'An Arundel Tomb'. In your answer, trace the way the poet develops his ideas during the course of the poem.
2. Copy the table below into your own notes and fill in critical comments about the last two quotations.

• Poetry Focus •

Philip Larkin

Key Quotes

The earl and countess lie in stone	The image conveys a sense of looking directly at the monument. Is the word 'lie' used ambiguously to suggest the illusion of the couple's love?
Their supine stationary voyage	Contrasting references to inactivity and action (death and life) are a distinctive feature of the poem.
A bright/Litter of birdcalls	Slender vowels and alliteration add to the vitality of this memorable image.
Washing at their identity	
What will survive of us is love	

The Whitsun Weddings

Philip Larkin

That Whitsun, I was late getting away:
   Not till about
One-twenty on the sunlit Saturday
Did my three-quarters-empty train pull out,
All windows down, all cushions hot, all sense 5
Of being in a hurry gone. We ran
Behind the backs of houses, crossed a street
Of blinding windscreens, smelt the fish-dock; thence
The river's level drifting breadth began,
Where sky and Lincolnshire and water meet. 10

All afternoon, through the tall heat that slept
   For miles inland,
A slow and stopping curve southwards we kept.
Wide farms went by, short-shadowed cattle, and
Canals with floatings of industrial froth; 15
A hothouse flashed uniquely: hedges dipped
And rose: and now and then a smell of grass
Displaced the reek of buttoned carriage-cloth
Until the next town, new and nondescript,
Approached with acres of dismantled cars. 20

At first, I didn't notice what a noise
   The weddings made
Each station that we stopped at: sun destroys
The interest of what's happening in the shade,
And down the long cool platforms whoops and skirls 25
I took for porters larking with the mails,
And went on reading. Once we started, though,
We passed them, grinning and pomaded, girls
In parodies of fashion, heels and veils,
All posed irresolutely, watching us go, 30

As if out on the end of an event
   Waving goodbye
To something that survived it. Struck, I leant
More promptly out next time, more curiously,
And saw it all again in different terms: 35

The fathers with broad belts under their suits
And seamy foreheads; mothers loud and fat;
An uncle shouting smut; and then the perms,
The nylon gloves and jewellery-substitutes,
The lemons, mauves, and olive-ochres that 40

Marked off the girls unreally from the rest.
   Yes, from cafés
And banquet-halls up yards, and bunting-dressed
Coach-party annexes, the wedding-days
Were coming to an end. All down the line 45
Fresh couples climbed aboard: the rest stood round;
The last confetti and advice were thrown,
And, as we moved, each face seemed to define
Just what it saw departing: children frowned
At something dull; fathers had never known 50

Success so huge and wholly farcical;
   The women shared
The secret like a happy funeral;
While girls, gripping their handbags tighter, stared
At a religious wounding. Free at last, 55
And loaded with the sum of all they saw,
We hurried towards London, shuffling gouts of steam.
Now fields were building-plots, and poplars cast
Long shadows over major roads, and for
Some fifty minutes, that in time would seem 60

Just long enough to settle hats and say
   I nearly died,
A dozen marriages got under way.
They watched the landscape, sitting side by side
– An Odeon went past, a cooling tower, 65
And someone running up to bowl – and none
Thought of the others they would never meet
Or how their lives would all contain this hour.
I thought of London spread out in the sun,
Its postal districts packed like squares of wheat: 70

There we were aimed. And as we raced across
   Bright knots of rail

Past standing Pullmans, walls of blackened moss
Came close, and it was nearly done, this frail
Travelling coincidence; and what it held 75
Stood ready to be loosed with all the power
That being changed can give. We slowed again,
And as the tightened brakes took hold, there swelled
A sense of falling, like an arrow-shower
Sent out of sight, somewhere becoming rain. 80

Philip Larkin

'now and then a smell of grass'

GLOSSARY

Whit (Pentecost) Sunday, the seventh after Easter, was a popular time for weddings.
19 *nondescript*: ordinary.
25 *skirls*: high-pitched cries.
26 *larking*: joking, carrying on.
28 *pomaded*: perfumed.
29 *parodies*: imitations.
30 *irresolutely*: hesitantly.
37 *seamy*: lined.
38 *smut*: rude or suggestive comments.
38 *perms*: waved hairstyles popular at the time.
40 *olive-ochres*: green and gold colours.
41 *unreally*: falsely.
44 *annexes*: reserved areas.
57 *gouts*: great spurts.
65 *Odeon*: popular cinema name.
73 *Pullmans*: luxury rail carriages (sleeping cars).
79 *arrow-shower*: short outburst of rain.

EXPLORATIONS

1 What is Larkin's attitude to the wedding parties that he describes in stanzas three and four? Refer to the text in your answer.
2 Select two visual images from the poem to show Larkin's eye for observational detail. Comment briefly on the effectiveness of each example.
3 Write a short personal response to 'The Whitsun Weddings', highlighting the impact it made on you.

• Poetry Focus •

Philip Larkin

STUDY NOTES

Larkin began writing 'The Whitsun Weddings' in 1957, and spent over a year drafting it. He said, 'You couldn't be on that train without feeling the young lives all starting off, and that just for a moment you were touching them. Doncaster, Retford, Grantham, Newark, Peterborough, and at every station more wedding parties. It was wonderful, a marvellous afternoon.' While the poem is lengthy by Larkin's standards, it moves typically from specific observation to an insightful reflection of love and marriage.

The poem's positive title immediately suggests celebration. Larkin's personal narrative makes use of everyday colloquial speech ('I was late getting away') to introduce this seemingly ordinary account of his afternoon journey from Hull to London. The opening lines of stanza one build to a steady rhythm, like a train leaving a railway station. At first, the poet's senses are engaged but not fully absorbed in his surroundings. However, his language ('The river's level drifting breadth') conveys the numbing drowsiness of a warm summer day. Larkin's **characteristic eye for detail** evokes the claustrophobic atmosphere inside the carriage: 'All windows down, all cushions hot'. The panoramic picture of the outside view 'Where sky and Lincolnshire and water meet' reveals his appreciation of nature and an enthusiasm for the English landscape.

Although the poet seems somewhat removed from the rest of society, his sense of place and expressive description continue into stanza two: 'Wide farms went by, short-shadowed cattle'. The June weather is personified ('the tall heat that slept'), adding to an already oppressive mood. Occasional run-through phrasing ('hedges dipped/And rose') echoes the movement of the train on its 'curve southwards'. Always a realist, Larkin includes a number of **unappealing images** associated with the industrial age: 'floatings of industrial froth' and 'acres of dismantled cars'. This convincing sense of the familiar is characteristic of a poet who is known for vividly recording life in post-war England.

Stanza three focuses on the various wedding groups arriving on the station platforms. Larkin gradually realises that the 'whoops and skirls' he hears on the platforms are the animated voices of 'grinning and pomaded' girls who are seeing off the honeymooners. **The poet's tone wavers** between derision of the guests' style ('parodies of fashion') and admiration of their glamorous 'heels and veils'.

Despite his ironic detachment, Larkin cannot help but be increasingly attracted ('more curiously') to the small dramas taking place around him. He observes the various groups – 'fathers with broad belts under their suits', 'mothers loud and fat'. For much of **stanza four**, **his attitude is condescending**, referring to one vulgar uncle 'shouting smut'. He is equally disdainful of the clothes on show ('lemons, mauves and olive-ochres') and the cheap 'jewellery-substitutes'.

The **poet's apparent class superiority** is also evident in **stanza five** as he begins to wonder about the tawdry wedding receptions that have been taking place in 'cafés' and 'banquet-halls up yards'. Despite all this derision, Larkin detects a more important undertone beneath the brash celebrations. All the newlywed couples are about to leave their familiar lives behind. The inherent sadness and inevitability of the moment are summed up as 'The last confetti and advice were thrown'. Meanwhile, real life resumes for the children after the enjoyment of the day, while proud fathers feel relieved that all the fuss is over. For Larkin himself, however, the occasion has brought him closer to the people he has been observing and criticising.

Stanza six marks a change in the poet's outlook. More sensitive than before, he imagines how the **older, more realistic wives view married life pragmatically** as 'a happy funeral', likely to bring both joy and sorrow. This 'secret' is not yet understood by the impressionable younger girls carefully 'gripping their handbags tighter' and who presumably have more romantic notions about marriage. Larkin sees them as facing 'a religious wounding', a typically ambiguous comment, suggesting both the wedding ritual and the likely hurt that lies ahead. From this moment, the poet associates himself more closely with the newlywed couples aboard the train ('Free at last'). He is no longer merely a detached observer as 'We hurried towards London'. The poem's rhythm gathers pace, perhaps reflecting his growing mood of optimism.

The lines maintain their momentum in **stanza seven** as Larkin's fellow-passengers relive the excitement of the day ('*I nearly died*'). The train journey has let the poet realise that **the people he has seen are all interconnected** ('their lives would all contain this hour'). This is coupled with the poignant understanding that it is only Larkin himself who is conscious of this fact ('none/Thought of the others they would never meet'). This overview of how the random lives of individuals form a greater pattern is teased out further as he uses an inventive rural simile to describe London's numerous 'postal districts packed like squares of wheat'.

• Poetry Focus •

Philip Larkin

At the start of **stanza eight**, there is little doubt that Larkin is aware of the full significance of this weekend outing. The 'dozen marriages' have made a lasting impact on the poet. As the train arrives at its destination, he reflects on 'this frail/Travelling coincidence'. **Is he simply saying that all of life can be viewed as a journey** where we meet people by chance, and that some of these encounters have the power to change us? The last lines reach a high point 'as the tightened brakes took hold' and the poem ends on a dramatic note ('A sense of falling'), suggesting both danger and adventure. The final image of the distant 'arrow-shower … becoming rain' is an exciting one, hinting at romance, beauty and even sadness. Elusive to the end, Larkin's poem invites us to consider the wonderful experience of life in all its richness.

ANALYSIS

It has been said that Philip Larkin's poetry is gloomy and pessimistic. In your opinion, is this true of 'The Whitsun Weddings'? Refer to the poem in your answer.

SAMPLE PARAGRAPH

Larkin is more of a realistic poet than a pessimistic one. In my opinion, he celebrated traditional English life in 'The Whitsun Weddings'. He has a love for the English landscape. Even the fish-dock in Hull get his attention. His description of the horizon 'where the sky over Lincolnshire and the water meet' is evidence of his love of his native land. He seems obsessed by the young wedding couples and their families when he sees them at the rail stations. He might be poking fun at them here and there, but it is all good-natured, never mean. Larkin laughs at the 'nylon gloves and the jewellery substitutes' and at the 'uncle shouting out smut' at the honeymooners. This is all very good-natured. And certainly not gloomy. I think the speaking tone he uses shows that he admires these happy wedding guests. He's almost envious of their enjoyment. Philip hears the 'whoops' of the 'mothers loud and very fat', but he seems to be just smiling at their sense of fun. Not that Larkin is a complete bundle of laughs. There are some serious bits, of course. However, he is just being real when he describes the secret comments of the experienced wives who see married life as 'a happy funeral'. Overall, I think Larkin is upbeat and celebrates working-class life.

EXAMINER'S COMMENT

While this lively paragraph makes a reasonable attempt to address the question in a focused way, some points lack development and the expression isn't always controlled. Some of the quotations are also incorrect. Grade-C standard.

CLASS/HOMEWORK EXERCISES

1. It has been said of Larkin that he observes 'ordinary people doing ordinary things'. To what extent do you agree with this statement in light of your reading of 'The Whitsun Weddings'?
2. Copy the table below into your own notes and fill in critical comments about the last two quotations.

Key Quotes

That Whitsun, I was late getting away	From the outset, Larkin's colloquial style and personal narrative approach draw in the reader.
I leant/ More promptly out next time	The image illustrates the poet's increasing fascination with the lives of the wedding parties.
The women shared/ The secret like a happy funeral	Larkin contrasts different reactions to the newlyweds. Does the realism of the older women reflect his own sceptical attitude towards marriage?
and none/ Thought of the others they would never meet	
like an arrow-shower/ Sent out of sight, somewhere becoming rain	

MCMXIV

Philip Larkin

Those long uneven lines
Standing as patiently
As if they were stretched outside
The Oval or Villa Park,
The crowns of hats, the sun   5
On moustached archaic faces
Grinning as if it were all
An August Bank Holiday lark;

And the shut shops, the bleached
Established names on the sunblinds,   10
The farthings and sovereigns,
And dark-clothed children at play
Called after kings and queens,
The tin advertisements
For cocoa and twist, and the pubs   15
Wide open all day;

And the countryside not caring:
The place names all hazed over
With flowering grasses, and fields
Shadowing Domesday lines   20
Under wheat's restless silence;
The differently-dressed servants
With tiny rooms in huge houses,
The dust behind limousines;

Never such innocence,   25
Never before or since,
As changed itself to past
Without a word – the men
Leaving the gardens tidy,
The thousands of marriages   30
Lasting a little while longer:
Never such innocence again.

Leaving Certificate English

Philip Larkin

'Those long uneven lines'

GLOSSARY

The title refers to the Roman numerals for 1914, the year that World War I began. It became known as the Great War, a landmark event in the 20th century.
4 *The Oval*: famous cricket ground near London.
4 *Villa Park*: Birmingham home ground of Aston Villa football club.
6 *archaic*: dated, old-fashioned.
8 *lark*: celebration, spree.
11 *farthings and sovereigns*: currency used at the time. The copper farthing was just a quarter of a penny, while the gold sovereign coin was worth £1.
15 *twist*: probably refers to a small piece of tobacco.
20 *Domesday*: medieval spelling of Doomsday (or Judgment Day); in 1086, William the Conqueror compiled a record of English land ownership in the Domesday Book.
24 *limousines*: luxury cars.

EXPLORATIONS

1 Suggest a reason to explain why the poet chose to write the title in Roman numerals. (Where else might the letters MCMXIV be seen?)
2 In your opinion, is Larkin's view of the past accurate and realistic or is it sentimental and idealised? Refer to the text in your answer.
3 What do you think is meant by the final line, 'Never such innocence again'? Briefly explain your answer.

STUDY NOTES

This elegiac poem, written in 1960, has often been read as a nostalgic account of a vanished English way of life. The Roman numerals of the title evoke war memorials and the detailed descriptions seem to suggest old photographs. The whole poem consists of one long sentence, giving a sense of timelessness and connecting readers with the men lining up for army service.

• Poetry Focus •

Philip Larkin

Larkin's meditation begins with a description of an old photograph of 'uneven lines' of British volunteers outside an army recruiting office at the start of World War I. In **stanza one**, the poet observes that the men are queuing happily, as if for a game of cricket or football. The **tragic irony of their fate** is suggested by the image of the sun shining on their 'moustached archaic faces' and their carefree expressions, 'Grinning' as if it was all just a 'lark'. Larkin's tone seems unclear. Does he admire the men's idealism and courage or is there a sense that these raw recruits are naïvely seeking adventure?

The holiday atmosphere continues in **stanza two** with a **wistful celebration of pre-war English life**. Larkin lists some of the hallmarks of a bygone era: 'farthings and sovereigns', 'children at play', 'cocoa and twist'. Trusted shops ('Established names') and public houses ('Wide open all day') add to this relaxed feeling of security. Overall, this idealised image of a long-lost England is one of innocence, freedom and stability.

The poet swaps the familiar town setting for the open countryside in **stanza three**. At first, the mood seems untroubled ('not caring'). The alliterative effect and soft sibilant sounds of 'flowering grasses, and fields' evoke England's green and pleasant land. But the positive mood is suddenly overshadowed by the reference to 'Domesday lines' – a chilling echo of the earlier 'uneven lines' of men whose lives are likely to end on the battlefield. The reality of mass war graves is further stressed by the unsettling image of the 'wheat's restless silence'. **Larkin's tone becomes increasingly critical** as he focuses on the class divisions ('differently-dressed servants') prevalent within English society. Images of 'tiny rooms in huge houses' and 'dust behind limousines' suggest that social inequality was hidden away hypocritically.

The powerfully emotive force of **stanza four** emphasises **the passing of an innocent age**: 'Never before or since'. Purposeful rhythm and repetition ('never' is used three times) reflect Larkin's shocking realisation that the war would mark a turning point in our understanding of man's inhumanity to man. The compelling image of countless naïve volunteers leaving their homes, unaware that their marriages would only last 'a little while longer', is undeniably poignant. Rather than being a hymn of sentimental nostalgia, the poem is dark with the shadow of unexpected death and we are left with an enduring sense of the human tragedy involved.

ANALYSIS

In your view, how well does Larkin's poem 'MCMXIV' convey the innocence of pre-war England?

SAMPLE PARAGRAPH

Many of Philip Larkin's poems on our course, e.g. 'Ambulances' and 'The Whitsun Weddings', give me a good insight into the past and ordinary English life. This is certainly true of his war poem 'MCMXIV'. The poem begins with a series of images showing long lines of young men signing up to enlist in the war. They are 'Grinning' and have no notion of the horrors before them. Their innocence is very well seen in the way Larkin shows them standing 'patiently' as though they were waiting to enter a football stadium. There is a photographic quality to his descriptions. Life seems simple, carefree. The poet suggests this with images of bank holidays, familiar shop advertisements, young children playing and the pubs 'Wide open all day'. But there is another, darker side to pre-war society – social division. Larkin reminds us of the 'differently-dressed servants' who are slaving away in 'tiny rooms' for the upper classes. By the end of the poem, he suggests that the innocent pre-war years were about to be replaced with a horrifying time of conflict, mass destruction and death. I found the final verse very effective, repeating the awful truth – 'Never such innocence again'. The peace and harmony of the past would be shattered for all time.

EXAMINER'S COMMENT

An assured personal response, focused throughout and well illustrated. Quotations are integrated effectively and the answer ranges widely over the positive and negative aspects of English life presented in the poem. Grade A.

CLASS/HOMEWORK EXERCISES

1. How does Larkin establish the underlying sense of death that pervades the poem? Refer closely to the text in your answer.
2. Copy the table below into your own notes and fill in critical comments about the last two quotations.

• Poetry Focus •

Philip Larkin

Key Quotes

Those long uneven lines	The description of the enlisting men, as yet undisciplined, is in contrast to the grim reality of what lies ahead.
An August Bank Holiday lark	The archaic word 'lark' (meaning fun) exposes the innocence of the volunteers. How much sympathy does Larkin have for them?
Under wheat's restless silence	This subtle image foreshadows the mass war graves of Europe. Sibilance adds to the poignant mood.
tiny rooms in huge houses	
Never such innocence again	

Ambulances

Closed like confessionals, they thread
Loud noons of cities, giving back
None of the glances they absorb.
Light glossy grey, arms on a plaque,
They come to rest at any kerb: 5
All streets in time are visited.

Then children strewn on steps or road,
Or women coming from the shops
Past smells of different dinners, see
A wild white face that overtops 10
Red stretcher-blankets momently
As it is carried in and stowed,

And sense the solving emptiness
That lies just under all we do,
And for a second get it whole, 15
So permanent and blank and true.
The fastened doors recede. *Poor soul*,
They whisper at their own distress;

For borne away in deadened air
May go the sudden shut of loss 20
Round something nearly at an end,
And what cohered in it across
The years, the unique random blend
Of families and fashions, there

At last begin to loosen. Far 25
From the exchange of love to lie
Unreachable inside a room
The traffic parts to let go by
Brings closer what is left to come,
And dulls to distance all we are. 30

• Poetry Focus •

Philip Larkin

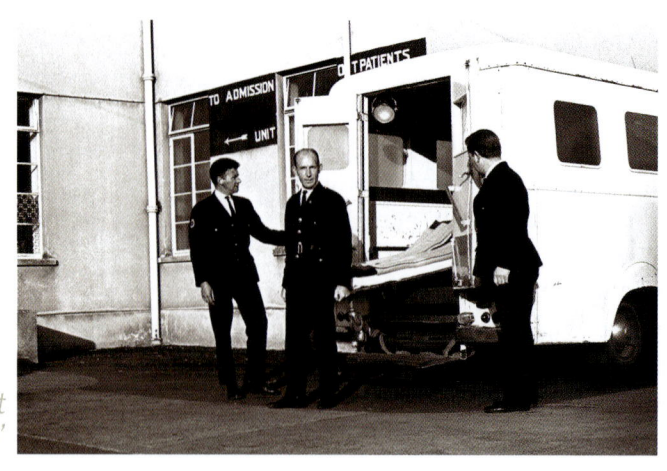

'They come to rest at any kerb'

GLOSSARY

1 *confessionals*: small, box-like rooms used by Catholic priests to hear confessions.
4 *plaque*: shiny metal sign on the side of the ambulance.
7 *strewn*: scattered around.
12 *stowed*: stored.
17 *recede*: move away.
22 *cohered*: brought together.

EXPLORATIONS

1 How does Larkin present the ambulances in stanza one? Are they mysterious? Comforting? Disturbing? Refer to the text in your answer.
2 From your reading of the second stanza, what evidence can you find of the poet's superb eye for interesting detail?
3 Critics have said that Philip Larkin's poems are more realistic than pessimistic. In your opinion, is this the case in 'Ambulances'? Give reasons for your answer.

STUDY NOTES

'Ambulances' is a reflection on life and mortality, written in the early 1960s when an ambulance was usually associated with bad news. Larkin once remarked that everything he wrote had 'the consciousness of approaching death in the background'.

What do you think of when you see an ambulance? A serious road accident or some other emergency? Do you feel a sense of fear or of hope? People usually become apprehensive when they hear an ambulance siren. Are they genuinely concerned or are they just being inquisitive and voyeuristic?

From the outset of 'Ambulances', the tone is uneasy. There is an immediate sense of threat from these anonymous 'grey' vans which prowl around 'Loud noons of cities'. Even in the hustle and bustle of urban life, nobody escapes. Larkin sees these vehicles as **symbols of death**. An ambulance can take anyone away at any time. The patient is confined and vulnerable in much the same way as everyone is unable to escape dying: 'All streets in times are visited'. The dramatic opening line of the *first stanza* compares the ambulance van to a confessional – a place where people experience spiritual rebirth and make their peace with God. This religious image forces readers to face up to the inevitability of death. The poet personifies the vehicles, but they are as unresponsive as a corpse, 'giving back/None of the glances they absorb'. Bystanders glance nervously at passing ambulances, perhaps hoping deep down that their time has not yet come. However, the randomness of death is starkly emphasised by the line 'They come to rest at any kerb'. We are all powerless against the **stark reality of our mortality**.

Stanza two demonstrates Larkin's keen eye for vivid detail as he describes the **reaction of onlookers** when an ambulance arrives and disturbs a quiet neighbourhood. The street is suddenly transformed. Normal life stops for a moment as people consider the significance of what is happening. Simple, colloquial language illustrates the sharp contrast between everyday life ('children strewn on steps or road') and the hidden terror of death as the patient (now an unknown body described as 'it') is carried out to the ambulance. The **colour images** highlight the anguish of life-threatening illness ('A wild white face') and danger ('Red stretcher-blankets').

Larkin's tone is much more reflective in *stanza three*. This is typical of his writing. The crowd of spectators watching the small drama taking place 'sense the solving emptiness/That lies just under all we do'. They have been forced to confront the one underlying truth that all life ends with the mystery of dying. The poet himself was an atheist who could only believe in the 'emptiness' of oblivion after death. Unlike the earlier third-person description in the opening stanzas, the introduction of the pronoun 'we' gives the poem a **universal significance**. Death is our common fate and, in Larkin's belief, makes life meaningless. This seems to be the central **moment of truth**, or epiphany, in the poem – the morbid discovery that human existence is futile. Modern secular society avoids death. It is a taboo subject that we only think about when we are forced to.

For Larkin, all of our daily concerns – cooking, playing, etc. – are merely ways of filling time until death transports us to a state of 'permanent and blank' nothingness. As the ambulance pulls away, the poet suggests that people's whispered sympathy ('*Poor soul*') for the patient is really a selfish expression of 'their own distress'. Such **irony is a common feature** of Larkin's cynical observations of everyday life.

In the **final two stanzas, the mood of depression deepens** as Larkin considers the dying patient experiencing 'the sudden shut of loss'. Stark imagery and a deliberate rhythm combine to suggest the great change that death will bring, separating the individual from family and identity. The sensation of being isolated inside the ambulance ('Unreachable inside a room') echoes the earlier alienation of the confessional and adds to the growing sense of panic. Death will eventually alter ('loosen') everything.

Although the syntax (order of words) is complex at the end, Larkin manages to give a clear impression of his own **sombre philosophy**. As with much of his work, he is able to take a particular circumstance and find a general truth in it. The poem ends on a sweetly serene note of disillusion. Although ambulances try to save lives, they are actually the messengers of unavoidable death. The final disarming image leaves a lingering sense of bleakness. As the traffic parts and the ambulance siren quickly fades away, death also 'dulls to distance all we are'. For Larkin, there is no higher purpose to human existence, no comforting afterlife.

ANALYSIS

Write a paragraph on Larkin's use of vivid and realistic images in 'Ambulances'.

SAMPLE PARAGRAPH

The opening lines of 'Ambulances' contain many authentic images of the vans weaving in and out of traffic as they 'thread' their way through a busy city. We are given an immediate sense of the everyday setting and the noisy street: 'Loud noons of cities'. This condensed image effectively conveys a realistic impression of the city-centre sounds at midday. Larkin adds drama to the scene by describing one 'Light glossy grey' ambulance suddenly coming to a 'rest at any kerb'. It is the immediate focus of attention. The poet fills in the dramatic scene with precise pictures of the various spectators. Women coming from the shops stop and stare. There is realistic detailed description of the 'smells of different dinners' and of the children who are innocently playing, 'strewn on steps or road'. However, Larkin's picture of the sick patient is the most convincing of all. 'A wild white face' staring up from the 'Red stretcher-blankets' suggests pain and fear. The vivid images create a compelling sense of the seriousness of what is happening.

EXAMINER'S COMMENT

As part of a full essay answer, this A-grade paragraph is firmly focused on how Larkin selects vibrant and energetic images to convey meaning and reinforce his themes. The quotations are effectively used to illustrate the poet's skill in creating key moments of drama surrounding the sudden arrival of the ambulance.

CLASS/HOMEWORK EXERCISES

1. How would you describe the dominant mood of 'Ambulances'? Using evidence from the poem, write a paragraph showing how Larkin creates this mood. (Model your answer on the sample paragraph above.)
2. Copy the table below into your own notes and fill in critical comments about the last two quotations.

Key Quotes

They come to rest at any kerb	The ambulance (representing death) can come at any time. This is a central theme in the poem.
children strewn on steps…/ A wild white face	Typically, Larkin's evocative and detailed imagery is taken from everyday life.
the solving emptiness	Everyone must eventually face up to the reality of death. Assonant and sibilant effects add poignancy to the phrase.
They whisper at their own distress	
Unreachable inside a room	

• Poetry Focus •

The Trees

Philip Larkin

The trees are coming into leaf
Like something almost being said;
The recent buds relax and spread,
Their greennesss is a kind of grief.

Is it they are born again   5
And we grow old? No, they die too.
Their yearly trick of looking new
Is written down in rings of grain.

Yet still the unresting castles thresh
In fullgrown thickness every May.   10
Last year is dead, they seem to say,
Begin afresh, afresh, afresh.

'The recent buds relax and spread'

EXPLORATIONS

1. Larkin compares and contrasts the world of nature in 'The Trees' with the world of man. List one similarity and one contrast and comment on their effectiveness. Support your views with reference to the poem.
2. 'Like something almost being said'. In your opinion, what is almost being said? To whom and by whom is it being said?
3. 'Begin afresh, afresh, afresh.' Do you think this line is optimistic or full of false hope?

STUDY NOTES

'The Trees' was written in 1967 and forms part of the *High Windows* collection. At this point, Larkin's personal life had become complicated. His mother was suffering from the early stages of Alzheimer's. This adds a special resonance to the last line of the poem. Do you think that people often long to 'Begin afresh, afresh, afresh'?

Larkin deals with the classic theme of **transience** (passing time) in this lyric poem. The language in the **opening stanza** is harmonious and sombre, as long vowel sounds ('a', 'o' and 'u') announce the arrival of spring. The event is seen as inevitable; Larkin conveys the feeling that this has happened so often before. The mystery of the leaves' tentative arrival is suggested in the simile 'Like something almost being said'. We know it's going to happen, but we don't know how or why. It just does. Note the use of 'we' – this is a message for all of us. The verbs 'relax and spread' vividly convey the abundant covering of leaves on the former bare branches. But this rejuvenation of nature is not greeted warmly by the poet, who states that it is 'a kind of grief'. For whom is there sorrow? Man is unable to renew himself. Is the poet perhaps thinking of lost opportunities, what might have been? Or perhaps he is thinking of loved ones who are sick. The slow three-beat rhythm (iambic tetrameter) perfectly suits this lyrical meditation on the theme of decay and death.

In the **second stanza**, Larkin asks a rhetorical question to explore this thought further: 'Is it that they are born again/And we grow old?' The stark answer comes in the broken line 'No, they die too'. He does not flinch from the unpalatable reality of the **finality of all living things**. Time passes relentlessly and mercilessly, and the passage through time is recorded 'in rings of grain' in the tree trunks. The trees' appearance of renewal is just that – appearance, a 'trick'. The rhyme here (*cddc*) is pertinent: 'born again' rhymes with 'rings of grain', emphasising that their trick of renewal is exposed in the tree trunk.

Larkin's tone changes abruptly in the **third stanza**. **The energy and life** of the blossoming trees is celebrated in the metaphor 'unresting castles'. Spring's dynamic growth is shown in the compound word 'fullgrown' and in the assonance of 'unresting' and 'thresh'. Life springs back 'every May'. The trees, symbols of courage, are giving a message of hope to mankind as they seem to say, 'Last year is dead'. There is no use grieving over what is gone; concentrate on the future. The trees' exhortation is charged with urgency in the appeal 'Begin afresh, afresh, afresh'. Is this what was hinted at in the earlier phrase,

'Like something almost being said'? The vibrant rhetoric of spring demands that we seize the day. The life-force of the trees is sending out the hope-filled message: don't give up. Is this longing for life attractive but false? Which is the abiding message of the poem, the **vitality of life or the inevitability of death? Could it be both?**

ANALYSIS

Larkin was dismissive of his insights in this poem. He mocked 'The Trees' as 'awful tripe'. Do you agree or disagree with this view? Support your opinion with references from the poem.

SAMPLE PARAGRAPH

Larkin wrote of his 'astounded delight at the renewal of the natural world'. This lyric, with its theme of transience, emphasises this view, but also brings it a step further. Here is no attractive, false idea of renewal. The poet realises that the trees will, after renewing themselves year after year (unlike humans), eventually die. The abrupt broken line 'No, they die too' boldly states this fact. He calls their rejuvenation a 'trick', as if there is something false or deceitful in what they do. The passage of inexorable time is marked in the material, decaying world in 'rings of grain'. This is definitely not 'tripe', but genuine insight into the nature of things, however unsavoury. I feel his imagination is caught by the vitality and dynamism of the growing trees, which he describes as 'unresting castles'. The onomatopoeic 'thresh' captures this swaying movement and sense of being vibrantly alive. The concluding line, with its repetitive appeal to 'Begin afresh, afresh, afresh', seems to me to be a plea for hope. Life should be lived to the brim. So the voice of the trees/the poet is telling us to seize the day. I believe that Larkin was very wrong to be so dismissive of this lyric. Each new day brings with it the possibility of wonder.

EXAMINER'S COMMENT

This focused paragraph eloquently argues the merits of Larkin's poem. A clear viewpoint is established, detailing a range of points. Expression and vocabulary are impressive. The judicious use of quotation adds weight to the response. Grade A.

CLASS/HOMEWORK EXERCISES

1. Larkin said, 'When you've read a poem, that's it, it's all quite clear what it means.' Having read 'The Trees', would you agree or disagree with this view? Support your answer with reference to the text.
2. Copy the table below into your own notes and fill in critical comments about the last two quotations.

Key Quotes

The trees are coming into leaf/ Like something almost being said	This simile vividly shows the tentative arrival of the new growth on the trees and hints at the mystery of life.
Is it that they are born again/ And we grow old?	Larkin poses a rhetorical question, teasing out the difference between the fate of the trees and humans.
Their yearly trick of looking new	The word 'trick' suggests deception and double-dealing on the part of the trees, as they 'seem' to be rejuvenated each year. They appear to be defeating time.
Yet still the unresting castles thresh	
Begin afresh, afresh, afresh	

• Poetry Focus •

The Explosion

Philip Larkin

On the day of the explosion
Shadows pointed towards the pithead:
In the sun the slagheap slept.

Down the lane came men in pitboots
Coughing oath-edged talk and pipe-smoke,   5
Shouldering off the freshened silence.

One chased after rabbits; lost them;
Came back with a nest of lark's eggs;
Showed them; lodged them in the grasses.

So they passed in beards and moleskins,   10
Fathers, brothers, nicknames, laughter,
Through the tall gates standing open.

At noon there came a tremor; cows
Stopped chewing for a second; sun,
Scarfed as in a heat-haze, dimmed.   15

The dead go on before us, they
Are sitting in God's house in comfort,
We shall see them face to face –

Plain as lettering in the chapels
It was said, and for a second   20
Wives saw men of the explosion

Larger than in life they managed –
Gold as on a coin, or walking
Somehow from the sun towards them,

One showing the eggs unbroken.   25

• 322 •

Philip Larkin

'Fathers, brothers, nicknames, laughter'

GLOSSARY

2 *pithead*: the top part of a mine.
3 *slagheap*: man-made hill formed from the waste of coal mining.
4 *pitboots*: heavy boots worn by miners.
8 *lark's eggs*: the eggs of the skylark, a native bird of England and Ireland.
10 *moleskins*: heavy material worn by working men.
15 *Scarfed*: wrapped up.

EXPLORATIONS

1 Does Larkin give a realistic picture of the working men? Choose two realistic details (images) that you found effective.
2 Would you consider this poem a religious poem? Why or why not?
3 Comment on the concluding image as a symbol of redemption.

STUDY NOTES

'The Explosion' documents a tragedy that can randomly happen to a community, but it offers a consolation that is not present in Larkin's other poems. The word 'explosion' brings to mind a loud bang, destruction, dead bodies. What other words do you associate with the word 'explosion'?

The **source** of this poem was a **documentary** Larkin watched on the coal-mining industry. The poem gives an account of an underground accident in which a number of miners lost their lives. Many of the miners' wives were supposed to have seen visions of their husbands at the moment of the explosion. Larkin also said, 'I heard a **song** about a mine disaster ... it made me want to write the same thing, a mine disaster with a vision of immortality at the end ... that's the point of the eggs.'

Philip Larkin

The poem **opens quietly as the scene is observed** in stanza one and we are gently led into the drama: 'On the day of the explosion'. Notice the word 'the'. This is a specific event that will affect specific people. The details give a premonition of disaster: 'Shadows pointed towards the pithead'. The alliteration of the explosive letter 'p' adds to the menace, as does the personification: 'slagheap slept'. The image of a sleeping monster that will wreak havoc if awoken is suggested. The alliteration of 's' emphasises the uneasy peace.

In **contrast**, along come the noisy miners, swearing and coughing in stanza two. An impression of proud, ordinary strong young men from the tough world of the mines is given in a few well-chosen details: 'pitboots', 'Coughing oath-edged talk and pipe-smoke'. The onomatopoeia in the line 'Shouldering off the freshened silence' gives an idea of their rough strength. They walk unknowing, but we know and this adds to the growing tension and suspense in the poem. **We are brought closer to the miners** in stanza three as we observe them playing about. One chases rabbits, but comes back with a 'nest of lark's eggs'. He 'shows' the eggs. These are men who are interested in and deeply respectful of nature. He 'lodged' the eggs in the grasses, where the mother bird could find them. We see the sensitivity in these tough men.

The miners are part of a **close-knit community**, as we learn in stanza four: 'Fathers, brothers, nicknames, laughter'. The poignancy is becoming unbearable for the reader as we realise all will be blown apart by the event that is about to occur. The 'tall gates' are waiting, 'standing open', almost like the gates of the underworld, inescapable. **These men meet their fate** in stanza five ('So they passed'). The language is almost biblical. The ending is becoming inevitable. Larkin records the accident calmly, without melodrama. Instead we are presented with the ripple effects of the explosion on nature: 'cows/Stopped chewing' and the sun 'dimmed' as it was supposed to have done at the crucifixion of Christ. Time stands still. The explosion only registered for a 'second'. This is in contrast with the world of the men, where nothing will ever be the same again. But the rescue and the grief are unmentioned. We are left to imagine the horror.

In the final part of the poem (stanzas six to nine), **the focus is changed**. Now we are looking at the wives and their reactions to the deaths. The passage from the Bible is in italics, words of comfort, a certainty of resurrection: '*We shall see them face to face*'. The wives believe this so strongly that they have a glimpse of their husbands and sons 'for a second'. Notice the difference of the reaction of the wives and the animals. The women's lives are irrevocably changed, but the animals resume their grazing. This terrible tragedy is of no consequence to the world of nature. They are unable to explain this vision 'Somehow'. These men are as they were and also are now **transformed**, 'Larger than in life'. They are walking in brilliant light. The sun is now the blazing sun of eternity. They are 'Gold as on a coin', a pure and enduring metal. The rhythm is stately and formal, which suits the religious viewpoint.

The **poem ends on a note of affirmation**, with the potent image of the unbroken eggs suggesting the hope of resurrection, the continuity of life and the strength of the ties of love. The last line stands alone, separated from the eight other three-line stanzas. Larkin's scepticism is absent. He is moved by sympathy for these men and their families. As the poet has said (in 'An Arundel Tomb'), 'What will survive of us is love'. This is the last poem in his last collection of poetry. Is it being suggested that love triumphs over death? Is this a modern religious poem?

ANALYSIS

Write a paragraph on Larkin's use of memorable images in 'The Explosion'.

SAMPLE PARAGRAPH

Larkin captures the scene on the day of the explosion with a few well-chosen visual details. He alerts the reader to the possibility of disaster with the sinister image of the 'shadows' which 'pointed towards the pithead', almost as if they were arrows of destiny marking the target of the miners. The air of menace is further emphasised with the memorable image of the slagheap as it 'slept' in the sun. The personification suggests a sleeping monster that will cause chaos if woken up. The image of the 'tall gates standing open' appealed to me, as it suggested the entry of the men into death's kingdom. The long vowel sounds slow the line. Death does not know time. These vowels, 'a' and 'o', lend a stately, solemn rhythm to the phrase, which reminds me of a ceremonial funeral march. The final image, contained in the floating last line, 'One showing the eggs unbroken', is full of optimism and hope, as it reminds me of Easter and the Resurrection of Christ. The image reflects a rare moment when Larkin has a positive attitude towards a Christian afterlife. The little eggs suggest renewal, the beginning of a new era. Larkin has laid aside his cynicism. The poem ends on this memorable image of transcendence, making the poem a beautiful religious credo.

Philip Larkin

EXAMINER'S COMMENT

This is a succinct and well-controlled paragraph. The student has a close knowledge of the text and has clearly understood the task. The writing is fluent throughout and makes effective use of pertinent quotation. Grade A.

CLASS/HOMEWORK EXERCISES

1. Write a paragraph on how the structure of the poem helps Larkin communicate his theme effectively. (Look at the arrangement of the stanzas scene by scene on the page, the use of run-on lines, the placement of key words, the use of italics and the separate last line.)
2. Copy the table below into your own notes and fill in critical comments about the last two quotations.

Key Quotes

So they passed in beards and moleskins	The use of detailed images adds a strong visual quality and realism to the description of the miners.
Fathers, brothers, nicknames, laughter	Larkin recognises and admires the ordinary lives of this hardworking mining community.
At noon, there came a tremor	There are no details about the actual explosion. The tone is detached and the poet seems stunned by the event.
We shall see them face to face	
the eggs unbroken	

Cut Grass

Philip Larkin

Cut grass lies frail:
Brief is the breath
Mown stalks exhale.
Long, long the death

It dies in the white hours   5
Of young-leafed June
With chestnut flowers,
With hedges snowlike strewn,

White lilac bowed,
Lost lanes of Queen Anne's lace,   10
And that high-builded cloud
Moving at summer's pace.

'Lost lanes of Queen Anne's lace'

GLOSSARY

2 *Brief is the breath*: life is short (the Bible says: 'all the glory of man is as flowers of grass').
8 *strewn*: covered untidily.
10 *Queen Anne's lace*: cow parsley, a white wild flower with lace-like blooms.

EXPLORATIONS

1 This poem gives a picture of a rural landscape. What colour predominates? List three examples. What is the colour white usually associated with? (Innocence, weddings, funeral flowers, purity, etc.) In your opinion, why does Larkin use this colour?

• Poetry Focus •

Philip Larkin

2   In your opinion, what is the mood of the poem? Does it change or not? Give evidence from the text to support your view.
3   Write a paragraph giving your own personal response to this poem. Refer closely to the text in your answer.

STUDY NOTES

'Cut Grass' is a lyric dealing with a recurring theme in Larkin's poetry, passing time and death. Written in 1971, it appeared in his collection *High Windows*. It is a calm poem that Larkin saw as a 'succession of images'. His verdict was, 'I like it all right'. Yet it was written at the end of Larkin's life, when he was very bitter about the state of England ('what an end to a great country'). He was critical of socialism and immigrants: 'I have always been right wing ... I identify with certain virtues (thrift, hard work, reverence, desire to preserve).'

The Bible states that 'All flesh is grass'. The title of 'Cut Grass' echoes this classic theme implicitly as we are reminded of the figure of Father Time/Death with his scythe. All living things are mown down. The setting of this poem is a meadow that has been recently mown. 'Cut grass lies frail' suggests the **fragility and brevity of life** against the relentless approach of inescapable death. The word 'frail' almost seems to expire as its sound drifts away at the end of the first line of stanza one. The short, unpredictable life of the grass is eloquently captured in the alliterative phrase 'Brief is the breath'. Explosive 'b' sounds reflect the action of breathing in and out. This personification, continued in the verb 'exhale', implies the parallel between our tenuous hold on life and that of all living things. The full stop at the end of this line underscores the reality of death and its finality. In contrast to this, the first stanza runs on into the next stanza to emphasise the fact that death is endless; it is not subject to time: 'Long, long the death'.

Stanza two tells us when the grass in the meadow dies, just at the moment when all other things are growing profusely. The trees are beginning to come into leaf and the hedges are covered in foaming whitethorn, like snow ('snowlike strewn'). The alliteration and run-on lines suggest the abundance of nature. **Nature has the ability to renew itself**, as the compound word 'young-leafed' suggests. We wonder: can man renew himself? The assonance ('hours', 'flowers') adds a poignant, melancholy note to this stanza, as in the midst of life is death.

In the **third stanza**, this abundance continues as the succession of beautiful white images mirror each other: 'White lilac bowed' flows into frothy 'lanes of Queen Anne's lace'. This wild flower appears every summer in out-of-the way lanes throughout rural England. Is this poem also an elegy for a disappearing England? The alliteration of 'l' suggests the meandering, winding lanes of the countryside. Towering white clouds add to this picture of rural serenity, as they glide effortlessly by, 'Moving at summer's pace'. But all will die in their own time. **This elegy is like a lament or requiem**, its long vowel sounds suggesting the lingering of the bereaved, unwilling to let the dead go. The poet's tone is sympathetic, resigned to the inevitable.

Here is no Christian consolation, no exhortation to live life passionately. The two-sentence poem is divided into short, abrupt sentences at the start which showcase the harsh finality of death. The poem then moves into the long run-on lines of the second sentence, which is stately and dignified and is suitable for a lament. The regular rhyme scheme (*abab, cdcd, efef*) underpins the fact that time passes and death comes; it is unavoidable. **Larkin clearly valued traditional English poetry forms**, as he valued England.

ANALYSIS

Larkin said he wrote two kinds of poems, 'the beautiful and true'. Discuss this statement, referring to the poem 'Cut Grass'. Support your view with references from the poem.

SAMPLE PARAGRAPH

In my opinion, Larkin has indeed written a poem that resonates with truth. There is no escaping the sad finality of all human existence, 'Brief is the breath'. The poet does not give us any consolation either in this elegy. The real truth of human mortality floats in our consciousness as timeless and as inevitable as the 'high-builded cloud' floats in the sky on a summer's day. I also think this poem is beautiful, as the succession of idyllic images which are truly English are presented to us. The smell of cut grass is suggested in the evocative line 'Mown stalks exhale'. The abundance and generosity of nature is shown in the alliterative phrase 'hedges snowlike strewn'. But for me the real beauty of the poem lies in the musical writing. It reminds me of a song lyric. The assonance of long vowel sounds ('Long, long') and slender vowels ('White lilac') evoke long, lazy summer evenings that are quintessentially English. The melancholic phrase 'Lost lanes' seems to be lamenting a lost way of life, as well as death, as the 'l' sound lingers on the ear. Larkin is a superb craftsman. The gentle fading sounds of the words 'frail' and 'exhale' both disappear, as all individual existence does into the inevitability of death. The finality of death is punctuated sternly by the full stop after 'exhale'. The compound words 'young-leafed', 'high-builded' show the beauty of life. The regular rhyme scheme (*abab, cdcd, efef*) moves as effortlessly as the clouds 'at summer's pace'. Larkin expresses a classic, true theme in a beautiful way. Like him, I like this poem 'all right'.

EXAMINER'S COMMENT

This paragraph addresses the two elements of the question (beautiful and true). It shows a real appreciation of poetic technique. Fluent and varied expression, particularly the impressive vocabulary, merits a grade A.

CLASS/HOMEWORK EXERCISES

1. Larkin's poems show 'loneliness, emptiness and mortality'. Do you agree that this is true of 'Cut Grass'? Refer to the text in your answer.
2. Copy the table below into your own notes and fill in critical comments about the last two quotations.

Key Quotes

Cut grass lies frail	Life is short for all living things.
Mown stalks exhale	The long vowel sounds ('a' and 'o') slow the pace of the line, emphasising the inevitability of passing time.
It dies in the white hours/ Of young-leafed June	Contrast adds a poignant tone. The rest of nature is very much alive, as referenced by the compound word 'young-leafed'.
Lost lanes of Queen Anne's lace	
And that high-builded cloud/Moving at summer's pace	

LEAVING CERT SAMPLE ESSAY

Q 'The appeal of Philip Larkin's poetry.'
Using the above title, write an essay outlining what you consider to be the appeal of Larkin's poetry. Refer to the poems by Philip Larkin that you have studied.

> **MARKING SCHEME GUIDELINES**
>
> Expect a clear focus on the appeal (or lack of it) of the poems by Larkin. Responses may concentrate on the poet's themes and/or style. Evidence of engagement/involvement with the work of the poet should be rewarded.
>
> Material may be drawn from the following:
> - The poet's distinctive personality; honesty, compassion.
> - His observations of the ordinary, everyday world.
> - Prominent themes: time, transience, love, death.
> - Powerful visual images, metaphors, sound effects.
> - Colloquial language, measured rhythm, controlled rhyme.
> - Use of irony, dark humour, dry wit.
> - Varying tones – optimism, nostalgia, disillusionment, etc.

SAMPLE ESSAY
(The Appeal of Larkin's Poetry)

1 Philip Larkin has a reputation as a gloomy poet who sees nothing positive about the world around him. 'Writing about unhappiness is the source of my popularity' (Larkin). Yet he is still one of the most highly regarded poets of the 20th century. His poems are memorable because they address everyday issues such as love, marriage and death. This is done through stories based on his own observations of the world around him. Best of all, he tackles these subjects in a fresh and honest way.

2 There is evidence in 'The Whitsun Weddings' that Larkin saw marriage in a very positive light. A wedding traditionally offered a chance for happiness. The poem has a narrative, colloquial quality that appeals to me. Larkin's insight into human behaviour is very interesting. It's as if we are listening to gossip. He witnesses several newlywed couples boarding the train at each station, with their families waving farewell to them. At the beginning, he seems critical and cynical at what is going on, with 'the mothers loud and fat', 'An uncle shouting smut' and the 'jewellery-substitutes'. But this is the kind of honest criticism that makes the poem true to life. He even notes the sad aspects of weddings, where children leave the family home. This is suggested by the phrase 'The last confetti'. However, Larkin finally describes the 'arrow-shower … somewhere becoming rain', a beautiful image clearly suggesting that there is hope for these couples.

3. The passing of time is a recurring theme in Larkin's poems. 'At Grass' takes a nostalgic look at another typical rural landscape where racehorses are quietly grazing. The poet creates a strangely calm scene with a cinematic image of the wide field. The two horses are imprecise figures far away in the distance: 'The eye can hardly pick them out'. The lines are slow moving and the punctuation holds up the pace: 'Then one crops grass, and moves about'. A strange sense of time passing is created with the use of dashes and the steady, even rhyme scheme. This forces the reader to closely observe what is being expressed, moment by moment. The attractive soft tone and gentle sounds are in keeping with the poem's wistful mood.

4. Larkin then draws in readers by giving us the history of these distinguished animals. They once won 'Cups and Stakes and Handicaps'. Short, snappy punctuation captures the tension and buzz of the racetrack. But all that glory and attention have now passed as they spend their final years in 'unmolesting meadows'. The mood of fulfilment brings the poem to a truly satisfying conclusion. Larkin contemplates what will happen when our 'fame' has ended. Will we all 'stand anonymous again'? What will happen to us when we are past our glory and our prime? The poet's tender sentiments illustrate his sensitive awareness of life's realities. However, like many of his poems, we can interpret the outlook as either positive or negative. For me, the poem is meaningful because it broadly celebrates life, but also regrets its passing.

5. What is interesting about Larkin's poems about death is that he openly writes about the one thing we all fear most. In 'Ambulances', Larkin begins looking at an ambulance's journey through a built-up town where the locals are busy getting on with their ordinary lives. But the ambulance is a reminder of how fragile life is. The poet's startling imagery reflects people's shock when they see this sick woman being stretchered out of her home. Her 'wild white face' is a reminder of how helpless and

fearful she is. People whisper 'Poor soul' but 'They whisper at their own distress'. What is impressive about Larkin is that he always gets to the truth. And the truth hurts. It's not that people don't feel sorry for the dying patient, it's more that they cannot really make sense of death.

6   *Overall, there is an engaging sense of realism and energy about Philip Larkin's poems. He is honest enough to face up to universal fears while still feeling sympathy for ordinary individuals. I believe that Larkin isn't as cynical as he is made out to be. He celebrates life and relationships in poems such as 'An Arundel Tomb', where he concludes: 'What will survive of us is love'. There are many examples of where he is sympathetic to people (e.g. the victims in 'The Explosion') because they are powerless against fate. I am convinced that Larkin fully deserves his reputation and that his poetry will continue to appeal to readers.*

(approx. 750 words)

GRADE: A2
P   = 15/15
C   = 12/15
L   = 12/15
M   = 5/5
Total = 44/50

EXAMINER'S COMMENT

This is a good, personal response that is focused and well supported. The candidate displays a clear knowledge of Larkin's work. Quotations are accurate and successfully integrated into the general commentary. Despite a lack of development of some points, the essay is well organised, wide ranging and very confidently written. Grade A.

SAMPLE LEAVING CERT QUESTIONS ON LARKIN'S POETRY (45–50 MINUTES)

1   What impact did the poetry of Philip Larkin make on you as a reader? In shaping your answer, you might consider some of the following:
    - The poet's main themes.
    - Language and imagery in the poems.
    - Your favourite poem or poems.

2. Some critics have claimed that Larkin is 'one of the most sensitive and compassionate of poets'. Would you agree with this estimation of the poems by Philip Larkin on your course? Support your point of view by relevant quotation or reference.
3. If you were asked to give a public reading of some of Philip Larkin's poems, which ones would you choose? Give reasons for your choices, supporting them by reference to the poems on your course.

SAMPLE ESSAY PLAN (Q3)

If you were asked to give a public reading of Philip Larkin's poems, which ones would you choose? Give reasons for your choices, supporting them by reference to the poems on your course.

- *Intro:* Sense of audience expected; mention recurring themes that are still relevant and some interesting aspects of Larkin's style.
- *Point 1:* 'Wedding-Wind' – adopts persona of new wife, concentration on joy, optimistic ending. We can appreciate this theme.
- *Point 2:* 'The Whitsun Weddings' – train journey, ordinary experience, steady rhythm of train – poet reflects on newlywed couples at end.
- *Point 3:* 'Ambulances' – imagery conveys graphic horror of violence and its indiscriminate nature.
- *Point 4:* 'The Trees' – celebrates human resilience and courage in the face of certain death. Use of present continuous tense, sibilance, even rhyme scheme underlines this positive outlook.
- *Point 5:* 'The Explosion' – illustrates how life can suddenly be disrupted by disaster. Vivid details convey the world of mining and the imminent dangers. Uplifting imagery.
- *Conclusion:* Larkin is a fine observer of ordinary lives/places, but he also challenges readers by exploring wider questions about life/death, sorrow/happiness.

EXERCISE

Develop one of the above points into a paragraph.

POINT 5 – SAMPLE PARAGRAPH

I feel that the poem 'The Explosion' is very much a description of a modern-day experience. After 9/11 and the London Underground Tube bombings, a working man returning home from work, unknowing that his life and those of his relatives will be disturbed by tragedy, strikes a deep fear in all of us. Do you feel safe in this modern world of random terrorism? The world of the miner is conveyed in a few well-chosen details, rather like close-ups on a TV news sequence: 'pitboots', 'in beards and moleskins'. After a day spent down the dusty mines, these miners were 'Coughing'. They are tough, their talk is 'oath-edged'. But the men are also part of a close-knit community: 'Fathers, brothers'. The personal angle, as the tabloids so often say, is given. They have 'nicknames', they are laughing. This adds to the poignancy of the scene. Then the focus is shifted to the aftermath of the tragedy. Again, a modern-day parallel strikes us. The people of London attended their memorial services for the dead and then returned to the Underground train stations. We marvelled at the courage of ordinary people under threat. So the wives of the dead drew comfort from 'We shall see them face to face'. The defiant human spirit is also shown in the uplifting image that ends the poem: 'One showing the eggs unbroken'. I am sure you will agree with the inclusion of this poem because it deals in such a true way with the unpredictability of life, a harsh fact, and the resilience of the ordinary man. These aspects of the tragedy become beautiful under the observant eyes of Larkin.

EXAMINER'S COMMENT

As part of a full essay answer, the student has written an impressive A-grade paragraph and gives a comprehensive explanation for the inclusion of 'The Explosion' in the public reading. Likening the poem to modern tragic events adds a compelling, unique dimension to the discussion. The response is well rooted in the text.

• Poetry Focus •

Philip Larkin

Last Words

'Larkin's poems are melancholy, melodious, disenchanted, bewitching, perfectly written and perfectly approachable.'

Seamus Heaney

'People marvelled that a poet they had never met could have spoken to them so intimately.'

Andrew Motion

'I want readers to feel yes, I've never thought of it that way, but that's how it is.'

Philip Larkin

'I lie here in a riot of sunlight watching the day break and the clouds flying. Everything is going to be all right.'

Derek Mahon (1941–)

Derek Mahon was born in Belfast and educated at Trinity College Dublin and Paris-Sorbonne. He has worked as a journalist in London and in New York, where he also taught at NYU. In his time, he has been a playwright, translator and critic. Mahon is one of several northern Protestant poets who came to prominence in the late 1960s and early 1970s. His poetry expresses the feelings of exile and the oppressiveness of history that characterise much of modern life. His is a pessimism that discovers great beauty in mundane locations (an abandoned shed filled with decomposing mushrooms, a lively fishing village, an offshore island) but despairs at their impermanence and eventual meaninglessness. Mahon's poems often project into a devastating future. Recurring settings in his work include desolate landscapes, deserted beaches and other closely observed scenes of immense isolation. This reflects his complex attitude to his own middle-class Ulster background. Despite its emergence from the turmoil of Northern Ireland, his poetic voice is formal, moderate and even restrained. Although he has self-consciously distanced himself from Ireland, Derek Mahon still manages to address this alienation from homeland. Part of his impressive art has been to apply exceptional technical ability and light humour to such serious themes as the past, identity, place, conflict, loneliness and modern culture.

• Poetry Focus •

PRESCRIBED POEMS (HIGHER LEVEL)

Derek Mahon

1 **'Grandfather' (p. 340)**

In this personal and nostalgic sonnet about his grandfather, Mahon presents a fascinating image of an old man who seems to have difficulty coming to terms with his retirement from the Belfast shipyards. The grandfather's character remains a mystery throughout: 'Nothing escapes him; he escapes us all'.

2 **'Day Trip to Donegal' (p. 345)**

This is another intensely personal poem. Mahon's visit to a coastal village in Donegal turns out to be an unsettling experience. On his return to his familiar Belfast home, he feels suddenly troubled and forsaken. He is haunted by a vivid nightmare and imagines himself 'alone far out at sea'.

3 **'Ecclesiastes' (p. 350)**

The central theme here is Mahon's complex relationship with his traditional Ulster Protestant culture. Using the language of a fundamentalist Christian preacher, the poet describes Belfast as a bleak, oppressive city. But he is unable to deny his roots and – almost against his will – feels at home there.

4 **'After the *Titanic*' (p. 355)**

This powerfully moving monologue allows us to hear the lonely voice of Bruce Ismay in his response to one of history's great sea tragedies. Ismay defends his actions on the terrible night of the disaster and appeals for understanding: 'Include me in your lamentations'.

5 **'As It Should Be' (p. 361)**

This highly ironic poem explores aspects of fanaticism and the cycle of violence in Irish history. A Free State officer gives his version of shooting a rebel soldier ('gunned him down in a blind yard'). Mahon satirises the arrogant officer's self-serving attempts to justify the killing.

6 **'A Disused Shed in Co. Wexford' (p. 366)**

Mahon's most famous evocation of the downtrodden and forgotten. He describes the 'thousand mushrooms' in the abandoned shed, finally exposed to daylight. Rich symbolism and sensuous images are used effectively to highlight the anguish of suffering people, begging us to 'speak on their behalf'.

7 'Rathlin' (p. 373)

Ireland's violent history – and the continuing cycle of conflict – is a recurring theme in Mahon's poetry. On a visit to Rathlin Island (now a natural bird sanctuary), Mahon recalls a late 16th-century massacre and discovers ghostly presences from the past. In the end, he wonders whether 'the future lies before us or behind'.

8 'The Chinese Restaurant in Portrush' (p. 378)

This beautiful and delicate poem, set in a small Chinese restaurant, reflects on a number of interesting themes: identity and home; loss and separation; and the Troubles. Overall, the poet seems to be celebrating the simple realities of everyday life.

9 'Kinsale' (p. 383)

This short, lyrical poem deals with another of Mahon's favourite themes: the tension between Ireland's past and its present. While the poet hints at the country's troubled history, he sees some reason for cautious optimism in modern-day Kinsale, where he can imagine 'a future, forbidden to no one'.

10 'Antarctica' (p. 387)

This poem is based on Captain Scott's dramatic and ill-fated expedition to the South Pole in 1912. One of the team members, Lawrence Oates, gave up his own life so that his companions might have a better chance of survival. Mahon sums up this futile act of heroism in the refrain: 'At the heart of the ridiculous, the sublime'.

• Poetry Focus •

Grandfather

Derek Mahon

They brought him in on a stretcher from the world,
Wounded but humorous; and he soon recovered.
Boiler-rooms, row upon row of gantries rolled
Away to reveal the landscape of a childhood
Only he can recapture. Even on cold   5
Mornings he is up at six with a block of wood
Or a box of nails, discreetly up to no good
Or banging round the house like a four-year-old –

Never there when you call. But after dark
You hear his great boots thumping in the hall   10
And in he comes, as cute as they come. Each night
His shrewd eyes bolt the door and set the clock
Against the future, then his light goes out.
Nothing escapes him; he escapes us all.

'row upon row of gantries rolled/Away'

GLOSSARY

3 *Boiler-rooms*: engine rooms in ships.
3 *gantries*: bridge-like scaffolds that support cranes, usually in a shipyard.
7 *discreetly*: carefully, circumspectly.
11 *cute*: sly, cunning.
12 *shrewd*: clever, perceptive.

EXPLORATIONS

1. Discuss the picture of the grandfather that is presented in the line 'Wounded but humorous; and he soon recovered'. In your opinion, is he a likeable character?
2. Derek Mahon uses colloquial language throughout this poem. Choose two examples and comment briefly on the effectiveness of each.
3. Write a short personal response to this poem. Refer closely to the text in your answer.

STUDY NOTES

'Grandfather' comes from Derek Mahon's first poetry collection, *Night Crossing* (1968). The poet's grandfather was a foreman boiler-maker in the famous Belfast shipyard, Harland and Wolff, where the *Titanic* was built. Mahon gives 'a voice to those who are marginalised in society' and instead of a picture of a faceless retired man, a wonderful character – eccentric, liberated and elusive – emerges from this compact sonnet. We hear the admiration and slight exasperation of the poet as he observes the busy, noisy presence of his grandfather in the house. Mahon values traditional poetic forms and he uses an amended sonnet form to comment imaginatively on a rather rebellious, 'cute' individual.

Derek Mahon is very conscious of his roots. He has said that 'the shipyards of Belfast are no less part' of the Irish experience 'than a country town in the Gaeltacht'. In a sense, he is celebrating industrialised, urban Belfast. Many of the **stereotypical characteristics of Northern Irish people** (tenacity, rebelliousness, self-reliance and a dry, wry sense of humour) are evident in the description of Mahon's grandfather, who had to retire from the Belfast shipyards after a work-related accident. The prepositions 'in', 'on' and 'from' in the **first line** contain and confine the storyline of the poem. Mahon's grandfather is now away from the world of work, incapacitated on a stretcher and forced to spend his time in the house.

His **indomitable spirit** is conveyed in the sparse **second line**: 'Wounded but humorous; and he soon recovered'. His good-humoured battle for health is captured in these few words. The harsh, masculine world of work is vividly depicted by images of 'Boiler-rooms' and 'gantries'. This tough environment now recedes, almost like a cartoon sequence: 'row upon row ... rolled/Away'. The strict, ordered world of physical work is replaced by the magical 'landscape of a childhood'. Freedom and relaxation beckon, but only to him, as 'Only he can recapture' it. Although he has been released from the obligations and burdens of the working world, he seems to be uncomfortable with the transition from work to leisure. Is there a sense that he feels redundant and ill at ease?

The grandfather's individuality is brilliantly captured by Mahon's adaptation of the sonnet form, mixing elements from the Petrarchan and Shakespearean tradition. The grandfather is not someone who conforms to the conventional notion of a 'normal' elderly person. The rhymes mirror this, as they slip and slide like the elusive grandfather ('world'/'rolled'; 'childhood'/'recovered'). **Line 5** paints a picture of **an old man who is still energetic, secretive and liberated**. He endures hardship without complaint ('Even on cold/Mornings'). An early riser ('up at six'), he is industrious and noisily goes about doing little jobs with his 'block of wood/Or a box of nails'. While there is more than a hint of frustration at his retirement, he still enjoys a childlike freedom ('like a four-year-old').

The **run-on line that bridges the octet and sestet** illustrates the old man's lively personality. Mahon bends the sonnet form in deference to this slippery character. The mild exasperation of the poet is evident when he remarks that his grandfather is 'Never there when you call'. The poem turns on the word 'But' and we see the grandfather at night. The colloquial phrase 'as cute as they come' firmly roots him in Belfast, referring both to **the charm and cunning of this eccentric character**. He performs the night duties of the house, securing it against harm, as he goes to 'bolt the door' and 'set the clock'. He is aware of the dangers 'after dark'. Finally he rests: 'then his light goes out'. The phrase refers not only to the switching off of his bedroom light, but also to the extinguishing of his energy. His earlier presence – captured in the percussive musical sounds of 'banging' and 'thumping' – is at last still and silent.

The **final line** is enigmatic and firmly places the grandfather centre stage: 'Nothing escapes him; he escapes us all'. This old man is aware of everything, yet **he retains his mystery, his uniqueness**. Throughout this personal reflection, Mahon's tone is both nostalgic and affectionate. His technical expertise is clearly evident in this sonnet. He plays with its form as 'discreetly' as his grandfather moves around the house.

ANALYSIS

'Derek Mahon's acute eye and precise ear are notable features of his poetry.' Discuss this view of the poet's work in relation to 'Grandfather'. Support your points with quotation from the text.

SAMPLE PARAGRAPH

I was surprised by the poem 'Grandfather'. I felt I could really see and hear this energetic individual as he went around living life on his own terms. The use of onomatopoeia in the verbs 'thumping' and 'banging', with their explosive letters 'p' and 'b', really made us hear this noisy individual as he went about 'like a four-year-old'. Yet, he was 'fixing things' with his 'block of wood/Or a box of nails'. I could also hear another voice, the slightly irritated voice of the poet. The grandfather was 'up at six'; he was 'discreetly up to no good'; he was 'Never there when you call'. This unconventional man lived to his own rhythm. Mahon caught this quirkiness in the way he shaped the sonnet: changing the rhyme scheme and running the octet into the sestet with a long dash, echoing the running of the grandfather around the house. Even the turn (volta) of the sonnet is as elusive as the grandfather. So the sight of the poem on the page does not conform to 'rules'; neither does this independent old man. The twanging tones of Northern Ireland are captured in the colloquial phrases 'up to no good' and 'as cute as they come'. Here is a poet with a 'precise ear'. Wonderfully detailed images are also presented to the reader. The rigid, structured world of men's work is shown by the phrase 'row upon row of gantries'. This old man still retains traces of his former life as his 'great boots' can be heard around the house. He still performs regular duties. 'Each night' he is careful to 'bolt the door' and 'set the clock'. Mahon paints the picture of an industrious man, cautious and unsettled. I really liked the last line, as I could see this clever, mischievous old man whom 'Nothing escapes' and I could sense that he was answerable to no one ('he escapes us all'). Mahon's closely observed character study conveys a memorable image of a remarkable man. I was surprised at how much I really liked the poem.

Derek Mahon

EXAMINER'S COMMENT

A clear treatment of the two aspects of the question: Mahon's 'acute eye' and 'precise ear'. The candidate showed a very good understanding of the poem. There was also real engagement and the response was ably supported by relevant quotation. Grade A.

CLASS/HOMEWORK EXERCISES

1. 'Derek Mahon is a poet who is more interested in people than places.' Comment on this statement in relation to 'Grandfather'. Refer closely to the text in your response.
2. Copy the table below into your own notes and fill in critical comments about the last two quotations.

Key Quotes

They brought him in on a stretcher	Mahon's grandfather retired from working in the Belfast shipyards because of a work-related accident. The poem describes the very active retirement of this man.
gantries rolled/Away to reveal the landscape of a childhood/Only he can recapture	The long run-on lines suggest an endless vista of time that originally belonged to the grandfather in boyhood and now belongs to him again in his retirement.
His shrewd eyes bolt the door	The personification of 'eyes' evokes the fierce energy of this independent, clever man. The curt, monosyllabic verb 'bolt' resounds as the old man locks out night's danger.
set the clock/Against the future	
Nothing escapes him; he escapes us all	

Day Trip to Donegal

We reached the sea in early afternoon,
Climbed stiffly out. There were things to be done,
Clothes to be picked up, friends to be seen.
As ever, the nearby hills were a deeper green
Than anywhere in the world, and the grave
Grey of the sea the grimmer in that enclave.

Down at the pier the boats gave up their catch,
A writhing glimmer of fish. They fetch
Ten times as much in the city as here,
And still the fish come in year after year –
Herring and mackerel, flopping about the deck
In attitudes of agony and heartbreak.

We left at eight, drove back the way we came,
The sea receding down each muddy lane.
Around midnight we changed-down into suburbs
Sunk in a sleep no gale-force wind disturbs.
The time of year had left its mark
On frosty pavements glistening in the dark.

Give me a ring, goodnight, and so to bed …
That night the slow sea washed against my head,
Performing its immeasurable erosions –
Spilling into the skull, marbling the stones
That spine the very harbour wall,
Muttering its threat to villages of landfall.

At dawn I was alone far out at sea
Without skill or reassurance – nobody
To show me how, no promise of rescue –
Cursing my constant failure to take due
Forethought for this; contriving vain
Overtures to the vindictive wind and rain.

• Poetry Focus •

Derek Mahon

'At dawn I was alone far out at sea'

GLOSSARY

- 5 *grave*: sombre, ominous.
- 6 *enclave*: enclosed area.
- 8 *writhing*: twisting.
- 14 *receding*: retreating, withdrawing.
- 22 *marbling*: polishing, staining.
- 23 *spine*: harbour wall.
- 24 *landfall*: the coastline.
- 29 *Forethought*: preparation.
- 29 *vain*: pointless.
- 30 *Overtures*: advances, proposals.
- 30 *vindictive*: bitter, vengeful.

EXPLORATIONS

1. Based on your reading of the first two stanzas, describe the poet's initial impressions of Donegal. Support the points you make with quotation from the text.
2. Choose one image (or phrase) from the poem that you thought was particularly striking. Briefly explain your choice.
3. In your opinion, what is the central theme of this poem? Refer closely to the text in your answer.

STUDY NOTES

This poem appeared in Mahon's first poetry collection, *Night Crossing* (1968). On a first reading, it appears to be a typical nature poem based on a simple account of an excursion to the windswept coast of Donegal. Many poems feature a journey motif, usually symbolic of the search for self-discovery, insight or meaning. In this case, more attention is given to the return trip and the dream that dominates the poem's final two stanzas.

• 346 •

In the **opening stanza**, Mahon wastes little time in setting the scene and providing atmosphere, as he describes his arrival in Donegal. Characteristically, **the language has a conversational quality** ('There were things to be done'). He and his friends are uncomfortable after the long journey ('Climbed stiffly out'). But their mood lightens a little as they begin to take in the beauty of their surroundings, the rural seaside scene and the impressive landscape: 'a deeper green/Than anywhere in the world'. There is, however, something unappealing about the place and the ocean is described in dubious terms: 'the grave/Grey of the sea the grimmer in that enclave'. The gentle alliteration of 'gr' emphasises the sound of nearby waves. Interestingly, Mahon paints the sea's greyness in terms of a moral value rather than colour; its grim nature is emphasised.

Stanza two focuses on details of the harbour where local fishermen are at work. The poet observes 'Herring and mackerel, flopping about the deck'. His precise, vivid description personifies the 'writhing glimmer of fish' and **his sympathies are drawn to their suffering** ('In attitudes of agony and heartbreak'). By reminding us of distressing emotional experiences, Mahon makes us consider the systematic mass slaughter of powerless animals, something most of us take for granted. The image of the dead and dying fish can also be seen as a symbol of human suffering throughout history.

Much of **stanza three** describes the return journey to Belfast. The account reads like a diary: 'We left at eight, drove back the way we came'. Mahon's sibilant effects capture the fading sound of the 'sea receding' in the distance. By midnight, he reaches his familiar home on the outskirts of the city. It is 'Sunk in a sleep no gale-force wind disturbs'. The descent into **this secure, inviting world – in contrast to the more threatening Donegal coast** – is emphasised by the reference to gears of the vehicle: 'we changed-down into suburbs'. However, the evidence of nature's mysterious beauty is still apparent 'On frosty pavements glistening in the dark'.

The opening line of **stanza four** marks a **noticeable turning point** for the poet. Having left his friends, he is exhausted by the journey and retires for the night: 'and so to bed'. Immediately, **the poem becomes intensely introspective**, as his thoughts are haunted by vivid memories of the day trip: 'the slow sea washed against my head'. Once again, the prominent sibilance suggests the insistent sound of the waves. In a nightmarish blend of actual events and his own heightened imagination, Mahon uses the powerfully eroding sea as a metaphor

Derek Mahon

for his growing sense of disquiet. Somewhere between sleep and waking, the relentless ocean is 'Spilling into the skull'. Disturbing references to the 'immeasurable' destruction of the coastline 'Muttering its threat' add to this increasingly uneasy mood of fear and discomfort.

After a restless night, Mahon wakes early. He feels isolated and alone ('far out at sea'). He is acutely aware that he has been cast adrift with 'no promise of rescue'. **Stanza five** is dominated by frustration and despair. **Repetition and broad vowel sounds echo the depth of desolation he feels**: 'Cursing my constant failure'. Run-on lines and an unrestrained rhythm also reflect the poet's edgy stream of consciousness. As a final futile gesture, he resorts to imploring 'the vindictive wind and rain' to save him. In associating his alienation with being lost at sea, the poet might well be suggesting other universal human fears, perhaps the fear of facing death alone. This dark ending illustrates how Derek Mahon can take a relatively simple subject (a day trip to Donegal) and turn it into a nightmare full of terrifying images.

ANALYSIS

'Mahon's poetry is memorable for its striking images, but he is primarily a poet who makes us think.' Discuss this view in relation to 'Day Trip to Donegal'. Refer closely to the poem in your answer.

SAMPLE PARAGRAPH

Like most poets, Derek Mahon is thought-provoking and sometimes puzzling. On first reading, 'Day Trip to Donegal' appears straightforward. The poet and his friends arrive at the coast. From the start, however, Mahon is deeply affected by the place. His vivid description seems exaggerated – the hills of Donegal are 'a deeper green/Than anywhere in the world'. I thought he painted a very disturbing picture of the grey sea and grim atmosphere. His image of the dying fish, flopping about in 'agony and heartbreak', makes us think of human suffering. In the last section of the poem, he associates his own sense of self with the sea. Like the fish, the ocean is personified – 'Muttering its threat'. On his return to the Belfast suburbs, Mahon has troubled dreams of his day out: 'That night the slow sea washed against my head'. The metaphor is extraordinary, reminding me of how deeply affected he has been by the sights and sounds of the Donegal coast. The final stanza made the greatest impact on me. Mahon comes across as a vulnerable figure 'alone far out at sea'. There is a suggestion that he is suddenly aware of his own desperate state – uncertain and lonely. His final cry to the 'vindictive wind and rain' is moving and mysterious. I was able to imagine his own loneliness, just like the grey sea off the coast of Donegal.

EXAMINER'S COMMENT

A very well-focused response, addressing both elements of the question. There is also good personal engagement. Accurate and appropriate quotations are skilfully used as a basis for insightful discussion throughout. The expression is varied, fluent and well controlled. Grade A standard.

CLASS/HOMEWORK EXERCISES

1. In your opinion, how was Derek Mahon affected by his visit to Donegal? Refer closely to the poem in your answer.
2. Copy the table below into your own notes and fill in critical comments about the last two quotations.

Key Quotes

Quote	Comment
There were things to be done,/ Clothes to be picked up, friends to be seen	Mahon's language has an everyday, conversational quality. The tone here is focused and purposeful.
Down at the pier the boats gave up their catch,/ A writhing glimmer of fish	Mahon has been credited with an observant eye and a sympathetic attitude. In this poem, he gives the fish human qualities, as if he can relate to their pain.
At dawn I was alone far out at sea/ Without skill or reassurance	In contrast to his earlier feelings, Mahon ends up agitated and helpless. The broad vowel sounds convey his sense of alienation.
As ever, the nearby hills were a deeper green/ Than anywhere in the world	
That night the slow sea washed against my head	

• Poetry Focus •

Ecclesiastes

Derek Mahon

God, you could grow to love it, God-fearing, God-
   chosen purist little puritan that,
for all your wiles and smiles, you are (the
   dank churches, the empty streets,
the shipyard silence, the tied-up swings) and   5
   shelter your cold heart from the heat
of the world, from woman-inquisition, from the
   bright eyes of children. Yes you could
wear black, drink water, nourish a fierce zeal
   with locusts and wild honey, and not   10
feel called upon to understand and forgive
   but only to speak with a bleak
afflatus, and love the January rains when they
   darken the dark doors and sink hard
into the Antrim hills, the bog meadows, the heaped   15
   graves of your fathers. Bury that red
bandana and stick, that banjo; this is your
   country, close one eye and be king.
Your people await you, their heavy washing
   flaps for you in the housing estates –   20
a credulous people. God, you could do it, God
   help you, stand on a corner stiff
with rhetoric, promising nothing under the sun.

'the empty streets'

GLOSSARY

Ecclesiastes is the name of an Old Testament book in the Bible; much of the philosophy in the book argued that life was essentially meaningless and should therefore be enjoyed.
2 *purist*: extremist.
2 *puritan*: highly moral person.
3 *wiles*: tricks.
4 *dank*: damp.
5 *tied-up swings*: playgrounds were closed on Sundays by Protestant-controlled local councils.
9 *zeal*: fanaticism, fervour.
10 *locusts and wild honey*: the simple food of biblical prophets and sinners doing penance.
13 *afflatus*: divine guidance.
17 *bandana and stick, that banjo*: symbols of rebellion and creativity.
21 *credulous*: unsuspecting, naïve.
23 *rhetoric*: oratory; exaggeration.

EXPLORATIONS

1 What impression of Protestantism is presented in the first five lines of the poem? Refer to the text in your answer.
2 Choose one example of irony from the poem and comment on its effectiveness.
3 In your opinion, does the poem end on an optimistic or pessimistic note? Briefly explain your answer, using reference to the text.

STUDY NOTES

'Ecclesiastes' is set in Derek Mahon's hometown of Belfast. The poem was first published in 1972, when sectarian violence was on the rise in Northern Ireland; it is as close as the poet gets to writing directly about the Ulster Protestant tradition. In the course of this satirical poem, Mahon reveals mixed feelings towards his roots and condemns the fanatical preaching that exploits 'credulous people'. Ironically, just like Bible-thumping preachers, poets also use the power of language to communicate with people.

The **opening lines** of the poem have the sense of an interior monologue, with Mahon (seemingly in ironic mood) reflecting on some familiar features of Ulster Protestantism: 'dank churches, the empty streets' (**line 4**). His portrayal of Northern Protestants is highly critical. They are 'God-fearing' but self-satisfied ('chosen') believers whose strict form of worship is strait-laced and cheerless. Sharp consonant sounds and the abrupt repetition of 'God' echo **the violent oratory of the more extreme religious preaching** heard in Belfast during the early 1970s. Nevertheless, the poet retains a close affiliation with his uncompromising heritage, despite all its austerity: 'God, you could grow to love it'. The colloquial language adds an authentic touch, as Mahon delves deeper into the reality of strict Protestant adherence. A salvation of sorts is offered, but it involves sacrificing human warmth and family life: 'the/bright eyes of children' (**line 8**).

This deeply sombre mood continues in **lines 9–10**, where the poet focuses on the 'fierce zeal' of some Protestant clergymen who 'wear black, drink water' and imagine themselves as biblical holy men living on 'locusts and wild honey'. The **scathing tone** satirises hard-line fundamentalists who are out of touch and lack compassion. Mahon's imagery becomes increasingly bleak; he sets this grim, doctrinal religion in its local context of 'January rains' and 'dark doors'. There is no disguising his deep distaste for the rigid inhumanity of die-hard puritans who never 'feel called upon to understand and forgive'. But while the presence of this extreme Protestant tradition is highlighted in the reference to 'the heaped/graves of your fathers', there is also a possibility that such intolerant attitudes might be dying out.

However, such change seems unlikely in the immediate future and the poet echoes the conservative voice of dull Ulster Protestant culture, which continues to oppose any signs of freedom or adventure: 'Bury that red/bandana and stick, that banjo' (**line 17**). As far as Mahon is concerned, Northern Ireland remains blinded by the past; it is still a place where powerful traditionalists can 'close one eye and be king'. This ironic observation recalls the old proverb: 'In the land of the blind, the one-eyed man is king.' **The tone – equally regretful and resentful – is typically ambivalent**, reflecting the poet's apparent love–hate relationship with his homeland.

In the poem's **final lines**, Mahon accepts that his own roots will always lie within the Ulster Protestant tradition: 'Your people await you'. Almost against his will, he is drawn to Belfast's ordinary working-class areas ('the housing estates') with 'a credulous people' who are easily led. The poet feels sympathy for his fellow Protestants, while rejecting their religious bigotry. Mahon leaves us with a **dramatic image of a street preacher** ('stiff/with rhetoric') ranting at passers-by and 'promising nothing under the sun'. This ridiculous figure seems to sum up all the intransigence and absurdity of small-minded religious teaching. There is little doubt that Mahon's preacher warns of a dark and dismal future for Northern Ireland.

ANALYSIS

'Derek Mahon's Northern Irish background provides a crucial context for much of his poetry.' Discuss this statement, with particular reference to 'Ecclesiastes'. Support the points you make with reference to the poem.

SAMPLE PARAGRAPH

Many of Mahon's best-known poems are named after places in Northern Ireland. 'Ecclesiastes' refers to a book of the Bible and would be familiar to many church-going Belfast Protestants of Mahon's generation. Mahon grew up in Belfast and religion has always played an important role there – and sometimes it has caused more harm than good. This poem was written at the start of the Troubles in 1972. In it, Mahon uses the strident voice of a fundamentalist preacher to express his criticism of the puritanical religion, which was based on fear and penance. He describes it as 'God-fearing' and 'puritanical'. Images of Protestant Belfast are bleak: 'dank churches', 'tied-up swings' and 'preachers wearing black'. At the same time, the poet's tone is one of understanding and even affection. He thinks of earlier Protestant generations who have settled in Co. Antrim: 'the heaped graves of your fathers'. Overall, his attitude is respectful and he realises that he too is part of that hardworking culture, just like the working classes in East Belfast's housing estates. Addressing himself, he agrees that he belongs here: 'Your people await you'. Although Mahon mocks the extreme, conservative aspects of his own Protestant culture, he still has a regard for it. To him, these 'credulous people' are hardworking and sincere. Their leaders might well be to blame, but not the ordinary Protestants themselves. Even though the poet finds some of their beliefs peculiar – like the deranged fanatic on the street corner – he maintains a sense of belonging to the tribe to which he himself belongs.

EXAMINER'S COMMENT

This is a solid response, which addresses the question throughout. There is evidence of good engagement with the poem – especially with the poet's ambivalent attitude to the Protestant tradition. While references are used well, some of the quotes are inaccurate. Grade B.

• Poetry Focus •

Derek Mahon

CLASS/HOMEWORK EXERCISES

1. 'Tensions and conflict are prominent themes in the poetry of Derek Mahon.' Discuss this view, with reference to 'Ecclesiastes'. Refer to the poem in your answer.
2. Copy the table below into your own notes and fill in critical comments about the last two quotations.

Key Quotes

God, you could grow to love it, God-fearing, God-/chosen purist little puritan	The forceful repetition and spitting consonants of these lines echo the angry sentiments of a ranting preacher.
the shipyard silence, the tied-up swings	Symbols of Belfast's past highlight the reality of sectarianism. It was taken for granted that shipyard jobs excluded Catholics and Protestant-controlled local councils closed all public parks on Sundays.
sink hard/into the Antrim hills	Mahon is very much aware of the enduring traditional presence of Ulster Protestants. This image suggests how they have made their mark and have become entrenched in the landscape over the centuries.
wear black, drink water, nourish a fierce zeal	
Bury that red/bandana and stick, that banjo	

After the *Titanic*

Derek Mahon

  They said I got away in a boat
And humbled me at the inquiry. I tell you
  I sank as far that night as any
Hero. As I sat shivering on the dark water
  I turned to ice to hear my costly   5
Life go thundering down in a pandemonium of
  Prams, pianos, sideboards, winches,
Boilers bursting and shredded ragtime. Now I hide
  In a lonely house behind the sea
Where the tide leaves broken toys and hat-boxes   10
  Silently at my door. The showers of
April, flowers of May mean nothing to me, nor the
  Late light of June, when my gardener
Describes to strangers how the old man stays in bed
  On seaward mornings after nights of   15
Wind, takes his cocaine and will see no-one. Then it is
  I drown again with all those dim
Lost faces I never understood, my poor soul
  Screams out in the starlight, heart
Breaks loose and rolls down like a stone.   20
  Include me in your lamentations.

'And humbled me at the inquiry'

• Poetry Focus •

Derek Mahon

GLOSSARY

Titanic: Huge ship built in Belfast, which sank on its maiden voyage in 1912. Over 1,500 people were killed in the greatest loss of lives in maritime history.
1 *I*: Bruce Ismay, managing director of the White Star Line, which owned the *Titanic*. He was one of the few male survivors of the tragedy.
2 *inquiry*: investigation.
6 *pandemonium*: turmoil, uproar.
7 *winches*: machines for hauling or lifting.
8 *ragtime*: early form of jazz, sometimes called 'ragged rhythm'; a reference to the bravery of the orchestra, which continued to play as the ship sank.
15 *seaward*: looking towards the sea.
16 *cocaine*: addictive drug.
21 *lamentations*: cries of grief.

EXPLORATIONS

1 From your reading of 'After the *Titanic*', do you feel any sympathy for Bruce Ismay? Support your response with suitable quotation from the text.
2 Comment on the poet's use of sound effects in lines 7–8.
3 Mahon is often praised for his vivid, memorable imagery. Choose two visual images that appeal to you in the poem. Comment on the effectiveness of each.

STUDY NOTES

'After the *Titanic*' comes from Derek Mahon's second collection, *Lives* (1975). It charts the journey of Joseph Bruce Ismay, managing director of the White Star Line, the shipping company that owned the *Titanic*. We encounter Ismay as he descends into the murky depths of his own private hell. Ismay was strongly criticised for his alleged failure to help drowning passengers and he was one of only a handful of men to escape the sinking ship. It is a long-standing maritime tradition that women and children must be saved first in an emergency. Mahon has a gift for entering into the lives of others, particularly lone, abandoned individuals like Bruce Ismay.

The original title of this poem was 'Bruce Ismay's Soliloquy'. As managing director of the White Star Line shipping company, Ismay stated that the *Titanic* was 'the latest thing in the act of shipbuilding'. It cost £1.5 million pounds to build and was the epitome of the elegance and self-confidence of the Edwardian age. However, on its first sailing to America in 1912, the ship collided with an iceberg and sank, with the loss of more than 1,500 lives, the largest ever loss of civilian life at sea. An **inquiry strongly criticised Ismay's decision** to escape the disaster in a lifeboat. As a result, he was widely ridiculed by both the

American and British press for apparently deserting the ship while women and children were still on board.

In this dramatic monologue, Derek Mahon **adopts the persona of this despondent man** as he attempts to refute the accusations levelled at him: 'They said I got away in a boat' (**line 1**). However, we quickly become aware of Ismay's self-absorption when we note the over-use of 'I', 'me' and 'my'. All the sentences in this poem relate to his life after the sinking of the *Titanic*. Ismay complains about how he has been viewed by the public. The finger of accusation has been pointed directly at him ('humbled me at the inquiry'), but he emphatically pleads his case ('I tell you'), insisting that he 'sank as far that night as any/Hero'.

But we cannot help wondering if Ismay protests too much. Other men had given their lives so that women and children could be saved. Mahon's **visual effects graphically illustrate the bitterly cold night** ('shivering on the dark water') as well as Ismay's own fear: 'I turned to ice'. This phrase in **line 5** rings ironically, as the reader is all too aware that the ship sank because it hit an iceberg. There is also the implication that Ismay's own life halted – froze – on the night of 14 April 1912. He spent the next 25 years reliving over and over again the horrifying events of that terrible disaster. Since that moment, he has been as cold as death.

The poet is a solitary observer. He **invites us to witness the horror and turmoil of the awful tragedy** through striking, unforgettable images in **lines 6–7**. The consonants in 'pandemonium', 'Prams' and 'pianos' are scattered by the dissonance of random items thrown together chaotically by the sinking ship: 'sideboards', 'winches'. The band played on boldly as the vessel sank and this is remembered in the phrase 'shredded ragtime'. The ragged rhythm of jazz is poignantly appropriate, as the syncopated beat echoes the breaking up of the huge liner. Mahon's choice of the adjective 'shredded' presents a sad picture of the musicians' torn sheet music floating on the surface of the dark Atlantic water. The poet asks us to reflect not only on the dreadful suffering of the ship's passengers on that fateful night, but also on Bruce Ismay's character ('my costly/Life'). This wealthy man is shown to be totally self-absorbed, in stark contrast to the stoical, brave musicians on the ship.

Line 8 brings the scene to the present: 'Now I hide'. Ismay has taken refuge from the hostile world in a 'lonely house behind the sea'. **The poet asks us to**

• Poetry Focus •

Derek Mahon

reflect sympathetically on his shame and isolation. For Ismay, there is no escaping the past. The sea itself brings constant, silent reminders of the women ('hat-boxes') and children ('broken toys') who have possibly drowned because of Ismay's selfish actions. Nonetheless, it is clear that he is now a broken man who has no interest in nature's passing show of seasonal change: 'The showers of/April, flowers of May mean nothing to me'. The harmony of the natural world is beautifully suggested by the assonance of 'flowers' and 'showers'. Ismay is acutely aware of the judgment of others. He recounts how his 'gardener/Describes to strangers' the reclusive routine of his day. Although the sun rises in spite of everything, Ismay spends his time in a drug-fuelled half-existence.

Towards the end of the poem, Mahon focuses on Ismay's increasing desolation. We are haunted by his stark admission: 'I drown again with all those dim/Lost faces' (**lines 17–18**). Surprisingly, Ismay also admits he 'never understood' them. Does this mean that he did not recognise the worth and dignity of the *Titanic* victims? Or did he see himself as superior to them? The **poem concludes with a hysterical outburst**, as Ismay recounts his anguish. Mahon's powerful verbs ('Screams',' Breaks', 'Rolls') dramatically capture the suffering of this guilt-ridden man. Broad vowel sounds ('loose', 'down', 'stone') haul the line downwards. It is as if Ismay is drowning in his own despair. The poet has created an atmosphere of haunting, lonely torment in which Ismay's tortured soul is collapsing.

The **last line** is a reference to the Book of Lamentations from the Bible, an **outpouring of grief** at the destruction of Jerusalem. The speaker in this book says that he has seen much affliction. Is Ismay likening himself to this person? Is it ironic that he is doing so? The final, shortest line of the poem could be seen as a misguided demand from a self-serving man: 'Include me in your lamentations'. This line could also be read as a plea for clemency for a desolate man who 'dies' every night. Is he a victim of the tragedy as well? Fortunately, the poet leaves readers to make up their own minds.

Derek Mahon has always been interested in form and structure, in 'purposefulness, instead of randomness'. He has stated: 'It's important to me what a poem looks like on a page.' **This poem has an irregular left-hand pattern, suggesting all is out of order: the sinking ship, the lost lives, the anguished Ismay. The untidy right-hand pattern is reminiscent of the debris carried by the waves,** which appears to Ismay as silent reminders of his 'crime'.

Run-on lines also suggest the sea's ebb and flow. Whether or not we sympathise with Bruce Ismay, there is no denying that Mahon has created a memorable poem from the 'products of a broken world'.

ANALYSIS

'In his poetry, Derek Mahon digs sympathetically into the psyche of a character.' Discuss this statement with reference to 'After the *Titanic*'. Use suitable reference and quotation in support of your answer.

SAMPLE PARAGRAPH

Derek Mahon is a poet who has a 'watchful heart' and who is fascinated by the ghostly voices of the past. He is drawn to lonely, deserted people on the edge of society. He enters into the lives of these people and gives them a voice. He believed in speech as the essence of identity. In 'After the *Titanic*', he speaks in the voice of Bruce Ismay, the vilified managing director of the White Star Line shipping company that owned the *Titanic*. Mahon speaks with the sad, self-pitying voice of Ismay. I was drawn into Ismay's personal torment. He made a decision to take a place on a lifeboat, against the long-standing tradition of women and children first. We realise he may have physically saved himself, but his soul died that night and he is forced to live as an outcast in a drug-induced stupor ('takes his cocaine and will see no-one'). Mahon also lets us glimpse the lives of the terrified passengers as the great liner sank. Through his striking imagery and explosive sound effects, I could imagine the horror of that night in 1912: 'a pandemonium of/Prams, pianos, sideboards, winches'. I was able to visualise the silent reminders of Ismay's night of shame as the sea 'leaves toys and hat-boxes' outside the door of his 'house behind the sea'. These are pathetic, painful reminders of the children and women who died when the *Titanic* sank. Mahon is not an overemotional poet. He shows us the dark side of Ismay – the wealthy, arrogant man concerned with his 'costly/Life'. The first person pronoun ('I') is used many times in the poem: 'I got away', 'I saw', 'I turned to ice', 'I drown again', showing the extent of this man's self-absorption. Mahon's use of dramatic verbs ('Screams out', 'Breaks loose', etc.) makes visible the nightmarish horror of Ismay's personal hell. The poet lets us hear this unhappy man demand to be remembered in the outpouring of grief for the victims. For me, Mahon draws a picture of a sad and very selfish man.

EXAMINER'S COMMENT

This is a well-developed answer, which shows a considered personal engagement with the poem. Interesting discussion points about how Mahon explores the psyche of Ismay's intense personality are well supported by the careful use of suitable quotation. Grade A.

CLASS/HOMEWORK EXERCISES

1. Mahon has said: 'I'm interested in at least the appearance of control.' In your opinion, how has the poet used a formal, polished style to engage the reader's emotions in 'After the *Titanic*'? Refer closely to the text in your response.
2. Copy the table below into your own notes and fill in critical comments about the last two quotations.

Key Quotes

As I sat shivering on the dark water	Mahon speaks in the querulous, self-pitying voice of Bruce Ismay. The poet has adopted this troubled man's persona to let the reader examine the events of that night from Ismay's perspective.
Boilers bursting and shredded ragtime	Alliteration of the explosive letter 'b' graphically captures the eruption of steam as the ship sank. This is an example of Mahon's skill in vivid, precise description. The forlorn picture of torn fragments of sheet music on the water highlights the tragedy.
The showers of/April, flowers of May mean nothing to me	The lyrical sound of nature is evoked through assonance ('flowers', 'showers'). To some extent, our sympathy is engaged for this pitiful man to whom nothing matters anymore.
heart/Breaks loose and rolls down like a stone	
Include me in your lamentations	

As It Should Be

Derek Mahon

We hunted the mad bastard
Through bog, moorland, rock, to the starlit west
And gunned him down in a blind yard
Between ten sleeping lorries
And an electricity generator.   5

Let us hear no idle talk
Of the moon in the Yellow River;
The air blows softer since his departure.

Since his tide-burial during school hours
Our children have known no bad dreams.   10
Their cries echo lightly along the coast.

This is as it should be.
They will thank us for it when they grow up
To a world with method in it.

'Through bog, moorland, rock'

GLOSSARY

3 *blind*: enclosed.
5 *electricity generator*: machine for producing electric current.
7 *the moon in the Yellow River*: reference to Denis Johnston's 1931 play, *The Moon in the Yellow River*, which is set in the Irish Free State. A new hydro-electric generator is being built; a revolutionary tries to blow it up and is later shot.
9 *tide-burial*: the carrying of a body out to sea by the tide.
14 *method*: law and order.

EXPLORATIONS

1. Mahon is a poet who is sympathetic to those who have failed. How is this evident in the description of the murdered man? Support your response with quotation from the poem.
2. Select one image that you found particularly interesting in the poem and comment on its effectiveness.
3. 'This is as it should be.' Do you agree with this speaker's statement in the poem? Support your discussion with textual reference.

STUDY NOTES

> Derek Mahon's *Lives* (1975) contains this frightening defence of violence. Once again, the poet enters into the mindset of an outsider – a murderer who states the truth 'as it should be'. Mahon lets us hear this man speak and invites us to form our own opinion about his beliefs and actions. The poet has said that he experienced 'contempt for what I felt was the barbarism on both sides' during the Northern Troubles. 'As It Should Be' has a very important message to the world today, which is torn apart by violent fundamentalism.

Mahon assumes the persona of the killer and the poem's dramatic opening stanza refers to the collective personal pronoun ('We'). This imbues the killer with the status of belonging to a group. He acted with their approval: 'We hunted the mad bastard'. The victim is dehumanised by the use of the word 'bastard', rather than his actual name. In the speaker's opinion, this man is 'mad', a lunatic. This suggests that he is easily expendable – anonymity makes it easier to hate. The desperate chase over barren land is described with economy and precision in the list: 'bog, moorland, rock'. The reader can imagine the frantic flight of this hunted man, desperately slipping and falling as he tries to escape his pursuers. Then the romantic, magical setting of the 'starlit west' is reached – a suitable location, perhaps, for a dreamy idealist.

The poem is based on a play by Denis Johnston, *The Moon in the Yellow River* (1931). In this drama set in the Irish Free State, a rebel character attempts to blow up a new hydro-electric generator. For the Free State, the building of Ardnacrusha Station was an important symbol of progress and independence. In the play, the rebel is shot by an officer of the Free State forces, which condone the killing. It can be dangerous to believe in dreams; in attempting to realise them, the status quo is upset. The new setting of the 'starlit west' reflects the idealistic notions of the 'mad bastard'. Does it also suggest breadth of vision, an open mind? The harsh setting of industrial power and progress ('sleeping lorries/And an electricity generator') is where the fugitive rebel is eventually murdered, 'in a blind yard'. The **matter-of-fact reporting of the killing is shocking**. The yard is a walled-up, secret place where terrible things can happen unremarked, unpunished. It is a place from which there is no escape. Is the speaker 'blind' also, only aware of his own narrow fanatical viewpoint? We are led to realise that freedom comes at a terrible price; the birth of a nation is not without pain.

The curt dismissal in the *second stanza* ('Let us hear no idle talk') is typical of the colloquial idiom used by extremists when they discount opposing points of view. Mahon's choice of the adjective 'idle' shows the contempt of the killer for any opinion except his own. It suggests a foolish action, like trying to catch the moon's reflection in a river. Short lines hint at the speaker's cynical sense of confidence. Despite the brutality of the victim's death, there is a glib attempt to justify the killing: 'The air blows softer since his departure'. **The tone is highly complacent.** Instead of acknowledging the vicious act for what it was, a less offensive term is used: 'departure'. Is the speaker deluding himself or his audience? Through subtle irony, Mahon is slowly making us aware of where his own sympathies lie.

The euphemistic self-justification continues in the *third stanza*, with a reference to the victim's 'tide-burial'. Mahon shows us that the victim did not even have the dignity of being buried, but was dumped at sea in broad daylight ('during school hours'). Is this simply self-deception? **The certain voice of the murderer** is evident when he states that 'Our children have known no bad dreams'. With this act, the younger generation is out of danger; it was all done for the children's good. Who could argue with that? The carefree innocence of youth is captured in this lyrical line: 'Their cries echo lightly along the coast'. This is what the killer says he has defended. But has he? Surely a man's blood now stains this coast? Although the poet does not comment directly, he is presenting an alternative perspective and inviting us to form our own opinions.

The *fourth stanza* rings out self-righteously in the tones of the Old Testament: 'This is as it should be'. The unwavering, headstrong voice shows no repentance. Now we start to question why it should be this way. Is this the best way? Will the children 'thank' the killers for such atrocities 'when they grow up'? Will these violent events ensure or damage the children's happiness? **Mahon awakens our critical faculties.** The chilling concluding image of a

Derek Mahon

'world with method in it' leaves the reader to wonder exactly whose order has been established in the world. The confident voice of the speaker has a decidedly hollow ring, as the value and morality of fundamentalism and fanaticism is held up for scrutiny. Characteristically, Derek Mahon has given a localised conflict a much greater universal significance.

ANALYSIS

'Derek Mahon uses polite, refined mockery to examine serious subject matter.' Discuss this statement in relation to the poem 'As It Should Be', supporting the points you make with reference to the text.

SAMPLE PARAGRAPH

Mahon wanted to be 'free from history'. In 'As It Should Be', he takes on the voice of an extremist to examine the serious issue of fundamentalism, the arrogant belief that one point of view matters to the exclusion of all others. The poet's technical excellence with language enables him to avoid overt commentary on the event, but through 'polite, refined mockery' of the murderer's own words, he shows the message to be seriously flawed. The sheer hatred of the killer is starkly captured in the strong verbs 'hunted' and 'gunned'. Bigotry is clearly heard in the phrase 'Let us hear no idle talk'. A lack of compassion for the victim is shown in the speaker's description of him as a 'mad bastard'. The self-delusional denial of callous murder is shown by his use of 'departure' and 'tide-burial' to describe the brutal killing. Mahon's awareness (and therefore our understanding) of the truth is contrasted effectively with the murderer's lack of self-awareness in the line: 'This is as it should be'. The reader immediately asks: why? The certainty of the speaker leaves the reader shaking his head in disbelief. The speaker declares that the children will be grateful for these horrific deeds 'when they grow up'. How could anyone condone a person being pursued like an animal ('Through bog, moorland, rock') and then executed without court or law, in a 'blind' alley? Mahon's cold, precise observation of the detached murderer allows us to look and be clearly aware of the man's human inadequacy. This dark, bigoted world of hatred is indeed a world with madness in it, rather than order ('a world with method in it') brightly illuminated by the refined sensibility of the poet.

EXAMINER'S COMMENT

A sound understanding of the poem and a clear sense of engagement is evident throughout. The answer carefully explores how Mahon's skill allows readers to see the real truth of the speaker's words. A little more discussion on irony would have been useful. Overall, there is effective use of succinct and pertinent quotation. Grade A.

CLASS/HOMEWORK EXERCISES

1. 'Although Derek Mahon's poetry is set in one place only, the emotions aroused by the poems have a much wider resonance.' Discuss this view of Mahon's work, with particular reference to the poem 'As It Should Be'. Refer closely to the text in your response.
2. Copy the table below into your own notes and fill in critical comments about the last two quotations.

Key Quotes

And gunned him down in a blind yard/ Between ten sleeping lorries/ And an electricity generator	The detached tone of this factual account of the murder is highlighted by the detail of 'ten' vehicles. Run-on lines suggest the unstoppable will of the murderer to carry out his dark deed.
The air blows softer since his departure	The lyrical use of soft consonants ('l' and 's') together with the broad vowel sounds ('a' and 'o') contrasts chillingly with the meaning of the line, as the killer states that life is better since the murder.
Since his tide-burial during school hours	A complete lack of respect for the dignity of another human being is shown by the dumping of the body at sea. The timing ('during school hours') adds further poignancy to the terrible scene, as we contrast the children's innocent lives with the grim action of the killer.
This is as it should be	
To a world with method in it	

• Poetry Focus •

A Disused Shed in Co. Wexford

Let them not forget us, the weak souls among the asphodels.
– Seferis, Mythistorema, tr. Keeley and Sherrard
(for J.G. Farrell)

Even now there are places where a thought might grow –
Peruvian mines, worked out and abandoned
To a slow clock of condensation,
An echo trapped for ever, and a flutter
Of wild flowers in the lift-shaft,   5
Indian compounds where the wind dances
And a door bangs with diminished confidence,
Lime crevices behind rippling rain-barrels,
Dog corners for bone burials;
And in a disused shed in Co. Wexford   10

Deep in the grounds of a burnt-out hotel,
Among the bathtubs and the washbasins
A thousand mushrooms crowd to a keyhole.
This is the one star in their firmament
Or frames a star within a star.   15
What should they do there but desire?
So many days beyond the rhododendrons
With the world waltzing in its bowl of cloud,
They have learnt patience and silence
Listening to the rooks querulous in the high wood. 20

They have been waiting for us in a foetor
Of vegetable sweat since civil war days,
Since the gravel-crunching, interminable departure
Of the expropriated mycologist.
He never came back, and light since then   25
Is a keyhole rusting gently after rain.
Spiders have spun, flies dusted to mildew
And once a day, perhaps, they have heard something –
A trickle of masonry, a shout from the blue
Or a lorry changing gear at the end of the lane. 30

Derek Mahon

There have been deaths, the pale flesh flaking
Into the earth that nourished it;
And nightmares, born of these and the grim
Dominion of stale air and rank moisture.
Those nearest the door growing strong –   35
'Elbow room! Elbow room!'
The rest, dim in a twilight of crumbling
Utensils and broken pitchers, groaning
For their deliverance, have been so long
Expectant that there is left only the posture.   40

A half century, without visitors, in the dark –
Poor preparation for the cracking lock
And creak of hinges. Magi, moonmen,
Powdery prisoners of the old regime,
Web-throated, stalked like triffids, racked by drought   45
And insomnia, only the ghost of a scream
At the flash-bulb firing-squad we wake them with
Shows there is life yet in their feverish forms.
Grown beyond nature now, soft food for worms,
They lift frail heads in gravity and good faith.   50

They are begging us, you see, in their wordless way,
To do something, to speak on their behalf
Or at least not to close the door again.
Lost people of Treblinka and Pompeii!
'Save us, save us,' they seem to say,   55
'Let the god not abandon us
Who have come so far in darkness and in pain.
We too had our lives to live.
You with your light meter and relaxed itinerary,
Let not our naive labours have been in vain!'   60

'stale air and rank moisture'

Derek Mahon

GLOSSARY

The inscription comes from *Mythistorema* (*The Myth of History*) by the Greek poet, George Seferis. The asphodel is a type of lily that was closely associated with death and the afterlife in Greek mythology. Mahon dedicates the poem to his friend J.G. Farrell, who had written about the demise of Anglo-Irish power in his civil war novel, *Troubles*.

6 *compounds*: enclosures, reserves.
7 *diminished*: weakened, reduced.
11 *a burnt-out hotel*: probably a reference to Farrell's novel, where a body is found in a shed beside a burnt-out hotel.
14 *firmament*: sky, heavens.
17 *rhododendrons*: vivid flowering shrubs.
20 *querulous*: argumentative, confrontational.
21 *foetor*: stench.
22 *civil war days*: the Irish Civil War (1922–23).
23 *interminable*: endless.
24 *expropriated*: rejected, dispossessed.
24 *mycologist*: expert on fungi, mushrooms, etc.
34 *rank*: rotten.
38 *pitchers*: pots.
43 *Magi*: wise men.
43 *moonmen*: astronauts (mycologists resemble astronauts in spacesuits).
45 *triffids*: fictional plants that threaten the world (from John Wyndham's science fiction novel, *The Day of the Triffids*).
45 *racked*: tortured.
46 *insomnia*: restlessness.
54 *Treblinka*: notorious Nazi death camp in Poland.
54 *Pompeii*: Italian city destroyed in 79 AD when Mount Vesuvius erupted.
59 *light meter*: photographic device to measure brightness.
59 *itinerary*: tourist route.
60 *naive*: foolish, innocent.

EXPLORATIONS

1 Choose two images of decay or decomposition in the poem. Comment on the effectiveness of each image.
2 Mahon shows an astonishing flair for metaphorical language in this poem. Discuss his use of metaphors, supporting your views with clear references to the text.
3 In your opinion, what is the central theme of this poem? Refer closely to the text in your response.

STUDY NOTES

The epigraph of the poem establishes its central theme: Mahon's deep concern about history's forgotten victims. 'Let them not forget us, the weak souls among the asphodels' is a compelling plea from the powerless. Just like 'After the *Titanic*' and 'As It Should Be', this poem – widely regarded as one of Mahon's finest – illustrates the poet's ability to give a voice to the silenced. 'A Disused Shed in Co. Wexford' is also a poem of great scope, which invites readers to reflect on the tragic lives of others.

Stanza one opens on a meditative note: 'Even now there are places where a thought might grow'. Mahon's preoccupation with seeking meaning is reflected in the intensely dramatic language. He manages to convey a **sense of time passing as well as a feeling of abandonment** in the 'Peruvian mines' and 'Indian compounds'. 'An echo trapped for ever' suggests silent spaces, long since deserted by forgotten generations. As he considers the lives of others and the mystery of time, Mahon seems acutely aware of the shared human experience that transcends the 'slow clock'. He associates the disused shed with other desolate places where confined people might have been exploited or oppressed.

This theme ('thought') is developed in **stanza two**, which personifies the 'thousand mushrooms' trapped in the darkness: 'What should they do there but desire?' Their overwhelming sense of longing is all the more poignant since they are resigned to their claustrophobic isolation and 'have learnt patience'. The poet recognises that they are hidden away from the outside 'world waltzing in its bowl of cloud', a powerful image evoking both the joy and mystique of creation. For Mahon, **the mushrooms are symbols of all those who have been marginalised over the centuries**. History has no shortage of abandoned communities. In Ireland alone, the poet might be thinking of Anglo-Irish Protestants in the Republic or of disaffected groups in Northern Ireland. At any rate, there is no doubt about the sympathetic mood in these lines and the compassionate tone for all who have suffered.

In **stanza three**, **the decaying mushrooms are associated with the stagnant period following Irish independence**: 'waiting for us in a foetor/Of vegetable sweat since civil war days'. Mahon uses another metaphor (the mycologist's departure) to illustrate how many people felt disowned and forsaken at this time. Images of waste and disintegration ('a keyhole rusting gently', 'flies dusted to mildew') contribute to an understanding of 'interminable' time. The poet also leaves us with a sense of desperate people's awareness of diminishing hope ('a shout from the blue') when faced with the harsh reality of irrevocable loss.

This feeling of anguish dominates **stanza four**. Mahon's continuing personification of the festering mushrooms vividly evokes the wretched endeavours of all those who experience oppression. References to 'pale flesh flaking', 'nightmares' and the 'Dominion of stale air' signify the deadly legacy of human suffering. The derelict shed is filled with 'rank moisture'. **Mahon's rich, sensuous language gives way to a more melodramatic, nightmarish scene** as he envisages the more resistant mushrooms forcing themselves ('Elbow room!') towards the light at the expense of those left 'groaning/For their deliverance'. But they are condemned to captivity forever and must accept that 'there is left only the posture' of escape.

The poet assumes the role of a tourist in **stanza five**. The visitor – the first in 'A half century' – is intrigued by the discovery of these hideously distorted mushrooms. To the outsider, they now resemble something from another weird world: 'Magi, moonmen'. There is even a sense of menace about these grotesque 'Powdery prisoners', which begin to resemble man-eating 'triffids'. **Mahon creates an increasingly surreal and hysterical atmosphere**, dramatising the suffering of the mushrooms, 'racked by drought/And insomnia', as they are confronted by the intruding sightseer with his camera. The scene is chaotic and confrontational as 'their feverish forms' face 'the flash-bulb firing-squad'. The inevitable presence of death is also evident in the sensuous account of how the decaying fungi have become 'soft food for worms'. In their final failure, all they can do is 'lift frail heads in gravity and good faith'.

Mahon combines the twin themes of history and separation in the highly charged **final stanza**. On behalf of the world's downtrodden and forgotten, the mushrooms 'are begging us, you see, in their wordless way,/To do something'. For the first time, he refers to specific victims: both of the Holocaust and of a great natural disaster ('Lost people of Treblinka and Pompeii'). In a powerful, pleading tone, the mushrooms now speak directly for the voiceless dead: 'Let the god not abandon us'. The poem ends as it began, with a final impassioned plea to the tourist ('with your light meter') to at least set the record straight. **Is Mahon also asking us to acknowledge the suffering ('darkness and pain') and all the other shameful events of history?** The last line echoes the plaintive epigraph: 'Let not our naive labours have been in vain!' Once again, this strange and stimulating poem can be read in many different ways. As always, readers must come to their own understanding and have the confidence to make their own personal responses.

ANALYSIS

'In many of his poems, Derek Mahon addresses issues concerning the world's marginalised and oppressed peoples.' Discuss how 'A Disused Shed in Co. Wexford' reflects this statement, using close reference to the text of the poem.

SAMPLE PARAGRAPH

I thought 'A Disused Shed in Co. Wexford' was a very powerful protest which encouraged me to relate to the suffering of other people. Inside the mushroom shed, Mahon himself imagines some of those who have been badly treated in history. The haunting images of the 'Peruvian mines' and 'Indian compounds' made me think of abandoned countries where 'lost people' have endured terrible experiences. As it is impossible to really understand what they went through, Mahon uses the decayed mushrooms as a symbol of all the corruption in the world which causes such pain. He hints at many voiceless groups, including those who suffered after the Irish Civil War. His tone is sympathetic to those who are brutally victimised – 'groaning for deliverance'. I could also sympathise with their troubles when he mentioned the death camps 'of Treblinka' and the forgotten victims of Pompeii. He personified the rotting mushrooms – 'their pale flesh' struggling for freedom – 'Elbow room!' Mahon's poem is a moving cry for help for all outsiders who are on the margins of society. I thought the ending was very moving when he said 'Let God not abandon them'. The poem was very disturbing and filled with haunting images of victims. The fact that the mushroom shed is disused for so long suggested that oppressed people are easily forgotten.

EXAMINER'S COMMENT

This is a reasonably well-focused paragraph, which explores Mahon's sympathies for oppressed groups. There is a sense of engaging personal response throughout. However, expression is a little awkward towards the end and the quotations are slightly inaccurate. Grade C.

CLASS/HOMEWORK EXERCISES

1. 'Although Mahon's poems can be challenging at times, they are essentially thought-provoking and meaningful.' In light of this statement, discuss 'A Disused Shed in Co. Wexford'. Support the points you make with reference to the poem.
2. Copy the table below into your own notes and fill in critical comments about the last two quotations.

• Poetry Focus •

Derek Mahon

Key Quotes

Even now there are places where a thought might grow	The first line is reflective. Typically, it is open to interpretation. For Mahon, the disused shed is the starting point for his own train of thought.
And a door bangs with diminished confidence	The image suggests emptiness and isolation. An underlying mood of failure is present throughout the poem.
'Save us, save us,' they seem to say	Repetition invites readers to share the poet's own awareness of the plight of suffering people. The pleading tone echoes the anguish of all who are in agony.
There have been deaths, the pale flesh flaking/ Into the earth that nourished it	
Grown beyond nature now, soft food for worms, / They lift frail heads in gravity and good faith	

Rathlin

A long time since the last scream cut short –
Then an unnatural silence; and then
A natural silence, slowly broken
By the shearwater, by the sporadic
Conversation of crickets, the bleak
Reminder of a metaphysical wind.
Ages of this, till the report
Of an outward motor at the pier
Shatters the dream-time, and we land
As if we were the first visitors here.

The whole island a sanctuary where amazed
Oneiric species whistle and chatter,
Evacuating rock-face and cliff-top.
Cerulean distance, an oceanic haze –
Nothing but sea-smoke to the ice-cap
And the odd somnolent freighter.
Bombs doze in the housing estates
But here they are through with history –
Custodians of a lone light which repeats
One simple statement to the turbulent sea.

A long time since the unspeakable violence –
Since Somhairle Buí, powerless on the mainland,
Heard the screams of the Rathlin women
Borne to him, seconds later, upon the wind.
Only the cry of the shearwater
And the roar of the outboard motor
Disturb the singular peace. Spray-blind,
We leave here the infancy of the race,
Unsure among the pitching surfaces
Whether the future lies before us or behind.

Derek Mahon

• Poetry Focus •

Derek Mahon

'As if we were the first visitors here'

GLOSSARY

Rathlin is a small island located off the coast of Co. Antrim. In the late 16th century, the island's entire population (estimated at over 600 people) was massacred by English invaders. Rathlin is now a well-known bird sanctuary and nature reserve.

4 *shearwater*: type of long-winged seabird.
4 *sporadic*: occasional.
6 *metaphysical wind*: mystical, supernatural.
7 *report*: echo.
9 *dream-time*: bliss; in Aboriginal mythology, dream-time is also called the *alcheringa*, the golden age when the first ancestors were created.
11 *sanctuary*: holy place of refuge; nature reserve.
12 *Oneiric*: dreamlike.
14 *Cerulean*: sky-blue.
16 *somnolent*: lifeless, drowsy.
16 *freighter*: cargo boat.
19 *Custodians*: guardians, protectors.
20 *turbulent*: stormy.
22 *Somhairle Buí*: Irish chieftain (Sorley Boy MacDonald) whose family and supporters were killed on Rathlin in the 1575 atrocity.
27 *singular*: unusual.
29 *pitching*: tossing.

EXPLORATIONS

1 Based on your reading of stanza one, describe the poet's initial response to Rathlin Island. Refer closely to the text in your answer.
2 Choose one phrase or image that you found particularly effective in the poem. Briefly explain why you chose it.
3 In your opinion, do the last three lines of the poem suggest hope or fear or both? Briefly explain your response.

STUDY NOTES

Like several other poems by Derek Mahon, 'Rathlin' describes a journey and its significance. Ireland's violent past is a recurring theme in his work. In this case, he touches on Rathlin's infamous massacres during the late 16th century and its present importance as a wildlife sanctuary. The poet contrasts the tranquillity he experiences on his visit with the horrendous events of 400 years earlier, when the island's population was killed by invaders. Reports claimed that the cries of the victims were carried to the mainland by the wind and that a local Irish chieftain, Somhairle Buí, heard them but was unable to help.

In the opening stanza, Mahon reflects on the unspeakable violence of a 16th-century bloodbath, which left an unnatural silence on Rathlin. In crafting a truly harrowing image – 'the last scream' of a dying islander – **the poet dramatises the slaughter and its traumatic aftermath**. His description is dominated by contrasting sounds. An eerie calm ('natural silence') is replaced by 'the sporadic/Conversation of crickets' – the sharp 'r' and 'c' onomatopoeic effects echoing their nocturnal chirping. Considering the island's disturbing past, it is grimly ironic that Rathlin has become a sanctuary for beautiful seabirds, such as the shearwater. Mahon senses that his own intrusive arrival in a noisy motorboat 'Shatters the dream-time'. But he remains acutely aware of how nothing can erase the brutality of history; 'the bleak/Reminder of a metaphysical wind'.

This deeply sombre mood continues in stanza two. The poet focuses on the island's serene beauty and its 'amazed' birdlife, unaccustomed to human visitors. There is an underlying sense that the birds' fearful response ('Evacuating rock-face and cliff-top') mirrors the reaction of the 16th-century inhabitants when faced with invaders. Mahon suggests the **subtle association between past and present** through vague images: 'Cerulean distance, an oceanic haze'. Here, sibilant and assonant sounds accentuate the gentle mood. This lethargic atmosphere is emphasised by random details, such as occasional 'sea-smoke' and 'the odd somnolent freighter'. But the tranquil security is shattered by an unexpected reference to Northern Ireland's continuing conflict: 'Bombs doze in the housing estates'. Although Rathlin may be 'through with history', violence is never far beneath the surface in the North. Even the 'lone' lighthouse that warns against 'the turbulent sea' seems to expose the vulnerability of this peaceful place.

Stanza three returns to the massacre. Mahon imagines the distraught chieftain, Somhairle Buí, standing on the mainland listening to the terrible 'screams of the Rathlin women' as they are butchered. This image reflects the desperate frustration of 'powerless' people everywhere to secure peace in times of conflict. Again, there is a contrast between that horrific past and the stillness of the present, where only the noises of the shearwater and the boat engine disturb the unusual calm. **The poem ends ambiguously**, as Mahon and his fellow travellers leave Rathlin, not knowing whether 'the future lies before us or behind'.

On the return journey over rough seas, the poet is 'Spray-blind' – perhaps another metaphor for his uncertainty. Is he distancing himself from violence? Or heading towards greater conflict on the mainland? In his own mind, he is leaving 'the infancy of the race'. The phrase is open to several interpretations. Innocent children were murdered in the 16th-century atrocities. Yet **Rathlin's newfound natural harmony might signal the start of a peaceful era where people can be more cautiously optimistic.** Some critics have stated that the metaphor of Rathlin's lighthouse sending its message to the restless sea suggests that the lessons of the past can be learned in the difficult times of the present. Perhaps the island symbolises the world at large in all its inconsolable tragedy. In the end, readers must find their own meaning and decide for themselves.

ANALYSIS

'The notion of history repeating itself is an important theme in Derek Mahon's poetry.' Discuss this view, with particular reference to 'Rathlin'. Support the points you make with quotations from the poem.

SAMPLE PARAGRAPH

The first line of Mahon's poem 'Rathlin' is a dramatic reference to an atrocity from the 1500s when innocent women and children were killed. He remembers 'the last scream cut short' before silence descended on the island. The opening statement about how 'unnatural silence' eventually becomes 'natural silence' is ironic, and foreshadows the response that people in Northern Ireland have made to more recent violence. Although Rathlin is a bird sanctuary nowadays, Mahon is realistic when he notes, 'Bombs doze in the housing estates'. To me, he is simply saying that sectarian violence has not gone away. I think there is a strong sense of irony in the statement: 'But here they are through with history'. In the final stanza, he returns to the 16th-century slaughter. It is a mirror image of what continues in his homeland, where ordinary people are 'powerless' to influence the conflict. The disturbing ending of the poem suggests that the cycle of violence is likely to continue. Mahon wonders 'Whether the future lies before us or behind'. In my opinion, he believes that history repeats itself and that peace is always temporary, 'singular'. The final image of his rough sea journey back to the mainland where he is 'Unsure among the pitching surfaces' emphasises this bleak reality.

EXAMINER'S COMMENT

This paragraph addresses the question directly and traces the progress of Mahon's theme through the poem. There is evidence of personal engagement and clear appreciation of the way images from the past are linked to the present. Apt quotations and fluent expression throughout. Grade A.

CLASS/HOMEWORK EXERCISES

1. 'Derek Mahon's poetry explores the mystery and significance that is hidden beyond appearances.' Discuss this view, with particular reference to 'Rathlin'. Support the points you make with reference to the poem.
2. Copy the table below into your own notes and fill in critical comments about the last two quotations.

Key Quotes

A long time since the last scream cut short	The poem begins with a dramatic reference to Rathlin's barbarous history. Emphatic words ('scream' and 'cut') emphasise the gruesome past.
Oneiric species whistle and chatter, / Evacuating rock-face and cliff-top	Sound effects are used to convey a clear sense of the rugged island landscape today. Sharp consonants ('r', 'c' and 't') echo the natural wildlife.
Spray-blind, / We leave here the infancy of the race	Mahon ends the poem ambiguously. He seems to suggest that people today are blind to reality, but he also hints that there is some hope of improvement.
the report/ Of an outward motor at the pier/ Shatters the dream-time	
Unsure among the pitching surfaces/ Whether the future lies before us or behind	

• Poetry Focus •

The Chinese Restaurant in Portrush

Derek Mahon

Before the first visitor comes the spring
Softening the sharp air of the coast
In time for the first seasonal 'invasion'.
Today the place is as it might have been,
Gentle and almost hospitable. A girl   5
Strides past the Northern Counties Hotel,
Light-footed, swinging a book-bag,
And the doors that were shut all winter
Against the north wind and the sea mist
Lie open to the street, where one   10
By one the gulls go window-shopping
And an old wolfhound dozes in the sun.

While I sit with my paper and prawn chow mein
Under a framed photograph of Hong Kong
The proprietor of the Chinese restaurant   15
Stands at the door as if the world were young,
Watching the first yacht hoist a sail
– An ideogram on sea-cloud – and the light
Of heaven upon the hills of Donegal;
And whistles a little tune, dreaming of home.   20

'dreaming of home'

Derek Mahon

GLOSSARY

Portrush is a predominantly Protestant seaside town in north Co. Antrim. Mahon often cycled there at weekends.

3 *'invasion'*: intrusion; arrival of a large number of people who do not belong to the region.

5 *hospitable*: friendly, welcoming to strangers.

12 *wolfhound*: oblique reference to Ulster conflicts and the legend of Cú Chulainn, who was known as the hound of Ulster. The sleeping hound suggests that rivalries have been laid aside, if only temporarily.

13 *prawn chow mein*: Chinese dish of fried noodles, seafood and vegetables.

15 *proprietor*: owner of a business.

18 *ideogram*: a character or symbol in writing that stands not for a word or sound but for a concept, idea or the thing itself; here the sail could be the character that paints the idea of home for the emigrant.

EXPLORATIONS

1 Comment on Mahon's use of sibilant sound effects in the first three lines of the poem.
2 Choose two details from the poem that suggest that the town of Portrush is 'Gentle and almost hospitable'. Briefly explain each choice.
3 Write a short personal response to the poem, in which you highlight the impact it made on you. Refer to the text in your answer.

STUDY NOTES

> 'The Chinese Restaurant in Portrush' examines the concept of home and belonging. Once again, the poet is the wry, solitary observer. Mahon has said, 'I could spend an afternoon happily staring.' This leisurely poem moves gracefully from a view of an off-season seaside town to a casual sketch of Mahon himself and the proprietor of the Chinese restaurant. What connects everyone and everything – both distant and local – is the illusory word, 'home'.

Derek Mahon is well known for his **characteristically keen sense of place**. This poem **opens** on a spring day in a small resort in Northern Ireland. Soft sibilant sounds ('spring', 'Softening', 'coast') convey **the mellowing nature of the new season on the quiet town of Portrush**. The expected influx of holidaymakers is regarded by both poet and residents as an 'invasion'. The arrival of tourist groups is seen as an intrusion – or even a violation. Over the centuries, Irish history has been marked by violent invasions and Mahon now seems relieved that he is living in relatively peaceful times, when 'the place is as it might have been'. However, prior to this holiday season, Portrush is 'Gentle'; it belongs to Mahon and the residents. Indeed, the town is 'almost hospitable'. The qualification clearly suggests that the small resort – and perhaps Ireland itself

– gives a hesitant welcome to its visitors. Overall, there is an underlying reticence in these **opening lines**.

The mood changes abruptly with the **dynamic image of a modern, purposeful girl** who 'Strides past'. Her 'Light-footed' determination is contained in the monosyllabic verb. She appears to belong here, as she confidently twirls her book-bag. To the poet, everything is unfolding as it should, signalling a new year and new experiences: 'the doors ... Lie open'. Are the references to books and open doors a suggestion that open minds are also needed here? The mood of expectation and hope increases as a droll note of humour creeps in with the allusion to gulls who 'go window-shopping' (**line 11**). But the inevitable, harsh reality of conflict in Northern Ireland is hinted at in the image of the 'old wolfhound' (**line 12**). This is a land where bitter rivalries lie deep, indicated by the mention of 'sharp air' and 'invasion'. For the present, however, the old mythical conflicts have been almost forgotten and there is peace: the hound 'dozes in the sun'. Mahon rarely deals directly with the sectarian Troubles of Northern Ireland. He has written, 'I felt very far from home in those years. In fact for a large part of my life I've been terrified of home.' Nevertheless, he does not feel like an outsider in Portrush and he distances himself instinctively from 'the first visitor'.

The second section of the poem is set in the quiet interior of the restaurant. **The mood becomes more personal and Mahon's tone is restrained** as he sketches a charming illustration of himself with his newspaper and prawn chow mein (**line 13**). The restaurant owner stands nearby, looking out 'as if the world were young'. Is there a hint that the world is now cynical and disappointed? However, the mood of optimism and renewal returns as the boats in the distance take to the sea again after the harsh winter. The proprietor watches 'the first yacht hoist a sail'. Now the poet imagines how a Chinese person might think. The sail becomes an ideogram, perhaps for place of birth. The owner is 'dreaming of home'. Did the sail remind him of this? The **relaxed atmosphere** is captured particularly in the phrase 'whistles a little tune'. The proprietor continues to dream as he admires the beautiful, idyllic countryside 'and the light/Of heaven upon the hills of Donegal'. As in much of the poem, run-on lines contribute to the gentle rhythm and enhance the wistful mood.

In the **final lines**, the view has moved from streetscape to horizon and beyond. Mahon challenges us by **placing a poem that celebrates home in the transient**. He is being gently sardonic by locating the poem in a tourist town, a place of coming and going. By contrast, the image of Hong Kong in its 'framed photograph' shows a fixed, idealised place. The city was then a British colony. Interestingly, like Northern Ireland, Hong Kong was displaced and was not part of its natural homeland. The poet seems to be suggesting that home is a place where one lives, where nurturing takes place. But in this poem, home seems an illusion, an unattainable dream. There is a sense of yearning as the Chinese man stands 'dreaming of home' (line 20). Does Mahon also share this yearning for that instinctive sense of belonging? Are Portrush, Hong Kong or Donegal really home for anyone in the poem?

ANALYSIS

'A sense of separation is central to the poetry of Derek Mahon.' Discuss the statement with particular reference to 'The Chinese Restaurant in Portrush'. Support your views with close reference to the text.

SAMPLE PARAGRAPH

Derek Mahon's poem 'The Chinese Restaurant in Portrush' describes a detached figure who tries to make sense of what home really means. He has set his poem in a transient place. He is visiting an Irish seaside holiday resort. It is off-season ('Before the first visitors arrive'), which adds to the sense of isolation. He cuts himself off from contact with others as he sits on his own with a shield, 'my paper'. He's eating Chinese food in a foreign restaurant. He is not in harmony with his environment. The picture of Hong Kong is 'framed'. This also adds to the image of home having been put on a pedestal. The city is idealised, just like our ideas about home. Hong Kong, like Northern Ireland, was cut off from its natural hinterland of China. Deep sadness is found throughout this poem as hints of what might have happened come to the surface: 'as it might have been', 'as if the world was young'. But Mahon doesn't seem at ease, as he refers to a symbol of conflict, the Irish wolfhound. However, his relationship with his birthplace also has an optimistic side as he observes the girl who 'strides' and the 'doors' which 'lie open'. Mahon is like the inward-looking residents in the town, he resents its changing character as the noisy day trippers are described as an 'invasion' – which is true. He feels different to these outsiders. The poet's voice is precise, using colloquial language – 'dozes in the sun'. In the end, I felt that nobody finds home in this poem, however much they try and dream. Both the Chinese immigrant and the local poet feel separated from where they feel they belong.

Derek Mahon

EXAMINER'S COMMENT

While this answer was on track some of the time, it drifted from the question in places. The repetitive style at the start (where too many sentences began with 'He') and the slightly inaccurate quotations were offset by some good critical discussion in the second half of the paragraph. Overall, a note-like response. Grade C.

CLASS/HOMEWORK EXERCISES

1. 'While Mahon makes readers face up to life's realities, he is never sentimental or self-pitying.' Discuss this view of Derek Mahon's poetry, with particular reference to 'The Chinese Restaurant in Portrush'. Refer closely to the text in your response.
2. Copy the table below into your own notes and fill in critical comments about the last two quotations.

Key Quotes

In time for the first seasonal 'invasion'	Mahon refers to the tourists who descend on Portrush every summer. He might also be thinking of Ireland's history. The tone is curt and unwelcoming.
Light-footed, swinging a book-bag	Precise detail conveys a picture of a young, carefree girl who does not feel the weight of history. The 'book-bag' suggests someone who looks outward, perhaps in contrast to some people in the area?
one/By one the gulls go window-shopping	Mahon's typically droll humour.
An ideogram on sea-cloud	
And whistles a little tune, dreaming of home	

Kinsale

Derek Mahon

The kind of rain we knew is a thing of the past –
deep-delving, dark, deliberate you would say,
browsing on spire and bogland; but today
our sky-blue slates are steaming in the sun,
our yachts tinkling and dancing in the bay   5
like racehorses. We contemplate at last
shining windows, a future forbidden to no one.

'our yachts tinkling and dancing in the bay'

GLOSSARY

The small town of Kinsale in Co. Cork is now a lively fishing port and tourist centre. Its historic importance goes back to the Battle of Kinsale in 1601 when English forces overcame the armies of the Ulster chieftains, Hugh O'Neill and Hugh O'Donnell. To a large extent, this marked the end of Gaelic rule in Ireland.

2 *deep-delving*: exploring the past.
3 *browsing on*: considering; surviving on.
3 *spire and bogland*: religion and land are traditional symbols of power in Irish history.

EXPLORATIONS

1 What is your reading of the first line of the poem?
2 Comment on Mahon's use of contrasting images in the poem. Refer to the text in your answer.
3 In your opinion, does the poem end on a positive or negative note? Give reasons for your answer.

• Poetry Focus •

Derek Mahon

STUDY NOTES

In 'Kinsale' the poet returns to the theme of Irish identity and imagines a future that is 'forbidden to no one'. Mahon lived in the Co. Cork seaside town for some years and would be well aware of its significance in the historical conflict between Ireland and England. Although he does not refer directly to the past in this short, celebratory poem, he makes effective use of symbols to suggest the contrast between modern Ireland and its turbulent history.

The **opening lines** are typically conversational. Mahon reflects on an earlier time, which he associates with wet, gloomy weather: 'The kind of rain we knew is a thing of the past'. **There is a sense of relief that the worst is over.** Alliteration emphasises the harsh conditions of the past: 'deep-delving, dark, deliberate'. From the outset, readers are quietly encouraged to agree with the poet's view ('you would say').

A deeply sombre tone is created by slow rhythm, intrusive punctuation and a polysyllabic adjective ('deliberate'). It is likely that the rain symbolises Mahon's view of Kinsale – and of Ireland – in the past. He may well be imagining a time of relative poverty, prior to the sudden prosperity of the late 20th century. He could also be reflecting on times of violence and failed rebellion, such as the Battle of Kinsale in 1601. At any rate, the underlying **mood of haunting oppression** is enhanced by further alliteration and broad vowel assonant sounds: 'browsing on spire and bogland'. The mention of church spires and native bogland suggests the powerful influences of religion and land in Irish history.

Line 3 marks a turning point in the poem. Mahon distances himself from the past and focuses on modern times. The metaphor of sunshine following rain is a fairly obvious symbol of celebration and optimism. However, the colourful images of present-day Kinsale are fresh and vibrant. A pulsating sibilance contributes to the changing atmosphere, as though the dreary past is evaporating before our eyes: 'sky-blue slates are steaming in the sun'. Mahon's **dynamic description reflects the feeling of renewed energy and prosperity** that is evident around Kinsale, where yachts are now 'tinkling and dancing in the bay/like racehorses'. The light, musical effects of the onomatopoeic verbs and the unusual simile suggest much about affluent lifestyles during Ireland's economic boom in the 1990s. Repetition of the inclusive pronoun 'our' also conveys a sense of communal confidence.

Derek Mahon

In contrast to the 'deep-delving' rain, refreshing light and cheerfulness dominate the poem's **final lines**. Mahon adopts the role of observer, looking at the new Ireland through 'shining windows'. It appears that Ireland's future will be a bright one, filled with hope and opportunity: 'forbidden to no one'. The poet has a cautious optimism regarding the years ahead. However, **readers might also 'contemplate' a more sceptical undertone**. Is Mahon warning against the complacency of newfound wealth? Perhaps he is suggesting that just as Irish people would be unwise to take the temporary sunshine for granted, we should never lose sight of Kinsale's darker history.

ANALYSIS

'The importance of place and identity are central themes in Derek Mahon's poetry.' Using suitable reference to the text, discuss this view with reference to 'Kinsale'.

SAMPLE PARAGRAPH

'Kinsale' reminded me of Mahon's poem 'Rathlin'. Each place has had a violent history that has impacted on Irish people. I thought it was interesting that the poet takes a broad view of Ireland – North and South – reminding us of the oppression and defeats suffered by the native Irish over the centuries. In 'Kinsale', Mahon uses the weather as a metaphor for the contrast between past and present. As a people, we have moved from 'deep-delving, dark' rain to bright sunny days and 'shining windows'. Although the poem is only seven lines long, it gives us a concise history lesson of how far the Irish nation has come from the times of colonisation. To me, this suggests the resilience of an independent people who have survived a difficult history. Mahon hints at the historical power of the Catholic Church, and at peasant farmers in his phrase 'spire and bogland'. He is also quite cynical of the more recent Celtic Tiger boom with its short-lived, vulgar wealth: 'yachts tinkling and dancing'. I thought he was far-sighted to condemn our country's tacky materialism at the end. His tone seems ironic when he criticises the 'shining windows'. As we all know, the rain is never too far away in Ireland. 'Kinsale' is a very interesting poem, which made me think twice about the way Irish people sometimes lose touch with reality.

• Poetry Focus •

Derek Mahon

EXAMINER'S COMMENT

A good, solid response that takes a clear and personal approach to the question. The opening comparison with 'Rathlin' provided an interesting context for exploring Mahon's themes of place and identity. Expression was controlled throughout and suitable quotations were used to support discussion points. Grade A.

CLASS/HOMEWORK EXERCISES

1. 'Many of Derek Mahon's poems reaffirm positive values, such as hope, open-mindedness and sympathy for others.' Comment on the validity of this statement, with particular reference to 'Kinsale'.
2. Copy the table below into your own notes and fill in critical comments about the last two quotations.

Key Quotes

The kind of rain we knew is a thing of the past	Mahon uses the rain as a metaphor for Ireland's troubled history – particularly times of conflict, poverty and failure.
our sky-blue slates are steaming in the sun	In contrast to the gloomy image of the past, vibrant colours and lively sibilance underline the upbeat mood of the newly confident Ireland he sees in Kinsale.
a future forbidden to no one	While a positive future is a possibility, it is not guaranteed. Is the poet warning us to expect more darkness in years to come?
browsing on spire and bogland	
our yachts tinkling and dancing in the bay/ like racehorses	

Antarctica

(for Richard Ryan)

'I am just going outside and may be some time.'
The others nod, pretending not to know.
At the heart of the ridiculous, the sublime.

He leaves them reading and begins to climb,
Goading his ghost into the howling snow;   5
He is just going outside and may be some time.

The tent recedes beneath its crust of rime
And frostbite is replaced by vertigo:
At the heart of the ridiculous, the sublime.

Need we consider it some sort of crime,   10
This numb self-sacrifice of the weakest? No,
He is just going outside and may be some time –

In fact, for ever. Solitary enzyme,
Though the night yield no glimmer there will glow,
At the heart of the ridiculous, the sublime.   15

He takes leave of the earthly pantomime
Quietly, knowing it is time to go.
'I am just going outside and may be some time.'
At the heart of the ridiculous, the sublime.

'At the heart of the ridiculous, the sublime'

• Poetry Focus •

Derek Mahon

GLOSSARY

Antarctica: region surrounding the South Pole.
(for Richard Ryan): Irish poet.
1 *'I am just going outside and may be some time'*: words of Lawrence Oates, a team member on Captain Scott's ill-fated expedition to the South Pole in 1912. Oates deliberately sacrificed his life so that companions might have a better chance of survival.
3 *ridiculous*: absurd, foolish, illogical.
3 *sublime*: majestic, noble, inspiring, heavenly.
5 *Goading*: pushing, urging, encouraging.
7 *rime*: greyish frost, ice.
8 *frostbite*: skin and body tissue numbed and damaged because of freezing conditions.
8 *vertigo*: dizziness, usually caused by looking down from a height.
13 *enzyme*: substance that acts as a trigger to promote a particular reaction; metaphor for Lawrence Oates.
16 *earthly pantomime*: life seen as an absurd, colourful show; a lively, slapstick comedy.

EXPLORATIONS

1. Choose two phrases that convey the freezing environment of the Antarctic in this poem. Comment briefly on the effectiveness of each.
2. The actual words spoken by Lawrence Oates before he went to his certain death are used repeatedly in the poem. In your opinion, what effect does this have on the reader?
3. Comment on the character of Captain Oates, as portrayed by Mahon in this poem. Do you think that the poet has given a positive or negative picture of Oates? Refer to the text in your answer.

STUDY NOTES

This poem is from Derek Mahon's 1986 collection, *Antarctica*. It is based on a true incident that took place during Captain Scott's famous expedition to the South Pole (1911–12), when he was narrowly beaten to the finish by the Norwegian, Roald Amundsen. Captain Lawrence Oates, a member of the team, developed gangrene as a result of severe frostbite in his feet. He asked to be left behind, but his companions refused. One night he left the tent with these words: 'I am just going outside and may be some time.' Believing that he was holding back the team, he deliberately went to his death. His sacrifice, sadly, did not prevent the others from dying. They failed to reach the safety of their well-stocked base camp by just 11 miles. This historical perspective adds another layer of poignancy to the poem. Mahon is interested in ghostly voices from the past. The poem is written in the form of a villanelle, with five tercets and a final quatrain.

This poem is set in the huge, hostile, empty space of the area surrounding the South Pole. **A dignified man, Lawrence Oates decides his tragic fate alone.** In the first tercet (three-line stanza), Oates's own words are used: 'I am just going outside and may be some time'. This heart-rending statement has the distant tone of a lost voice from the past, echoing down the generations. Readers are aware that Oates's sacrifice ultimately proved futile. The first and third lines form two refrains, which are woven effortlessly throughout the poem and are combined in the concluding couplet. The reaction of Oates's team members is now shown: 'The others nod'. Respecting his decision, they are aware of what he is about to do, although they are 'pretending not to know'. In the third line, we hear Mahon's voice: 'At the heart of the ridiculous, the sublime'. The poet is quietly meditating on the fact that even though a gesture appears absurd and foolish ('ridiculous'), nevertheless it can contain heroic and high-minded elements ('the sublime').

In the second stanza, the poet paints a picture of a determined, selfless man pushing himself against the extremes of winter weather: 'Goading his ghost into the howling snow'. The alliteration of the hard 'g' emphasises the physical effort this courageous man is making. Mahon's use of the present tense makes the scene realistically dramatic. The assonance of the broad 'o' vowel vividly impersonates the screaming snowstorm. This is the **hostile environment** into which Oates has chosen to go. The poet repeats Oates's words when he observes: 'He is just going outside and may be some time'.

The third tercet shows the scene from the perspective of Oates: the tent disappears, 'recedes' with a crusting of hoar frost. Everything is dissolved into a whirlpool of white. The numbing pain of his frostbite is now replaced by the giddy sensation of vertigo as he loses his sense of balance in the spiralling snowstorm.

Mahon **questions whether this act is a 'crime'** in the fourth tercet. Suicide was once regarded as the greatest sin a man could commit, as it was the ultimate act of despair. But an emphatic 'No' from the poet dispels any critical questioning of 'This numb self-sacrifice of the weakest'.

The poet's use of a dash and run-on lines points deliberately into the grim fifth stanza. He emphasises the fact that Oates is gone 'for ever'. Although the men in this tragic story are not named directly, they symbolise the greater good of which humanity is sometimes capable. Mahon's resolute rhythm mirrors the slow, decisive trudging of the disappearing man. He presents a chilling, harrowing image of this man as a 'Solitary enzyme'. Oates is seen as an example of humanity's capacity for noble self-sacrifice, a **lone force capable of altering states**. He has become a catalyst for good. Humanity is ennobled by the supreme generosity of a man giving his life for the good of others. Although there was no glimmer of hope for this man, he was and is an inspiration for us all.

In the **final quatrain** Oates's quiet, dignified departure is described: 'He takes leave of the earthly pantomime'. **The absurdity of life** is stressed by use of the word 'pantomime', with its connotations of slapstick comedy and children's laughter. This man's calm realisation that 'it is time to go' leaves us awestruck. The poem concludes with the two refrains: Oates's **self-effacing, courageous words** ('I am just going outside and may be some time') and the poet's thoughtful comment ('At the heart of the ridiculous, the sublime').

The **formal structure** of the poem is in keeping with the stiff-upper-lip personality of Captain Oates and it also **graces his act with ritual and ceremony**. Mahon has chosen a villanelle form. There is irony here: the villanelle is traditionally associated with light-hearted poems celebrating idyllic country life, which contrasts dramatically with Antarctica's frozen wasteland. The tightly controlled rhyme scheme (*aba*) echoes the self-determination of Oates ('He takes leave', 'time to go'). There is another significant contrast in the poem: between the words 'sublime' and 'ridiculous', which appear four times each. They represent the two views of Oates's behaviour. However, 'sublime' is given emphasis – it is rhymed throughout ('time', 'climb', 'rime', 'crime', 'enzyme', 'pantomime'). Indeed, Mahon concludes with this reverberating adjective ('sublime'), as a final tribute to the remarkable dignity and extraordinary courage of Lawrence Oates.

ANALYSIS

It has been said that Derek Mahon's poetry has a distinctive sense of terminal pathos, which arouses emotions of deep pity and sorrow in the reader. Comment on this view of the poet's work, referring to the poem 'Antarctica'. Support your comments with reference to the text.

SAMPLE PARAGRAPH

Mahon's poetry is peopled with loners who have been unsuccessful. Yet Captain Lawrence Oates, in his solitary act of self-sacrifice, epitomises in a heart-wrenching manner the individual's capacity for greatness. Poetry widens a reader's imagination and it can be a force for moral good. The incredible, selfless act of Oates shines out with hope in a dark, selfish world ('there will glow'). I was filled with admiration for this man when he calmly says: 'I am just going outside and may be some time'. The understated tone resonates quietly, yet forcefully; and the phrase is more powerful as I realise that these are Oates's actual last words, as recorded by the leader of the expedition in his diary. In our greedy, materialistic world, it is good to hear words that lighten the darkness. The reader's heart is caught by the forlorn phrase 'Solitary enzyme'. The small, determined figure ('Goading his ghost into the howling snow') shows the heroic endurance of a man who just keeps going, 'Though the night yield no glimmer'. I felt deep pity for this man when 'frostbite is replaced by vertigo'. Out in the howling wastes of the South Pole, he stumbles in unimaginable agony. The tent, the only source of comfort, is disappearing – 'receding beneath its crust of rime', the repetition of 'r' mimicking the encroaching ice. Judging the man's action in a logical way, it was foolish, 'ridiculous', particularly in hindsight. The sacrifice was in vain, since the other explorers perished. But the reader's feelings are aroused by the self-control of Oates who simply 'takes leave of the earthly pantomine'. The 'sublime' act of love, giving one's life for the good of others, fills the reader with deep pity, but also with great pride in the human race.

EXAMINER'S COMMENT

A well-illustrated answer focusing clearly on the task. Quotes are integrated effectively into critical comments. There is also a strong sense of personal engagement with the poem. The expression is mature and controlled throughout. Varied vocabulary enlivens the response. Grade A.

CLASS/HOMEWORK EXERCISES

1. Compare and contrast the character of Captain Oates with another loner from Mahon's poetry on your course. Which character appeals to you more? Explain your response, giving references from the text to support your views.
2. Copy the table below into your own notes and fill in critical comments about the last two quotations.

• Poetry Focus •

Derek Mahon

Key Quotes

'*I am just going outside and may be some time*'	These words are an example of controlled understatement from a brave and dignified man. The adverb 'just' (i.e. only) suggests a lack of histrionics in this generous act.
He leaves them reading and begins to climb, /Goading his ghost into the howling snow; /He is just going outside and may be some time	The rigid rhyme scheme (*aba*) adds to the reality of the tragic event. The environment and the man are both inflexible. Broad vowel sounds echo the snowstorm, personified as a menacing enemy taunting Captain Oates from outside the security of the tent.
The tent recedes beneath its crust of rime	Mahon's precision in describing a dramatic setting is evident here. The repeated slender vowel 'e' suggests that the tent is becoming smaller and more distant from Oates as it is swallowed by the encroaching ice.
He takes leave of the earthly pantomime/ Quietly	
At the heart of the ridiculous, the sublime	

LEAVING CERT SAMPLE ESSAY

> **Q** 'Derek Mahon's poetry is chiefly concerned with exploring relationships between people and places.' Discuss this statement, supporting the points you make with reference to the poems by Mahon on your course.

MARKING SCHEME GUIDELINES

Reward responses that demonstrate clear evidence of personal engagement/ involvement with the poetry of Derek Mahon.

Some of the following areas might be addressed:
- Compelling insights into Irish history and culture.
- Interesting perspective on political and/or religious conflict.
- Importance of home and background in the poems.
- Empathy with lonely, marginalised people.
- Significance of dramatic settings and/or landscapes.
- Intensity/complexity of themes.
- Revealing moods and atmospheres.
- Eloquent patterns of imagery, symbolism and/or language.

SAMPLE ESSAY (Mahon Explores Relationships between People and Places)

1 *Derek Mahon was by far the most interesting poet I studied. I enjoyed reading his poems about outsiders and lonely people. He writes about lonely places, such as Rathlin, a disused farm-shed in Wicklow and Antarctica. But these remote locations all seemed to excite his imagination and get him wondering about people's lives. His poems about Donegal, Kinsale and Portrush were very thought-provoking as well. It's obvious that places are important to Mahon as starting points for human experiences throughout history. There was a real sense of the violence of the past in his poems. I also got the impression that he is fascinated by the history and atmosphere of places. For him, they provide settings for understanding the lives of people.*

2 *Our class started with one of Mahon's more accessible poems, 'Grandfather', which was fairly typical of the poet in its apparent simplicity. It was set in the poet's hometown of Belfast and briefly sketched his grandfather's uneasy* *lifestyle after being forced to retire – 'Wounded but humorous' – from years of work in the shipyards. What was interesting about the poem was the fact that the old man seemed so totally unable to relax. Mahon described his new lifestyle as an imitation of the old working routine –'Mornings he is up at six'. It was really a subtle insight into the grandfather's character. The image of him 'banging round the house like a four-year-old' captured the relationship between Mahon and the old man. The tone was sympathetic, showing that Mahon almost treated his grandfather like a mischievous child who was a little too lively to be trusted, but whom he still loved. I also sensed the poet's understanding of his grandfather's sadness. The old man might have felt useless, at a loose end, as he was coming close to death – setting 'the clock/Against the future'.*

3 *I have to say that 'A Disused Shed In Co. Wexford' was the toughest of Mahon's poems. But it turned out to be the one I remember best. The isolated setting is similar to his descriptions of Rathlin Island or the Donegal coastline in that it sets off his imagination. He states this at the start of the poem – 'now there are places where a thought might grow'. Mahon relates the desolate building to other places where people have been mistreated. The old empty shed reminds him of 'Peruvian mines' where peasants slaved their lives away underground. His sympathy is also evident when he thinks of 'Indian compounds where the wind dances'. The piles of decaying mushrooms are seen as symbols of wasted lives. Mahon personifies them to highlight their predicament – 'They have been waiting for us in a foetor'.*

4 *The poet's reference to 'civil war days' is clearly meant to make readers reflect on the experiences of victims during that painful period in Ireland's past. From history, we know that it was a time of complex relationships. Irish people were bitterly divided during the 1920s and the Anglo-Irish Protestants felt isolated and abandoned. But Mahon keeps us thinking about other victims. Towards the end of the poem, he depicts the mushrooms as 'pale flesh flaking' and 'Powdery prisoners'. In a surreal sequence, he compares them to imaginary man-eating plants – 'triffids, racked by drought'. To me, he was suggesting that all through history, there are countless examples of uncontrollable mass violence between people. The graphic images he uses are horrifying and intense –'the ghost of a scream'. I thought the poem ended powerfully when he described the tragic lives of 'Lost people of Treblinka and Pompeii'. Their defeated cries ('Save us') were particularly moving. Overall, Mahon's disused shed had a lasting effect on me in that it really highlighted man's inhumanity to man.*

5 Some of his poems are much more upbeat, of course, and he can celebrate the beauty of places as well. In both 'Kinsale' and 'The Chinese Restaurant in Portrush', he helps us to visualise places where people can get on with their ordinary lives. Images of 'sky-blue slates' and 'yachts tinkling and dancing in the bay' are signs of today's more prosperous Ireland. I felt that he was much more optimistic about life here. His description of the slates 'steaming in the sun' reflect his more upbeat outlook. The sibilance added a light, musical effect as well. Again, Mahon's clever symbolism of the 'shining windows' suggests 'a future forbidden to no one'. Springtime in Portrush also contributed to the positive atmosphere. Although there is a sense that both the Chinese restaurant manager and Mahon himself are dreaming of a home elsewhere, the mood in the poem is generally upbeat. The two men admire 'the hills of Donegal'; Mahon enjoys watching the street where 'the gulls go window-shopping'; and the restaurant owner 'whistles a little tune'.

6 Donegal is clearly one of Mahon's favourite spots and a source of inspiration for him. I liked the contrasting moods in his poem 'Day Trip to Donegal'. I especially enjoyed how the place had both positive and disturbing effects on him. The poet saw the local landscape as 'deeper green/Than anywhere in the world'. He also appeared to be entranced by the grey sea and shocked by the 'writhing' fish in the harbour. What was interesting was how the poem showed Mahon's own relationship with Donegal. In the end, he was haunted by the day trip and felt nothing but isolation – 'I was alone and far out at sea'.

7 Many of Derek Mahon's poems use particular places to reflect on human relationships and behaviour. Irish locations especially offer a context or basis for exploring history and the tensions between himself and the world. In a way, his poems also encouraged me to think a little more about the past and the experiences of those who suffered oppression. Reading Mahon might not have provided answers, but it encouraged me to ask questions about the relationships between people and places.

(approx. 990 words)

GRADE: A1
P   = 15/15
C   = 15/15
L   = 15/15
M   = 5/5
Total = 50/50

• Poetry Focus •

Derek Mahon

EXAMINER'S COMMENT

This is a confident response to a challenging question. The personal approach is sustained and discussion is relevant throughout. Points are clearly presented, supported by suitable reference and expression is well controlled. The organised structure reflects a planned approach and a familiarity with Mahon's poems.

SAMPLE LEAVING CERT QUESTIONS ON MAHON'S POETRY (45–50 MINUTES)

1. Write the text of a talk you would give on your local radio station about the impact that Derek Mahon's poetry has made on you. You should refer to both subject matter and style. Support the points you make with reference to the poetry on your course.

2. 'Derek Mahon – an original and distinctive voice.'
   Using the above title, write an introduction to the poetry of Derek Mahon. Your introduction should focus on the poet's themes and his language use. Support your points with suitable reference to the poems by Mahon that you have read.

3. 'Mahon presents readers with challenging ideas in a style that is always subtle and delicate.' To what extent do you agree or disagree with this assessment of Mahon's poetry? Support your points with reference to the poems you have studied.

SAMPLE ESSAY PLAN (Q2)

'Derek Mahon – an original and distinctive voice.'
Using the above title, write an introduction to the poetry of Derek Mahon. Your introduction should focus on the poet's themes and his language use. Support your points with suitable reference to the poems by Mahon that you have read.

- *Intro:* Overview of Mahon's prominent themes: identity, history, places, alienation, outsiders, etc. Individual style, precise language use, memorable imagery and symbolism, etc.

- *Point 1:* Importance of the poet's Ulster Protestant background. 'Ecclesiastes' shows his ambivalent attitude to this tradition. In 'As It Should Be', he

	satirises fanaticism and bigotry. Characteristic use of colloquial language.
Point 2:	Mahon's ability to put himself in the place of others, especially outsiders such as Ismay in 'After the *Titanic*'. Being haunted by the past is a recurring theme in his poetry. Sound effects and metaphor used effectively.
Point 3:	Significance of places in his poems – Kinsale, Belfast, Donegal, Portrush, Rathlin. Varieties of tone leave readers to find their own meaning in the poems. Frequent echoes of the traumatic and ghostly voices from the past return to haunt the present.
Point 4:	'Antarctica' examines alienation and the nature of heroism. Dramatic setting, use of repetition, ambiguous tone.
Point 5:	Key poems – 'A Disused Shed in Co. Wexford' and 'Day Trip to Donegal' – define Mahon's personal views and illustrate many stylistic qualities. Rich symbolism, sensuous imagery, effective onomatopoeic effects, dark and intense moods, etc.
Conclusion:	Lively, thought-provoking ideas; addresses dangerous issues; remarkable breadth of vision; fresh, contemporary voice; distinctive use of language.

EXERCISE

Develop one of the above points into a paragraph.

POINT 2 – SAMPLE PARAGRAPH

A notable feature of Mahon's poetry is his ability to assume the persona of someone in exceptional circumstances and to present an alternative perspective. In 'After the *Titanic*', Mahon lets the poem's central character speak for himself. It struck me that the poet is attracted to troubled individuals like Bruce Ismay who, in his own way, is also a victim of the *Titanic* tragedy. His resentful tone is evident from the start: 'They said I got away in a boat'. Ismay's memories of the tragedy are intense: 'I sat shivering on the dark water'. Mahon lets us hear Ismay's self-interested version of the tragic night in this dramatic monologue and I felt a certain amount of sympathy for this recluse in his 'lonely house behind the sea'. What impresses me about Mahon is the way he gives voice to unlikely viewpoints and challenges our prejudices. Ismay emerges from this poem as a troubled figure who is unable to escape the 'Lost faces I never understood'. His deep depression and hopelessness are conveyed by the haunting images of 'broken toys' that are discarded on a local beach. The poet's originality is marked by this ability to suggest loss of innocent life. He also recreated the 'pandemonium' of the disaster through harsh aural images: 'Boilers bursting and shredded ragtime'. In his inimitable way, Mahon's metaphorical language summed up Ismay's terror: 'I sank as far that night as any'. By taking an original approach to one guilty survivor's experience, the poet made me much more aware of the greater tragedy that took the lives of so many people and continues to shock today.

EXAMINER'S COMMENT

The paragraph maintains a strong focus on addressing the question of Mahon's distinctive qualities. The personal approach is well judged and there is unmistakable evidence of close engagement with the poem. Reference and quotations are integrated fluently into the discussion and expression is clear throughout. Grade A.

Last Words

'Our bravest and most stylish wielder of the singing line.'

Michael Longley

'He [Mahon] has been reported as saying that much of the best of contemporary American poetry has been written by rap artists: "At least it rhymes".'

Patrick Cotter

'I am a recovering Protestant. Belfast, in particular, will always be a part of me, that dark, unlovely town.'

Derek Mahon

*'Out of the ash
I rise with my red hair
And I eat men like air.'*

Sylvia Plath (1932–63)

Born in Boston, Massachusetts, in 1932, **Sylvia Plath** is a writer whose best-known poems are noted for their intense focus and vibrant, personal imagery. Her writing talent – and ambition to succeed – was evident from an early age. She kept a journal during childhood and published her early poems in literary magazines and newspapers. After studying Art and English at college, Plath moved to Cambridge, England, in the mid-1950s. Here she met and later married the poet Ted Hughes. The couple had two children, Frieda and Nicholas, but the marriage was not to last. Plath continued to write through the late 1950s and early 1960s. During the final years of her life, she produced numerous confessional poems of stark revelation, channelling her long-standing anxiety and doubt into poetic verses of great power and pathos. At her creative peak, Sylvia Plath took her own life on 11 February 1963.

• Poetry Focus •

Sylvia Plath

PRESCRIBED POEMS (HIGHER LEVEL)

1 'Black Rook in Rainy Weather' (p. 402)

Plath uses the description of the rook to explore poetic inspiration and her joy when creative 'miracles' occur.

2 'The Times Are Tidy' (p. 407)

Disillusioned with the blandness of her times, this bitter social commentary contrasts the uneventful 1950s with the idealistic fairytale world of the past.

3 'Morning Song' (p. 411)

The poem records Plath's feelings after the birth of her daughter and focuses on the wonder of the mother–child relationship.

4 'Finisterre' (p. 416)

A highly descriptive poem dominated by disturbing themes of decay and death. Plath and her husband visited Finisterre on the north-west coast of France in 1960.

5 'Mirror' (p. 421)

The central themes are self-knowledge and ageing. In the first stanza, the poet is the mirror; in the second, she is the woman looking into it.

6 'Pheasant' (p. 425)

Another personal poem about man's relationship with nature. Plath believed that respect for life's natural order was vital.

7 'Elm' (p. 429)

An intensely introspective poem, rich in dark imagery and symbolism. The poet personifies the elm tree, giving it a voice.

8 'Poppies in July' (p. 434)

One of Plath's bleakest poems, contrasting the vitality of the poppies with her own exhausted longing to escape a world of pain.

9. 'The Arrival of the Bee Box' (p. 438)

This narrative addresses several key themes, including power, freedom and oppression.

10. 'Child' (p. 443)

In this short poem, Plath observes the innocence of childhood, but is overcome by personal feelings of failure and hopelessness.

• Poetry Focus •

Black Rook in Rainy Weather

Sylvia Plath

On the stiff twig up there
Hunches a wet black rook
Arranging and rearranging its feathers in the rain.
I do not expect a miracle
Or an accident   5

To set the sight on fire
In my eye, nor seek
Any more in the desultory weather some design,
But let spotted leaves fall as they fall,
Without ceremony, or portent.   10

Although, I admit, I desire,
Occasionally, some backtalk
From the mute sky, I can't honestly complain:
A certain minor light may still
Lean incandescent   15

Out of kitchen table or chair
As if a celestial burning took
Possession of the most obtuse objects now and then –
Thus hallowing an interval
Otherwise inconsequent   20

By bestowing largesse, honor,
One might say love. At any rate, I now walk
Wary (for it could happen
Even in this dull ruinous landscape); skeptical,
Yet politic; ignorant   25

Of whatever angel may choose to flare
Suddenly at my elbow. I only know that a rook
Ordering its black feathers can so shine
As to seize my senses, haul
My eyelids up, and grant   30

A brief respite from fear
Of total neutrality. With luck,

Trekking stubborn through this season
Of fatigue, I shall
Patch together a content   35

Of sorts. Miracles occur,
If you care to call those spasmodic
Tricks of radiance miracles. The wait's begun again,
The long wait for the angel,
For that rare, random descent.   40

'Hunches a wet black rook'

GLOSSARY

8 *desultory*: unexceptional, oppressive.
10 *portent*: omen.
15 *incandescent*: glowing.
19 *hallowing*: making holy.
20 *inconsequent*: of no importance.
21 *largesse*: generous, giving.
25 *politic*: wise and likely to prove advantageous.
37 *spasmodic*: occurring in bursts.

EXPLORATIONS

1 What is the mood of the poet? How does the weather described in the poem reflect this mood?
2 In your opinion, why do you think Plath sees light coming from ordinary household objects such as kitchen tables and chairs?
3 What do you think the final stanza means? Consider the phrase 'The wait's begun again'. What is the poet waiting for?

• Poetry Focus •

STUDY NOTES

'Black Rook in Rainy Weather' was written while Plath was studying in Cambridge in 1956. It contains many of her trademarks, including the exploration of emotions, the use of weather, colour and natural objects as symbols, and the dreamlike world. She explores a number of themes: fear of the future, lack of identity and poetic inspiration.

Stanza one begins with the straightforward description of a bird grooming itself, which the poet observes on a rainy day. But on closer inspection, the mood of the poem is set with the words 'stiff' and 'Hunches'. The bird is at the mercy of the elements ('wet') and there is no easy movement ('stiff'). **This atmospheric opening is dull and low key**. The black rook is a bird of ill omen. But the bird is presenting its best image to the world as it sits 'Arranging and rearranging its feathers'. Plath longed to excel in both life and art. If she were inspired, the rook would take on a new light as if on fire. But she doesn't see this happening. Even the weather is 'desultory' in the fading season of autumn. Poetic inspiration is miraculous; it is not ordinary. The world is experienced in a heightened way. Notice the long line which seems out of proportion with the rest as she declares that she doesn't expect any order or 'design' in the haphazard weather. The decaying leaves will fall with no ritual, without any organisation, just as they will. **This is a chaotic world**, a random place with no design, just as poetic inspiration happens by chance. It is also accidental, like the falling leaves. We cannot seek it, we receive it. It is active, we are passive.

After this low-key opening, the poem starts to take flight in stanzas three and four when the poet states: 'I desire'. Plath employs a witty metaphor as she looks for 'some backtalk' from the 'mute sky'. **She would like to connect with it**. It could happen on her walk, or even at home if she were to experience a 'certain minor light' shining from an ordinary, everyday object like a chair. The association of fire and light makes an ordinary moment special. It is 'hallowing'; it is giving generously ('largesse'). She is hoping against hope. Plath may be sceptical, but she is going forward carefully in case she misses the magic moment. **She must stay alert and watchful**. She must be 'politic', wise.

Stanzas six, seven and eight discuss poetic inspiration. Plath doesn't know if it will happen to her or how it will happen. Two contrasting attitudes are at loggerheads: hope and despair. The rook might inspire her: '**Miracles occur**'. If she were motivated, it would relieve 'total neutrality', this nothingness she feels when living uninspired. Although she is tired, she is insistent, 'stubborn'.

The poet will have to 'Patch' something together. She shows human vulnerability, but she is trying. This determination is a different tone from the negative one at the beginning.

Literature was as important to Plath as friends and family. What she can't live without, therefore, is inspiration – a dark, passionless existence. **Depression** is an empty state with no feeling or direction, yet her view of creativity is romantic. It is miraculous, available only to a chosen few. 'The long wait for the angel' has begun. Notice the constant use of the personal pronoun 'I'. This is a poet who is very aware of self and her own personal responses to events and feelings. The outside world becomes a metaphor for her own interior world.

Plath uses both archaic language and slang as if reinforcing the randomness of the world. This is also mirrored in the run-on lines. All is haphazard, but carefully arranged, so even the extended third-to-last line stretches out as it waits for the 'random descent' of inspiration. In this **carefully arranged disorder**, two worlds are seen. One is negative: 'desultory', 'spotted', 'mute', 'dull', 'ruinous', 'stubborn', 'fatigue'. This is indicative of her own bleak mood. The other world is positive: 'fire', 'light', 'incandescent', 'celestial', 'hallowing', 'largesse', 'honor', 'love', 'shine'. Here is the possibility of radiance.

ANALYSIS

'Plath's poems are carefully composed and beautifully phrased.' Write a paragraph in response to this statement, illustrating your answer with close reference to the poem 'Black Rook in Rainy Weather'.

SAMPLE PARAGRAPH

Just like the rook, Plath 'arranges and rearranges' her words with infinite care to communicate the contrast between the dull life of 'total neutrality' which occurs when she is not inspired, when nothing sets 'the sight on fire'. I particularly admire how she artfully arranges disorder in the poem. This mirrors the chance of poetic inspiration. Long lines poke untidily out of the first three stanzas, seeking the 'minor light' to 'Lean incandescent' upon them. I also like how the lines run in a seemingly untidy way into each other, as do some stanzas. Stanza three goes into four, as it describes the chance of a light coming from an ordinary object, such as a kitchen chair, which is seen only if the poet is inspired. The alliteration of 'rare, random' in the last line mirrors the gift of poetic technique which will be given to the poet if she can receive the blessed benediction of poetic inspiration. 'Miracles occur'.

EXAMINER'S COMMENT

Close reading of the poem is evident in this original response to Plath's poetic technique. Quotations are very well used here to highlight Plath's ability to create disordered order. Grade-A standard.

CLASS/HOMEWORK EXERCISES

1. In your opinion, has the poet given up hope of being inspired? Use reference to the poem in your answer.
2. Copy the table below into your own notes and fill in critical comments about the last two quotations.

Key Quotes

But let spotted leaves fall as they fall,/ Without ceremony	Decaying leaves drop as they will without any ritual to mark the event.
As if a celestial burning took/Possession of the most obtuse objects now and then	Poetic inspiration allows Plath to see the most ordinary things in a state of heightened awareness. They appear transformed into objects of beauty.
A brief respite from fear/ Of total neutrality	A major concern of the poet is the distress of losing her inspiration.
If you care to call those spasmodic/ Tricks of radiance miracles	
that rare, random descent	

The Times Are Tidy

Sylvia Plath

Unlucky the hero born
In this province of the stuck record
Where the most watchful cooks go jobless
And the mayor's rôtisserie turns
Round of its own accord.   5

There's no career in the venture
Of riding against the lizard,
Himself withered these latter-days
To leaf-size from lack of action:
History's beaten the hazard.   10

The last crone got burnt up
More than eight decades back
With the love-hot herb, the talking cat,
But the children are better for it,
The cow milks cream an inch thick.   15

'riding against the lizard'

GLOSSARY

2 *province*: a remote place.
2 *stuck record*: the needle would sometimes get jammed on a vinyl music album.
4 *rôtisserie*: meat on rotating skewer.
7 *lizard*: dragon.
11 *crone*: old witch.

Poetry Focus

Sylvia Plath

EXPLORATIONS

1. What is suggested by the poem's title? Is Plath being cynical about modern life? Develop your response in a short paragraph.
2. Select one image from the poem that suggests that the past was much more dangerous and exciting than the present. Comment on its effectiveness.
3. Do you agree or disagree with the speaker's view of modern life? Give reasons for your answer.

STUDY NOTES

> 'The Times Are Tidy' was written in 1958. In this short poem, Plath casts a cold eye on contemporary life and culture, which she sees as bland and unadventurous. The poem's ironic title clearly suggests Plath's dissatisfaction with the over-regulated society of her day.

Do you think you are living in an heroic age or do you believe that most people have lost their sense of wonder? Is there anyone in public life whom you really admire? Perhaps you despair of politicians, particularly when their promises sound like a 'stuck record'.

Stanza one is dominated by hard-hitting images reflecting how the world of fairytale excitement has disappeared. From the outset, **the tone is scornful and dismissive**. Plath believes that any hero would be totally out of place amid the mediocrity of our times. True talent ('the most watchful cooks') is largely unrewarded. The unexpected imagery of the 'stuck record' and the mayor's rotating spit symbolise complacent monotony and lack of progress, particularly during the late 1950s, when Plath wrote the poem. Both images convey a sense of purposeless circling, of people going nowhere. It seems as though the poet is seething with frustration at the inertia and conformity of her own life and times.

Plath's **darkly embittered sense of humour** becomes evident in **stanza two**. She laments the current lack of honour and courage – something which once existed in the world of fairytales. Unlike the past, contemporary society is compromised. There are no idealistic dragon-slayers any more. The worker who dares to stand up and criticise ('riding against the lizard') is risking demotion. The modern dragon – a metaphor for the challenges we face – has even been reduced to a mere lizard. Despite this, we are afraid of confrontation and prefer to retreat. The verb 'withered' suggests the weakness and decay of our safe, modern world. The poet openly complains that 'History's beaten the hazard'. Over time, we have somehow defeated all sense of adventure and daring. These qualities belong in the distant past.

In **stanza three**, Plath continues to contrast past and present. Witches are no longer burned at the stake. This might well suggest that superstition has disappeared, and with it, all imagination. The last two lines are ironic in tone, reflecting the poet's deep **disenchantment with the excesses of our consumer society**. The final image – 'the cow milks cream an inch thick' – signifies overindulgence. At one time, it was thought that supernatural forces could reduce the milk yield from cows.

The poet clearly accepts that **society has changed for the worse**. Children may have everything they want nowadays, but they have lost their sense of wonder and excitement. She laments the loss of legendary heroism. Medieval dragons and wicked witches (complete with magic potions and talking cats) no longer exist. Her conclusion is that life today is decidedly less interesting than it used to be. Unlike so much of Plath's work, the personal pronoun 'I' is not used in this poem. However, the views expressed are highly contemptuous and the weary, frustrated tone clearly suggests that Plath herself feels unfulfilled.

ANALYSIS

Write a paragraph on Plath's critical tone in 'The Times Are Tidy'.

SAMPLE PARAGRAPH

The tone of voice in 'The Times Are Tidy' is almost irrationally critical of modern life. Plath has nothing good to say about today's world as she sees it. The poem's title is glib and self-satisfied, just like the neatly organised society that Plath seems to despise. The opening comment – 'Unlucky the hero born/In this province' – emphasises this negative tone. The poet's mocking attitude becomes increasingly disparaging as she rails against the unproductive images of easy living – 'the stuck record' and 'the mayor's rôtisserie'. Plath goes on to contrast today's apathetic society with the more spirited medieval era, when knights in armour existed. The poet deliberately omits all the positive aspects of modern life and chooses to give a very one-sided view of the world. Plath ends on a sarcastic note, sneering at the advances of our world of plenty – 'cream an inch thick'. The voice here – and indeed, throughout the entire poem – is both sardonic and superior.

EXAMINER'S COMMENT

This A-grade paragraph demonstrates strong interpretive skills and is firmly focused on Plath's judgmental tone. The supporting references range widely and effectively illustrate the poet's critical attitude. Quotations are particularly well integrated and the management of language is assured throughout.

CLASS/HOMEWORK EXERCISES

1. Outline the main theme in 'The Times Are Tidy'. In your answer, trace the way the poet develops her ideas during the course of the poem.
2. Copy the table below into your own notes and fill in critical comments about the last two quotations.

Key Quotes

Unlucky the hero born/ In this province	Plath is clearly disillusioned with the unheroic world in which she lives.
the mayor's rôtisserie turns/ Round of its own accord	The image of automation suggests how complacent and predictable life has become. Nothing seems to change.
History's beaten the hazard	Ironically, like the beasts of legend, excitement and romance have been crushed in these 'tidy' modern times.
But the children are better for it	
The cow milks cream an inch thick	

Morning Song

Sylvia Plath

Love set you going like a fat gold watch.
The midwife slapped your footsoles, and your bald cry
Took its place among the elements.

Our voices echo, magnifying your arrival. New statue.
In a drafty museum, your nakedness   5
Shadows our safety. We stand round blankly as walls.

I'm no more your mother
Than the cloud that distills a mirror to reflect its own slow
Effacement at the wind's hand.

All night your moth-breath   10
Flickers among the flat pink roses. I wake to listen:
A far sea moves in my ear.

One cry, and I stumble from bed, cow-heavy and floral
In my Victorian nightgown.
Your mouth opens clean as a cat's. The window square   15

Whitens and swallows its dull stars. And now you try
Your handful of notes;
The clear vowels rise like balloons.

'The clear vowels rise like balloons'

GLOSSARY

2 *midwife*: a person trained to assist at childbirth.
3 *elements*: primitive, natural, atmospheric forces.
9 *Effacement*: rub out, make inconspicuous, obliterate.
11 *pink roses*: images on the wallpaper.
18 *vowels*: speech sounds made without stopping the flow of the breath.

Sylvia Plath

EXPLORATIONS

1. Comment on the suitability and effectiveness of the simile in line 1.
2. What is the attitude of the mother to the new arrival? Does her attitude change in the course of the poem? Refer to the text in your answer.
3. A metaphor links two things so that one idea explains or gives a new viewpoint about the other. Choose one metaphor from the poem and comment on its effectiveness.

STUDY NOTES

> 'Morning Song' was written in 1961. Plath explores the complex issues of the relationship between a mother and a child, celebrating the birth of the infant but also touching on deep feelings of loss and separation.

Do all mothers immediately welcome and fall in love with a new baby? Are some of them overwhelmed or even depressed after giving birth? Are parents often anxious about the new responsibilities a baby brings?

Plath wrote this poem after two intensely personal experiences, celebrating the birth of her daughter, Frieda, who was 10 months old when she wrote the poem, and shortly after a miscarriage. The poem is realistic and never strays into sentimentality or cliché. The title 'Morning' suggests a new beginning and 'Song' a celebration.

Stanza one describes the arrival of the child into the world in a strong, confident, rhythmic sentence announcing the act of creation: 'Love set you going'. The simile comparing the child to a 'fat gold watch' suggests a plump baby, a rich and precious object. The broad vowel effects emphasise the physical presence of the baby. The 'ticking' sound conveys action and dynamism, but also the passage of time. The child is now part of the mortal world where change and death are inevitable. At this moment of birth, the baby is the centre of attention as the midwife and parents surround her. But this is a cruel world, as we see from the words 'slapped' and 'bald'. The child is now part of the universe as she takes her place among the 'elements'. The verbs in this stanza are in the past tense – **the mother is looking back at the event**. The rest of the poem is written in the present tense, which adds to the immediacy of the experience.

Stanza two has a feeling of disorientation, as if the mother feels separated from the child now that she has left the womb. There is a nightmarish, surreal quality to the lines 'Our voices echo, magnifying your arrival'. Plath sees the child as a new exhibit ('New statue') in a museum. Commas and full stops break up the flow of the lines and **the tone becomes more stilted and detached**. The child as a work of art is special and unique, but the museum is 'drafty', again a reference to the harshness of the world. The baby's vulnerability is stressed by its 'nakedness'. The midwife's and parents' frozen response is caught in the phrase 'blankly as walls'. They anxiously observe, unsure about their ability to protect. This baby also represents a threat to their relationship as she 'Shadows' their safety. The child is perceived as having a negative impact on the parents, perhaps driving them apart rather than uniting them.

Stanza three catches the **complex relationship between child and mother**. Plath feels she can't be maternal ('no more your mother'). This is vividly shown in the image of the cloud that rains, creating a puddle. **But in the act of creation, it destroys itself and its destruction is reflected in the pool of water**. Throughout her life, the poet was haunted by a fear of her own personal disintegration and annihilation. Does she see a conflict between becoming a mother and remaining a writer? She also realises as the child grows and matures that she will age, moving closer to death, and this will be reflected in the child's gaze. The mood of this stanza is one of dislocation, estrangement and powerlessness. Notice how the three lines of the stanza run into each other as the cloud disappears.

In **stanza four**, the tone changes to one of intimate, maternal love as the caring mother becomes alert to her child's needs. The situation described is warm and homely – the 'flat pink roses' are very different to the chill 'museum' of a previous stanza. The fragile breathing of the little child is beautifully described as 'your moth-breath/Flickers'. **Onomatopoeia in 'Flickers' mimics the tiny breathing noises of the child**. The mother is anticipating her baby's needs as she wakes ('listen'). The breathing child evokes happy memories of Plath's seaside childhood ('A far sea moves in my ear'). The infant cries and the attentive mother springs into action. She laughs at herself as she describes the comical figure she makes, 'cow-heavy and floral'. She feels awkward as she 'stumble[s]' to tend her child, whose eager mouth is shown by a startling image ('clean as a cat's') as it opens wide to receive the night feed of milk.

The stanza flows smoothly over into **stanza five**, just as nature flows to its own rhythm and does not obey clocks or any other man-made rules. Night becomes morning as the child swallows the milk and the window swallows the stars.

Children demand a parent's time and energy. **The child now defines herself** with her unique collection of sounds ('Your handful of notes'). This poem opened with the instinctive, elemental 'bald' cry of a newborn, but closes on a lovely, happy image of music and colour, as the baby's song's notes 'rise like balloons'.

ANALYSIS

The poem opens with the word 'Love'. Is this poem about parental love or parental anxiety?

SAMPLE PARAGRAPH

This poem contains both as the tone varies from the confident assertion that 'Love' was the source of the child to the curiously disengaged tone of the second stanza, where the parents 'stand round blankly as walls'. The enormity of the event of the birth of their child into a harsh world, 'drafty museum', seems to overwhelm them, particularly the mother. In the third stanza, she declares that she is not the child's mother, and explores her feelings of annihilation through the complex image of the disintegrating cloud, which creates only to be destroyed in the act of creation. However, the poem ends on a positive, loving note as the attentive mother feeds her child on demand, listening to her baby's song 'rise like balloons'. This poem realistically deals with the conflicting emotions new parents experience at a birth.

EXAMINER'S COMMENT

The short paragraph deals confidently with both attitudes in a well-sustained argument effectively using pertinent quotes. These references range widely over much of the poem and the expression is very well controlled. Grade B.

CLASS/HOMEWORK EXERCISES

1. Look at the different sounds described in the poem, such as 'slapped', 'bald cry', 'A far sea moves', 'The clear vowels rise', and comment on their effectiveness.
2. Copy the table below into your own notes and fill in critical comments about the last two quotations.

Key Quotes

The midwife slapped your footsoles	After a birth, the nurse slaps the child to make it cry and clear the mucus from its mouth and nose.
your nakedness/Shadows our safety	The baby's vulnerability is a threat to the parents' relationship.
cow-heavy and floral/In my Victorian nightgown	A slightly comic picture of a mother heavy with breast milk in a long, patterned, high-neck nightdress.
Our voices echo, magnifying your arrival	
And now you try/Your handful of notes	

Finisterre

Sylvia Plath

This was the land's end: the last fingers, knuckled and rheumatic,
Cramped on nothing. Black
Admonitory cliffs, and the sea exploding
With no bottom, or anything on the other side of it,
Whitened by the faces of the drowned.   5
Now it is only gloomy, a dump of rocks –
Leftover soldiers from old, messy wars.
The sea cannons into their ear, but they don't budge.
Other rocks hide their grudges under the water.

The cliffs are edged with trefoils, stars and bells   10
Such as fingers might embroider, close to death,
Almost too small for the mists to bother with.
The mists are part of the ancient paraphernalia –
Souls, rolled in the doom-noise of the sea.
They bruise the rocks out of existence, then resurrect them.   15
They go up without hope, like sighs.
I walk among them, and they stuff my mouth with cotton.
When they free me, I am beaded with tears.

Our Lady of the Shipwrecked is striding toward the horizon,
Her marble skirts blown back in two pink wings.   20
A marble sailor kneels at her foot distractedly, and at his foot
A peasant woman in black
Is praying to the monument of the sailor praying.
Our Lady of the Shipwrecked is three times life size,
Her lips sweet with divinity.   25
She does not hear what the sailor or the peasant is saying –
She is in love with the beautiful formlessness of the sea.

Gull-colored laces flap in the sea drafts
Beside the postcard stalls.
The peasants anchor them with conches. One is told: 30
'These are the pretty trinkets the sea hides,
Little shells made up into necklaces and toy ladies.
They do not come from the Bay of the Dead down there,
But from another place, tropical and blue,
We have never been to.   35
These are our crêpes. Eat them before they blow cold.'

• Leaving Certificate English •

Sylvia Plath

'and the sea exploding'

GLOSSARY

1 *land's end*: literally 'Finisterre'; the western tip of Brittany.	19 *Our Lady of the Shipwrecked*: the mother of Christ prayed for sailors.
3 *Admonitory*: warning.	30 *conches*: shells.
10 *trefoils*: three-leaved plants.	31 *trinkets*: cheap jewellery.
13 *paraphernalia*: discarded items.	36 *crêpes*: light pancakes.
14 *doom-noise*: hopeless sounds.	

EXPLORATIONS

1 Would you agree that this is a disquieting poem that is likely to disturb readers? Refer to the text in your answer.
2 There are several changes of tone in this poem. Describe two contrasting tones, using close reference to the text.
3 What does the poem reveal to you about Sylvia Plath's own state of mind? Use reference to the text in your response.

STUDY NOTES

'Finisterre' was written in 1960 following a visit by Plath to Brittany, France. As with many of her poems, the description of the place can be interpreted both literally and metaphorically.

The sea has always inspired poets and artists. It is at times welcoming, menacing, beautiful, peaceful and mysterious. Throughout her short life, Sylvia Plath loved the ocean. She spent her childhood years on the Atlantic coast just north of Boston. This setting provides a source for many of her poetic ideas. Terror and death loom large in her descriptive poem 'Finisterre', in which the pounding rhythm of storm waves off the Breton coast represents **Plath's inner turmoil**.

Stanza one opens dramatically and immediately creates a disturbing atmosphere. Plath describes the rocky headland as being 'knuckled and rheumatic'. In a series of powerful images ('the last fingers', 'Black/Admonitory cliffs', 'and the sea exploding'), the poet recreates the uproar and commotion of the scene. The **grisly personification** is startling, linking the shoreline with suffering and decay. There is a real sense of conflict between sea and land. Both are closely associated with death ('the faces of the drowned'). The jagged rocks are compared to 'Leftover soldiers' who 'hide their grudges under the water'. There is a noticeable tone of regret and protest against the futility of conflict, which is denounced as 'old, messy wars'.

Plath's **negative imagery** is relentless, with harsh consonant sounds ('knuckled', 'Cramped', 'exploding') emphasising the force of raging storm waves. The use of contrasting colours intensifies the imagery. As the 'sea cannons' against the headland, the atmosphere is 'only gloomy'. It is hard not to see the bleak seascape as a reflection of Plath's own unhappy state.

In **stanza two**, the poet turns away from the cruel sea and focuses momentarily on the small plants clinging to the cliff edge. However, these 'trefoils, stars and bells' are also 'close to death'. If anything, they reinforce the **unsettling mood** and draw the poet back to the ocean mists, which she thinks of as symbolising the souls of the dead, lost in 'the doom-noise of the sea'. Plath imagines the heavy mists transforming the rocks, destroying them 'out of existence' before managing to 'resurrect them' again. In a **surreal sequence**, the poet enters the water ('I walk among them') and joins the wretched souls who lie there. Her growing sense of panic is suggested by the stark admission: 'they stuff my mouth with cotton'. The experience is agonising and leaves her 'beaded with tears'.

Plath's thoughts turn to a marble statue of 'Our Lady of the Shipwrecked' in **stanza three**. Once again, in her imagination, she creates a **dramatic narrative** around the religious figure. This monument to the patron saint of the ocean should offer some consolation to the kneeling sailor and a grieving peasant woman who pray to the mother of God. Ironically, their pleas are completely ignored – 'She does not hear' their prayers because 'She is in love with the beautiful formlessness of the sea'. The feeling of hopelessness is all pervading. Is the poet expressing her own **feelings of failure and despondency** here? Or is she also attacking the ineffectiveness of religion? The description of the statue is certainly unflattering. The figure is flighty and self-centred: 'Her marble skirts blown back in two pink wings'. In contrast, the powerful ocean remains fascinating.

In the **fourth stanza**, Plath describes the local Bretons who sell souvenirs to tourists. Unlike the previous three stanzas, **the mood appears to be much lighter** as the poet describes the friendly stall-keepers going about their business. It is another irony that their livelihood (selling 'pretty trinkets') is dependent on the sea and its beauty. Like the statue, the locals seem unconcerned by the tragic history of the ocean. Indeed, they are keen to play down 'the Bay of the Dead' and explain that what they sell is imported 'from another place, tropical and blue'. In the final line, a stall-holder advises the poet to enjoy the pancakes she has bought: 'Eat them before they blow cold'. Although the immediate mood is untroubled, **the final phrase brings us** back to the earlier – and more disturbing – parts of the poem where Plath described the raging storms and the nameless lost souls who have perished at sea.

ANALYSIS

Write a paragraph on Sylvia Plath's use of detailed description in 'Finisterre'.

SAMPLE PARAGRAPH

The opening images of the rocks – 'the last fingers, knuckled and rheumatic' – are of decrepit old age. The strong visual impact is a regular feature of Sylvia Plath's writing. The first half of the poem is filled with memorable details of the windswept coastline. In her careful choice of descriptive terms, Plath uses broad vowels to evoke a pervading feeling of dejection. Words such as 'drowned', 'gloomy', 'rolled' and 'doom' help to create this dismal effect. The dramatic aural image, 'The sea cannons', echoes the roar of turbulent waves crashing onto the rocks. Plath's eye for close observation is also seen in her portrait of the holy statue – 'Her lips sweet with divinity'. The poem ends with a painstaking sketch of the Breton traders selling postcards and 'Little shells made up into necklaces and toy ladies'. The local people seem to have come to terms with 'the Bay of the Dead' and are getting on with life. Overall, the use of details throughout the poem leaves readers with a strong sense of place and community.

EXAMINER'S COMMENT

Quotations are very well used here to highlight Plath's ability to create specific scenes and moods through precise description. The examples range over much of the poem and the writing is both varied and controlled throughout. Grade A standard.

CLASS/HOMEWORK EXERCISES

1. It has been said that vivid, startling imagery gives a surreal quality to 'Finisterre'. Using reference to the poem, write a paragraph responding to this statement.
2. Copy the table below into your own notes and fill in critical comments about the last two quotations.

Key Quotes

Admonitory cliffs, and the sea exploding/ With no bottom	Striking and dramatic images are a recurring feature throughout the poem.
Souls, rolled in the doom-noise of the sea	The poem is dominated by the underlying themes of fear, hopelessness and death.
They go up without hope, like sighs	Plath personifies the mists as the helpless souls of those who have been lost at sea.
Now it is only gloomy, a dump of rocks	
These are our crêpes. Eat them before they blow cold	

Mirror

Sylvia Plath

I am silver and exact. I have no preconceptions.
Whatever I see I swallow immediately
Just as it is, unmisted by love or dislike.
I am not cruel, only truthful –
The eye of a little god, four-cornered.   5
Most of the time I meditate on the opposite wall.
It is pink, with speckles. I have looked at it so long
I think it is part of my heart. But it flickers.
Faces and darkness separate us over and over.

Now I am a lake. A woman bends over me,   10
Searching my reaches for what she really is.
Then she turns to those liars, the candles or the moon.
I see her back, and reflect it faithfully.
She rewards me with tears and an agitation of hands.
I am important to her. She comes and goes.   15
Each morning it is her face that replaces the darkness.
In me she has drowned a young girl, and in me an old woman
Rises toward her day after day, like a terrible fish.

'The eye of a little god, four-cornered'

GLOSSARY
1 *exact*: accurate, giving all details; to insist on payment.
1 *preconceptions*: thoughts already formed.
11 *reaches*: range of distance or depth.
14 *agitation*: shaking, anxious.

EXPLORATIONS

1 Select two images that suggest the dark, sinister side of the mirror. Would you consider that these images show an unforgiving way of viewing oneself?

2   What are the parallels and contrasts between a mirror and a lake? Develop your response in a written paragraph.
3   Write your own personal response to this poem, referring closely to the text in your answer.

STUDY NOTES

> 'Mirror' was written in 1961 as Sylvia Plath approached her twenty-ninth birthday. In this dark poem, Plath views the inevitability of old age and death, our preoccupation with image and our search for an identity.

Do you think everyone looks at themselves in a mirror? Would you consider that people are fascinated, disappointed or even obsessed by what they see? Does a mirror accurately reflect the truth? Do people actually see what is reflected or is it distorted by notions and ideals they or society have? Consider the use of mirrors in fairytales: 'Mirror, mirror on the wall, who's the fairest of them all?' Mirrors are also used in myths, such as the story of Narcissus, who drowned having fallen in love with his reflection, and *Through the Looking Glass* is a famous children's book. Mirrors are also used in horror films as the dividing line between fantasy and reality.

In this poem, Plath often gives us a startling new angle on an everyday object. The function of a mirror is to reflect whatever is put in front of it. **Stanza one** opens with a ringing declaration by the mirror: 'I am silver and exact'. This **personification has a sinister effect** in the poem as the mirror describes an almost claustrophobic relationship with a particular woman. The voice of the mirror is clear, direct and precise. It announces that it reports exactly what there is without any alteration. We have to decide if the mirror is telling the truth, as it says it has no bias ('no preconceptions'). It does not judge, it reflects the image received. The mirror adopts the position of an impartial observer, but it is active, almost ruthless ('I swallow'). It is not cruel, but truthful.

Yet how truthful is a mirror image, as it flattens a three-dimensional object into two dimensions? The image sent out has no depth. The voice of the mirror becomes smug as it sees itself as the ruler of those reflected ('The eye of a little god'). Our obsession with ourselves causes us to worship at the mirror that reflects our image. In the modern world, people are often disappointed with their reflections, wishing they were thinner, younger, better looking. But **the mirror insists it tells the truth**, it doesn't flatter or hurt. The mirror explains how it spends its day gazing at the opposite wall, which is carefully described as 'pink, with speckles'. It feels as if the wall is part of itself. This reflection is disturbed by the faces of people and the dying light. The passage of time is evoked in the phrase 'over and over'.

In **stanza two**, the mirror now announces that it is 'a lake'. Both are flat surfaces that reflect. However, a lake is another dimension, it has depth. There is **danger**. The image is now drawn into its murky depths. The woman is looking in and down, not just at. It is as if she is struggling to find who she really is, what her true path in life is. Plath frequently questioned who she was. Expectations for young women in the 1950s were limiting. Appearance was important, as were the roles of wife, mother and homemaker. But Plath also wanted to write: 'Will I submerge my embarrassing desires and aspirations, refuse to face myself?' The mirror becomes irritated and jealous of the woman as she turns to the deceptive soft light of 'those liars, the candles or the moon'. The mirror remains faithful, reflecting her back. **The woman is dissatisfied with her image**. In her insecurity, she weeps and wrings her hands. Plath always tried to do her best, to be a model student, almost desperate to excel and be affirmed. Is there a danger in seeking perfection? Do we need to be kind to ourselves? Do we need to love ourselves? Again, the mirror pompously announces 'I am important to her'.

The march of time passing is emphasised by 'comes and goes', 'Each morning' and 'day after day'. The woman keeps coming back. The mirror's sense of its importance is shown by the frequent use of 'I' and the repetition of 'in me'. As time passes, the woman is facing the truth of her human condition as her reflection changes and ages in the mirror. Her youth is 'drowned', to be replaced by a monstrous vision of an old woman 'like a terrible fish'. **The lonely drama of living and dying is recorded with a dreamlike, nightmarish quality**. There is no comforting rhyme in the poem, only the controlled rhythm of time. The mirror does not give what a human being desires: comfort and warmth. Instead, it impersonally reminds us of our mortality.

ANALYSIS

What is your personal response to the relationship between the mirror and the woman? Support your views with reference to the poem.

SAMPLE PARAGRAPH

I feel the mirror is like an alter ego, which is coolly appraising the woman in an unforgiving way. The mirror is 'silver'. This cold metal object is

Sylvia Plath

heartless. Although the mirror repeatedly states that it does not judge, 'I have no preconceptions', the woman feels judged and wanting: 'She rewards me with tears and an agitation of hands'. I think the relationship between the woman and the mirror is dangerous and poisonous. She does indeed 'drown' in the mirror, as she never feels good enough. Is this the payment the mirror exacts? The complacent mirror rules her like a tyrannical 'little god, four-cornered'. It reminds me of how today we are never satisfied with our image, always wanting something else, more perfect. Plath also strove to be perfect. This obsessive relationship shows a troubled self, a lack of self-love. Who is saying that the older woman is 'like a terrible fish'? I think the mirror has become the voice of a society which values women only for their looks and youth, rather than what they are capable of achieving.

EXAMINER'S COMMENT

In this fluent and personal response, the candidate has given a distinctive and well-supported account of the uneasy relationship between the mirror and the woman. Grade A answer.

CLASS/HOMEWORK EXERCISES

1. How are the qualities of terror and despair shown in the imagery of the poem?
2. Copy the table below into your own notes and fill in critical comments about the last two quotations.

Key Quotes

I have no preconceptions	The mirror states that it objectively reflects reality.
The eye of a little god, four-cornered	Plath's metaphor emphasises how this rectangular mirror considers itself very important.
Searching my reaches for what she really is	The woman looks deeply into the mirror at her reflection.
I am silver and exact	
in me an old woman/Rises toward her day after day, like a terrible fish	

Pheasant

You said you would kill it this morning.
Do not kill it. It startles me still,
The jut of that odd, dark head, pacing

Through the uncut grass on the elm's hill.
It is something to own a pheasant,								5
Or just to be visited at all.

I am not mystical: it isn't
As if I thought it had a spirit.
It is simply in its element.

That gives it a kingliness, a right.								10
The print of its big foot last winter,
The tail-track, on the snow in our court –

The wonder of it, in that pallor,
Through crosshatch of sparrow and starling.
Is it its rareness, then? It is rare.								15

But a dozen would be worth having,
A hundred, on that hill – green and red,
Crossing and recrossing: a fine thing!

It is such a good shape, so vivid.
It's a little cornucopia.									20
It unclaps, brown as a leaf, and loud,

Settles in the elm, and is easy.
It was sunning in the narcissi.
I trespass stupidly. Let be, let be.

'in its element'

• Poetry Focus •

GLOSSARY

1 *You*: probably addressed to Plath's husband.
3 *jut*: extending outwards.
7 *mystical*: spiritual, supernatural.
13 *pallor*: pale colour.
14 *crosshatch*: criss-cross trail.
20 *cornucopia*: unexpected treasure.
23 *narcissi*: bright spring flowers.

EXPLORATIONS

1 Explain Sylvia Plath's attitude to nature based on your reading of 'Pheasant'.
2 Compile a list of the poet's arguments for not killing the pheasant.
3 Write a paragraph on the effectiveness of Plath's imagery in the poem.

STUDY NOTES

'Pheasant' was written in 1962 and reflects Plath's deep appreciation of the natural world. Its enthusiastic mood contrasts with much of her more disturbing work. The poem is structured in eight tercets (three-line stanzas) with a subtle, interlocking rhyming pattern (known as terza rima).

The poem opens with an urgent plea by Plath to spare the pheasant's life: 'Do not kill it'. In the first two stanzas, the tone is tense as the poet offers a variety of reasons for sparing this impressive game bird. She is both shocked and excited by the pheasant: 'It startles me still'. Plath admits to feeling honoured in the presence of the bird: 'It is something to own a pheasant'. The broken rhythm of the early lines adds an abruptness that heightens the sense of urgency. **Plath seems spellbound by the bird's beauty** ('The jut of that odd, dark head') now that it is under threat.

But the poet is also keen to play down any sentimentality in her attitude to the pheasant. Stanza three opens with a straightforward explanation of her attitude: 'it isn't/As if I thought it had a spirit'. Instead, **she values the bird for its graceful beauty and naturalness**: 'It is simply in its element'. Plath is keen to show her recognition of the pheasant's right to exist because it possesses a certain majestic quality, 'a kingliness'.

In stanza four, the poet recalls an earlier winter scene when she marvelled at the pheasant's distinctive footprint in the snow. The bird has made an even greater impression on Plath, summed up in the key phrase 'The wonder of it' at the start of stanza five. She remembers **the colourful pheasant's distinguishing marks against the pale snow**, so unlike the 'crosshatch' pattern of smaller birds, such as the sparrow and starling. This makes the pheasant particularly 'rare' and valuable in Plath's eyes.

The poet can hardly contain her regard for the pheasant and her tone becomes increasingly enthusiastic in stanza six as she dreams of having first a 'dozen' and then a 'hundred' of the birds. In a few **well-chosen details**, she highlights their colour and energy ('green and red,/Crossing and recrossing') and adds an emphatic compliment: 'a fine thing!' Her delight continues into stanza seven, where Plath proclaims her ceaseless admiration for the pheasant: 'It's a little cornucopia', an inspirational source of joy and surprise.

Throughout the poem, Plath has emphasised that the pheasant rightly belongs in its natural surroundings, and this is also true of the final lines. Stanza eight is considered and assured. From the poet's point of view, **the pheasant's right to live is beyond dispute**. While the bird is 'sunning in the narcissi', she herself has become the unwelcome intruder: 'I trespass stupidly'. Plath ends by echoing the opening appeal to spare the pheasant's life: 'Let be, let be'. The quietly insistent repetition and the underlying tone of unease are a final reminder of the need to respect nature.

It has been suggested that the pheasant symbolises Plath's insecure relationship with Ted Hughes. For various reasons, their marriage was under severe strain in 1962 and Plath feared that Hughes was intent on ending it. This interpretation adds a greater poignancy to the poem.

ANALYSIS

There are several mood changes in 'Pheasant'. What do you consider to be the dominant mood in the poem? Refer to the text in your answer.

SAMPLE PARAGRAPH

The mood at the beginning of 'Pheasant' is nervous and really uptight. Plath seems to have given up hope about the pheasant. It is facing death. She repeats the word 'kill' and admits to being shocked at the very thought of what the bird is facing. She herself seems desperate and fearful. This is shown by the short sentence, 'Do not kill it'. But the outlook soon changes. Plath describes the pheasant 'pacing' and 'in its element'. But she seems less stressed as she describes the 'kingliness' of the pheasant. But the mood soon settles down as Plath celebrates the life of this really beautiful bird. The mood becomes calmer and ends in almost a whisper, 'Let be, let be'. The dominant mood is calm and considered in the poem.

EXAMINER'S COMMENT

This is a reasonably well-focused response to the question. The candidate points out the change of mood following the first stanza. Some worthwhile references are used to show the poem's principal mood. The expression, however, is flawed in places (e.g. using 'but' to start sentences). The standard is C-grade overall.

CLASS/HOMEWORK EXERCISES

1. Plath sets out to convince the reader of the pheasant's right to life. Does she succeed in her aim? Give reasons for your answer.
2. Copy the table below into your own notes and fill in critical comments about the last two quotations.

Key Quotes

pacing/Through the uncut grass on the elm's hill	Plath is a keen observer of the pheasant and uses details to capture its steady movement.
That gives it a kingliness, a right	Man's relationship with the world of nature is central to 'Pheasant'.
It is such a good shape	The poem contains many direct statements that reflect Plath's clear sense of appreciation.
I am not mystical	
It unclaps, brown as a leaf	

Elm

For Ruth Fainlight

I know the bottom, she says. I know it with my great tap root:
It is what you fear.
I do not fear it: I have been there.

Is it the sea you hear in me,
Its dissatisfactions?
Or the voice of nothing, that was your madness?

Love is a shadow.
How you lie and cry after it
Listen: these are its hooves: it has gone off, like a horse.

All night I shall gallop thus, impetuously,
Till your head is a stone, your pillow a little turf,
Echoing, echoing.

Or shall I bring you the sound of poisons?
This is rain now, this big hush.
And this is the fruit of it: tin-white, like arsenic.

I have suffered the atrocity of sunsets.
Scorched to the root
My red filaments burn and stand, a hand of wires.

Now I break up in pieces that fly about like clubs.
A wind of such violence
Will tolerate no bystanding: I must shriek.

The moon, also, is merciless: she would drag me
Cruelly, being barren.
Her radiance scathes me. Or perhaps I have caught her.

I let her go. I let her go
Diminished and flat, as after radical surgery.
How your bad dreams possess and endow me.

I am inhabited by a cry.
Nightly it flaps out
Looking, with its hooks, for something to love.   30

I am terrified by this dark thing
That sleeps in me;
All day I feel its soft, feathery turnings, its malignity.

Clouds pass and disperse.
Are those the faces of love, those pale irretrievables?   35
Is it for such I agitate my heart?

I am incapable of more knowledge.
What is this, this face
So murderous in its strangle of branches? –

Its snaky acids hiss.   40
It petrifies the will. These are the isolate, slow faults
That kill, that kill, that kill.

'I am terrified by this dark thing'

GLOSSARY

The wych elm is a large deciduous tree, with a massive straight trunk and tangled branches. It was once a favourite timber of coffin makers. Plath dedicated the poem to a close friend, Ruth Fainlight, another American poet.
1 *the bottom*: lowest depths.
1 *tap root:* the main root.

15 *arsenic*: poison.
18 *filaments*: fibres, nerves.
24 *scathes*: injures, scalds.
33 *malignity*: evil.
34 *disperse*: scatter widely.
35 *irretrievables*: things lost forever.
40 *snaky acids*: deceptive poisons.
41 *petrifies*: terrifies.

EXPLORATIONS

1. There are many sinister nature images in this poem. Select two that you find particularly unsettling and comment on their effectiveness.
2. Trace and examine how love is presented and viewed by the poet. Support the points you make with reference to the text.
3. Write your own individual response to this poem, referring closely to the text in your answer.

STUDY NOTES

Written in April 1962, 'Elm' is one of Sylvia Plath's most challenging and intensely dramatic poems. Plath personifies the elm tree to create a surreal scene. It 'speaks' in a traumatic voice to someone else, the 'you' of line 2, the poet herself – or the reader, perhaps. Both voices interact throughout the poem, almost always expressing pain and anguish. Critics often associate these powerful emotions with the poet's own personal problems – Plath had experienced electric shock treatment for depression. However, this may well limit our understanding of what is a complex exploration of many emotions.

The opening stanza is unnerving. The poet appears to be dramatising an exchange between herself and the elm by imagining what the tree might say to her. The immediate effect is eerily surreal. From the start, **the narrative voice is obsessed with instability and despair**: 'I know the bottom'. The tree is described in both physical terms ('my great tap root' penetrating far into the ground) and also as a state of mind ('I do not fear it'). The depth of depression imagined is reinforced by the repetition of 'I know' and the stark simplicity of the chilling comment 'It is what you fear'.

The bizarre exchange between the two 'speakers' continues in stanza two. The elm questions the poet about the nature of **her mental state**. Does the wind blowing through its branches remind her of the haunting sound of the sea? Or even 'the voice of nothing' – the numbing experience of madness?

Stanzas three and four focus on the dangers and disappointments of love – 'a shadow'. The tone is wary, emphasised by the comparison of a wild horse that has 'gone off'. The relentless sounds of the wind in the elm will be a bitter reminder, 'echoing' this loss of love 'Till your head is a stone'. **Assonance** is effectively used here to heighten the sense of hurt and abandonment.

Sylvia Plath

For much of the middle section of the poem (**stanzas five** to **nine**), the elm's intimidating voice continues to dramatise a series of horrifying experiences associated with madness. The tree has endured extreme elements – rain ('the sound of poisons'), sunshine ('Scorched to the root'), wind ('of such violence') and also the moon ('Her radiance scathes me'). **The harsh imagery and frenzied language** ('burn', 'shriek', 'merciless') combine to create a sense of shocking destructiveness.

Stanzas 10 and **11** mark a turning point where the voices of the tree and the poet become indistinguishable. This is achieved by the seemingly harmless image of an owl inhabiting the branches, searching for 'something to love'. The speaker is haunted by 'this dark thing'. The **poet's vulnerability** is particularly evident in her stark admission: 'I feel its soft, feathery turnings, its malignity'. Plath has come to relate her unknown demons to a deadly tumour.

In the **last three stanzas**, the poet's voice seems more distant and calm before the final storm. The image of the passing clouds ('the faces of love') highlight the notion of rejection as the root cause of Plath's depression. The poem ends on a visionary note when she imagines being confronted by a 'murderous' snake that appears in the branches: 'It petrifies the will'. The scene of **growing terror builds to a hideous climax** until her own mental and emotional states (her 'slow faults') end up destroying her. The intensity of the final line, 'That kill, that kill, that kill', leaves readers with a harrowing understanding of Plath's paralysis of despair.

ANALYSIS

Do you think that 'Elm' has a surreal, nightmarish quality? In your response, refer to the text to support your views.

> **SAMPLE PARAGRAPH**
>
> I would agree that Sylvia Plath has created a very disturbing mood in the poem, 'Elm'. Giving the tree a speaking voice of its own is like something from a child's fairy story. Plath compares love to a galloping horse. The poem is mainly about depression and madness. So it's bound to be out of the ordinary. The speaker in the poem is confused and asks weird questions, such as 'Is it the sea you hear inside me?' She is obsessive and totally paranoid. Everything is against her, as far as she imagines it. The weather is seen as an enemy even, 'the rain is like arsenic' and 'sounds like

poisons'. The end is as if she is having a bad dream with imagining a fierce hissing snake in the tree coming after her. This represents Plath's deepest nightmare, the fear of loneliness. The whole poem is surreal and confusing – especially the images.

EXAMINER'S COMMENT

This paragraph includes some worthwhile references to the poem's disturbing aspects. The points are note-like, however, and the writing style lacks control. Some of the quotations are also inaccurate. C-grade standard.

CLASS/HOMEWORK EXERCISES

1. What evidence of Plath's deep depression and hypersensitivity is revealed in the poem 'Elm'? Refer closely to the text in your answer.
2. Copy the table below into your own notes and fill in critical comments about the last two quotations.

Key Quotes

I know it with my great tap root	Through the 'voice' of the elm, Plath uses the tree metaphor to suggest her own depths of despair.
My red filaments burn and stand, a hand of wires	This image of suffering may relate to the poet's own experience of electric shock treatment for depression.
A wind of such violence/Will tolerate no bystanding	Many searing images in the poem suggest a world that has been wasted by nuclear conflict.
the atrocity of sunsets	
Its snaky acids hiss	

• Poetry Focus •

Poppies in July

Sylvia Plath

Little poppies, little hell flames,
Do you do no harm?

You flicker. I cannot touch you.
I put my hands among the flames. Nothing burns.

And it exhausts me to watch you   5
Flickering like that, wrinkly and clear red, like the skin of a mouth.

A mouth just bloodied.
Little bloody skirts!

There are fumes that I cannot touch.
Where are your opiates, your nauseous capsules?   10

If I could bleed, or sleep! –
If my mouth could marry a hurt like that!

Or your liquors seep to me, in this glass capsule,
Dulling and stilling.

But colorless. Colorless.   15

'You flicker. I cannot touch you'

GLOSSARY
1 *hell flames*: most poppies are red, flame-like.
9 *fumes*: the effects of drugs.
10 *opiates*: sleep-inducing narcotics.
10 *nauseous*: causing sickness.
13 *liquors*: drug vapours.
13 *capsule*: small container.
15 *colorless*: drained, lifeless.

EXPLORATIONS

1. Examine the title, 'Poppies in July', in light of the main subject matter in the poem. Is the title misleading? Explain your answer.
2. What evidence can you find in 'Poppies in July' that the speaker is yearning to escape?
3. Colour imagery plays a significant role in the poem. Comment on how effectively colour is used.

STUDY NOTES

> Like most confessional writers, Sylvia Plath's work reflects her own personal experiences, without filtering any of the painful emotions. She wrote 'Poppies in July' in the summer of 1962, during the break-up of her marriage.

The **first stanza** is marked by an uneasy sense of foreboding. The speaker (almost certainly Plath herself) compares the blazing red poppies to 'little hell flames' before directly confronting them: 'Do you do no harm?' **Her distress is obvious** from the start. The poem's title may well have led readers to expect a more conventional nature poem. Instead, the flowers are presented as being highly treacherous, and all the more deceptive because they are 'little'.

Plath develops the fire image in **lines 3–6**. However, even though she places her hands 'among the flames', she finds that 'Nothing burns' and she is forced to watch them 'flickering'. It almost seems as though she is so tired and numb that **she has transcended pain** and can experience nothing: 'it exhausts me to watch you'. Ironically, the more vivid the poppies are, the more lethargic she feels.

The uncomfortable and disturbed mood increases in the **fourth stanza** with **two startling images**, both personifying the flowers. Comparing the poppy to 'A mouth just bloodied' suggests recent violence and physical suffering. The 'bloody skirts' metaphor is equally harrowing. There is further evidence of the poet's overpowering weariness in the prominent use of broad vowel sounds, for example in 'exhausts', 'mouth' and 'bloodied'.

In the **fifth stanza**, Plath's disorientated state turns to a distracted longing for escape. Having failed to use the vibrancy of the poppies to distract her from her pain, she now craves the feeling of oblivion or unconsciousness. But although she desires the dulling effects of drugs derived from the poppies, her **tone is hopelessly cynical** as she describes the 'fumes that I cannot touch'.

The mood becomes even more distraught in **lines 11–12**, with the poet begging for any alternative to her anguished state. 'If I could bleed, or sleep!' is an emphatic plea for release. It is her final attempt to retain some control of her life in the face of an overwhelming sense of powerlessness. Plath's **growing alienation** seems so unbearably intense at this point that it directly draws the reader's sympathy.

The **last three lines** record the poet's surrender, perhaps a kind of death wish. Worn down by her inner demons and the bright colours of the poppies, Plath lets herself become resigned to a 'colorless' world of nothingness. Her **complete passivity** and helplessness are emphasised by the dreamlike quality of the phrase 'Dulling and stilling'. As she drifts into a death-like 'colorless' private hell, there remains a terrible sense of betrayal, as if she is still being haunted by the bright red flowers. The ending of 'Poppies in July' is so dark and joyless that it is easy to see why the poem is often seen as a desperate cry for help.

ANALYSIS

'Poppies in July' is one of Plath's most disturbing poems. What aspects of the poem affected you most?

SAMPLE PARAGRAPH

'Poppies in July' was written at a time when Plath was struggling with the fact that her husband had deserted her. This affected her deeply and it is clear that the poppies are a symbol of this excruciating time. Everything about the poem is negative. The images of the poppies are nearly all associated with fire and blood. Plath's language is alarming when she compares the poppies to 'little hell flames' and also 'the skin of a mouth'. The most disturbing aspect is Plath's own unstable mind. She seems to be in a kind of trance, obsessed by the red colours of the poppies, which remind her of blood. I got the impression that she was nearly going insane in the end. She seems suicidal – 'If I could bleed'. For me, this is the most disturbing moment in the poem. I can get some idea of her troubled mind. Plath cannot stand reality and seeks a way out through drugs or death. The last image is of Plath sinking into a dull state of drowsiness, unable to cope with the world around her.

EXAMINER'S COMMENT

Overall, a solid B-grade response which responds personally to the question. While the candidate dealt well with the disturbing thought in the poem, there could have been a more thorough exploration of Plath's style and how it enhances her theme of depression.

CLASS/HOMEWORK EXERCISES

1. Would you agree that loneliness and pain are the central themes of 'Poppies in July'? Refer to the text of the poem when writing your response.
2. Copy the table below into your own notes and fill in critical comments about the last two quotations.

Key Quotes

You flicker. I cannot touch you	The contrast between the poppies' energy and Plath's own passive state is a memorable feature of the poem.
And it exhausts me to watch you	Plath's overwhelming sense of despair is central to the poem.
Flickering like that, wrinkly and clear red	The vivid imagery used to describe the poppies is highly disturbing.
Where are your opiates, your nauseous capsules?	
If my mouth could marry a hurt like that	

• Poetry Focus •

The Arrival of the Bee Box

Sylvia Plath

I ordered this, this clean wood box
Square as a chair and almost too heavy to lift.
I would say it was the coffin of a midget
Or a square baby
Were there not such a din in it.   5

The box is locked, it is dangerous.
I have to live with it overnight
And I can't keep away from it.
There are no windows, so I can't see what is in there.
There is only a little grid, no exit.   10

I put my eye to the grid.
It is dark, dark,
With the swarmy feeling of African hands
Minute and shrunk for export,
Black on black, angrily clambering.   15

How can I let them out?
It is the noise that appalls me most of all,
The unintelligible syllables.
It is like a Roman mob,
Small, taken one by one, but my god, together!   20

I lay my ear to furious Latin.
I am not a Caesar.
I have simply ordered a box of maniacs.
They can be sent back.
They can die, I need feed them nothing, I am the owner.   25

I wonder how hungry they are.
I wonder if they would forget me
If I just undid the locks and stood back and turned into a tree.
There is the laburnum, its blond colonnades,
And the petticoats of the cherry.   30

They might ignore me immediately
In my moon suit and funeral veil.

I am no source of honey
So why should they turn on me?
Tomorrow I will be sweet God, I will set them free.   35

The box is only temporary.

'It is the noise that appalls me'

GLOSSARY

10 *grid*: wire network.
13 *swarmy*: like a large group of bees.
22 *Caesar*: famous Roman ruler.
29 *laburnum*: tree with yellow hanging flowers.
29 *colonnades*: long groups of flowers arranged in a row of columns.
32 *moon suit*: protective clothing worn by beekeepers; all-in-one suit.

EXPLORATIONS

1 How would you describe the poet's reaction to the bee box – fear or fascination, or a mixture of both? Write a paragraph for your response, referring to the poem.
2 Select two surreal images from the poem and comment on the effectiveness of each.
3 Would you describe this poem as exploring and overcoming one's fears and anxieties? Is the ending optimistic or pessimistic, in your opinion?

STUDY NOTES

'The Arrival of the Bee Box' was written in 1962, shortly after Plath's separation from her husband. Her father, who died when she was a child, had been a bee expert and Plath and her husband had recently taken up beekeeping. She explores order, power, control, confinement and freedom in this deeply personal poem.

Sylvia Plath

The poem opens with a simple statement: 'I ordered this'. Straightaway, the emphasis is on order and control. The poet's tone in stanza one is both matter of fact and surprised: 'I was the one who ordered this' and also 'Did I really order this?' **This drama has only one character, Plath herself.** We observe her responses and reactions to the arrival of the bee box. Notice the extensive use of the personal pronoun 'I'. We both see and hear the event.

The box is described as being made of 'clean wood' and given a homely quality with the simile 'Square as a chair'. But then a surreal, dreamlike metaphor, 'the coffin of a midget/Or a square baby', brings us into a **nightmare world**. The abnormal is suggested by the use of 'midget' and deformity by 'square baby'. The coffin conveys not only death, but also entrapment and confinement, preoccupations of the poet. The box has now become a sinister object. A witty sound effect closes the first stanza, as 'din in it' mimics the sound of the bees. They are like badly behaved children.

Stanza two explores the **poet's ambivalent attitude to the box**. She is fascinated by it, as she is curious to see inside ('I can't keep away from it'). Yet she is also frightened by it, as she describes the box as 'dangerous'. She peers in. The third stanza becomes claustrophobic and oppressive with the repetition of 'dark' and the grotesque image of 'the swarmy feeling of African hands/Minute and shrunk for export'. The milling of the bees/slaves is vividly captured as they heave around in the heat in an atmosphere of menace and oppression, hopelessly desperate.

We hear the bees in stanza four. The metaphor of a Roman mob is used to show how if they are let loose they will create **chaos and danger**. The assonance of 'appalls' and 'all' underlines the poet's terror. The phrase 'unintelligible syllables', with its onomatopoeia and its difficult pronunciation, lets us hear the angry buzzing. Plath is awestruck at their collective force and energy: 'but my god, together!' Notice the use of the exclamation mark.

The poet tries to listen, but only hears 'furious Latin' she does not understand. She doubts her capacity to control them, stating that she is 'not a Caesar', the powerful ruler of the Romans, in stanza five. She regards them as 'maniacs'. Then she realises that if she has ordered them, she can return them: 'They can be sent back'. **She has some control of this situation.** Plath can even decide their fate, whether they live or die: 'I need feed them nothing'. She has now redefined the situation as she realises that she is 'the owner'. They belong to her.

The feminine, nurturing side of her now emerges as she wonders 'how hungry they are'. The stereotype of the pretty woman surfaces in the description of the bees' natural habitat of trees in stanza six. Plath thinks if she releases them, they would go back to the trees, 'laburnum' and 'cherry'. She herself would then merge into the landscape and become a tree. This is a reference to a Greek myth where Daphne was being pursued by Apollo. After begging the gods to be saved, they turned her into a tree.

Now she refers to herself in her beekeeping outfit of veil and boiler suit in stanza seven. She rhetorically asks why they would attack her, as she is not a source of sustenance ('I am no source of honey'). **She decides to be compassionate**: 'Tomorrow I will be sweet God, I will set them free'. She realises that they are imprisoned only for now: 'The box is only temporary'.

This poem can also be read on another level. The box could represent the poet's attempt to be what others expect, the typical 1950s woman – pretty, compliant, nurturing. The bees could represent the dark side of her personality, which both fascinated and terrified Plath. She has to accept this: 'I have to live with it overnight'. **The box is like Pandora's box**: safe when locked, but full of danger when opened. Although she finds this disturbing, she also feels she must explore it in the interests of developing as a poet. The references to the doomed character of Daphne and the 'funeral veil' echo chillingly. Would these dark thoughts, if given their freedom, drive her to suicide? The form of this poem is seven stanzas of five lines. One line stands alone, free like the bees or her dark thoughts. If the box represents Plath's outside appearance or body, it is mortal, it is temporary. Will the thoughts, if freed from the body, stop?

ANALYSIS

How does this poem address the themes of order and power? Write a paragraph in response. Support your views with reference to the text.

SAMPLE PARAGRAPH

The poem opens with a reference to order, 'I ordered this'. It is an assertion of power, a deliberate act by 'I'. Throughout the poem the repetition of 'I' suggests a person who consciously chooses to act in a certain way. 'I put my eye to the grid', 'I lay my ear to furious Latin'. It is as if the poet wishes to confront and control her fears over the contents of the box. This box contains live, buzzing bees, whose wellbeing lies in the hands of the poet.

'I need feed them nothing, I am the owner'. Although she realises that she is not 'Caesar', the mighty Roman ruler, she can choose to be 'sweet God'. She alone has the power to release the bees, 'The box is only temporary'. This poem can also be read as referring to the control a person exercises when confronting their innermost fears and desires. These thoughts can be ignored or faced. The person owns these thoughts and can choose to contain them or confront them. Plath feared her own dark side, but felt it should be explored to enable her to progress as a poet. For her 'The box is only temporary'.

EXAMINER'S COMMENT

This note-like response summarises parts of the poem that allude to order and power. However, it fails to address the question about the poet's approach to the central themes. There is little discussion about Plath's attitude to power. Grade C.

CLASS/HOMEWORK EXERCISES

1. How does Plath create a dramatic atmosphere in 'The Arrival of the Bee Box'?
2. Copy the table below into your own notes and fill in critical comments about the last two quotations.

Key Quotes

I have to live with it overnight/ And I can't keep away from it	The poet refers to the intense relationship she has with the box, from which she cannot escape.
With the swarmy feeling of African hands/ Minute and shrunk for export	The bees are described as miniature African slaves who are imprisoned as they are sent off to another country.
I am not a Caesar	Plath admits that she would be unable to control these angry bees if released.
Tomorrow I will be sweet God	
The box is only temporary	

• Leaving Certificate English •

Child

Sylvia Plath

Your clear eye is the one absolutely beautiful thing.
I want to fill it with color and ducks,
The zoo of the new

Whose name you meditate –
April snowdrop, Indian pipe,   5
Little

Stalk without wrinkle,
Pool in which images
Should be grand and classical

Not this troublous   10
Wringing of hands, this dark
Ceiling without a star.

'The zoo of the new'

GLOSSARY
4 *meditate*: reflect.
5 *Indian pipe*: American woodland flower.
7 *Stalk*: plant stem.
9 *classical*: impressive, enduring.
10 *troublous*: disturbed.

EXPLORATIONS

1. What was your own immediate reaction after reading 'Child'? Refer to the text in your answer.
2. Which images in the poem are most effective in contrasting the world of the child and the world of the adult?
3. Plath uses various sound effects to enhance her themes in 'Child'. Comment briefly on two interesting examples.

STUDY NOTES

> Sylvia Plath's son was born in January 1962. A year later, shortly before the poet's own death, she wrote 'Child', a short poem that reflects her intense feelings about motherhood.

The first line of stanza one shows the **poet's emphatic appreciation of childhood innocence**: 'Your clear eye is the one absolutely beautiful thing'. The tone at first is hopeful. Her love for the new child is generous and unconditional: 'I want to fill it with color'. The childlike language is lively and playful. Plath plans to give her child the happiest of times, filled with 'color and ducks'. The vigorous rhythm and animated internal rhyme in the phrase 'The zoo of the new' are imaginative, capturing the sense of **youthful wonder**.

In stanza two, the poet continues to associate her child with all that is best about the natural world. The baby is like the most fragile of flowers, the 'April snowdrop'. The assonance in this phrase has a musical effect, like a soft lullaby. Yet her own fascination appears to mask a deeper concern. Plath feels that such a perfect childhood experience is unlikely to last very long. Despite all her positive sentiments, what she wants for **the vulnerable child** seems directly at odds with what is possible in **a flawed world**.

Run-on lines are a recurring feature of the poem and these add to the feeling of freedom and innocent intensity. Stanza three includes two **effective comparisons**, again taken from nature. Plath sees the child as an unblemished 'Stalk' that should grow perfectly. A second quality of childhood's pure innocence is found in the 'Pool' metaphor. We are reminded of the opening image – the child's 'clear eye', always trusting and sincere.

The poet would love to provide a magical future for her young child, so that the pool would reflect 'grand and classical' images. However, as a loving mother, she is trapped between her **idealism** – the joy she wants for her child – and **a distressing reality** – an awareness that the child's life will not be perfectly happy. This shocking realisation becomes clear in stanza four and overshadows her hopes completely. The final images are stark and powerful – the pathetic 'Wringing of hands' giving emphasis to her helplessness. The last line poignantly portrays the paradox of the tension between Plath's dreams for the child in the face of the despair she feels about the oppressive world: this 'Ceiling without a star'. This dark mood is in sharp contrast with the rest of the poem. The early celebration has been replaced by anguish and an overwhelming sense of failure.

ANALYSIS

Do you think 'Child' is a positive or negative poem? Refer to the text in explaining your response.

SAMPLE PARAGRAPH

I think Plath's poem, 'Child', is essentially about a mother's inadequacy. The poet wants the best for her innocent son. Although the first half of the poem focuses on her wishes to protect him, this changes at the end. Plath starts off by wanting to fill the boy's life with happy experiences (bright colours and toys) and keep him close to nature. There are numerous references to nature right through the poem and Plath compares her son to an 'April snowdrop'. This tender image gave me a very positive feeling. Everything about the child is wonderful at first. He is 'absolutely beautiful'. This all changes at the end of the poem. The mood turns negative. Plath talks of being confined in a darkened room which has a 'Ceiling without a star'. This is in total contrast with the images early on which were of the bright outdoors. The poet was positive at the start. This has been replaced with negative feelings. The ending is dark and 'troublous' because Plath knows that her child will grow up and experience pain just as she has.

EXAMINER'S COMMENT

This paragraph addresses the question well and offers a clear response. The candidate effectively illustrates the changing mood from optimism to pessimism and uses apt quotations in support. The style of writing is a little note-like and pedestrian. A basic B-grade standard.

CLASS/HOMEWORK EXERCISES

1. Write a paragraph comparing 'Child' with 'Morning Song'. Refer to theme and style in both poems.
2. Copy the table below into your own notes and fill in critical comments about the last two quotations.

Key Quotes

Your clear eye	The newborn child is innocent and is still unaffected by the corrupt world.
I want to fill it with color and ducks	The childlike language reflects the mother's desire to be part of her child's innocent world.
Stalk without wrinkle	Simple, memorable images typify Plath's sense of the child's perfection.
Not this troublous/Wringing of hands	
this dark/Ceiling without a star	

LEAVING CERT SAMPLE ESSAY

> **Q** **'Reading Sylvia Plath's poetry can be an uncomfortable experience.'**
>
> **Write a personal response to the above statement. Your answer should focus clearly on her themes and the manner in which she explores them. Support your points by reference to the poetry of Sylvia Plath on your course.**

MARKING SCHEME GUIDELINES

Reward responses that show clear evidence of personal engagement with the poems. The key term ('uncomfortable experience') may be addressed implicitly or explicitly. Candidates may choose to focus on the positive aspects of Plath's poetry. Allow for a wide range of approaches in the answering.

Material might be drawn from the following:
- Recurring themes of nature, disillusionment, transience, etc.
- Complexity of mother–child relationships.
- Contrasting images and tones.
- Startling and unusual language.
- The poet's life and how it links with her poetry.

SAMPLE ESSAY
(Reading Sylvia Plath's Poetry)

1. *The poetry of Sylvia Plath awakes a multitude of emotions in the reader, many of them disturbing. Plath's engulfing depression led her to take a view of the world that is alarming and often perverse. However, Plath's great understanding of life and love for her children led her to write poems that bring both joy and contentment to the reader. It is this diversity of approach that makes Plath one of the finest poets of the modern age.*

2. *Motherhood had a highly potent effect on Plath as a person. This is presented to the reader in the poem 'Morning Song', which is addressed to her daughter. She refers to her child with three words: 'fat gold watch'. This image suggests that the baby is valuable, to be treasured and praised. However, the image of a watch*

may symbolise the dark undercurrent that time is passing, it is slipping away for both mother and daughter. This ambiguity exists in much of Plath's work and, when examined, may be a cause for distress and discomfort for the reader. The poet chooses to present the notion that her daughter is a work of art with the words 'New statue./In a drafty museum'. It is into this harsh world that her child will venture, a disturbing thought for both the poet and the reader.

3. *The final image of the poem is of the baby herself trying a 'handful of notes'. The poet refers to the 'vowels' as they 'rise like balloons'. While the image seems to be a warm, content one, the image of a balloon seems to suggest something fragile, flimsy and transient. Even in her upbeat poems, Plath subtly presents disconcerting thoughts to the reader. The poem 'Black Rook in Rainy Weather' arises from the poet's feelings of contentment with life. She expresses this with the words 'I do not expect a miracle/Or an accident'. This inner peace leads the poet to rejoice in the mundane and urge us 'to let spotted leaves fall as they fall,/Without ceremony'. The poet becomes aware that 'Miracles occur' even if they are only 'spasmodic/Tricks of radiance'.*

4. *'Poppies in July' is undoubtedly one of the most disturbing poems by Plath. It deals with the horrors of her depression. The title seems to suggest a joyful image, but this could not be further from the truth. Plath refers to the poppies as 'little hell flames', seeing them as instruments which add to her suffering. Plath, it seems, would rather feel pain than feel nothing at all. She is horrified when she puts her hand 'among the flames' and 'Nothing burns'. Plath longs to find the poppies 'Dulling and stilling' and for everything to be 'colorless'. This poem gives a vivid description of how Plath feels choked by her destructive feelings. The depth of the poet's despair is evident in the troubling effect 'Poppies in July' has on the reader.*

5. *Plath explores a similar experience in 'Elm', which starts with the words, 'I know the bottom ... I know it with my great tap root'. The reference to a root suggests that the poet not only knew the lowest point, but draws her entire existence from that dark, hopeless place. We are told that Plath has 'suffered the atrocity of sunsets'. This hatred of something generally considered to be beautiful and joyous is a startling indication of the depth of her depression. Plath sees her sorrow as something that exists within herself – it is interior – and reveals that all day she feels 'its dark, feathery turnings, its malignity'. This horrifying image portrays the utter helplessness of the poet. It fills the reader with dread and fear, as Plath herself must have felt about her helplessness when she wrote the poem.*

6 'Child' was written to Plath's son shortly before she died. She expresses the wish that life should not be 'this troublous/Wringing of hands, this dark/Ceiling without a star'. The absence of the star symbolises the absence of any hope. We get the sense that Plath will never manage to break free of this depression and it is this thought that horrifies the reader.

7 Even in poems that seem peaceful and loving, the echoes of Plath's depression exist as undercurrents. The explicit nature of her darker poems affects the reader deeply, revealing to them the horrors and terrible reality of utter despair. Few, if any, could read Plath's poetry and remain unchanged by it.

(approx. 740 words)

```
GRADE: A2
P     = 13/15
C     = 13/15
L     = 12/15
M     = 5/5
Total = 43/50
```

EXAMINER'S COMMENT

A solid answer showing an excellent knowledge of Plath's poetry. The emphasis on the effect that the poems have on the reader is sustained throughout. Some points are well developed, often in detail (e.g. in paragraph 2) and apt quotations are well used. Apart from some repetition (paragraph 5), the overall expression is fluent and varied.

SAMPLE LEAVING CERT QUESTIONS ON PLATH'S POETRY (45–50 MINUTES)

1. 'Introducing Sylvia Plath'. Using this title, write an article for your school magazine. Support your points by close reference to the prescribed poems by Plath that you have studied.
2. 'Although Plath's poetry deals with intense experiences, her skill with language ensures that she is always in control of her subject matter.' Discuss this view, supporting your points with the aid of suitable reference to the poems by Plath on your course.

3 'Sylvia Plath's poems emerge from an unsettled world of anguish and personal torment.' Do you agree with this assessment of her poetry? Write a response, supporting your points with reference to the poems by Plath that you have studied.

SAMPLE ESSAY PLAN (Q2)

'Although Sylvia Plath's poetry deals with intense experiences, her skill with language ensures that she is always in control of her subject matter.' Discuss this view, supporting your points with the aid of suitable reference to the poems by Plath on your course.

- *Intro:* Identify the elements to be addressed – Plath's intensely disturbing themes and her innovative use of language.

- *Point 1:* Inner torment of 'Elm' presented through complex imagery and unsettling symbolism, allowing the reader to appreciate a nightmare world.

- *Point 2:* Contrast is effectively used in 'Poppies in July'. The speaker's deep yearning to escape is highlighted by the startling imagery of the flowers.

- *Point 3:* The depression in 'Black Rook in Rainy Weather' is also emphasised by conflicting images from nature and religion.

- *Point 4:* 'Child' and 'Morning Song' express strong themes about intense relationships through her mastery of language.

- *Conclusion:* Many poems deal with extreme emotional states, but Plath's poetic technique never lapses.

EXERCISE

Develop one of the above points into a paragraph.

POINT 2 – SAMPLE PARAGRAPH

'Poppies in July' is an intense poem about Plath's desperation to escape from her unhappy world. It begins on a disturbing note. The speaker is troubled by the sight of poppies, which she calls 'little hell flames'. The references to Hell and fire are developed through the rest of the poem, suggesting an extremely disturbed mind. The image of the red flames is both dramatic and terrifying – and typical of Plath's intense poetry. Readers can sense a standoff between the poppies and Plath herself. The flowers almost seem to mock the poet: 'You flicker. I cannot touch you'. Other images in the poem add to our understanding of the poet's deep pain – 'A mouth just bloodied' and 'fumes that I cannot touch'. Plath describes the poppies in a way that reveals her own troubled mental state. She is exhausted, almost beyond despair. We see her control of language when she contrasts the colour of the poppies with her own lifeless mood. We are left with a genuine sense of Plath's anguish. Unlike the blazing red flowers, the poet herself is 'colorless'.

EXAMINER'S COMMENT

This is a well-focused paragraph that concentrates on Plath's ability to use language in an inventive and controlled fashion. The contrast between the vivid appearance of the poppies and the poet's own bleak mood is very well illustrated. There is also a sense of engagement with the feelings expressed in the poem. A very good A-grade standard.

Last Words

'Her poems have that heart-breaking quality about them.'
Joyce Carol Oates

'Artists are a special breed. They are passionate and temperamental. Their feelings flow into the work they create.'
J. Timothy King

'I am a genius of a writer; I have it in me. I am writing the best poems of my life.'
Sylvia Plath

'I have spread my dreams under your feet.'

W.B. Yeats (1865–1939)

William Butler Yeats was born in Dublin in 1865. The son of a well-known Irish painter, John Butler Yeats, he spent much of his childhood in Co. Sligo. As a young writer, Yeats became involved with the Celtic Revival, a movement against the cultural influences of English rule in Ireland that sought to promote the spirit of our native heritage. His writing drew extensively from Irish mythology and folklore. Another great influence was the Irish revolutionary Maud Gonne, a woman as famous for her passionate nationalist politics as for her beauty. She rejected Yeats, who eventually married another woman, Georgie Hyde Lees. However, Maud Gonne remained a powerful figure in Yeats's writing. Over the years, Yeats became deeply involved in Irish politics and despite independence from England, his work reflected a pessimism about the political situation here. He also had a lifelong interest in mysticism and the occult. Appointed a senator of the Irish Free State in 1922, he is remembered as an important cultural leader, as a major playwright (he was one of the founders of Dublin's Abbey Theatre) and as one of the greatest 20th century poets. Yeats was awarded the Nobel Prize in 1923 and died in 1939 at the age of 73.

• Poetry Focus •

W.B. Yeats

PRESCRIBED POEMS (HIGHER LEVEL)

1 'The Lake Isle of Innisfree' (p. 456)

Written when Yeats lived in London and was homesick for Ireland, the poem celebrates the simple joys of nature and the search for peace.

2 'September 1913' (p. 460)

In this nostalgic poem, Yeats contrasts the disillusionment he feels about the Ireland of his own day with the romanticised past.

3 'The Wild Swans at Coole' (p. 465)

Based on the symbolism of the swans, Yeats reviews his emotional state. He reflects on deep personal concerns: love, ageing and the loss of poetic inspiration.

4 'An Irish Airman Foresees his Death' (p. 470)

This war poem is written as a monologue in the 'voice' of Yeats's friend, Major Robert Gregory. Its themes include heroism, nationalism and the youthful desire for excitement.

5 'Easter, 1916' (p. 474)

Yeats explores a variety of questions and issues provoked by the 1916 Rising. In re-evaluating his own views, he struggles to balance heroic achievement with the tragic loss of life.

6 'The Second Coming' (p. 481)

The poem addresses the chaos brought about by violence and political change. Having witnessed war in Europe, Yeats feared that civilisation would break down completely.

7 'Sailing to Byzantium' (p. 486)

Yeats's wide-ranging themes (including old age, transience, death, immortality and art) are all associated with the importance of finding spiritual fulfilment.

8 *from* **Meditations in Time of Civil War: 'The Stare's Nest by my Window' (p. 492)**

Written in response to the Irish Civil War, the poem tries to balance the destruction of conflict with the regenerative power of nature.

9 **'In Memory of Eva Gore-Booth and Con Markiewicz' (p. 496)**

Yeats's tribute to the Gore-Booth sisters is a lament for lost youth and beauty. He also reflects on the decline of the Anglo-Irish Ascendancy.

10 **'Swift's Epitaph' (p. 501)**

In this short translation from the original Latin inscription commemorating Jonathan Swift, Yeats honours a courageous writer who also came from the Anglo-Irish tradition.

11 **'An Acre of Grass' (p. 504)**

Yeats refuses to grow old quietly. Instead, he takes inspiration from William Blake and Michelangelo to continue using his creative talents in search of truth.

12 *from* **'Under Ben Bulben' (p. 508)**

Written shortly before his death, the poem is often seen as Yeats's last will and testament. It includes a summary of his beliefs and ends with the poet's own epitaph.

13 **'Politics' (p. 512)**

A short satirical poem in which Yeats rejects political activity, preferring romantic love.

• Poetry Focus •

The Lake Isle of Innisfree

W.B. Yeats

I will arise and go now, and go to Innisfree,
And a small cabin build there, of clay and wattles made:
Nine bean-rows will I have there, a hive for the honey-bee,
And live alone in the bee-loud glade.

And I shall have some peace there, for peace comes dropping slow,   5
Dropping from the veils of the morning to where the cricket sings;
There midnight's all a glimmer, and noon a purple glow,
And evening full of the linnet's wings.

I will arise and go now, for always night and day
I hear lake water lapping with low sounds by the shore;   10
While I stand on the roadway, or on the pavements grey,
I hear it in the deep heart's core.

'I hear lake water lapping with low sounds by the shore'

GLOSSARY

2 *Innisfree*: island of heather.
   clay and wattles: rods and mud were used to build small houses.
7 *midnight's all a glimmer*: stars are shining very brightly in the countryside.
8 *linnet*: songbird.
10 *lapping*: gentle sounds made by water at the edge of a shore.
12 *heart's core*: essential part; the centre of the poet's being.

EXPLORATIONS

1. This poem was voted number one in a recent *Irish Times* poll of the top 100 poems. Why do you think it appeals to so many readers?
2. What does the poem reveal to you about Yeats's own state of mind? Use reference to the text in your response.
3. How does the second stanza describe the rhythm of the passing day? Use quotations to illustrate your response.

STUDY NOTES

> 'The Lake Isle of Innisfree' was written in 1890. Yeats was in London, looking in a shop window at a little toy fountain. He was feeling very homesick. He said the sound of the 'tinkle of water' reminded him of 'lake water'. He was longing to escape from the grind of everyday life and he wrote an 'old daydream of mine'.

This timeless poem has long been a favourite with exiles everywhere, as **it expresses a longing for a place of deep peace**. The tone in **stanza one** is deliberate, not casual, as the poet announces his decision to go. There are biblical overtones here: 'I will arise and go to my father,' the prodigal son announces. This lends the occasion solemnity. Then the poet describes the idyllic life of self-sufficiency: 'nine bean-rows' and 'a hive for the honey-bee'. These details give the poem a **timeless quality** as the poet lives 'alone in the bee-loud glade'.

Stanza two describes Innisfree so vividly that the future tense of 'I will arise' gives way to the present: 'There midnight's all a glimmer'. The **repetition** of 'peace' and 'dropping' suits the subject, as it lulls us into this tranquil place to which we all aspire to go at some point in our lives. **Beautiful imagery** brings us through the day, from the gentle white mists of the morning which lie like carelessly thrown veils over the lake to the blazing purple of the heather under the midday sun. The starry night, which can only be seen in the clear skies of the countryside, is vividly described as 'midnight's all a glimmer', with **slender vowel sounds** suggesting the sharp light of the stars. The soft 'l', 'm' and 'p' sounds in this stanza create a gentle and magical mood.

The **third stanza** repeats the opening, giving the air of a solemn ritual taking place. The **verbal music** in this stanza is striking, as the broad vowel sounds slow down the line, 'I hear lake water lapping with low sounds by the shore', emphasising peace and tranquility. Notice the alliteration of 'l' and the assonance of 'o' all adding to the serene calm of the scene. The only **contemporary detail** in the poem is 'pavements grey', suggesting the relentless concrete of the city. The exile's awareness of what he loves is eloquently expressed as he declares he hears the sound 'in the deep heart's core'. Notice the monosyllabic ending, which drums home how much he longs for this place. Regular end rhyme (*abab*) and the regular four beats in each fourth line reinforce the harmony of this peaceful place.

ANALYSIS

What musical sounds did you find effective in this poem? Write a paragraph, illustrating your answer with references to the text.

SAMPLE PARAGRAPH

Yeats said that this poem was his 'first lyric with anything in its rhythm of my own music'. 'The Lake Isle of Innisfree' has a solemn, deliberate tone. It even has biblical overtones. The steady end rhyme ('Innisfree', 'honey-bee') adds to this stately music. The poet uses broad vowels to slow down the pace of the poem. This is an idyllic place where time almost stands still, 'alone in the bee-loud glade'. The repetition of 'peace' and 'dropping' creates a dreamy, soporific effect in this 'old daydream' of Yeats's. The brightly shining stars and the rapid movement of the bird's wings provide contrast as busy slender vowels in 'midnight's all a glimmer' and 'linnet's wings' tremble on the page. The soft 'l' sounds and alliteration in the line 'I hear lake water lapping with low sounds by the shore' bring us back to the calm, magical scene. I thought the consonance of 'la' and 'lo' also added to this effect. The final line beats out its message with five strong monosyllabic words: 'In the deep heart's core'. The phrase underlines the longing of the emigrant. This contrasts wonderfully with the slipping away of reality in 'pavements grey' as the exile relives his heart's desire.

EXAMINER'S COMMENT

A good understanding of the techniques used by a poet to create music and the effect this has on the poem is displayed in the answer. Quotations are very well used here to back up this personal response. Grade-A standard.

CLASS/HOMEWORK EXERCISES

1. Pick out two images from the poem that appeal to you and discuss the reasons for their appeal.
2. Copy the table below into your own notes and fill in critical comments about the last two quotations.

Key Quotes

Nine bean-rows will I have there	Throughout the poem, Yeats is nostalgic for his homeland. He is yearning to return to the simple life he once enjoyed.
Dropping from the veils of the morning	The use of assonance emphasises the serene atmosphere of this magical place as the white mist lies over the lake.
noon a purple glow	The midday reflection of the heather in the water under the blazing midday sun is typical of the poet's effective visual imagery.
I will arise and go now	
I hear it in the deep heart's core	

• Poetry Focus •

September 1913

W.B. Yeats

What need you, being come to sense,
But fumble in a greasy till
And add the halfpence to the pence
And prayer to shivering prayer, until
You have dried the marrow from the bone;   5
For men were born to pray and save:
Romantic Ireland's dead and gone,
It's with O'Leary in the grave.

Yet they were of a different kind,
The names that stilled your childish play,   10
They have gone about the world like wind,
But little time had they to pray
For whom the hangman's rope was spun,
And what, God help us, could they save?
Romantic Ireland's dead and gone,   15
It's with O'Leary in the grave.

Was it for this the wild geese spread
The grey wing upon every tide;
For this that all that blood was shed,
For this Edward Fitzgerald died,   20
And Robert Emmet and Wolfe Tone,
All that delirium of the brave?
Romantic Ireland's dead and gone,
It's with O'Leary in the grave.

Yet could we turn the years again,   25
And call those exiles as they were
In all their loneliness and pain,
You'd cry, 'Some woman's yellow hair
Has maddened every mother's son':
They weighed so lightly what they gave.   30
But let them be, they're dead and gone,
They're with O'Leary in the grave.

• Leaving Certificate English •

W.B. Yeats

'Romantic Ireland's dead and gone'

GLOSSARY

1 *you*: merchants and business people.
8 *O'Leary*: Fenian leader, one of Yeats's heroes.
9 *they*: the selfless Irish patriots.
17 *the wild geese*: Irish independence soldiers forced into exile in Europe after 1690.
20 *Edward Fitzgerald*: 18th-century Irish aristocrat and revolutionary.
21 *Robert Emmet and Wolfe Tone*: Irish rebel leaders. Emmet was hanged in 1803. Tone committed suicide in prison after being sentenced to death in 1798.

EXPLORATIONS

1 Comment on the effectiveness of the images used in the first five lines of the poem.
2 How would you describe the tone of this poem? Is it bitter, sad, ironic, angry, etc.? Refer closely to the text in your answer.
3 Were the patriots named in the poem heroes or fools? Write a paragraph in response to Yeats's views.

STUDY NOTES

'September 1913' is typical of Yeats's hard-hitting political poems. Both the content and tone are harsh as the poet airs his views on public issues, contrasting the idealism of Ireland's heroic past with the uncultured present.

Yeats had been a great supporter of Sir Hugh Lane, who had offered his extensive art collection to the city of Dublin, provided the paintings would be on show in a suitable gallery. When the authorities failed to arrange this, Lane

W.B. Yeats

withdrew his offer. The controversy infuriated Yeats, who criticised Dublin Corporation for being miserly and anti-cultural. For him, it represented a **new low in the country's drift into vulgarity and crass commercialism**. The year 1913 was also a year of great hardship, partly because of a general strike and lock-out of workers. Poverty and deprivation were widespread at the time, particularly in Dublin's tenements.

The **first stanza** begins with a derisive **attack on a materialistic society** that Yeats sees as being both greedy and hypocritical. Ireland's middle classes are preoccupied with making money and slavish religious devotion. The rhetorical opening is sharply sarcastic, as the poet depicts the petty penny-pinching shopkeepers who 'fumble in a greasy till'. Yeats's tone is as angry as it is ironic: 'For men were born to pray and save'. Images of the dried bone and 'shivering prayer' are equally forceful – the poor are exploited by ruthless employers and a domineering Church. This disturbing picture leads the poet to regret the loss of 'Romantic Ireland' in the concluding refrain.

Stanza two develops the contrast between past and present as Yeats considers the **heroism and generosity of an earlier era**. Ireland's patriots – 'names that stilled' earlier generations of children – could hardly have been more unlike the present middle class. Yeats clearly relates to the self-sacrifice of idealistic Irish freedom fighters: 'And what, God help us, could they save?' These disdainful words echo the fearful prayers referred to at the start of the poem. The heroes of the past were so selfless that they did not even concern themselves with saving their own lives.

The wistful and nostalgic tone of **stanza three** is obvious in the rhetorical question about all those Irish soldiers who had been exiled in the late 17th century. Yeats's high regard for these men is evoked by comparing them to 'wild geese', a plaintive metaphor reflecting their nobility. Yet the poet's admiration for past idealism is diminished by the fact that **such heroic dedication was all for nothing**. The repetition of 'for this' hammers home Yeats's contempt for the pious materialists of his own imperfect age. In listing a roll of honour, he singles out the most impressive patriots of his own class, the Anglo-Irish Ascendancy. For the poet, Fitzgerald, Emmet and Tone are among the most admirable Irishmen. In using the phrase 'All that delirium of the brave', Yeats suggests that their passionate dedication to Irish freedom bordered on a frenzied or misplaced sense of daring.

This romanticised appreciation continues into the **final stanza**, where the poet imagines the 'loneliness and pain' of the heroic dead. His empathy towards them is underpinned by an **even more vicious portrayal of the new middle class**. He argues that the establishment figures of his own time would be unable to comprehend anything about the values and dreams of 'Romantic Ireland'. At best, they would be confused by the ludicrous self-sacrifice of the past. At worst, the present generation would accuse the patriots of being insane or of trying to impress friends or lovers. Perhaps Yeats is illustrating the cynical thinking of his time, when many politicians courted national popularity. 'Some woman's yellow hair' might well refer to the traditional symbol of Ireland as a beautiful woman.

The poet's disgust on behalf of the patriots is rounded off in the last two lines: 'But let them be, they're dead and gone'. The refrain has been changed slightly, adding further emphasis and a **sense of finality**. After reading this savage satire, we are left with a deep sense of Yeats's bitter disillusionment towards his contemporaries. The extreme feelings expressed in the poem offer a dispirited vision of an unworthy country. It isn't surprising that some critics have accused Yeats of over-romanticising the heroism of Ireland's past, of being narrow minded and even elitist. At any rate, the poem challenges us to examine the values of the state we are in, our understanding of Irish history and the meaning of heroism.

ANALYSIS

'September 1913' is based on contrasting images of meanness and generosity. Which set of images makes the greater impact? Write your response in a paragraph, referring closely to the text in your answer.

SAMPLE PARAGRAPH

Although W.B. Yeats ridicules the greedy shopkeepers and landlords of Dublin, he makes a much greater impression in describing the patriots of old Ireland – 'names that stilled your childish play'. The image stops us in our tracks. We can imagine how children used to hold men like Wolfe Tone and Robert Emmet in such great respect. Yeats uses the beautiful image of the wild geese spreading 'The grey wing upon every tide' to describe the dignified flight of Irish soldiers who refused to accept colonial rule. The poet's simple imagery is taken from the world of nature and has a vivid quality that makes us aware of the poet's high opinion of those heroes who were prepared to die for their beliefs.

• Poetry Focus •

W.B. Yeats

EXAMINER'S COMMENT

Clearly written and very well supported, this B grade response addresses the question directly. There is evidence of close engagement with the poem. In addition, the expression is varied, fluent and controlled throughout. However, further development of key contrast points would be expected for a top grade.

CLASS/HOMEWORK EXERCISES

1. How relevant is 'September 1913' to present-day Ireland? Refer to the text of the poem when writing your response.
2. Copy the table below into your own notes and fill in critical comments about the last two quotations.

Key Quotes

What need you, being come to sense	Rhetorical questions satirise those smug people who knew how to exploit situations to their advantage.
Romantic Ireland's dead and gone	In his refrain, Yeats is caught between deep disillusionment towards his contemporaries and admiration for a more idealistic age.
All that delirium of the brave	The heroes of the past were extraordinarily courageous – but does the paradox suggest that they were also out of control?
You have dried the marrow from the bone	
For this that all that blood was shed	

The Wild Swans at Coole

The trees are in their autumn beauty,
The woodland paths are dry,
Under the October twilight the water
Mirrors a still sky;
Upon the brimming water among the stones   5
Are nine-and-fifty swans.

The nineteenth autumn has come upon me
Since I first made my count;
I saw, before I had well finished,
All suddenly mount   10
And scatter wheeling in great broken rings
Upon their clamorous wings.

I have looked upon those brilliant creatures,
And now my heart is sore.
All's changed since I, hearing at twilight,   15
The first time on this shore,
The bell-beat of their wings above my head,
Trod with a lighter tread.

Unwearied still, lover by lover,
They paddle in the cold   20
Companionable streams or climb the air;
Their hearts have not grown old;
Passion or conquest, wander where they will,
Attend upon them still.

But now they drift on the still water,   25
Mysterious, beautiful;
Among what rushes will they build,
By what lake's edge or pool
Delight men's eyes when I awake some day
To find they have flown away?   30

W.B. Yeats

• Poetry Focus •

W.B. Yeats

'The bell-beat of their wings above my head'

GLOSSARY

5 *brimming*: filled to the very top or edge.
12 *clamorous*: loud, confused noise.
18 *Trod ... tread*: walked lightly; carefree.
19 *lover by lover*: swans mate for life; this highlights Yeats's loneliness.
21 *Companionable*: friendly.
24 *Attend upon them still*: waits on them yet.

EXPLORATIONS

1 Why do you think the poet chose the season of autumn as his setting? What changes occur at this time of year? Where are these referred to in the poem?
2 In your opinion, what are the main contrasts between the swans and the poet? Describe two, using close reference to the text.
3 What do you think the final stanza means? Consider the phrase 'I awake'. From what does the poet awake?

STUDY NOTES

'The Wild Swans at Coole' was written in 1916. Yeats loved spending time in the West, especially at Coole, the home of Lady Gregory, his friend and patron. He was 51 when he wrote this poem, which contrasts the swans' beauty and apparent seeming immortality with Yeats's ageing, mortal self.

The poem opens with a tranquil, serene scene of **autumnal beauty** in the park of Lady Gregory's home in Galway. This romantic image is described in great detail: the 'woodland paths are dry'. It is evening, 'October twilight'. The water is 'brimming'. The swans are carefully counted, 'nine-and-fifty'. The use of the soft letters 'l', 'm' and 's' emphasise the calm of the scene in stanza one.

In stanza two, the poem moves to the personal as he recalls that it is 19 years since he first counted the swans. The word 'count' links the two stanzas. The poet's counting is interrupted as these mysterious creatures all suddenly rise into the sky. Run-through lines suggest the flowing movement of the rising swans. Strong verbs ('mount', 'scatter') reinforce this elemental action. The great beating wings of the swans are captured in the onomatopoeic 'clamorous wings'. They are independent and refuse to be restrained. The ring is a symbol of eternity. The swans are making the same patterns as they have always made; they are unchanging. Stanza two is linked to stanza three by the phrases 'I saw' and 'I have looked'. Now the poet tells us his 'heart is sore'. He has taken stock and is **dissatisfied with his emotional situation**. He is 51, alone and unmarried and concerned that his poetic powers are lessening: **'All's changed'**. All humans want things to remain as they are, but life is full of change. He has lost the great love of his life, the beautiful Irish activist, Maud Gonne. He also laments the loss of his youth, when he 'Trod with a lighter tread'. Nineteen years earlier, he was much more carefree. The noise of the beating wings of the swans is effectively captured in the compound word 'bell-beat'. The alliterative 'b' reinforces the steady, flapping sound. The poet is using his intense personal experiences to express universal truths.

The swans in stanza four are **symbols of eternity**, ageless, 'Unwearied still'. They are united, 'lover by lover'. They experience life together ('Companionable streams'), not on their own, like the poet. He envies them their defiance of time: 'Their hearts have not grown old'. They do what they want, when they want. They are full of 'Passion or conquest'. By contrast, he is indirectly telling us, he feels old and worn out. The **spiral imagery** of the 'great broken rings' is reminiscent of the spirals seen in ancient carvings representing eternity. Yeats believed there was a cyclical pattern behind all things. The swans can live in two elements, water and air, thus linking these elements together. They are living, vital, immortal, unlike their surroundings. The trees are yellowing ('autumn beauty') and the dry 'woodland paths' suggest the lack of creative force which the poet is experiencing. Yeats is heartbroken and weary. Only the swans transcend time.

Stanza five explores a **philosophy of life**, linked to the previous stanza by the repetition of 'still'. The swans have returned to the water, 'Mysterious, beautiful'. The poem ends on a speculative note as the poet asks where they will

'Delight men's eyes'. Is he referring to the fact that **they will continue to be a source of pleasure to someone else** long after he is dead? The swans appear immortal, a continuing source of happiness as they practise their patterns, whereas the poet is not able to continue improving his own writing, as he is mortal. The poet is slipping into the cruel season of winter while the swans infinitely 'drift on the still water'.

ANALYSIS

Poets use patterns to communicate their message. With reference to 'The Wild Swans at Coole', write a paragraph on Yeats's use of pattern, referring to imagery, sound effects, rhyme, etc.

SAMPLE PARAGRAPH

The rhyme scheme in 'The Wild Swans at Coole' is *abcbdd*. When I look at the words which these rhymes stress, I see another layer in this poem. The marked contrast between the dry woodland paths, which are so suggestive of the drying up of creativity, and the water which 'Mirrors a still sky' is very effective. The water is teeming with life. In the second stanza the poet is anchored to the land as he makes his 'count', while the swans are free to fly at a moment's notice, 'All suddenly mount'. When Yeats first went to Coole, he was suffering from a broken heart and this is echoed in the rhyming lines 'And now my heart is sore', 'The first time on this shore'. Although the swans are in the 'cold', they have not 'grown old'. Finally, he wonders where these 'Mysterious and beautiful' creatures will be: 'By what lake's edge or pool'. Similarly, another layer of meaning is created by the rhyme of the last two lines of each stanza. I particularly liked the rhyme in the last stanza: 'when I awake some day/To find they have flown away'. This sums up for me the sadness of the poet as he realises he is mortal, whereas they are immortal. It may even suggest his dread that his poetic inspiration, which is as mysterious and beautiful as the swans, may suddenly desert him too. I think examining the carefully worked patterns of the poem increases both our enjoyment of the poem as well as our understanding of the poet's message.

• Leaving Certificate English •

EXAMINER'S COMMENT

The student has engaged in a personal way to answer this question. Detailed attention has been given to the poet's use of rhyme. An effective, well-developed discussion that makes good use of quotations to sustain the argument. Confident expression adds to the A-grade standard.

CLASS/HOMEWORK EXERCISES

1 Is the poem more concerned with the poet than the swans? Write a paragraph responding to this statement, referring to the text.
2 Copy the table below into your own notes and fill in critical comments about the last two quotations.

Key Quotes

The woodland paths are dry	Using symbolism, Yeats expresses his fears of ageing and the loss of his poetic imagination.
And now my heart is sore	Yeats admits to being dissatisfied with his life. The assonance adds to the poignancy.
All's changed	Political changes included World War I, the 1916 Rising and the Civil War. Personal changes included the loss of his great love (Maud Gonne) and his youth.
Unwearied still, lover by lover	
Mysterious, beautiful	

• 469 •

• Poetry Focus •

An Irish Airman Foresees his Death

W.B. Yeats

I know that I shall meet my fate
Somewhere among the clouds above;
Those that I fight I do not hate,
Those that I guard I do not love;
My country is Kiltartan Cross,   5
My countrymen Kiltartan's poor,
No likely end could bring them loss
Or leave them happier than before.
Nor law, nor duty bade me fight,
Nor public men, nor cheering crowds,   10
A lonely impulse of delight
Drove to this tumult in the clouds;
I balanced all, brought all to mind,
The years to come seemed waste of breath,
A waste of breath the years behind   15
In balance with this life, this death.

'I balanced all'

GLOSSARY

The Irish airman in this poem is Major Robert Gregory (1881–1918), son of Yeats's close friend, Lady Gregory. He was shot down and killed while on service in northern Italy.

3 *Those that I fight*: the Germans.
4 *Those that I guard*: Allied countries, such as England and France.
5 *Kiltartan*: townland near the Gregory estate in Co. Galway.
7 *likely end*: outcome.
12 *tumult*: turmoil; confusion.

EXPLORATIONS

1 'This poem is not just an elegy or lament in memory of the dead airman. It is also an insight into the excitement and exhilaration of warfare.' Write your response to this statement, using close reference to the text.
2 Write a paragraph on Yeats's use of repetition throughout the poem. Refer to the text in your answer.
3 Imagine you are Robert Gregory. Write a short diary entry reflecting your thoughts and feelings about becoming a fighter pilot. Base your comments on the text of the poem.

STUDY NOTES

> **Thousands of Irishmen fought and died in the British armed forces during the First World War. Robert Gregory was killed in Italy at the age of 37. The airman's death had a lasting effect on Yeats, who wrote several poems about him.**

Is it right to assume anything about young men who fight for their countries? Why do they enlist? Do they always know what they are fighting for? In this poem, Yeats expresses what he believes is the airman's viewpoint as he comes face to face with death. This **fatalistic attitude** is prevalent in the emphatic opening line. The poem's title also leads us to believe that the speaker has an intuitive sense that his death is about to happen. But despite this premonition, he seems strangely resigned to risking his life.

In lines 3–4, he makes it clear that he neither hates his German enemies nor loves the British and their allies. His thoughts are with the people he knows best back in Kiltartan, Co. Galway. Major Gregory recognises the irony of their detachment from the war. The ordinary people of his homeland are unlikely to be affected at all by whatever happens on the killing fields of mainland Europe. Does he feel that he is abandoning his fellow countrymen? What is the dominant tone of lines 7–8? Is there an underlying bitterness?

In line 9, the speaker takes time to reflect on why he joined the air force and immediately dismisses the obvious reasons of conscription ('law') or patriotism ('duty'). As a volunteer, Gregory is more openly cynical of the 'public men' and 'cheering crowds' he mentions in line 10. Like many in the military who have experienced the realities of warfare, **he is suspicious of hollow patriotism** and has no time for political leaders and popular adulation.

So why did Robert Gregory choose to endanger his life by going to war? The answer lies in the key comments 'A lonely impulse of delight' (**line 11**) and 'I balanced all' (**line 13**). The first phrase is paradoxical. The airman experiences not just the excitement, but also the isolation of flying. At the same time, his 'impulse' to enlist as a fighter pilot reflects both his **desire for adventure** as well as his regret.

The **last four lines** explain the real reason behind his decision. It was neither rash nor emotional, but simply a question of balance. Having examined his life closely, Gregory has chosen the heroism of a self-sacrificing death. It is as though he only feels truly alive during the 'tumult' of battle. Yeats's language is particularly evocative at this point. Awesome air battles are effectively echoed in such dynamic phrasing as 'impulse of delight' and 'tumult in the clouds'. This **sense of freedom and power** is repeatedly contrasted with the dreary and predictable security of life away from the war – dismissed out of hand as a 'waste of breath'. From the airman's perspective, as a man of action, dying in battle is in keeping with 'this life' that he has chosen. Such a death would be his final adventurous exploit.

Some commentators have criticised Yeats's poem for glorifying war and pointless risk-taking. Others have suggested that the poet successfully highlights Anglo-Irish attitudes, neither exclusively Irish nor English. The poet certainly raises interesting questions about national identity and ways of thinking about war. However, in elegising Robert Gregory, he emphasises **the airman's daring solitude**. Perhaps this same thrill lies at the heart of other important choices in life, including the creative activity of artists. Is there a sense that the poet and the pilot are alike, both of them taking calculated risks in what they do?

ANALYSIS

What do you think is the poem's dominant or central mood? Write your response in a paragraph, referring closely to the text in your answer.

SAMPLE PARAGRAPH

The title itself suggests fear. However, the airman accepts his impending death as if it is a natural result. 'Fate' suggests destiny, the unavoidable. The rest of the poem is dominated by a strong mood of resignation. The slow repetitive rhythm is like a chant or a prayer. This airman has a fatalistic temperament. He seems completely relaxed and reasonable when he says 'Those that I fight I do not hate'. In a way, he seems to have distanced himself from everything and everyone. He appears to have something of a death wish and his mood becomes very disillusioned towards the final section. For him, the past and future are a 'waste'. In general, his mood is quite resigned to death.

EXAMINER'S COMMENT

This candidate focuses well on the negative moods within the poem. Apt quotes are also effectively used in reference. The paragraph might have included some mention of the contrasting euphoria of war. The language towards the end is also slightly stilted. Overall, a B grade standard.

CLASS/HOMEWORK EXERCISES

1. Do you consider 'An Irish Airman Foresees his Death' to be an anti-war poem? Give reasons for your answer.
2. Copy the table below into your own notes and fill in critical comments about the last two quotations.

Key Quotes

I know that I shall meet my fate	The narrator, Robert Gregory, accepts that he will be killed in battle, yet his desire to take risks is more powerful.
My countrymen Kiltartan's poor	Examine the narrator's tone throughout the poem. Is it sincere, sympathetic, ironic, cynical?
A waste of breath	The speaker's disenchantment with ordinary life is emphasised. Is this disturbing?
Nor law, nor duty bade me fight	
In balance with this life, this death	

• Poetry Focus •

Easter, 1916

W.B. Yeats

I have met them at close of day
Coming with vivid faces
From counter or desk among grey
Eighteenth-century houses.
I have passed with a nod of the head   5
Or polite meaningless words,
Or have lingered awhile and said
Polite meaningless words,
And thought before I had done
Of a mocking tale or a gibe   10
To please a companion
Around the fire at the club,
Being certain that they and I
But lived where motley is worn:
All changed, changed utterly: 15
A terrible beauty is born.

That woman's days were spent
In ignorant good-will,
Her nights in argument
Until her voice grew shrill.   20
What voice more sweet than hers
When, young and beautiful,
She rode to harriers?
This man had kept a school
And rode our wingèd horse;   25
This other his helper and friend
Was coming into his force;
He might have won fame in the end,
So sensitive his nature seemed,
So daring and sweet his thought.   30
This other man I had dreamed
A drunken, vainglorious lout.
He had done most bitter wrong
To some who are near my heart,
Yet I number him in the song;   35
He, too, has resigned his part
In the casual comedy;

He, too, has been changed in his turn,
Transformed utterly:
A terrible beauty is born.

Hearts with one purpose alone
Through summer and winter seem
Enchanted to a stone
To trouble the living stream.
The horse that comes from the road,
The rider, the birds that range
From cloud to tumbling cloud,
Minute by minute they change;
A shadow of cloud on the stream
Changes minute by minute;
A horse-hoof slides on the brim,
And a horse plashes within it;
The long-legged moor-hens dive,
And hens to moor-cocks call;
Minute by minute they live:
The stone's in the midst of all.

Too long a sacrifice
Can make a stone of the heart.
O when may it suffice?
That is Heaven's part, our part
To murmur name upon name,
As a mother names her child
When sleep at last has come
On limbs that had run wild.
What is it but nightfall?
No, no, not night but death;
Was it needless death after all?
For England may keep faith
For all that is done and said.
We know their dream; enough
To know they dreamed and are dead;
And what if excess of love
Bewildered them till they died?
I write it out in a verse –
MacDonagh and MacBride

Poetry Focus

W.B. Yeats

And Connolly and Pearse
Now and in time to be,
Wherever green is worn,
Are changed, changed utterly:
A terrible beauty is born.   80

'All changed, changed utterly'

GLOSSARY

On 24 April 1916, Easter Monday, about 700 Irish Republicans took over several key buildings in Dublin. These included the Four Courts, Bolands Mills, the Royal College of Surgeons and the General Post Office. The rebellion lasted six days and was followed by the execution of its leaders. The Rising was a pivotal event in modern Irish history.

1 *them*: the rebels involved in the Rising.
14 *motley*: ridiculous clothing.
17 *That woman*: Countess Markiewicz, friend of Yeats and a committed nationalist.
24 *This man*: Padraig Pearse, poet and teacher, was shot as a leader of the Rising.
25 *wingèd horse*: Pegasus, the mythical white horse that flies across the sky, was a symbol of poetic inspiration.
26 *This other*: Thomas MacDonagh, writer and teacher, executed in 1916.
31 *This other man*: Major John MacBride was also executed for his part in the rebellion. He was the husband of Maud Gonne.
33 *most bitter wrong*: there were recurring rumours that MacBride had mistreated Maud Gonne.
67 *needless death*: Yeats asks if the Rising was a waste of life, since the British were already considering independence for Ireland.
76 *Connolly*: Trade union leader and revolutionary, executed in 1916.

EXPLORATIONS

1. Describe the atmosphere in the opening stanza of the poem. Refer closely to the text in your answer.
2. 'Easter, 1916' has many striking images. Choose two that you find particularly interesting and briefly explain their effectiveness.
3. On balance, does Yeats approve or disapprove of the Easter Rising? Refer to the text in your answer.

STUDY NOTES

> Yeats, who was in London at the time of the Rising, had mixed feelings about what had happened. He was clearly fascinated but also troubled by this heroic and yet in some ways pointless sacrifice. He did not publish the poem until 1920.

In the **opening stanza**, Yeats recalls how he used to meet some of the people who were later involved in the Easter Rising. He was unimpressed by their 'vivid faces' and he remembers routinely dismissing them with 'Polite meaningless words'. His admission that he **misjudged these insignificant Republicans** as subjects for 'a mocking tale or a gibe' among his clever friends is a reminder of his derisive attitude in 'September 1913'. Before 1916, Yeats had considered Ireland a ridiculous place, a circus 'where motley is worn'. But the poet confesses that the Rising transformed everything – including his own condescending apathy. In the stanza's final lines, Yeats introduces what becomes an ambivalent refrain ending in 'A terrible beauty is born'.

This sense of shock and the need to completely re-evaluate his views is developed in **stanza two**. The poet singles out individual martyrs killed or imprisoned for their activities, among them his close friend Countess Markiewicz. He also mentions Major John MacBride, husband of Maud Gonne, who had refused Yeats's proposal of marriage. Although he had always considered MacBride as little more than a 'drunken, vainglorious lout', Yeats now acknowledges that he too has been distinguished by his bravery and heroism. The poet wonders about the usefulness of all the passion that sparked the rebels to make such a bold move, but his emphasis is on the fact that **the people as well as the whole atmosphere have changed**. Even MacBride, whom he held in utter contempt, has grown in stature.

In **stanza three**, Yeats takes powerful images from nature and uses them to explore the meaning of Irish heroism. The metaphor of the stubborn stone in

• Poetry Focus •

W.B. Yeats

the stream might represent the defiance of the revolutionaries towards all the forces around them. **The poet evokes the constant energy and dynamism of the natural world**, focusing on the changes that happen 'minute by minute'. Image after dazzling image conjures up a vivid picture of unpredictable movement and seasonal regeneration (as 'hens to moor-cocks call') and skies change 'From cloud to tumbling cloud'.

For the poet, the Rising presented many contradictions, as he weighs the success of the revolt against the shocking costs. In contrasting the inflexibility of the revolutionaries with the 'living stream', he **indicates a reluctant admiration for the rebels' dedication**. Does Yeats suggest that the rebels risked the loss of their own humanity, allowing their hearts to harden to stone? Or is he also thinking of Maud Gonne and blaming her cold-hearted rejection of him on her fanatical political views?

In the final stanza, the poet returns to the metaphor of the unmoving stone in a flowing stream to warn of the dangers of fanaticism. The rhetorical questions about the significance of the rebellion reveal **his continuing struggle to understand** what happened. Then he asks the single most important question about the Rising: 'Was it needless death after all', particularly as 'England may keep faith' and allow Ireland its independence, all of which would prompt a more disturbing conclusion, i.e. that the insurgents died in vain.

Yeats quickly abandons essentially unanswerable questions about the value of the Irish struggle for freedom. Instead, he simply pays tribute to the fallen patriots by naming them tenderly, 'As a mother names her child'. The final assertive lines commemorate the 1916 leaders in dramatic style. Setting aside his earlier ambivalence, Yeats acknowledges that these patriots died for their dreams. The hushed tone is reverential, almost sacred. The rebels have been transformed into martyrs who will be remembered for their selfless heroism 'Wherever green is worn'. The insistent final refrain has a stirring and increasingly disquieting quality. The poem's central paradox, 'A terrible beauty is born', concludes that **all the heroic achievements of the 1916 Rising were at the tragic expense of human life**.

ANALYSIS

Write a paragraph outlining Yeats's feelings about the Irish patriots as expressed in the final stanza of 'Easter, 1916'. Support the points you make with suitable reference or quotation.

SAMPLE PARAGRAPH

The final verse reveals many of Yeats's unanswered questions and confused thinking about the 1916 patriots. However, he sees that his own role is to record what he knows to be true and to 'write it out in a verse'. This allows him to pay his own tribute to the 1916 leaders whom he lists formally, almost like a graveside oration. The slow, deliberate rhythm is deeply respectful. The mood is serious, almost sombre, in keeping with the poet's newfound respect for the dead heroes. Yeats ends with the keynote comment, 'A terrible beauty is born'. This oxymoron derives its power from the obvious contrast between the terms. He believed that the Easter Rising was terrible because of all the unnecessary suffering that had occurred. Nevertheless, Yeats accepts that there was a transforming beauty that took the rebels, and perhaps many others, out of their lives of 'casual comedy' into the tragic drama of real life.

EXAMINER'S COMMENT

This short paragraph is well focused and supported. The candidate touches on several interesting aspects of the poet's mixed feelings about 1916. The references to features of style contribute much to this well-written A-grade response.

CLASS/HOMEWORK EXERCISES

1. Yeats emphasises change of one kind or another throughout 'Easter, 1916'. List the main changes and comment briefly on them.
2. Copy the table below into your own notes and fill in critical comments about the last two quotations.

• Poetry Focus •

W. B. Yeats

Key Quotes

All changed, changed utterly:/A terrible beauty is born	The 1916 Rising, in all its idealism and brutality, had transformed not just Ireland, but Yeats's own attitudes.
Enchanted to a stone	The poet uses the metaphor to show both the determination of the rebels and their unswerving fanaticism.
they dreamed and are dead	Yeats has been forced to accept that the 1916 rebels were idealists who made the ultimate sacrifice.
polite meaningless words	
Being certain that they and I/ But lived where motley is worn	

The Second Coming

Turning and turning in the widening gyre
The falcon cannot hear the falconer;
Things fall apart; the centre cannot hold;
Mere anarchy is loosed upon the world,
The blood-dimmed tide is loosed, and everywhere   5
The ceremony of innocence is drowned;
The best lack all conviction, while the worst
Are full of passionate intensity.

Surely some revelation is at hand;
Surely the Second Coming is at hand.   10
The Second Coming! Hardly are those words out
When a vast image out of *Spiritus Mundi*
Troubles my sight: somewhere in sands of the desert
A shape with lion body and the head of a man,
A gaze blank and pitiless as the sun,   15
Is moving its slow thighs, while all about it
Reel shadows of the indignant desert birds.
The darkness drops again; but now I know
That twenty centuries of stony sleep
Were vexed to nightmare by a rocking cradle,   20
And what rough beast, its hour come round at last,
Slouches towards Bethlehem to be born?

W.B. Yeats

'somewhere in sands of the desert/A shape with lion body and the head of a man'

W.B. Yeats

GLOSSARY

The Second Coming: This is a reference to the Bible. It is from Matthew and speaks of Christ's return to reward the good.

1 *in the widening gyre*: Yeats regarded a cycle of history as a gyre. He visualised these cycles as interconnecting cones that moved in a circular motion widening outwards until they could not widen any further, then a new gyre or cone formed from the centre of the circle created. This spun in the opposite direction to the original cone. The Christian era was coming to a close and a new disturbed time was coming into view. In summary, the gyre is a symbol of constant change.
2 *falcon*: a bird of prey, trained to hunt by the aristocracy.
2 *falconer*: the trainer of the falcon. If the bird flies too far away, it cannot be directed.
4 *Mere*: nothing more than; just; only.
4 *anarchy*: lack of government or order. Yeats believed that bloodshed and a worship of bloodshed were the end of an historical era.
5 *blood-dimmed*: made dark with blood.
12 *Spiritus Mundi*: Spirit of the World, the collective soul of the world.
14 *lion body and the head of a man*: famous statue in Egypt; an enigmatic person.
17 *desert birds*: birds of prey.
19 *twenty centuries*: Yeats believed that two thousand years was the length of a period in history.
20 *vexed*: annoyed; distressed.
20 *rocking cradle*: coming of the infant Jesus.
21 *rough beast*: the Anti-Christ.
22 *Bethlehem*: birthplace of Christ. It is usually associated with peace and innocence, and it is terrifying that the beast is going to be born there. The spiral has reversed its spinning. A savage god is coming.

EXPLORATIONS

1 This poem suggests that politics are not important. Does the poet convince you? Write a paragraph in response, with reference to the text.
2 Yeats uses symbols to express some of his most profound ideas. What symbols in this poem appeal to you? Use reference to the text in your response.
3 'Yeats is yearning for order, and fearing anarchy.' Discuss two ways in which the poem illustrates this statement. Support your answer with reference to the text.

STUDY NOTES

'The Second Coming' is a terrifying, apocalyptic poem written in January 1919 against a background of the disintegration of three great European empires at the end of the First World War and against the catastrophic War of Independence in Ireland. These were bloody times. Yeats yearned for order and feared anarchy.

Sparked off by both disgust at what was happening in Europe as well as his interest in the occult, Yeats explores, in stanza one, what he perceives to be the failure at the heart of society: 'Things fall apart'. In his opinion, **the whole world was disintegrating** into a bloody, chaotic mess. This break-up of civilisation is described in metaphorical language. For Yeats, the 'gyre' is a symbol representing an era. He believed contrary expanding and contracting forces influence people and cultures and that the Christian era was nearing its end. Images of hunting show how the old world represented its failing – 'The falcon cannot hear the falconer'. We have lost touch with Christ, just as the falcon loses touch with the falconer as he swings into ever-increasing circles. This bird was trained to fly in circles to catch its prey. The circular imagery, with the repetitive '-ing', describes the continuous, swirling movement. Civilisation is also 'Turning and turning in the widening gyre' as it buckles and fragments.

The **tension** is reflected in a list of contrasts: 'centre' and 'fall apart', 'falcon' and 'falconer', 'lack all conviction' and 'intensity', 'innocence' and 'anarchy'. The strain is too much: 'the centre cannot hold'. The verbs also graphically describe this chaotic world: 'Turning and turning', 'loosed', 'drowned', 'fall apart'. Humans are changing amidst the chaos: 'innocence is drowned'. **Anarchy** is described in terms of a great tidal wave, 'the blood-dimmed tide', which sweeps everything before it. The compound word reinforces the overwhelming nature of the water. Yeats feels that the 'best', the leaders and thinkers, have no energy; they are indifferent and 'lack all conviction'. On the other hand, the 'worst', the cynics and fanatics, are consumed with hatred and violence, 'full of passionate intensity'.

Disillusioned, Yeats thinks **a new order has to be emerging**. He imagines a Second Coming. He repeats the word 'Surely' in a tone of both belief and fear in stanza two. 'The Second Coming' is usually thought of as a time when Christ will return to reward the good, but the image Yeats presents us with is terrifying. **A blank, pitiless creature emerges**. It is straight from the Book of Revelations: 'And I saw a beast rising out of the sea'. This was regarded as a sign that the end of the world was near. Such an unnatural hybrid of human and animal is the Anti-Christ, the opposite force of the gentle infant Jesus who signalled the end of the Greek and Roman Empires. The 'gaze blank' suggests its lack of intelligence. The phrase 'pitiless as the sun' tells us the creature has no empathy or compassion. It 'Slouches'. It is a brutish, graceless monstrosity.

The **hostile environment** is a nightmare scenario of blazing desert sun, shifting sands and circling predatory birds. The verbs suggest everything is out of focus:

W.B. Yeats

'Reel', 'rocking', 'Slouches'. 'The darkness drops again' shows how disorder, disconnectedness and the 'widening gyre' have brought us to nihilism. This seems to be a prophetic statement, as fascism was to sweep the world in the mid-20th century. Then Yeats has a moment of epiphany: 'but now I know'. Other eras have been destroyed before. The baby in the 'rocking cradle' created an upheaval that resulted in the end of 'twenty centuries of stony sleep'.

Yeats believed that a **cycle of history** lasted two thousand years in a single evolution of birth, growth, decline and death. All change causes upheaval. The Christian era, with its qualities of innocence, order, maternal love and goodness, is at an end. The new era of the 'rough beast' is about to start. It is pitiless, destructive, violent and murderous. This new era has already begun: 'its hour come round at last'. It is a savage god who is coming, uninvited. The spiral has reversed its motion and is now spinning in the opposite direction. The lack of end rhyme mirrors a world of chaos. Yeats looks back over thousands of years. We are given a thrilling and terrifying prospect from a vast perspective of millennia.

ANALYSIS

Yeats declared that a poet should think like a wise man, but express himself as one of the common people. Write a paragraph in response to this view, using close reference to 'The Second Coming'.

SAMPLE PARAGRAPH

I feel that the themes of stability and anarchy are wisely considered by Yeats. When I look at the events of the mid to late 20th century from the perspective of the 21st century, I see a very prophetic voice warning of the dangers of the cynic, 'lack all conviction', and the fundamentalist fanatic, 'while the worst/Are full of passionate intensity'. The rise of fascism, the Second World War, the Vietnam War, the atom bomb – none of these were known when Yeats wrote this poem in 1919. Things did 'fall apart' and 'darkness' did drop again. However, the human spirit, *Spiritus Mundi*, rose again, and I would suggest that he was wrong to be so gloomy. Out of the turmoil and chaos of the Second World War came a cry. 'Surely some revelation is at hand'. But it was not the 'rough beast' with a 'gaze blank and pitiless as the sun'. Instead we had the foundation of the European Union, which has led to a long peace and stability. So, unlike Yeats's doom-laden prophecy, I think the 'centre' did 'hold'. In my opinion, the references to the Bible, Matthew, 'The Second Coming', and the Book of Revelations, 'I saw a beast', the phrases 'widening gyre', '*Spiritus Mundi*' and the image of the Sphinx are not the language of the common man. It is very interesting to discover the meaning behind these phrases, but this is not the language of everyday speech. So although I do agree that Yeats did think like a wise man, I feel he was too pessimistic about the human race. I also think that although his expressions are powerful and thought provoking, they are not the language of the common man. This is in keeping with Yeats's view that the nobles and aristocrats should rule, not the masses.

EXAMINER'S COMMENT

This impressive response focused clearly on the task, which was to consider Yeats's wisdom and his ability to express himself as one of the common people. A real sense of individual engagement with the poem came across in this well-argued answer. A grade.

CLASS/HOMEWORK EXERCISES

1. This is a political poem. What kind of political vision does it convey? Illustrate your answer with reference to the text.
2. Copy the table below into your own notes and fill in critical comments about the last two quotations.

Key Quotes

Things fall apart	Yeats believed that civilisation is breaking up and a new, brutish order will be established.
The ceremony of innocence is drowned	This metaphor highlights that the rituals and celebration of goodness represented by the Christian era are swept away by anarchy.
When a vast image out of Spiritus Mundi/ Troubles my sight	The awesome sight that comes from the collective bank of memory of the human race.
Turning and turning in the widening gyre	
Surely the Second Coming is at hand	

• Poetry Focus •

Sailing to Byzantium

I

That is no country for old men. The young
In one another's arms, birds in the trees
– Those dying generations – at their song,
The salmon-falls, the mackerel-crowded seas,
Fish, flesh, or fowl, commend all summer long		5
Whatever is begotten, born, and dies.
Caught in that sensual music all neglect
Monuments of unageing intellect.

II

An aged man is but a paltry thing,
A tattered coat upon a stick, unless		10
Soul clap its hands and sing, and louder sing
For every tatter in its mortal dress,
Nor is there singing school but studying
Monuments of its own magnificence;
And therefore I have sailed the seas and come		15
To the holy city of Byzantium.

III

O sages standing in God's holy fire
As in the gold mosaic of a wall,
Come from the holy fire, perne in a gyre,
And be the singing-masters of my soul.		20
Consume my heart away; sick with desire
And fastened to a dying animal
It knows not what it is; and gather me
Into the artifice of eternity.

IV

Once out of nature I shall never take		25
My bodily form from any natural thing,
But such a form as Grecian goldsmiths make

Of hammered gold and gold enamelling
To keep a drowsy Emperor awake;
Or set upon a golden bough to sing   30
To lords and ladies of Byzantium
Of what is past, or passing, or to come.

'the holy city of Byzantium'

GLOSSARY

Sailing to Byzantium: for Yeats, this voyage would be one taken to find perfection. This country only exists in the mind. It is an ideal. The original old city of Byzantium was famous as a centre of religion, art and architecture.

1 *That*: Ireland – all who live there are subject to ageing, decay and death.
3 *dying generations*: opposites are linked to show that in the midst of life is death.
7 *sensual music*: the young are living life to the full through their senses and are neglecting the inner spiritual life of the soul.
9 *paltry thing*: worthless, of no importance. Old age is not valued in Ireland.
10 *tattered coat*: an old man is as worthless as a scarecrow.
10–11 *unless/Soul clap its hands and sing*: man can only break free if he allows his spirit the freedom to express itself.
13–14 *Nor is there ... own magnificence*: all schools of art should study the discipline they teach, while the soul should study the immortal art of previous generations.
17 *O sages*: wise men, cleansed by the holy fire of God.
19–24 *Come ... artifice of eternity*: Yeats asks the sages to teach him the wonders of Byzantium and gather his soul into the perfection of art.
19 *perne in a gyre*: spinning; turning very fast.
22 *fastened to a dying animal*: the soul trapped in a decaying body.
32 *past, or passing, or to come*: in eternity, the golden bird sings of transience (passing time).

• Poetry Focus •

EXPLORATIONS

1. This poem tries to offer a form of escape from old age. Does it succeed? Write a paragraph in response, with support from the text.
2. Why are the 'Monuments of unageing intellect' of such importance to Yeats? What does this imply about contemporary Ireland?
3. The poem is defiant in its exploration of eternity. Discuss, using reference or quotation.

STUDY NOTES

> 'Sailing to Byzantium' confronts the universal issue of old age. There is no easy solution to this problem. Yeats found the idea of advancing age repulsive and longed to escape. Here he imagines an ideal place, Byzantium, which allowed all to enjoy eternal works of art. He celebrates what man can create and he bitterly condemns the mortality to which man is subject.

Yeats wrote, 'When Irishmen were illuminating the Book of Kells … Byzantium was the centre of European civilization … so I symbolise the search for the spiritual life by a journey to that city.'

The poet declares the theme in the **first stanza** as he confidently declaims that the world of the senses is not for the old – they must seek another way which is timeless, **a life of the spirit and intellect**. The word 'That' tells us he is looking back, as he has already started his journey. But he is looking back wistfully at the world of the lovers ('the young/In one another's arms') and the world of teeming nature ('The salmon-falls, the mackerel-crowded seas'). The compound words emphasise the dynamism and fertility of the life of the senses, even though he admits the flaw in this wonderful life of plenty is mortality ('Those dying generations'). The life of the senses and nature is governed by the harsh cycle of procreation, life and death.

The poet asserts in the **second stanza** that **what gives meaning to a person is the soul**, 'unless/Soul clap its hands and sing'. Otherwise an elderly man is worthless, 'a paltry thing'. We are given a chilling image of the thin, wasting frame of an old man as a scarecrow in tattered clothes. In contrast, we are shown the wonders of the intellect as the poet tells us that all schools of art study what they compose, what they produce – 'Monuments of unageing intellect'. These works of art are timeless; unlike the body, they are not subject to decay. Thus, music schools study great music and art schools study great paintings. The life of the intellect and spirit must take precedence over the life of the senses. Yeats will no longer listen to the 'sensual music' that is appropriate only for the young, but will study the carefully composed 'music' of classic art.

In Byzantium, the buildings had beautiful mosaics, pictures made with little tiles and inlaid with gold. One of these had a picture of martyrs being burned. Yeats addresses these wise men ('sages') in **stanza three**. He wants them to whirl through time ('perne in a gyre') and come to **teach his soul how to 'sing'**, how to live the life of the spirit. His soul craves this ('sick with desire'), **but it is trapped in the decaying, mortal body** ('fastened to a dying animal'). This is a horrendous image of old age. The soul has lost its identity: 'It knows not what it is'.

He pleads to be saved from this using two interesting verbs, 'Consume' and 'gather'. Both suggest a desire to be taken away. A fire consumes what is put into it and changes the form of the substance. Yeats wants a new body. He pleads to be embraced like a child coming home: 'gather me'. But where will he go? He will journey into the cold world of art, 'the artifice of eternity'. 'Artifice' refers to the skill of those who have created the greatest works of art, but it also means artificial, not real. **Is the poet suggesting that eternity also has a flaw**?

The **fourth stanza** starts confidently as Yeats declares that 'Once out of nature', he will be transformed into the ageless perfect work of art, the **golden bird**. This is the new body for his soul. Now he will sing to the court. But is the court listening? The word 'drowsy' suggests not. Isn't he singing about transience, the passing of time: 'what is past, or passing, or to come'? Has this any relevance in eternity? Is there a perfect solution to the dilemma of old age?

Yeats raises these questions for our consideration. He has explored this problem by contrasting the abundant life of the young with the 'tattered coat' of old age. He has shown us the golden bird of immortality in opposition to the 'dying animal' of the decaying body. The poet has lulled us with end-rhymes and half-rhymes. He has used groups of threes – 'Fish, flesh, or fowl', 'begotten, born, and dies', 'past, or passing, or to come' – to argue his case. At the end of the poem, do we feel that Yeats genuinely longs for the warm, teeming life of the senses with all its imperfections rather than the cold, disinterested world of the 'artifice of eternity'?

ANALYSIS

'Yeats is often concerned with finding ways of escape from the sorrows and oppressions which are so much a part of life.' What evidence do you find for this statement in 'Sailing to Byzantium'?

SAMPLE PARAGRAPH

I believe that Yeats was preoccupied with the inescapable fact of ageing and death. This poem, 'Sailing to Byzantium', concerns a voyage to perfection. In ordinary life there is no perfection, a fact that Yeats recognises in the phrase 'dying generations'. All must die so that more can be born into the abundant, mortal world of nature. He rages against the weaknesses of old age: an old man is a 'tattered coat upon a stick', 'a paltry thing'. The body is a 'dying animal'. Terrible, grotesque imagery vividly describes the ravages of the ageing process. Yeats intends to turn his back on this and seek immortality, hence his journey to Byzantium. This city, in his opinion, is the perfect city, as it was the cradle of European civilisation and religious philosophy. He wants the figures that are in the golden mosaics to come and instruct him how to live this life of the intellect: 'gather me'. He wants to escape the sorrows and oppressions of ordinary life. Then he paints an idyllic picture of himself, now in the shape of a golden bird, singing his songs. But this world seems cold, 'artifice of eternity', lifeless and a poor contrast to the warm, heaving, teeming 'salmon-falls, mackerel-crowded seas' world of stanza one. I don't believe Yeats has found the perfect solution to the problem of ageing. Is there one?

EXAMINER'S COMMENT

A close reading of the poem is evident in this response to Yeats's search for escape. Engagement is evident in the response and was well supported by quotations. The student showed confidence in the concluding remarks. A-grade standard.

CLASS/HOMEWORK EXERCISES

1. Yeats often places himself at the centre of his work. Do you find this to be true in 'Sailing to Byzantium'? Give reasons for your answer.
2. Copy the table below into your own notes and fill in critical comments about the last two quotations.

Key Quotes

That is no country for old men	Yeats feels that Ireland is not a suitable place to live when old.
all neglect/Monuments of unageing intellect	Young people, because they are in the vigour of their youth, are only concerned with living life through their senses and have no time for matters of the mind or soul.
perne in a gyre	Twist in a spiralling motion. A spiral is an ancient symbol for immortality. The image suggests that Yeats will actively seek spiritual fulfillment.
Into the artifice of eternity	
I shall never take/My bodily form from any natural thing	

• Poetry Focus •

from Meditations in Time of Civil War: The Stare's Nest by my Window

W.B. Yeats

The bees build in the crevices
Of loosening masonry, and there
The mother birds bring grubs and flies.
My wall is loosening; honey-bees,
Come build in the empty house of the stare.   5

We are closed in, and the key is turned
On our uncertainty; somewhere
A man is killed, or a house burned,
Yet no clear fact to be discerned:
Come build in the empty house of the stare.   10

A barricade of stone or of wood;
Some fourteen days of civil war;
Last night they trundled down the road
That dead young soldier in his blood:
Come build in the empty house of the stare.   15

We had fed the heart on fantasies,
The heart's grown brutal from the fare;
More substance in our enmities
Than in our love; O honey-bees,
Come build in the empty house of the stare.   20

'days of civil war'

GLOSSARY

Stare is another name for the starling, a bird with distinctive dark brown or greenish-black feathers.

3 *grubs*: larvae of insects.

12 *civil war*: the Irish Civil War (1922–23) between Republicans who fought for full independence and supporters of the Anglo-Irish Treaty.

13 *trundled*: rolled.

17 *fare*: diet (of dreams).

18 *enmities*: disputes; hatred.

EXPLORATIONS

1. Comment on how Yeats creates an atmosphere of concern and insecurity in stanzas two and three.
2. In your opinion, how effective is the symbol of the bees as a civilising force amid all the destruction of war? Support your answer with close reference to the poem.
3. How would you describe the dominant mood of the poem? Is it positive or negative? Refer closely to the text in your answer.

STUDY NOTES

The Irish Civil War prompted Yeats to consider the brutality and insecurity caused by conflict. It also made him reflect on his own identity as part of the Anglo-Irish Ascendancy. The poet wrote elsewhere that he had been shocked and depressed by the fighting during the first months of hostilities, yet he was determined not to grow bitter or to lose sight of the beauty of nature. He wrote this poem after seeing a stare building its nest in a hole beside his window.

Much of the poem is dominated by the images of building and collapse. **Stanza one** introduces this tension between creativity ('bees build') and disintegration ('loosening'). In responding to the bitter civil war, Yeats finds suitable **symbols in the nurturing natural world to express his own hopes**. Addressing the bees, he asks that they 'build in the empty house of the stare'. He is desperately conscious of the political vacuum being presently filled by bloodshed. His desperate cry for help seems heartfelt in tone. There is also a possibility that the poet is addressing himself – he will have to revise his own attitudes to the changing political realities caused by the war.

In **stanza two**, Yeats expresses a sense of being **threatened by the conflict** around him: 'We are closed in'. The use of the plural pronoun suggests a community under siege. He is fearful of the future: 'our uncertainty'. Is the

• Poetry Focus •

poet reflecting on the threat to his own immediate household or to the once-powerful Anglo-Irish ruling class? The constant rumours of everyday violence are highlighted in the stark descriptions: 'A man is killed, or a house burned'. Such occurrences almost seem routine in the grim reality of war.

Stanza three opens with a **haunting image**, the 'barricade of stone', an enduring symbol of division and hostility. The vehemence and inhumanity of the times is driven home by the stark report of soldiers who 'trundled down the road' and left one 'dead young soldier in his blood'. Such atrocities add greater depth to the plaintive refrain for regeneration: 'Come build in the empty house of the stare'.

In the **final stanza**, Yeats faces up to the root causes of war: 'We had fed the heart on fantasies'. Dreams of achieving independence have led to even greater hatred ('enmities') and intransigence than could have been imagined. It is a tragic irony that the Irish nation has become more divided than ever before. The poet seems despairing as he accepts the failure represented by civil conflict: 'The heart's grown brutal'. It is as though he is reprimanding himself for daring to imagine a brave new world. His **final plea for healing** and reconstruction is strengthened by an emphatic 'O' to show Yeats's depth of feeling: 'O honey-bees,/Come build in the empty house of the stare'.

ANALYSIS

'Images of ruin and renewal are in constant opposition in this poem.' Write a paragraph in response to this statement, supporting your points with reference from the text.

SAMPLE PARAGRAPH

'The Stare's Nest by my Window' is mainly about conflict, and particularly the Irish Civil War. It is not surprising that the poem contains many symbols and images of ruin and destruction. Yeats watches the bees are building a nest in 'loosening masonry' outside his window. It's ironic. Something new is happening among the ruins. The bees are constructing. Building for the future. It is symbolic that something positive is taking place. This is a key theme in the poem. Yeats is hopeful in spite of the war. The poet's use of symbolism contrasts the two forces of ruin and renewal when he says 'build in the empty house'. There are other images of ruin e.g. the 'house burned' and the ruined life of the 'young soldier in his blood'. These images remind us of what happens in wartime. But Yeats seems to argue that we can learn from nature. He hopes that just as the birds take care of their young, Ireland will recover from war. In the future there will be renewal after all the ruin.

EXAMINER'S COMMENT

There are a number of focused points made in this paragraph and there is a reasonable attempt to use supporting references. The expression is disjointed at times and the point about symbolism is repeated unnecessarily. A solid C-grade standard.

CLASS/HOMEWORK EXERCISES

1. Repetition is an important feature in this poem. Comment on its effectiveness in enhancing our understanding of the poet's themes.
2. Copy the table below into your own notes and fill in critical comments about the last two quotations.

Key Quotes

The mother birds bring grubs and flies	Details of nurturing in nature are used as a contrast to the background violence and devastation of warfare.
Yet no clear fact to be discerned	Many Irish people were confused by the Civil War and families were sometimes bitterly divided.
Come build in the empty house of the stare	Yeats emphasises the need to rebuild the country after the conflict and establish a new civilised order.
My wall is loosening	
The heart's grown brutal	

In Memory of Eva Gore-Booth and Con Markiewicz

The light of evening, Lissadell,
Great windows open to the south,
Two girls in silk kimonos, both
Beautiful, one a gazelle.
But a raving autumn shears   5
Blossom from the summer's wreath;
The older is condemned to death,
Pardoned, drags out lonely years
Conspiring among the ignorant.
I know not what the younger dreams –   10
Some vague Utopia – and she seems,
When withered old and skeleton-gaunt,
An image of such politics.
Many a time I think to seek
One or the other out and speak   15
Of that old Georgian mansion, mix
Pictures of the mind, recall
That table and the talk of youth,
Two girls in silk kimonos, both
Beautiful, one a gazelle.   20

Dear shadows, now you know it all,
All the folly of a fight
With a common wrong or right.
The innocent and the beautiful
Have no enemy but time;   25
Arise and bid me strike a match
And strike another till time catch;
Should the conflagration climb,
Run till all the sages know.
We the great gazebo built,   30
They convicted us of guilt;
Bid me strike a match and blow.

— W.B. Yeats

• Leaving Certificate English •

W.B. Yeats

'that old Georgian mansion'

GLOSSARY

1 *Lissadell*: the Gore-Booth family home in Co. Sligo.
3 *kimonos*: traditional Japanese robes.
4 *gazelle*: graceful antelope.
5 *shears*: cuts.
9 *Conspiring*: plotting; scheming.
11 *Utopia*: a perfect world.
22 *folly*: foolishness.
28 *conflagration*: blazing inferno.
29 *sages*: philosophers.
30 *gazebo*: ornamental summer house, sometimes seen as a sign of extravagance.

EXPLORATIONS

1 What mood does Yeats create in the first four lines of the poem? Explain how he achieves this mood.
2 Would you agree that this is a poem of contrasts? How does Yeats use contrasts to express his thoughts and feelings? Support your points with relevant reference.
3 What picture of Yeats himself emerges from this poem? Use close reference to the text to support the points you make.

STUDY NOTES

Yeats wrote this poem about the two Gore-Booth sisters shortly after their deaths. He was 62 at the time. Eva was a noted campaigner for women's rights and Constance was a revolutionary who took part in the 1916 Rising. She later became the first woman elected to the British House of Commons at Westminster. The poet had once been fascinated by their youthful grace and beauty, but he became increasingly opposed to their political activism. Although the poem is a memorial to the two women, it also reveals Yeats's own views about the changes that had occurred in Ireland over his lifetime.

W.B. Yeats

Stanza one begins on a nostalgic note, with Yeats recalling a magical summer's evening in the company of the Gore-Booth sisters. The details he remembers suggest **a world of elegance and privilege** in the girls' family home, Lissadell House, overlooking Sligo Bay. 'Great windows' are a reminder of the grandeur to be found in the Anglo-Irish 'Big House'. Eva and Constance are portrayed as being delicately beautiful, their elusive femininity indicated by the exotic 'silk kimonos' they wear. The poet compares one of the girls to 'a gazelle', stylishly poised and graceful.

The abrupt contrast of mood in **line 5** disrupts the tranquil scene. Yeats considers the harsh effects of time and how it changes everything. He describes autumn (personified as an overenthusiastic gardener) as 'raving' and uncontrollable. The metaphor illustrates the way **time destroys** ('shears') the simple perfection of youth ('Blossom'). Typically, Yeats chooses images from the natural world to express his own retrospective outlook.

In **lines 7–13**, the poet shows his **deep contempt** for the involvement of both the Gore-Booth sisters in revolutionary politics. As far as Yeats is concerned, their activism 'among the ignorant' was a great mistake. These beautiful young women wasted their lives for a 'vague Utopia'. The graphic image of one of the girls growing 'withered old and skeleton-gaunt' is also used to symbolise the unattractive political developments of the era. Repulsed by the idea, Yeats retreats into the more sophisticated world of Lissadell's 'old Georgian mansion'.

The **second stanza** is in marked contrast to the first. Yeats addresses the spirits ('shadows') of Eva and Constance. The tone of voice is unclear. It appears to be compassionate, but there is an undertone of weariness as well. He goes on to scold the two women for wasting their lives on 'folly'. Yeats seems angry that their innocence and beauty have been sacrificed for nothing. It is as though he feels **they have betrayed both their own femininity and their social class**. If they had only known it, their one and only enemy was time.

In the **final lines** of the poem, Yeats dramatises his feelings by turning all his **resentment against time** itself. He associates the failed lives of the women with the decay of the Anglo-Irish Ascendancy. The energetic rhythm and repetition reflect his fury as he imagines striking match after match ('And strike another till time catch') and is consumed in a great 'conflagration'. The poet imagines that the significance of this inferno will eventually be understood by those who are wise, the 'sages'. In the last sentence, Yeats considers how 'They' (the enemies of the Anglo-Irish Ascendancy) hastened the end of a grand cultural era in Ireland. The 'great gazebo' is a symbol of the fine houses and gracious living that were slowly disappearing. The poem ends on a defiant note ('Bid me strike a match and blow'), with Yeats inviting the ghosts of Eva and Constance to help him resist the devastating effects of time.

ANALYSIS

To what extent is the poem a lament for the loss of youth and beauty? Refer closely to the text in your answer.

SAMPLE PARAGRAPH

'In Memory of Eva Gore-Booth and Con Markiewicz' is largely focused on the effects of time as an agent of destruction. Yeats begins by describing the two sisters as 'two girls'. I think his nostalgic portrayal of the time he shared with them at Lissadell is filled with regret. He remembers the summer evenings relaxing together 'and the talk of youth'. Yeats contrasts the beautiful girls in their silk kimonos with the way they were in their later years – 'withered old and skeleton-gaunt'. The image is startling, evidence of how he views the ravages of time. It is all the more shocking when compared with the exquisite kimonos – symbols of lost beauty. I think Yeats is also regretful of his own lost youth. At the end of the poem, he shows his anger at ageing and argues that youth has 'no enemy but time'.

EXAMINER'S COMMENT

Although short, this is a well-focused paragraph which directly addresses the question. The references and quotes are carefully chosen and show a clear engagement with the poem. The use of the unnecessary 'I think' weakens the expression slightly. Otherwise, a good B-grade response.

CLASS/HOMEWORK EXERCISES

1. From your reading of the poem, how would you describe Yeats's true feelings towards the two women? Support the points you make with reference and/or quotation.
2. Copy the table below into your own notes and fill in critical comments about the last two quotations.

• Poetry Focus •

W. B. Yeats

Key Quotes

The light of evening, Lissadell, / Great windows open to the south	These beautiful opening lines recreate the leisurely lifestyle associated with the Anglo-Irish gentry, the class to which Yeats belonged.
That table and the talk of youth	This is another reminder of the potential the sophisticated Gore-Booth sisters once had.
All the folly of a fight	In much of his poetry, Yeats was highly critical of the revolutionary activism of his time. This is underlined by the emphatic alliteration.
Two girls in silk kimonos	
Arise and bid me strike a match	

Swift's Epitaph

Swift has sailed into his rest;
Savage indignation there
Cannot lacerate his breast.
Imitate him if you dare,
World-besotted traveller; he   5
Served human liberty.

'Swift's Epitaph'

Glossary

Swift: Jonathan Swift, satirist and clergyman, author of *Gulliver's Travels* and dean of St Patrick's Cathedral. The original inscription in Latin is on his memorial in the cathedral. Yeats liked to spend time there.

Epitaph: inscription for a tomb or memorial.

1 *his rest*: suggestion of afterlife; death is not an end.

2 *Savage indignation*: the driving force of Swift's satirical work. He believed in a society where wrong was punished and good rewarded.

3 *lacerate*: cut; tear.

5 *World-besotted*: obsessed with travelling or with material concerns rather than spiritual matters.

5–6 *he | Served human liberty*: Yeats believed Swift served the liberty of the intellect, not liberty for the common people. Yeats associated democracy with organised mobs of ignorant people.

EXPLORATIONS

1. How would you describe the tone of this poem?
2. Comment on the poet's use of the verb 'lacerate'. What do you think Yeats is trying to convey?

STUDY NOTES

'Swift's Epitaph' is a translation from the original Latin epitaph composed by Swift for himself. Yeats adds a new first line to the original. He regarded this epitaph as the 'greatest … in history'.

W.B. Yeats admired Swift, who was proud and solitary and belonged to the Anglo-Irish tradition, as did Yeats himself. He regarded the Anglo-Irish as superior. He once said, 'We have created most of the modern literature of this country. We have created the best of its political intelligence.' **Yeats's additional first line** to the epitaph conveys a dignified sailing into the spiritual afterlife by the deceased Swift. The rest of the poem is a **translation** from the Latin original. Swift is now free from all the negative reactions he was subjected to when alive: 'Savage indignation there/Cannot lacerate his breast'. Swift's self-portrait conveys the impression of a man of fierce **independence and pride**. 'Imitate him if you dare' is the challenge thrown down like a gauntlet to the reader to try to be like him. 'World-besotted traveller' can be read as a man who has travelled extensively in his imagination as well as in reality. His contribution to humanity is summed up in the final sentence: 'he/Served human liberty'. **He freed the artist** from the masses so that the artist could 'make liberty visible'. The tone of this short, compressed poem is proud and defiant, like Swift.

ANALYSIS

What impression of Swift do you get from this poem by Yeats? Write a paragraph in response, supporting your views with reference to the text.

SAMPLE PARAGRAPH

I thought that Swift was a confident, fearless man who dared to voice his own truth. The tone of the poem, from its opening, 'Swift has sailed into his rest', suggests a man who knew what he was doing and did it with style. It suggests a spiritual man, 'into his rest'. He is embarking on an afterlife of some sort. He was a man who braved the censure of the world, 'Savage indignation there/Cannot lacerate his breast'. He dared to say what he felt he had to say. A challenge is thrown down to the reader, 'Imitate him if you dare'. Obviously, both Swift and Yeats considered that Swift would be a hard act to follow. The phrase 'world-besotted traveller' could mean that the poet considered that modern man was too obsessed with material possessions, while Swift was concerned with loftier matters such as the moral good. The final sentence, 'he/Served human liberty', states that he improved the human condition by making us all free. This is where I, as a 21st-century reader, part company with the epitaph. Swift did not fight for freedom as we understand it. It could be argued that he only believed in liberty for a select few, the Anglo-Irish Protestants. Yeats's tone is one of admiration for this courageous man, but modern man would not agree with this elitist view of freedom for a select group. Also the confident challenge to the reader to match Swift 'if you dare' comes across to me as arrogance. While I admire Swift's fearlessness, I do not admire his elitism or arrogance.

EXAMINER'S COMMENT

An original A-grade response to the question. The paragraph raises interesting discussion points about both writers. There is detailed support throughout and a fluent control of language in arguing the case vigorously.

CLASS/HOMEWORK EXERCISES

1. Is Yeats's use of the sailing metaphor effective? Briefly explain your answer.
2. Copy the table below into your own notes and fill in critical comments about the last two quotations.

Key Quotes

Swift has sailed into his rest	Swift has now entered the next life. The tone reflects Yeats's admiration and respect.
Savage indignation there/Cannot lacerate his breast	He is free from criticism now. Ironically, Swift's own savage criticism is now also at rest.
Imitate him if you dare	A challenge is given to the reader. Is the tone confrontational or superior?
World-besotted traveller	
he/Served human liberty	

• Poetry Focus •

An Acre of Grass

W.B. Yeats

Picture and book remain,
An acre of green grass
For air and exercise,
Now strength and body goes;
Midnight, an old house   5
Where nothing stirs but a mouse.

My temptation is quiet.
Here at life's end
Neither loose imagination,
Nor the mill of the mind   10
Consuming its rag and bone,
Can make the truth known.

Grant me an old man's frenzy.
Myself must I remake
Till I am Timon and Lear   15
Or that William Blake
Who beat upon the wall
Till Truth obeyed his call;

A mind Michael Angelo knew
That can pierce the clouds   20
Or inspired by frenzy
Shake the dead in their shrouds;
Forgotten else by mankind
An old man's eagle mind.

'An acre of green grass'

• Leaving Certificate English •

> **GLOSSARY**
>
> 2 *acre*: the secluded garden of Yeats's home, where he spent his final years.
> 5 *an old house*: the house was in Rathfarnham, Co. Dublin.
> 9 *loose imagination*: vague, unfocused ideas.
> 13 *frenzy*: wildly excited state.
> 15 *Timon and Lear*: two of Shakespeare's elderly tragic heroes, both of whom raged against the world.
> 16 *William Blake*: English visionary poet and painter (1757–1827).
> 19 *Michael Angelo*: Michelangelo, Italian Renaissance artist (1475–1564).
> 22 *shrouds*: burial garments.

EXPLORATIONS

1 How does Yeats create a mood of calm and serenity in the opening stanza?
2 Briefly explain the change of tone in stanza three.

STUDY NOTES

> Written in 1936 when Yeats was 71, the poet expresses his resentment towards ageing gracefully. Instead, he will dedicate himself to seeking wisdom through frenzied creativity. People sometimes take a narrow view of the elderly and consider them completely redundant. In Yeats's case, he is determined not to let old age crush his spirit.

Stanza one paints a picture of retirement as a surrender to death. Yeats's life has been reduced to suit his basic needs. 'Picture and book' might refer to the poet's memories. Physically weak, he feels like a prisoner whose enclosed garden area is for 'air and exercise'. There is an underlying **feeling of alienation and inactivity**: 'nothing stirs'.

In **stanza two**, the poet says that it would be easy to give in to the stereotypical image of placid contentment: 'My temptation is quiet', especially since old age ('life's end') has weakened his creative powers. **Yeats admits that his 'loose imagination' is not as sharp as it was when he was in his prime.** He no longer finds immediate inspiration ('truth') in everyday experiences, which he compares to life's 'rag and bone'.

The **third stanza** opens on a much more dramatic and forceful note as the poet confronts his fears: 'Grant me an old man's frenzy'. Yeats's personal prayer is totally lacking in meekness. Instead, he urges himself to focus enthusiastically on his own creative purpose – 'frenzy'. **He pledges to 'remake' himself** in the image of such heroic figures as Timon, Lear and William Blake. The passionate tone and run-on lines add to his sense of commitment to his art.

W.B. Yeats

• Poetry Focus •

In **stanza four**, Yeats develops **his spirited pursuit of meaningful old age** by reflecting on 'A mind Michael Angelo knew'. The poet is stimulated and encouraged to follow the great artist's example and 'pierce the clouds'. The image suggests the daring power of imagination to lift the spirit in the search for truth and beauty. The final lines build to a climax as Yeats imagines the joys of 'An old man's eagle mind'. Such intense creativity can 'Shake the dead' and allow the poet to continue experiencing life to its fullest.

ANALYSIS

Based on your reading of the poem, comment on Yeats's response to old age. Refer to the text in your answer.

SAMPLE PARAGRAPH

Yeats takes a highly unusual approach to ageing in 'An Acre of Grass'. He seems to be happy to sit reading in his quiet 'acre of grass'. Everything seems to be very organised, a little too organised for his liking. In the first few lines, we get a picture of someone close to second childhood, with his 'picture and book'. Late at night, he is awake and feels that 'nothing stirs but a mouse'. This is like the mind of a little child and it is what Yeats rebels against. He does not want to fade away. He really wants to keep being a poet and seek truth. To him, it is 'an old man's frenzy'. This suggests that he would prefer to be thought of as mad, but to keep producing his poems rather than fade away quietly. He wants to be like King Lear, the old king in Shakespeare's play who fought to the bitter end. Yeats wants to live life to the full, not fade away quietly. He wants to write his poetry and make use of his active mind until he takes his last breath. I admire his energy even though he seems a grumpy old man. His tone is fierce and defiant throughout most of the poem. He will not fade away on his acre of grass.

EXAMINER'S COMMENT

There is some very good discussion in this paragraph and a clear sense of individual engagement. The idea of Yeats rejecting second childhood is well supported. The style of writing lacks control at times and there are some awkward expressions and repetition ('fade away'). An average C grade.

CLASS/HOMEWORK EXERCISES

1. How would you describe the structure of this poem? Formal or informal? Regular or irregular? How does the poem's structure and form emphasise Yeats's message about old age?
2. Copy the table below into your own notes and fill in critical comments about the last two quotations.

Key Quotes

Midnight, an old house/Where nothing stirs but a mouse	Yeats creates an atmosphere of stillness and emptiness associated with lonely old age.
Here at life's end	Central to the poem is Yeats's awareness of death, which makes him determined to make the most of life.
the mill of the mind/Consuming its rag and bone	Yeats distils language in this powerful observation, which contains alliteration, personification and metaphor.
Grant me an old man's frenzy	
An old man's eagle mind	

• Poetry Focus •

from Under Ben Bulben

W.B. Yeats

V

Irish poets, learn your trade,
Sing whatever is well made,
Scorn the sort now growing up
All out of shape from toe to top,
Their unremembering hearts and heads   5
Base-born products of base beds.
Sing the peasantry, and then
Hard-riding country gentlemen,
The holiness of monks, and after
Porter-drinkers' randy laughter;   10
Sing the lords and ladies gay
That were beaten into the clay
Through seven heroic centuries;
Cast your mind on other days
That we in coming days may be   15
Still the indomitable Irishry.

VI

Under bare Ben Bulben's head
In Drumcliff churchyard Yeats is laid,
An ancestor was rector there
Long years ago; a church stands near,   20
By the road an ancient Cross.
No marble, no conventional phrase,
On limestone quarried near the spot
By his command these words are cut:

Cast a cold eye   25
On life, on death.
Horseman, pass by!

GLOSSARY
2 *whatever is well made*: great art.
6 *base*: low; unworthy.
16 *indomitable*: invincible; unbeatable.
17 *Under bare Ben Bulben's head*: defiant symbol of the famous mountain.
19 *ancestor*: the poet's great-grandfather.
27 *Horseman*: possibly a symbolic figure from local folklore.

'Under bare Ben Bulben's head'

W.B. Yeats

EXPLORATIONS

1. Comment on the tone used by Yeats in giving advice to other writers. Refer to the text in your answer.
2. From your reading of the poem, explain the kind of 'Irishry' that Yeats wishes to see celebrated in poetry. Support the points you make with reference or quotation.
3. Describe the mood of Drumcliff churchyard as visualised by the poet. Use close reference to the text to show how Yeats uses language to create this mood.

STUDY NOTES

This was one of Yeats's last poems. Sections V and VI of the elegy sum up his personal views on the future of Irish poetry and also include the enigmatic epitaph he composed for his own gravestone. Using art as a gateway to spiritual fulfillment is characteristic of the poet.

Section V is a hard-hitting address by Yeats to his contemporaries and all the poets who will come after him. He encourages them to set the highest 'well made' standards for their work. His uncompromisingly negative view of contemporary writing ('out of shape from toe to top') is quickly clarified. The reason why modern literature is in such a state of confusion is that the poets' 'unremembering hearts and heads' have **lost touch with tradition**. The formality and discipline of great classic poetry have been replaced by unstructured writing and free verse. The authoritative tone becomes even more scathing as Yeats castigates the inferiority of his peers as 'Base-born products'.

It is not only intellectual artistic tradition that the poet admires; he finds another valuable tradition in the legends and myths of old Ireland. Yeats urges his fellow writers to 'Sing the peasantry'. But he also advises them to **absorb**

other cultural traditions. Here he includes the 'Hard-riding country gentlemen' of his own Anglo-Irish class and the 'holiness of monks' – those who seek truth through ascetic or spiritual means. Even the more sensuous 'randy laughter' of 'Porter-drinkers' can be inspirational. For Yeats, the peasant and aristocratic traditions are equally worth celebrating. Irish history is marked by a combination of joy, heroism, defeat and resilience. Yet despite (or perhaps because of) his harsh criticism of the present generation, there is little doubt about the poet's passionate desire to encourage new writing that would reflect the true greatness of 'indomitable Irishry'.

Section VI is a great deal less dogmatic. Writing in the third person, Yeats describes his final resting place in Drumcliff. The voice is **detached and dignified**. Using a series of unadorned images, he takes us to the simple churchyard at the foot of Ben Bulben. The mountain stands as a proud symbol of how our unchanging silent origins outlive human tragedy. It is to his Irish roots that the poet ultimately wants to return. His wishes are modest but curt – 'No marble'. Keen to avoid the well-worn headstone inscriptions, Yeats provides his own incisive epitaph. The three short lines are enigmatic and balance opposing views, typical of so much of his poetry. The poet's last warning ('*Cast a cold eye*') reminds us to live measured lives based on a realistic understanding of the cycle of life and death. The beautiful Christian setting, subdued tone and measured rhythm all contribute to the quiet dignity of Yeats's final farewell.

ANALYSIS

Some people have criticised this poem as 'a bitter old man's snobbish rant'. Write your response to this comment, supporting your views with reference to the text.

SAMPLE PARAGRAPH

It's easy to see why Yeats could be accused of being elitist and superior. As he nears death, he is clearly not concerned with political correctness. He knows his own worth as the leading Irish writer of his times. He gets straight to the point in advising younger poets – 'learn your trade'. If I was an unpublished writer, I would take him seriously, rather than feeling precious. Yeats does not suffer fools easily and he has no respect for shoddy work that is 'out of shape'. His tone can be harsh, even shrill on occasions, but he is stressing a basic lesson that good writing must be disciplined. Rather than seeing him as someone who is ranting, I appreciate the way Yeats shows his interest in standards. His attitude is actually inclusive. He wants young poets to learn from every source available to them – sacred texts, the Protestant and peasant Catholic traditions, and from the 'Porter-drinkers' of Ireland. I can see no bitterness here. His own funeral instructions are actually humble. He does not demand a hero courageous tomb, just a simple plot in a country graveyard. To me, Yeats comes across as a man who is neither arrogant nor snobbish, but as a legendary writer concerned about Irish literature.

EXAMINER'S COMMENT

This is a very spirited and well-sustained personal response that reflects a clear viewpoint. Points are supported robustly with apt quotations and the arguments range over the whole poem. In the main, expression is fluent and controlled. An impressive A-grade standard.

CLASS/HOMEWORK EXERCISES

1. Is Yeats's epitaph in keeping with the views he expresses throughout the rest of the poem? Explain your answer using reference to the text.
2. Copy the table below into your own notes and fill in critical comments about the last two quotations.

Key Quotes

Irish poets, learn your trade	Yeats is enthusiastic about the need for poets to return to the formal, classical tradition that will again celebrate Ireland's heroic and spiritual values.
Base-born products of base beds	The poet is contemptuous of modern poetry, much of which he believed came from inferior writers. Repetition emphasises his disdain.
Sing the lords and ladies gay	Yeats associated aesthetic values and the place of art in society with the gracious lifestyle of the Anglo-Irish class.
By the road an ancient Cross	
Cast a cold eye/On life, on death	

• Poetry Focus •

Politics

'In our time the destiny of man presents its meanings in political terms.' – Thomas Mann

How can I, that girl standing there,
My attention fix
On Roman or on Russian
Or on Spanish politics,
Yet here's a travelled man that knows   5
What he talks about,
And there's a politician
That has both read and thought,
And maybe what they say is true
Of war and war's alarms,   10
But O that I were young again
And held her in my arms.

'But O that I were young again / And held her in my arms'

GLOSSARY

Politics: winning and using power to govern society.
Thomas Mann was a German novelist who argued that the future of man was determined by states and governments.
3–4 *On Roman or on Russian / Or on Spanish politics*: a reference to the political upheavals of Europe in the 1930s.

EXPLORATIONS

1. This poem suggests that politics are not important. Does the poet convince you? Write a paragraph in response, with reference to the text.
2. Where does the language used in the poem convey a sense of deep longing? How effective is this?

STUDY NOTES

'Politics' is a satire written in 1939 when Yeats was 73 in response to a magazine article. He said it was based on 'a moment of meditation'.

A **satire** uses ridicule to expose foolishness. A magazine article praised Yeats for his 'public' work. The poet was delighted with this word, as one of his aims had always been to 'move the common people'. However, the article went on to say that Yeats should have used this 'public' voice to address public issues such as politics. Yeats disagreed, as he had always regarded politics as dishonest and superficial. He thought professional politicians manipulated through 'false news'. This is evident from the ironic comment, 'And maybe what they say is true'. Here we see the poet's indifference to these matters.

This poem addresses **real truths**, the proper material for poems, the universal experience of **human relationships**, not the infinite abstractions that occupied politicians ('war and war's alarms'). Big public events, Yeats is suggesting, are not as important as love. The girl in the poem is more important than all the politics in the world: 'How can I … My attention fix/On Roman or on Russian/Or on Spanish politics'? So Yeats is overthrowing the epigraph at the beginning of the poem where the novelist Thomas Mann is stating that people should be concerned with political matters. Politics is the winning and using of power to govern the state. Yeats is adopting the persona of the distracted lover who is unable to focus on the tangled web of European politics in the 1930s. This poem was to be placed in his last poetry collection, almost like a farewell, as he states again that what he desires is youth and love.

But this poem can also give another view. Is the 'she' in the poem Ireland? Yeats has addressed public issues in poems such as 'Easter, 1916' and 'September 1913' and he was already a senator in the Irish government. As usual, he leaves us with questions as he draws us through this deceptively simple poem with its **ever-changing tones** that range from the questioning opening to mockery, doubt and finally longing. The **steady rhyme** (the second line rhymes with the fourth and so on) drives the poem forward to its emphatic **closing wish**, the cry of an old man who wishes to recapture his youth and lost love.

ANALYSIS

Do you agree with Yeats that only youth and love matter? Discuss, using reference to the poem.

SAMPLE PARAGRAPH

I think Yeats is expressing a deep-seated desire in all of us. We all want to be concerned with our own lives ('My attention fix'), not on the mess that the political world seems to be in, 'Roman or on Russian/Or on Spanish politics'. It is the same today. How often have we turned off the news in disgust or because we just couldn't take any more 'Of war and war's alarms'? And yet I would like to suggest another view on this. We get the governments we deserve. Democracy is fragile when good people are inattentive. So although I agree with Yeats's sentiments and can fully understand his closing wish, 'But O that I were young again/And held her in my arms', I feel that we have to sometimes safeguard the destiny of man. We are the generation that is on watch now for the protection of the environment and the safety of humanity. I think Thomas Mann has a point as he says, 'In our time the destiny of man presents its meanings in political terms'.

EXAMINER'S COMMENT

The student has engaged personally with the question and has presented a considered argument using relevant quotations effectively. The answer reads well and adjectives (such as 'fragile' and 'inattentive') are well chosen. Grade A.

CLASS/HOMEWORK EXERCISES

1. Comment on the rhythm of the poem, paying particular attention to the use of run-on lines.
2. Copy the table below into your own notes and fill in critical comments about the last two quotations.

Key Quotes

How can I, that girl standing there,/ My attention fix	The poet is declaring that his attention is on his personal concerns rather than public concerns such as politics.
On Roman or on Russian	The alliterative 'r' emphasises Yeats's tone of frustration.
And maybe what they say is true/ Of war and war's alarms	The poet is unsure of the truth of politicians' speeches.
And there's a politician/ That has both read and thought	
But O that I were young again/ And held her in my arms	

LEAVING CERT SAMPLE ESSAY

> **Q** Write an article for a school magazine introducing the poetry of W.B. Yeats to Leaving Certificate students. Tell them what he wrote about and explain what you liked about his writing, suggesting some poems that you think they would enjoy reading. Support your points by reference to the poetry by Yeats that you studied.

MARKING SCHEME GUIDELINES

Candidates are free to adopt a register they consider appropriate to the task. The task contains three closely related elements, which may be addressed separately or together. It is not necessary that these elements be given equal treatment.
- What he wrote about (themes, concerns, subject matter).
- What you liked about his writing.
- Suggest enjoyable poems.

Reward responses that show clear evidence of engagement with the poems and/or poet.

Some of the following areas might be addressed:
- Political and personal perspective of the poems.
- Variety of the themes.
- Strength of Yeats's vision.
- Depth and range of his feelings.
- Features of style, such as language, imagery, symbolism, sound, etc.

SAMPLE ESSAY
(Introduction to Yeats)

1 *Allow me to introduce to you a man of passion with a love for art and a great admiration for Ireland's heroes. Seamus Heaney described this man as 'a dreamer, an idealist'. This man, just like many of you, longed for a retreat from all the pressures of civilisation, and I feel we can all identify with him. This man is W.B. Yeats.*

• Poetry Focus •

W.B. Yeats

(2) Many of you today may be feeling fed up with school, home, life in general. Yeats felt the same way and longed to escape oppressive city life. This retreat from the irksome routine of the everyday is evoked in Yeats's most well-known poem, 'The Lake Isle of Innisfree'. After you have read these lines, close your eyes and imagine the scene, the colours, 'midnight's all a glimmer, and noon a purple glow'. Imagine the sounds: 'I hear lake water lapping with low sounds by the shore'. The tranquil atmosphere is summoned by 'and peace comes dropping slow'. Suddenly we are in an idyllic paradise as the soothing effect of the lines quietens our frazzled brains. Yeats stored this hypnotic image in his mind and returned to it every time he needed escape, 'While I stand on the roadway, or on the pavements grey'. He heard it in 'the deep heart's core'. We all, like Yeats, have a place or long to have a place, either physical or mental, that we retreat to when the pressure gets too much.

(3) We are all Celtic Cubs, and if the title was missing from 'September 1913', we could read this poem as a scathing attack on New Ireland, avaricious, selfish and materialistic. But Yeats wrote this poem primarily in response to the 1913 lock-out and the failure to fund the Hugh Lane Gallery with its collection of wonderful modern art. The anger spits off the page as he graphically describes these self-centred people concerned with outward appearances only. The phrase 'fumble in a greasy till' shows their dependence on money. Equally depressing is their attitude to religion which does not sustain them, but 'dries the marrow from the bone'. O'Leary, the Irish Fenian poet, is what an Irishman should be, someone who thought of his country, not himself. The refrain 'It's with O'Leary in the grave' drives this message home, as Yeats gets angrier ('Was it for this?') at the inability of the contemporary Irish to understand the bigger picture. Bitterly he resigns himself to the fact that his contemporaries just don't understand and he warns them not to judge these heroes by their own standards, 'But let them be ... They're with O'Leary in the grave'.

(4) 'Easter, 1916' is, I admit, a difficult poem, but it is worth the struggle. I particularly liked the fact that Yeats was big enough to admit he was wrong. The people he had condemned in the previous poem were capable of great sacrifices and indeed 'A terrible beauty' was born. Even Major MacBride who had married Maud Gonne, the love of Yeats's life, 'A drunken vainglorious lout', was

included in 'the song'. The structure of the poem is very clever, four verses, two with 24 lines, two with 16 lines, commemorating the date of the rebellion, the 24th of April 1916. Yeats admires the revolutionary spirit and their dream for independence for Ireland. But his choice of 'the stone' as a symbol of this spirit warns of danger. Sacrifice can turn a heart to stone. When is enough enough? 'O when may it suffice?' We see this every day in current political struggles. The poem ends with a litany, a list of holy names, of the dead: they are 'changed' and will be remembered 'wherever green is worn'.

5. My personal favourite is 'Sailing to Byzantium'. Yeats wrote some of his best poetry in his final years, as he raged against old age and death. He writes from an unusual perspective, looking back as he embarks on a journey. He realises he has to go because 'That is no country for old men'. The alliteration shows a fertile land teeming with passionate young life. 'Fish, flesh, or fowl, commend all summer long/Whatever is begotten, born, and dies'. Pitiful images describe old age, 'A tattered coat upon a stick', something that is only used to scare birds. Again, as in our first poem, Yeats longs to escape. He decides that he will not have a body that is natural because then it is subject to age. Instead, he chooses one that is an 'artifice'. But even in Paradise there is a problem. The emperor is 'drowsy' to whom Yeats, in his new form of a golden bird, sings. His heart really wishes to be with 'the young/In one another's arms'. I thought it was very interesting how a man could write so openly about growing old. It has very modern echoes when we see the acres of media space devoted to actually preventing ageing!

6. Before reading this article, you probably had a stereotypical image of Yeats as a serious young man staring sternly out through old-fashioned glasses. Who would have guessed the spirit and passion that lay beneath the stern exterior? Truly Yeats is a poet who sings to us 'Of what is past, or passing, or to come' and we are wide awake to listen.

(approx. 880 words)

Grade: A1		
P	=	15/15
C	=	15/15
L	=	15/15
M	=	5/5
Total	=	50/50

EXAMINER'S COMMENT

The candidate fulfilled the task eloquently and displayed a robust personal engagement with the poetry. The answer ranged widely to discuss Yeats's subject matter, what was interesting about the writing and the most enjoyable poems. Excellent use of accurate quotation throughout. A very impressive response.

SAMPLE LEAVING CERT QUESTIONS ON YEATS'S POETRY (45–50 MINUTES)

1. Give your personal estimation of the poetry of W.B. Yeats. Support your answer with reference to the poems on your course.
2. Consider the versions of Ireland that emerge from Yeats's poems. Do these versions form a consistent picture or not? Support your answer with close reference to the poems.
3. If you were asked to give a public reading of some of Yeats's poems, which ones would you choose? Give reasons for your choices, supporting them by reference to the poems by Yeats that you have studied.

SAMPLE ESSAY PLAN (Q1)

Give your personal estimation of the poetry of W.B. Yeats. Support your answer with reference to the poems on your course.

- *Intro:* A personal response is required; mention both content and style in the response. Public and personal poems are interesting and thought provoking.
- *Point 1:* 'September 1913' – public poem, accusatory. Note the changing refrain, litany, rhetorical questions, bitter tone, nostalgic view of Irish history.
- *Point 2:* 'Easter, 1916' – another public poem, an attempt to answer questions about the Rising. All had changed. Yeats admits he was wrong.
- *Point 3:* 'The Wild Swans at Coole' – autumnal retrospection as he realises how his life had changed in 19 years. Laments loss of youth, passion and love.
- *Point 4:* 'Sailing to Byzantium' – theme of ageing, use of contrast to convey theme.
Declamatory opening, uncertainty a sign of his humanity.

- *Conclusion*: Yeats – ideal past contrasted with unsatisfactory present, attitude to Irish patriotism, escape, ageing. Raises questions rather than providing answers.

EXERCISE

Develop one of the above points into a paragraph.

POINT 4 – SAMPLE PARAGRAPH

I find the poem 'Sailing to Byzantium' very intriguing. Here was a man who hated the weaknesses brought on by old age: 'An aged man is but a paltry thing'. Yet with passion and fire, he defies time: 'Once out of nature I shall never take/My bodily form from any natural thing'. The rhythmic phrasing of threes conveys the natural harmony of youth and fertility: 'Fish, flesh, or fowl'. This is the world of which Yeats wants to be a part, 'The young in one another's arms'. But that is not life. He presents us with the contrasting truth as he states, 'That is no country for old men'. Again, contrast is used as the beauty of 'artifice', 'the gold mosaic of a wall' is lined up against the brute reality of the soul 'fastened to a dying animal'. Through his clever contrasts, the poet explores the dilemma of ageing, which will come to us all, even though at 17 it seems very remote to me. I was also interested in Yeats's discovery of a flaw in Paradise. Now Yeats is immortal as his soul has taken the bodily form of a golden bird, 'such a form as Grecian goldsmiths make/Of hammered gold and gold enamelling'. However, the audience for his songs/poems, the Emperor, is 'drowsy'. He is not paying attention. Yeats is now raising the question: Is Paradise, 'artifice', all that it is supposed to be? Who will listen as Yeats sings of the great truths, 'Of what is past, or passing, or to come'? All great poets raise questions about life and existence for us to consider. Yeats is no exception.

EXAMINER'S COMMENT

As part of a full essay answer, this is a competent A-grade paragraph which offers a personal response firmly rooted in the text. The paragraph centres on the use of contrast used by Yeats to explore ageing, and both style and content are examined effectively. Very well supported by suitable quotes.

W.B. Yeats

Poetry Focus

Last Words

'He had this marvellous gift for beating the scrap metal of the day-to-day life into a ringing bell.'

Seamus Heaney

'Yeats's poetry is simple and eloquent to the heart.'

Robert Louis Stevenson

'I have spent my life saying the same thing in different ways.'

W.B. Yeats, writing to his wife

Glossary of Common Literary Terms

alliteration: the use of the same letter at the beginning of each word or stressed syllable in a line of verse, e.g. 'boilers bursting'.

assonance: the use of the same vowel sound in a group of words, e.g. 'bleared, smeared with toil'.

aubade: a celebratory morning song, sometimes lamenting the parting of lovers.

blank verse: unrhymed iambic pentameter, e.g. 'These waters, rolling from their mountain-springs'.

conceit: an elaborate image or far-fetched comparison, e.g. 'This flea is you and I, and this/Our marriage bed'.

couplet: two successive lines of verse, usually rhymed and of the same metre, e.g. 'So long as men can breathe or eyes can see,/So long lives this, and this gives life to thee'.

elegy: a mournful poem, usually for the dead, e.g. 'Sleep in a world your final sleep has woken'.

emotive language: language designed to arouse an emotional response in the reader, e.g. 'For this that all that blood was shed?'

epiphany: a moment of insight or understanding, e.g. 'Somebody loves us all'.

free verse: unrhymed and unmetred poetry, often used by modern poets, e.g. 'but the words are shadows and you cannot hear me./You walk away and I cannot follow'.

imagery: descriptive language or word-pictures, especially appealing to the senses, e.g. 'He was speckled with barnacles,/fine rosettes of lime'.

irony: when one thing is said and the opposite is meant, e.g. 'For men were born to pray and save'.

lyric: short musical poem expressing feeling.

metaphor: image that compares two things without using the words 'like' or 'as', e.g. 'I am gall, I am heartburn'.

onomatopoeia: the sound of the word imitates or echoes the sound being described, e.g. 'The murmurous haunt of flies on summer eves'.

• Poetry Focus •

paradox: a statement that on the surface appears self-contradictory, e.g. 'I shall have written him one/poem maybe as cold/ And passionate as the dawn'.

persona: the speaker or voice in the poem. This is not always the poet, e.g. 'I know that I shall meet my fate/Somewhere among the clouds above'.

personification: where the characteristics of an animate or living being are given to something inanimate, e.g. 'The yellow fog that rubs its back upon the window panes'.

rhyme: identical sound of words, usually at the end of lines of verse, e.g. 'I get down on my knees and do what must be done/And kiss Achilles' hand, the killer of my son'.

rhythm: the beat or movement of words, the arrangement of stressed and unstressed, short and long syllables in a line of poetry, e.g. 'I will arise and go now, and go to Innisfree'.

sestina: a six-stanza, six-line poem with the same six end words occurring throughout. The final stanza contains these six words. '*Time to plant tears,* says the almanac:/The grandmother sings to the marvellous stove/and the child draws another inscrutable house'.

sibilance: the whispering, hissing 's' sound, e.g. 'Singest of summer in full-throated ease'.

sonnet: a 14-line poem. The Petrarchan or Italian sonnet is divided into eight lines (octave) which present a problem or situation. The remaining six lines (sestet) resolve the problem or present another view of the situation. The Shakespearean sonnet is divided into three quatrains and concludes with a rhyming couplet, either summing up what preceded or reversing it.

symbol: a word or phrase representing something other than itself, e.g.' A tattered coat upon a stick'.

theme: the central idea or message in a poem.

tone: the type of voice or attitude used by the poet towards his or her subject, e.g. 'O but it is dirty'.

villanelle: a five-stanza poem of three lines each, with a concluding quatrain, using only two end rhyming words throughout, e.g. 'I am just going outside and may be some time,/At the heart of the ridiculous, the sublime'.

ACKNOWLEDGMENTS

The authors and publisher are grateful to the following for permission to reproduce copyrighted material:

'The Fish', 'The Bight', 'At the Fishhouses', 'The Prodigal', 'Questions of Travel', 'The Armadillo', 'Sestina', 'First Death in Nova Scotia', 'Filling Station', 'In the Waiting Room' from THE COMPLETE POEMS 1927–1979 by Elizabeth Bishop. Copyright © 1979, 1983 by Alice Helen Methfessel. Reprinted by permission of Farrar, Straus and Giroux, LLC;

The poems 'The Forge', 'Bogland', 'The Tollund Man', 'Mossbawn: Sunlight', 'A Constable Calls', 'The Skunk', 'The Harvest Bow', 'The Underground', 'Postscript', 'A Call', 'Tate's Avenue', 'The Pitchfork' and 'Lightenings viii' by Seamus Heaney are reprinted by kind permission of Faber & Faber Ltd;

The poems 'Thinking of Mr D.', 'Dick King', 'Mirror in February', 'Chrysalides','VI Littlebody' from *Glenmacnass*, 'Tear', 'Hen Woman', 'His Father's Hands', 'Model School, Inchicore' from *Settings*, 'VII' from *The Familiar* and 'Echo' from *Belief and Unbelief* are taken from Thomas Kinsella: *Collected Poems*, Carcanet Press 2001 and reprinted by kind permission of Carcanet Press Limited;

The poems 'Wedding-Wind', 'At Grass', 'Church Going', 'An Arundel Tomb', 'The Whitsun Weddings', 'MCMXIV', 'Ambulances', 'The Trees', 'The Explosion' and 'Cut Grass' by Philip Larkin are reprinted by kind permission of Faber & Faber Ltd;

The poems 'Grandfather', 'Day Trip to Donegal', 'Ecclesiastes', 'After the *Titanic*', 'As It Should Be', 'A Disused Shed in Co. Wexford', 'Rathlin', 'The Chinese Restaurant in Portrush', 'Kinsale' and 'Antarctica' by Derek Mahon are reprinted by kind permission of the author and The Gallery Press, Loughcrew, Oldcastle, County Meath, Ireland from *Collected Poems* (1999);

The poems 'Black Rook in Rainy Weather', 'The Times Are Tidy', 'Morning Song', 'Finisterre', 'Mirror', 'Pheasant', 'Elm', 'Poppies in July', 'The Arrival of the Bee Box' and 'Child' by Sylvia Plath are reprinted by kind permission of Faber & Faber Ltd;

The poems by W.B. Yeats are reproduced by kind permission of A P Watt on behalf of Gráinne Yeats.

The authors and publisher have made every effort to trace all copyright holders, but if any has been inadvertently overlooked we would be pleased to make the necessary arrangement at the first opportunity.